Hands-On Full-Stack Web Development with ASP.NET Core

Learn end-to-end web development with leading frontend frameworks, such as Angular, React, and Vue

Tamir Dresher
Amir Zuker
Shay Friedman

Packt>

BIRMINGHAM - MUMBAI

Hands-On Full-Stack Web Development with ASP.NET Core

Copyright © 2018 Packt Publishing

All rights reserved. No part of this book may be reproduced, stored in a retrieval system, or transmitted in any form or by any means, without the prior written permission of the publisher, except in the case of brief quotations embedded in critical articles or reviews.

Every effort has been made in the preparation of this book to ensure the accuracy of the information presented. However, the information contained in this book is sold without warranty, either express or implied. Neither the author(s), nor Packt Publishing or its dealers and distributors, will be held liable for any damages caused or alleged to have been caused directly or indirectly by this book.

Packt Publishing has endeavored to provide trademark information about all of the companies and products mentioned in this book by the appropriate use of capitals. However, Packt Publishing cannot guarantee the accuracy of this information.

Commissioning Editor: Kunal Chaudhari
Acquisition Editor: Noyonika Das
Content Development Editor: Francis Carneiro
Technical Editor: Surabhi Kulkarni
Copy Editor: Safis
Project Coordinator: Sheejal Shah
Proofreader: Safis Editing
Indexer: Rekha Nair
Graphics: Alishon Mendonsa
Production Coordinator: Arvindkumar Gupta

First published: October 2018

Production reference: 1301018

Published by Packt Publishing Ltd.
Livery Place
35 Livery Street
Birmingham
B3 2PB, UK.

ISBN 978-1-78862-288-2

www.packtpub.com

Mapt

mapt.io

Mapt is an online digital library that gives you full access to over 5,000 books and videos, as well as industry leading tools to help you plan your personal development and advance your career. For more information, please visit our website.

Why subscribe?

- Spend less time learning and more time coding with practical eBooks and Videos from over 4,000 industry professionals

- Improve your learning with Skill Plans built especially for you

- Get a free eBook or video every month

- Mapt is fully searchable

- Copy and paste, print, and bookmark content

Packt.com

Did you know that Packt offers eBook versions of every book published, with PDF and ePub files available? You can upgrade to the eBook version at www.packt.com and as a print book customer, you are entitled to a discount on the eBook copy. Get in touch with us at customercare@packtpub.com for more details.

At www.packt.com, you can also read a collection of free technical articles, sign up for a range of free newsletters, and receive exclusive discounts and offers on Packt books and eBooks.

Contributors

About the authors

Tamir Dresher is the chief architect of Clarizen, a leading SaaS company in work collaboration and project management. Prior to that, he was a senior architect and leader of the cloud division at CodeValue, Israel. Tamir has helped organizations and start-ups create scalable distributed systems with .NET and is a prominent member of Israel's Microsoft developers' community. He was awarded Microsoft MVP for his contributions as a conference speaker, organizing developer-community events, and authoring *Rx . NET in Action*. As part of his role as Professor of Software Engineering at the Ruppin Academic Center, Tamir loves teaching and mentoring students and speaking at international conferences. His Twitter handle is @tamir_dresher.

I want to thank those people who have been close to me and supported me, especially my wife, Gabriela, and my children, Shira, Yonatan, and Eyal. You are the ones who have given me the power to push forward. I love you.

Amir Zuker, a founder of CodeValue and its web division leader, is a senior software architect specializing in .NET and web-related technologies. Amir has headed up large development teams, conducted lectures and workshops, and has tackled various technological obstacles head-on in both frontend and backend products, including cloud, on-premise, and IoT solutions. A qualified instructor and consultant, he has helped dozens of companies build their systems from the ground up, including areas of recruitment, business analysis, architecture, design, implementation, testing, and DevOps. You can reach out to him via Twitter, @AmirZuker.

Shay Friedman is the CTO and VP, R&D, of Jifiti. With 20 years' experience in the software development world, Shay spearheads and manages the many technologies that Jifiti utilizes on a daily basis. Prior to that, Shay co-founded Pickspace, a VC-backed start-up in the field of real-estate tech. As CTO, he led the company's development efforts and helped it become a world leader in co-working space-related technologies. Prior to Pickspace, Shay co-founded CodeValue, one of the leading tech consulting companies in Israel, where he managed the web division, consulted dozens of companies, conducted training courses, and more. Shay is a renowned international speaker, loves playing basketball, and is endeavoring to improve his guitar playing.

I would like to thank my wife, Chen, and my beautiful family for their endless support and love. You give meaning to my words.

About the reviewers

Shama Hoque has more than 8 years' experience as a software developer and mentor, with a master's in software engineering from Carnegie Mellon University.

She specializes in full stack development with JavaScript, and currently makes web-based prototypes for R&D start-ups in California, while training aspiring software engineers and teaching web development to CS undergrads in Bangladesh.

She is also the author of Packt's *Full Stack React Projects* book, released in May 2018.

> *I would like to thank my family for their unconditional support and encouragement for everything I take on, and my students for continuously inspiring me to keep learning.*

Antonio Esposito is a Microsoft Certified Trainer, software architect, father, son, and lover of cooking and eating. He has been addicted to computer programming from age eight, a developer since 2002, and a speaker from 2010. He has moved across Europe in the last fifteen years working as freelance consultant or speaker for companies such as UniCredit Bank, Ferrari F1 Racing Team, Microsoft Italy, IBM, and many others. He actively attends as a speaker at a lot of conferences, such as MCT Summit and WPC Italy. He is already an author for Packt with *Learning .NET High Performance Programming* in 2014 and *Reactive Programming for .NET Developers* in 2015.

Paul Johnson has been writing software since the early 1980s on machines ranging from the ZX81 and servers to his trusty Mac, and has used more languages than he can remember. He is a qualified scuba diver and college lecturer. Paul lives with his wife, kids, and pets, and listens to an inordinate amount of rock and metal on Primordial Radio. This is his third book for Packt.

He is an avid biker and volunteers for the Merseyside and Cheshire Blood Bikes on a regular basis and is also currently working on a proposal for his 4th book with Packt.

Packt is searching for authors like you

If you're interested in becoming an author for Packt, please visit `authors.packtpub.com` and apply today. We have worked with thousands of developers and tech professionals, just like you, to help them share their insight with the global tech community. You can make a general application, apply for a specific hot topic that we are recruiting an author for, or submit your own idea.

Table of Contents

Preface

This book is intended for junior developers who are seeking to improve their web development skills and become full-stack developers.

It teaches the new way of writing web applications via the concepts of single-page applications and REST APIs. After reading and practicing with the book, you will be able to build both the backend and frontend parts of web applications, thereby becoming a full-stack developer.

Who this book is for

This book is intended for C# programmers interested in developing, and further enhancing, their skills in the development of web applications running in the cloud. Additionally, novice web developers who wish to learn the modern way of writing web apps using several leading frameworks will benefit a great deal from this book.
This book is for junior developers with prior experience in writing C# applications, and will teach you the basics of creating backend applications with ASP.NET Core, and frontend applications with modern technologies.

What this book covers

Chapter 1, *Becoming a Full-Stack .NET Developer*, explains the meaning of full-stack development and what technologies will be covered throughout the rest of the book.

Chapter 2, *Setting Up Your Development Environment*, guides you through the installation of tools that you will use throughout this book.

Chapter 3, *Creating a Web Application with ASP.NET Core*, teaches the basics of ASP.NET Core as a framework for creating web applications.

Chapter 4, *Building REST APIs with ASP.NET Core Web API*, explains why REST architectural styles are preferable when it comes to creating backends and teaches you how to create a REST API with ASP.NET Core.

Chapter 5, *Persisting Data with Entity Framework*, defines the data model you will use for the GiveNTake sample application this book creates, and teaches you how to store and query data from a relational database using EF Core.

Chapter 6, *Securing the Backend Server,* teaches you how to make your service more secure and how to add authentication and authorization so that you can control who will use your APIs.

Chapter 7, *Troubleshooting and Debugging,* covers a number of techniques that will be valuable when you develop your backend application and that will allow you to troubleshoot potential issues.

Chapter 8, *Getting Started with Frontend Web Development,* covers the history, as well as current and future developments, in the web development field, focusing on HTML, CSS, and JavaScript. At the same time, it illustrates the app that you will build throughout the book and demonstrates a classic implementation of that using jQuery.

Chapter 9, *Getting Started with TypeScript,* covers TypeScript, which is designed and maintained by Microsoft. In this chapter, we will cover the fundamentals of TypeScript, such as types, interfaces, classes, modules, decorators. TypeScript uses static typing and assists tremendously with maintainability and productivity.

Chapter 10, *App Development with Angular,* explains what Angular is, along with its features, and then teaches you how to build web apps using Angular as it takes you through a detailed step-by-step tutorial in building an actual app.

Chapter 11, *Implementing Routing and Forms,* teaches you additional features in Angular, specifically, its rich support for routing and forms as you add these to the app you built in the previous chapter.

Chapter 12, *App Development with React,* explains what React is, along with its features, and then teaches you how to build web apps using React as it takes you through a detailed step-by-step tutorial in building an actual app.

Chapter 13, *App Development with Vue,* explains what Vue is, along with its features, and then teaches you how to build web apps using Vue as it takes you through a detailed step-by-step tutorial in building an actual app.

Chapter 14, *Moving Your Solution to the Cloud,* reviews the meaning of the cloud and guides you in the first steps of creating your account in Microsoft Azure.

Chapter 15, *Deploying to Microsoft Azure,* explains the steps you need to carry out in order to deploy and host your application in Microsoft Azure and teaches you how to automate the process.

Chapter 16, *Taking Advantage of Cloud Services*, demonstrates a number of valuable services that the Azure cloud has to offer that will make it easier for you to scale your service based on demand, troubleshoot problems, and create multiple environments for the purpose of testing new features.

To get the most out of this book

You should have experience of, and feel comfortable with, programming with C#.

Prior knowledge of ASP.NET or other .NET web technologies, along with HTML and JavaScript, is recommended.

Download the example code files

You can download the example code files for this book from your account at www.packt.com. If you purchased this book elsewhere, you can visit www.packt.com/support and register to have the files emailed directly to you.

You can download the code files by following these steps:

1. Log in or register at www.packt.com.
2. Select the **SUPPORT** tab.
3. Click on **Code Downloads & Errata**.
4. Enter the name of the book in the **Search** box and follow the onscreen instructions.

Once the file is downloaded, please make sure that you unzip or extract the folder using the latest version of:

- WinRAR/7-Zip for Windows
- Zipeg/iZip/UnRarX for Mac
- 7-Zip/PeaZip for Linux

The code bundle for the book is also hosted on GitHub at https://github.com/ PacktPublishing/Hands-On-Full-Stack-Web-Development-with-ASP.NET-Core. In case there's an update to the code, it will be updated on the existing GitHub repository.

We also have other code bundles from our rich catalog of books and videos available at https://github.com/PacktPublishing/. Check them out!

Download the color images

We also provide a PDF file that has color images of the screenshots/diagrams used in this book. You can download it here: `https://www.packtpub.com/sites/default/files/downloads/9781788622882_ColorImages.pdf`.

Conventions used

There are a number of text conventions used throughout this book.

`CodeInText`: Indicates code words in text, database table names, folder names, filenames, file extensions, pathnames, dummy URLs, user input, and Twitter handles. Here is an example: "For example, if you need to use `System.IO`, you can get it from NuGet as a separate library, without the need to add and load the entire `System` assembly."

A block of code is set as follows:

```
public static IWebHostBuilder CreateWebHostBuiler(string[] args) =>
    WebHost.CreateDefaultBuilder(args)
        .UseStartup<Startup>();
```

When we wish to draw your attention to a particular part of a code block, the relevant lines or items are set in bold:

```
WebHost.CreateDefaultBuilder(args)
    .UseContentRoot(Path.Combine(Directory.GetCurrentDirectory(),
    "/client"))
    .UseStartup<Startup>()
    .Build();
```

Any command-line input or output is written as follows:

```
dotnet new web
```

Bold: Indicates a new term, an important word, or words that you see on screen. For example, words in menus or dialog boxes appear in the text like this. Here is an example: "Open Visual Studio and go to **File** | **New** | **Project**...."

Warnings or important notes appear like this.

Tips and tricks appear like this.

Get in touch

Feedback from our readers is always welcome.

General feedback: If you have questions about any aspect of this book, mention the book title in the subject of your message and email us at customercare@packtpub.com.

Errata: Although we have taken every care to ensure the accuracy of our content, mistakes do happen. If you have found a mistake in this book, we would be grateful if you would report this to us. Please visit www.packt.com/submit-errata, selecting your book, clicking on the Errata Submission Form link, and entering the details.

Piracy: If you come across any illegal copies of our works in any form on the internet, we would be grateful if you would provide us with the location address or website name. Please contact us at copyright@packt.com with a link to the material.

If you are interested in becoming an author: If there is a topic that you have expertise in and you are interested in either writing or contributing to a book, please visit authors.packtpub.com.

Reviews

Please leave a review. Once you have read and used this book, why not leave a review on the site that you purchased it from? Potential readers can then see and use your unbiased opinion to make purchase decisions, we at Packt can understand what you think about our products, and our authors can see your feedback on their book. Thank you!

For more information about Packt, please visit `packt.com`.

Becoming a Full-Stack .NET Developer

1

The **World Wide Web (WWW)** has changed tremendously since its beginning. In less than 30 years, it has morphed from a document-sharing space into a sophisticated platform that joins the world together. The role of developers, the ones behind the scenes of this global craze, has also changed accordingly.

Having started with the title *Web Master* — a job that required some knowledge of HTML and a little bit of Perl — the web developer role has changed into *full-stack developer*. A short title with a big meaning. As a full-stack developer, you're required to master many programming languages, markup languages, and tools — and that is before you even start working on the actual project at hand. It's an extremely challenging role, yet one of the most satisfying in the software industry.

In this chapter, we'll demystify what it means to be a full-stack developer and go through the basic concepts and ideas such a developer needs to know. We will cover the following topics:

- The full-stack developer
- Backend fundamentals
- Frontend fundamentals

The full-stack developer

Full-stack developer is a term that describes a developer who is experienced with the entire stack of application development — the backend side, which also includes the database, and the frontend side, which is commonly known as the user interface. It sounds like only a few selected developers who have a vast amount of knowledge and incredible, almost mythical, skills are qualified to bear this title - full-stack. However, the truth is different—nobody can know everything, and the secret is to pick a specific stack of technologies and deep dive into them. Being a full-stack developer will allow you to develop any kind of application, and thus opens up an endless amount of opportunities.

Full-stack development

Full-stack development refers to a client-server architecture model, or, as it's more commonly known, the frontend and backend. These are different in almost every single aspect. Backend development refers to writing code for the server side—handling data, providing APIs, managing security, deployment, and more. Frontend development refers to writing code for the client side—in our case, web clients running in users' browsers, working on the user interface, presentation logic, browser compatibility, performance, responsiveness, and more.

The backend and frontend parts do not usually share code; it might be written in entirely different programming languages, and run on different types of machines and in geographical locations. They communicate through the network via the HTTP protocol with the help of standards, ideas, practices, and architectural styles such as REST and JSON. The most notable difference between the backend and the frontend is the intended end user that interacts with each one of them—the backend interface serves computer systems, while the frontend interface serves human beings, as shown in the following diagram:

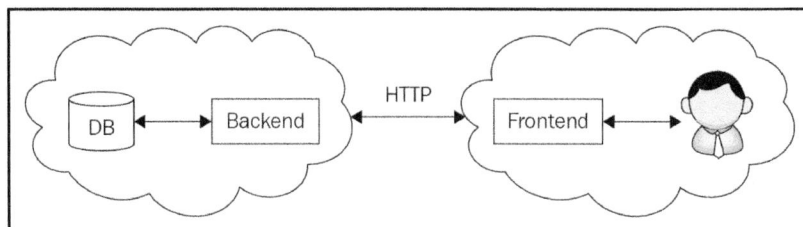

Being a full-stack developer means that you are an all-around developer who understands the different concepts and responsibilities of each part and, moreover, is able to take an idea and implement it from the very first line of code to a finished and deployed product.

In order to begin diving into full-stack development, let's get familiar with the concepts, responsibilities, and technologies for each part of the stack.

Backend fundamentals

The backend side of a system is one or more applications running on machines that are commonly referred to as servers. The purpose of these applications is to serve requests coming from other applications—clients—and execute the necessary steps to accomplish the given request (validate the input, verify the requester's permissions, query and update rows in the database, run algorithms and workflows, and, at the end, return a response that the client side can then use to determine how to proceed.

The backend side of a project is like the soil in a flower field—if the soil is healthy, it enables a flourishing field with lovely flowers. However, if the soil is dry and not taken care of, the flowers will die and the field will cease to exist.

In our case, the field is the backend server and the flowers are our users—the backend needs to be reliable, secure, fast, and scalable in order to support many happy users and to create a successful product.

The world of backend development is extensive — there are a vast amount of programming languages and technologies that you can choose from. Each of them looks at this world from a slightly different angle, enabling different targets. For example, C# is a very powerful language that comes with plenty of handy tools, JavaScript allows you to write the backend and the frontend using the same programming language, and Python is suitable for systems based on math and complex algorithms.

Fortunately, whatever the technology of choice is, its interface to external systems will follow the same protocols as other backend systems — HTTP and JSON, which allow the creation of RESTful APIs. This enables strict separation of concerns between the backend and the frontend — each of them can be created using a different set of technologies but they will still be able to communicate flawlessly.

Hypertext Transfer Protocol

Hypertext Transfer Protocol (HTTP) is the foundation of communication on the WWW. It defines the format of messages and the way they are transmitted between the client and the server.

HTTP has two sides to communication — the client and the server. On web applications, the client is the user's web browser and the server is the backend server. Communication happens when the client creates a message called an HTTP request, sends it to the server, and the server, in turn, responds with an HTTP response, as shown in the following diagram:

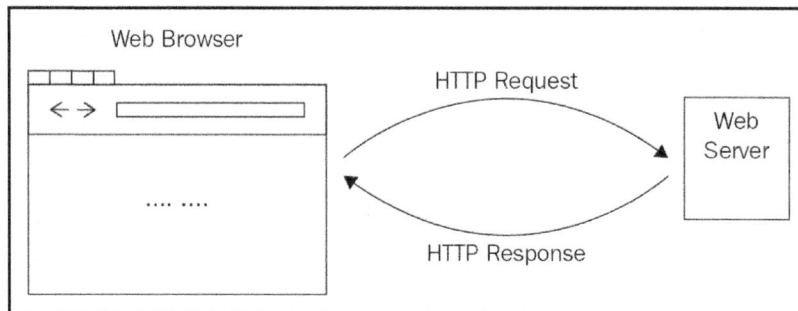

Each HTTP request consists of a few pieces of information:

- **URI**: The web address or IP address that identifies the server. For example, `http://example.com` or `http://192.168.0.1`.
- **Method:** The action that should be taken upon the requested resource. For example, `GET` indicates data retrieval and `POST` indicates data creation.
- **Body**: Contains the data to be sent to the server, if any. The most popular data format for HTTP requests is JSON but, generally, data can be formatted in any format that the server understands.
- **Headers**: An optional set of metadata key-value pairs that add information to a request.

The server retrieves this request, executes related logical steps (commonly known as business logic), and forms an HTTP response to be sent back to the client. This response includes a few details:

- **Status code**: A three-digit integer that describes the result of the request. For example, 200 means OK, 500 means there was an error in the server, and 404 means the requested resource was not found.

- **Body**: The data sent back from the server, if any. As with the request body, JSON is the common data format, but any other format is valid as well.
- **Headers**: An optional set of metadata key-value pairs that add information about the response.

HTTP is a stateless protocol

The HTTP protocol is a stateless one. This means that every HTTP request the server receives is independent and does not relate to requests that came prior to it. For example, imagine the following scenario: a request is made for the first ten user records, then another request is made for the next ten records.

On a stateful protocol, the server remembers each client position inside the result-set, and therefore the requests will be similar to:

- Give me the first ten user records
- Give me the next ten records

On a stateless protocol, the requests will be a bit different. The server doesn't hold the state of its client, and therefore the client's position in the result-set needs to be sent as part of the requests:

- Give me user records on index 1 to 10
- Give me user records on index 11 to 20

The slight difference between these examples represents the different approaches. On stateful protocols, you assume that the server knows everything about the previous requests, while on a stateless protocol you assume the opposite—the server doesn't know anything about the previous requests, which is why you send all the necessary information with each and every request.

On the one hand, this makes web service development more challenging, since creating fast, stateless service is not an easy task. On the other hand, this enables services to scale out quickly and support millions of users rather easily.

HTTP/2

HTTP was created by Sir Tim Berners-Lee, the founder of the World Wide Web, back in 1989. The first version, HTTP 1.0, was introduced in 1996, followed by HTTP 1.1, which was introduced in 1997. HTTP 1.1 is still the most common version of HTTP out there.

In May 2015, HTTP/2 was released, which provided several improvements and enhancements to the old HTTP 1.1 protocol, such as server-to-client `push` messages and binary data support, to name just a couple. Ever since, it has been adopted by many websites and is slowly becoming the standard version of choice for websites.

Representational State Transfer

Representational state transfer (REST) is an architectural style for resource-oriented services. It is used by most web applications today to standardize communication between the client and the server. If HTTP was the *spoken language*, REST would be a set of rules for that language.

REST-based web services, also known as RESTful APIs, have a few constraints they need to follow:

- **Consistent interface**: Every entity is a resource that will have a unique endpoint— a unique base URL. All operations on a resource will be available via that URL.
- **URL and HTTP methods**: When a resource URL is combined with an HTTP method, it describes an operation performed on the resource. For example, GET means retrieving data, POST means creating data, and DELETE means deleting data.
- **Statelessness**: Just like the HTTP protocol, RESTful services are stateless. This means that each request is independent and information regarding previous requests is never used.
- **Cacheable**: For each response, the server defines whether it is cacheable or not. Once a response is set as cacheable, the client caches it and uses the data from the cache instead of requesting it from the server again and again.

For example, in an application that manages students, we could have the following services:

URL	HTTP Method	Description
/students	GET	Retrieve all students
/students	POST	Create a new student
/students/123	GET	Retrieve student with ID 123
/students/123	PUT	Update student with ID 123
/students/123	DELETE	Delete student with ID 123

REST has become the de facto style of communication between the backend and the frontend. This is especially because it is a simple concept, yet very powerful — it makes the backend understandable to other developers and simple to modify and scale, and supports multiple types of clients, including web and mobile.

ASP.NET Core

ASP.NET Core is a free, open-source web framework developed by Microsoft. It provides features that enable building the backend for modern web applications, as well as web APIs. The programming language that is used for the development of ASP.NET Core is C# or any other .NET-based programming language.

ASP.NET Core is a redesign of the popular ASP.NET **Model View Controller** (**MVC**) and ASP.NET Web API frameworks. The result is a leaner and more modular framework that can run on the full .NET Framework on Windows and .NET Core on other platforms.

Both parts of the framework, MVC and Web API, help in creating modern web applications. MVC is for building traditional web applications in which rendering is done on the server-side, but also supports integration with modern JS libraries and client-side rendering. ASP.NET offers many web development features out of the box, such as security, data validation, deployment, and more. ASP.NET Web API is for creating RESTful web services that serve modern frontend applications, mobile apps, and any other endpoints.

ASP.NET Core is a popular choice but is definitely not alone in the world of backend development. It is similar to other frameworks such as Laravel (PHP), Spring (Java), Ruby on Rails (Ruby), Django (Python), and others. Each has its own advantages and disadvantages. I chose ASP.NET Core for this book as it is one of the top frameworks out there, runs on the powerful C# language, and has wonderful IDE support.

Frontend fundamentals

The frontend is where users interact with your system. There's a lot to consider and prepare for in the frontend since users, unlike machines, are not homogeneous and this affects their experience when using a website—some have technical experience and some do not; some are young while others are older. The design should be inviting, the flow of work should be clear, and the way things work should help the user be effective and avoid mistakes.

We achieve these targets by working with three technologies that complement each other: HTML, **Cascading Style Sheets (CSS)**, and JavaScript — the undisputed kings of the WWW:

- **HTML**: Describes what exists on a page
- **CSS**: Describes how a page looks
- **JavaScript**: Describes how a page behaves

These technologies have been the foundation of the internet almost since the day it was born. They have been growing and maturing ever since, adding much-needed features that enable more complex systems to be written on top of them.

As a result, frontend development frameworks have started to pop up in the last decade. Their goal is to take advantage of HTML, CSS, and JavaScript and bring them to the next level. These frameworks have added conventions, programming models, and advanced patterns and techniques, and have generally enabled developers to create massive systems using web technologies in a productive and stable way.

These advances indicated the beginning of a big shift in web development architecture—from traditional, server-centric architecture to **Single-page application (SPA)**, client-server architecture.

Since the beginning of the WWW, the way web applications has been developed was server-centric, with minimal to no code running on the client. For example, the following sequence describes the usual flow of work:

1. The user browses to a web address.
2. The server gets the request, generates HTML for the user, and sends it back.
3. The browser gets the HTML and displays it to the user. The user sees the web page and clicks a button.
4. The server receives the button click, generates HTML that matches the button click, and returns it. In the meantime, the user sees an empty browser screen.
5. The browser gets the HTML and displays it to the user. The user sees the web page.

On the one hand, this was easier to code and maintain, since all the code was located on the server. On the other hand, this way is slow and provides a poor user experience for the user.

This architecture was used mainly because browsers didn't support features required for rich client development. Once that started to change with new versions of HTML, CSS, and JavaScript, the shift toward full client-server architecture began too.

The new architecture is known as SPA, which is basically client-server architecture. It was named SPA because of its differences from traditional web applications. In traditional web applications, the user navigates between different pages that are retrieved separately from the server upon request. In SPA applications, there is only one page, which contains the entire application, and every UI change is made locally via JavaScript. A usual flow of work in SPA architecture will look like the following:

1. The user navigates to a web address.
2. The server responds with HTML and multiple JavaScript files that contain the client-side application code.
3. The browser gets the files and displays the web page to the user. The user sees it and clicks a button.
4. JavaScript code on the client handles the click and calls the server side for data. In the meantime, the user sees a loading animation.
5. The server gets the request for data, retrieves the required data, and sends it back to the client.
6. JavaScript gets the response from the server, generates matching HTML, and displays it to the user. The user sees the updated web page.

This architecture enables rich client development that works quickly and smoothly. However, it does make it more complicated to develop web applications, as developers are required to master both client and server technologies.

Hypertext Markup Language

Hypertext markup language (HTML) has been a part of web development since the very beginning of the WWW in 1989. At the beginning, it was used to display simple documents, but as the web grew, HTML matured and adjusted to support not just documents, but also full-blown applications.

HTML is a markup language, which means that it does not have programming language-specific dynamic capabilities such as variables, loops, or functions. Its sole responsibility is to statically describe the content of a web page.

The most recent version, HTML5, added long-awaited features such as new types of form controls, canvas, native video capabilities, and numerous new JavaScript APIs.

CSS

CSS is a style sheet language that is used to describe how HTML elements look. It is one of the pillars of web development, and provides many features for web developers that enable the creation of web applications that look great and adapt themselves to both mobile and desktop use.

CSS is a markup language and, like HTML, it does not support dynamic features such as variables and loops. Having said that, CSS does have some capabilities that enable it to change the look of an element based on its state, such as when a mouse is hovering over it, or based on an environment detail such as screen width.

In recent years, there has been interesting progress in the world of CSS. Since CSS is used in every single web application today, developers required more advanced capabilities for development — features such as variables, hierarchy, mixins (grouping CSS declarations for better reusability), and others — that were absent from CSS. As a result, new languages have been created, such as SCSS and LESS. These languages are supersets of CSS—they add much-needed features to the CSS development process and compile to CSS to be interpreted by browsers.

The last version of CSS, CSS3, added features such as web fonts, animations, transformations, and transitions that made the web application experience much smoother and more user-friendly.

JavaScript

JavaScript is the third part of the web development triangle — HTML, CSS, and JavaScript. It is a dynamic multi-paradigm programming language that is natively supported by all web browsers. It is used to add dynamic capabilities to web pages and to control the behavior of its elements.

The JavaScript language is an implementation of its standard, ECMAScript. Almost every browser has its own implementation of the ECMAScript standard. For example, Chrome has V8, Safari has WebKit, and Edge has Chakra.

JavaScript is the basis of all web application development frameworks, such as Angular, React, and others. Additionally, apart from frontend development, it has been adapted for backend development via the Node.js runtime environment.

The ES2015 version brought major enhancements to the language with new syntax for classes and modules, the `for-of` loop, arrow functions, and more. The latest version, ES2017, introduced the anticipated `async/await` feature.

TypeScript

TypeScript is a programming language developed by Microsoft, and is used primarily as a JavaScript substitute for development. The language adds features and enhancements to the JavaScript language that help in creating and maintaining large code bases.

TypeScript compiles (or, more correctly, transpiles) to JavaScript, which can then be interpreted by browsers or any other JavaScript runtime environments.

TypeScript adds static typing capabilities to JavaScript, such as type declaration and interfaces. In addition, it enables developers to use new JavaScript syntax from the latest, or even future, ECMAScript releases, and compile them to JavaScript, which can be interpreted by today's web browsers.

TypeScript has become very popular in the last couple of years, and is even used to develop the Angular framework itself. Though it is not required for SPA-based application development, it makes code clearer and more maintainable, which is why it is highly popular among developers.

JavaScript frontend frameworks

Writing your frontend with pure JavaScript is possible, and it was the way websites were developed for many years. Over the years, several libraries have emerged incorporating different controls and allowing code reusability. As they have grown, some of these libraries have merged together to create a framework that helps developers to create complete websites from start to end, while also providing answers to many aspects required by modern websites, such as routing, authentication, data binding, state management, and so on.

In this book, we will concentrate on three of the most popular JavaScript frameworks today: Angular, React, and Vue.js.

Angular

Angular (`https://angular.io/`) is an SPA frontend web application development platform developed by Google and the open source community. It is the successor of the popular AngularJS framework, which dominated the SPA platform world at the beginning of the decade.

Angular takes HTML, CSS, and JavaScript and puts them in the context of application development with modular, component-based architecture, conventions, and utilities. It consists of a few basic concepts:

- **Modules**: Containers of Angular code
- **Data binding**: A mechanism that automatically reflects changes in the code on the UI, and vice versa
- **Components**: An HTML template combined with JavaScript code that controls it
- **Directives**: Add behavior to HTML elements of Angular components
- **Services**: Units of work that are additional to UI development, such as data handling or logging

Angular is one of the most popular frameworks today for web application development, and even has frameworks built on top of it such as NativeScript, which enables native mobile development based on an Angular code.

React

React, released and managed by Facebook, is a JavaScript SPA framework focusing on components, serving the purpose of a view engine. Contrary to Angular, React is less opinionated on how you build an entire app and requires a milder learning curve, albeit it's just a view engine. React enables building encapsulated and reusable components using its notorious and controversial JSX, a **domain-specific language** (**DSL**) that allows you to write the view of the component in JavaScript alongside the component logical code.

React was released to the public in 2013 and it has made a great impact in the field, introducing great concepts to web apps, such as JSX, Virtual DOM, unidirectional data flow and great performance.

Notably, React is not just for web apps. React follows the notion of *Learn-Once-Write-Everywhere*. Meaning, you can leverage React to write apps that target different platforms, for example using React Native for cross-platform native mobile apps and React360 for VR.

Moreover, the innovation and collaboration around React is astonishing and its community is paramount. React is just a component library, thus enthusiast followers have created complementary libraries to provide other aspects related to app development, such as state management, routing, and isomorphic rendering. Some of which have too made a noticeable influence in the field as well, for example, Flux and Redux.

Ever since its release, React has been gaining popularity at a steady pace, taking its place as the leading SPA framework for quite some time now.

Vue.js

Vue.js (`https://vuejs.org/`), commonly referred to as Vue and pronounced view, is a JavaScript framework that aims to be approachable, with a less steep learning curve than other frameworks. Vue is based on the **Model–view–viewmodel** (**MVVM**) (`https://en.wikipedia.org/wiki/Model%E2%80%93view%E2%80%93viewmodel`) UI architecture and is focused on the *ViewModel* layer. It connects the *View* and the *Model* via two-way data bindings.

Vue consists of the following features and ideas:

- **Data binding (reactiveness)**: A mechanism that automatically reflects changes in the code on the UI and vice versa
- **Components**: An HTML template combined with JavaScript code that controls it
- **Directives**: Prefixed HTML attributes that tell Vue.js to do something about a DOM element
- **Filters:** Functions used to process raw values before updating the view

Summary

The full-stack developer is a master of backend and frontend technologies, and most of all, of the core concepts involved in building web applications. In this chapter, we have gone through the definition of full-stack development and learned what it takes to become a full-stack developer.

The full-stack development field has grown and matured tremendously in the last decade. From static informative websites, it has evolved into full-featured applications, which have almost entirely replaced the previous industry kings, desktop applications, making full-stack development the land of opportunity in the software development world.

Setting Up Your Development Environment

2

Writing code can be a complex job — you need to be precise, make as few mistakes as possible, prepare for failure, and, of course, get the job done. Tools such as an **Integrated Development Environment (IDE)** are important, because they can help in all of these tasks, and therefore, choosing the right one is a crucial decision in a project's life.

Just as the technologies themselves have been growing and maturing, so have the full-stack development tools. However, it is not enough for them to be amazing and simply exist—as a professional full-stack developer, it is your job to know these tools from top to bottom, and use them accordingly.

In this chapter, we will prepare our work environment, and install the following necessary applications and tools for full-stack development with the ASP.NET Core and JavaScript frameworks:

- Visual Studio
- Node.js and npm
- TypeScript
- Google Chrome
- Fiddler

Visual Studio

Visual Studio is an IDE that we will use for writing both our backend and frontend code. With more than 20 years of existence, it is one of the most advanced development environments today.

There are plenty of IDEs, and it is up to you to try a few of them and keep the one you feel most comfortable with. For me, Visual Studio is the best choice when writing .NET code, so I chose to work with it throughout this book. Nevertheless, if you prefer a different IDE, keep using it.

Installing Visual Studio Community

Visual Studio Community edition is the free version of Visual Studio. It is more than enough for what we need, but if you're a part of an enterprise company or a big team, you might want to consider the paid versions.

To install Visual Studio Community, open your browser and browse to `https://www.`
`visualstudio.com/vs/community`, and then click on the **Download VS Community 2017** button. There are versions for both the Windows and macOS operating systems to choose from.

Once the download is complete, locate the downloaded file and run it. You might be asked by the Windows **User Account Control** system to allow the file to make changes to your computer — click **Yes** to continue:

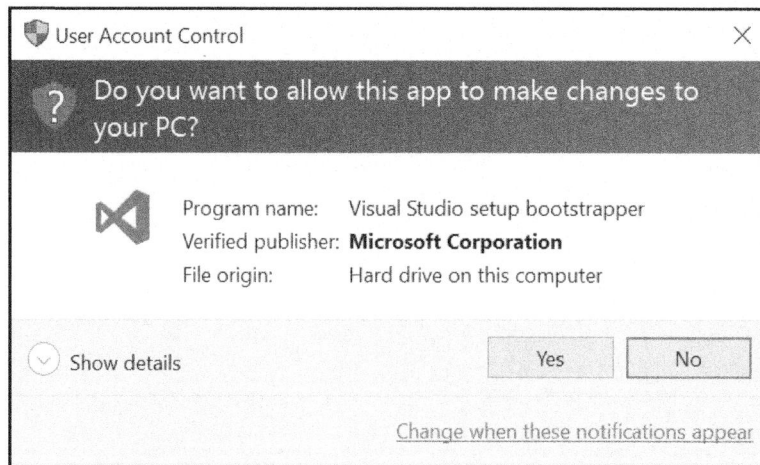

After the installation begins, follow these steps:

1. When installation starts, you will see the following welcome screen:

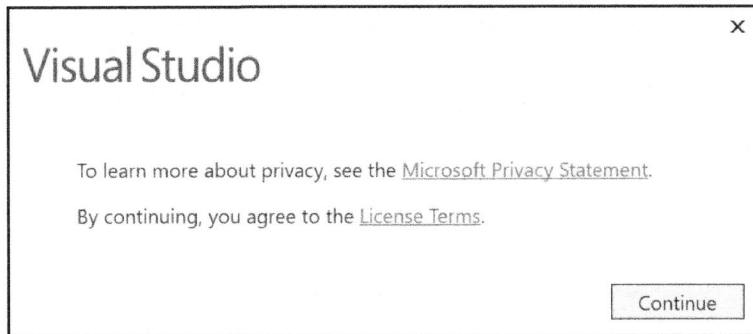

Click **Continue** to agree to the **License Terms** and continue to the next steps.

2. An installation window will appear, where you are asked to choose the workloads you will need during development. Scroll down the list and choose **ASP.NET and web development**, **Azure development**, and **.NET Core cross-platform development**, as shown here:

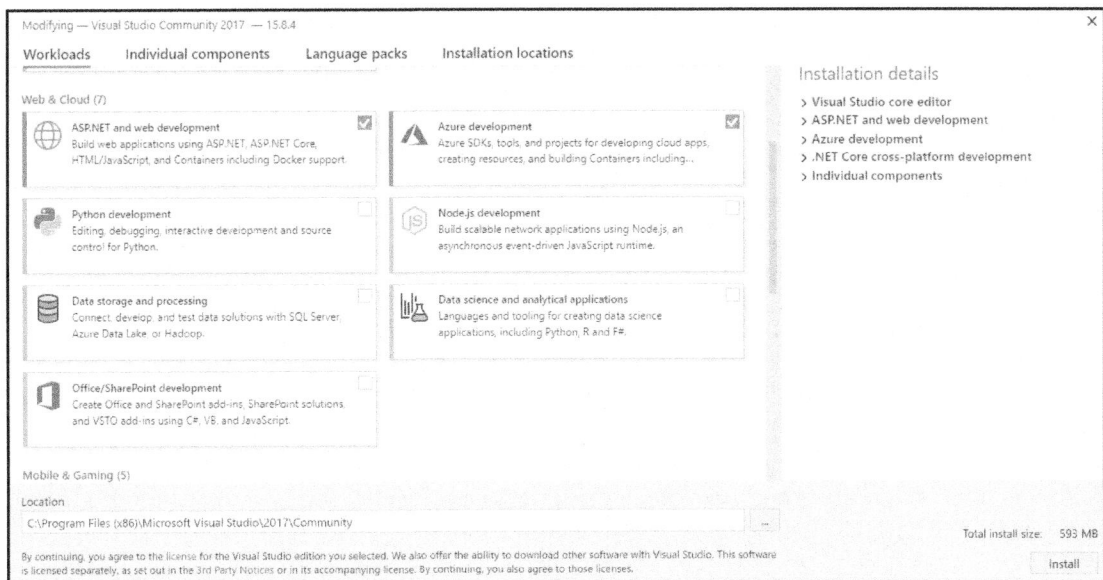

3. Click the **Install** button in the bottom-right of the screen to start the installation process.

4. The installation might take several minutes to complete. You can get an idea of how much more time is needed by looking at the progress indicator:

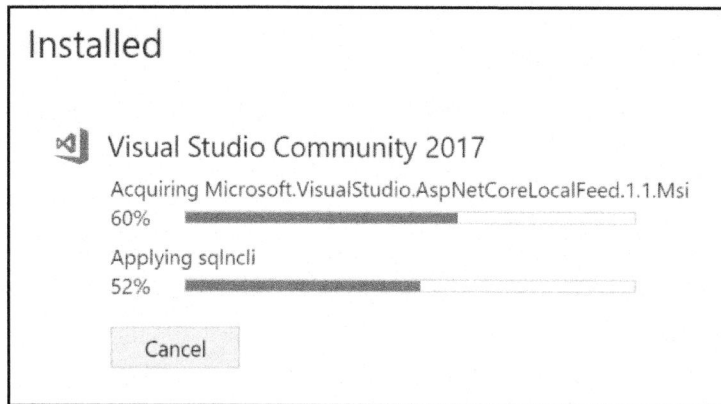

Installed

Visual Studio Community 2017

Acquiring Microsoft.VisualStudio.AspNetCoreLocalFeed.1.1.Msi
60%

Applying sqlncli
52%

Cancel

5. When the installation is done, you might be asked to restart your computer. If so, go ahead:

Reboot required

Success! One more step to go. Please restart your computer before you start Visual Studio Community 2017.

Get troubleshooting tips   Restart   Not now

6. After restarting, click on **Start | All Programs | Visual Studio 2017** to open Visual Studio Community.
7. If the installation was successful, you will be asked to sign in. At the moment, this is not important, so you can skip this step by clicking **Not now, maybe later**.

8. In the next window, shown in the following screenshot, select **Web Development** in the **Development Settings** drop-down menu, choose your favorite color theme, and click **Start Visual Studio**:

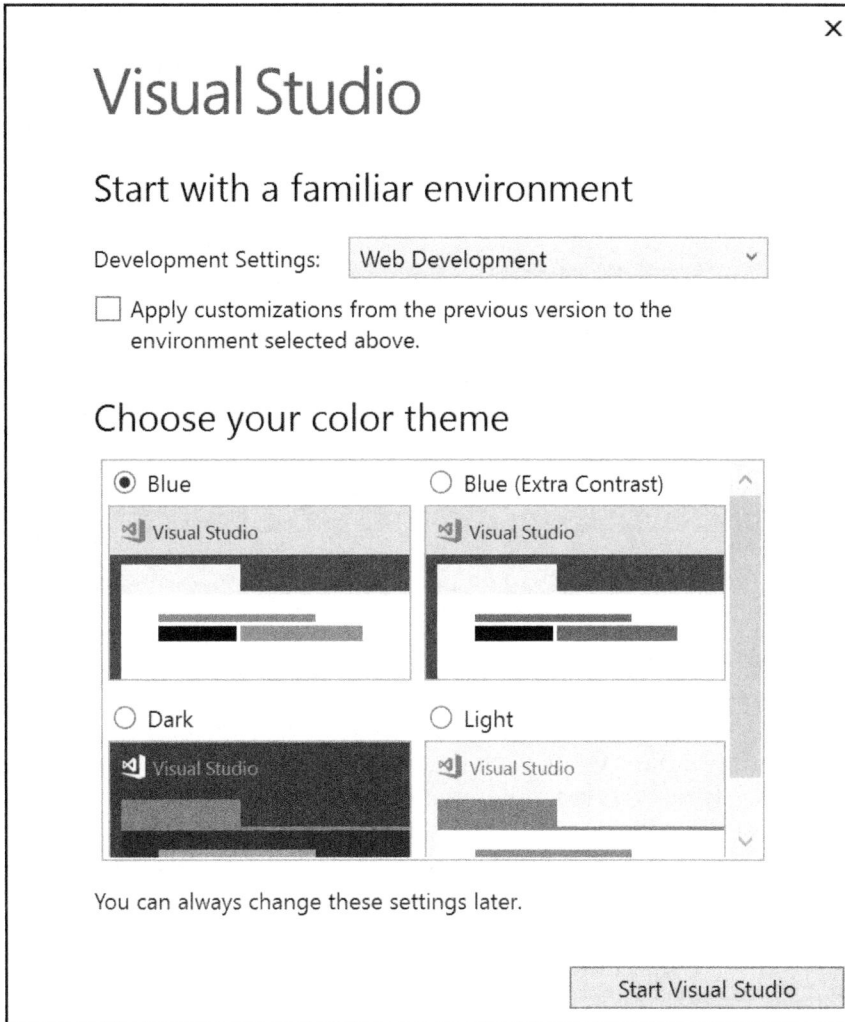

9. Visual Studio will run some initialization processes and then start, as shown here:

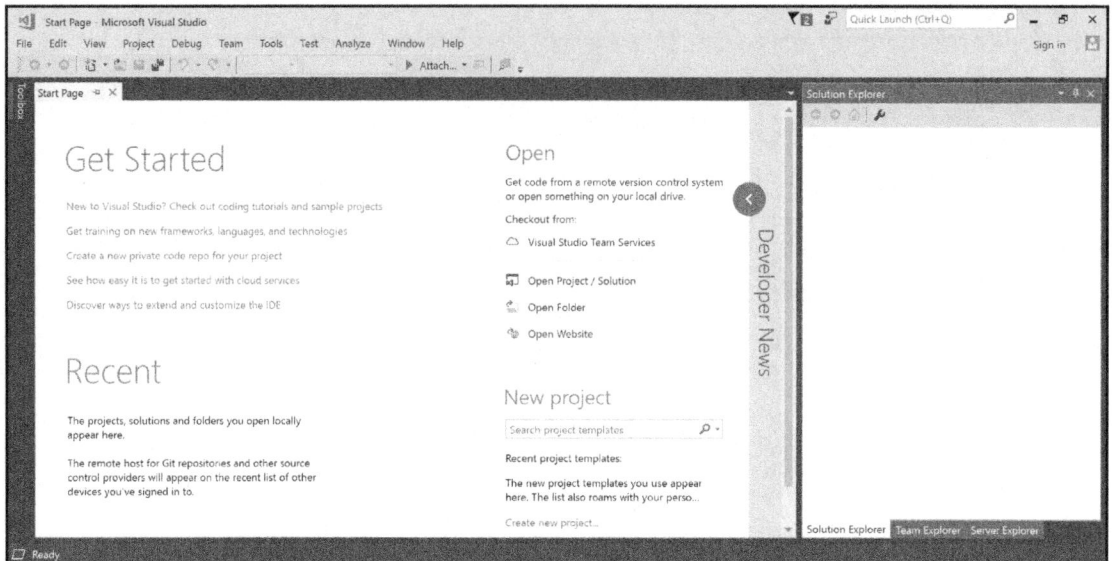

Now that you have Visual Studio installed, let's continue installing the other tools.

Node.js and npm

Node.js is a JavaScript runtime environment. It is a technology that enables you to run JavaScript code directly on your computer, without the need for a browser. It has gained popularity, Node.js is the technology responsible for these servers actually running, as well as being behind countless web development utilities. Throughout this book, we will use it for the latter option.

npm is a large repository of JavaScript libraries and utilities—almost 500,000 in the time of writing — that you can easily install and add to your project or computer.

Installing Node.js

To install Node.js, follow these steps:

1. Open your browser and navigate to `https://nodejs.org/en/download`.
2. Find the installer that matches your operating system, and click on it to download it.
3. When the download is complete, execute the downloaded file to open the installation wizard, which should look like the following:

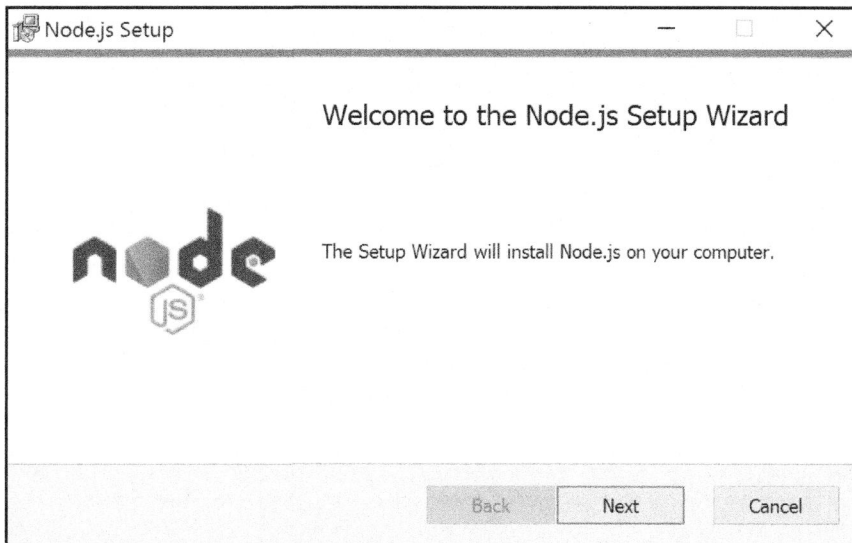

4. Click **Next** to move forward in the wizard steps until the installation begins:

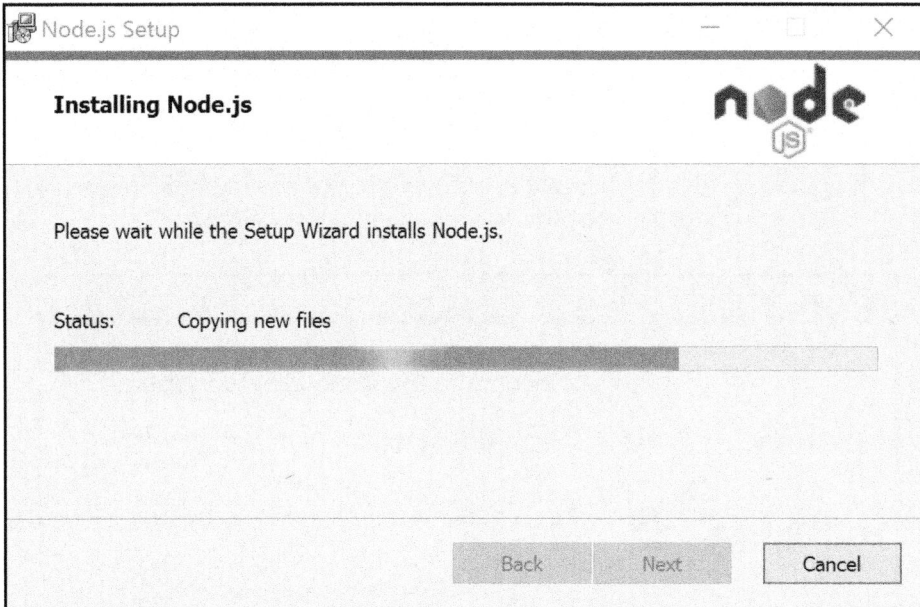

5. Once the Node.js installation is done, click **Finish** to close the wizard:

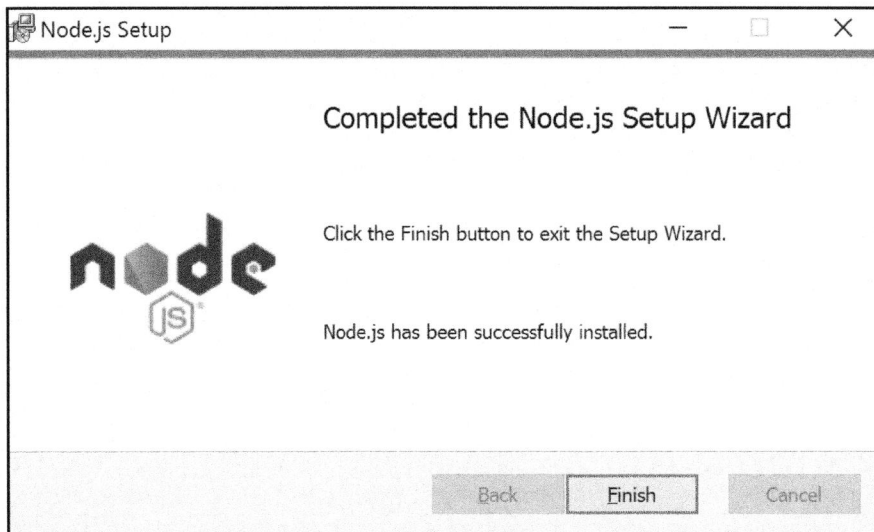

6. To test that Node.js was installed successfully, click Start | **All Programs** | **Windows System** | **Command Prompt**.

7. In the Command Prompt window, write the following command and press *Enter*:

```
node --version
```

You should see the version of the installed Node.js platform, as shown here:

```
Command Prompt                                        —    □    ×
Microsoft Windows [Version 10.0.10586]
(c) 2015 Microsoft Corporation. All rights reserved.

C:\Users\shayi>node --version
v6.11.3

C:\Users\shayi>
```

Installing Node.js also installs npm, so there are no further steps needed.

TypeScript

TypeScript is a programming language for large web applications. It adds new static typing features to JavaScript, as well as implementing upcoming features of the JavaScript language to enable developers to use them today.

Browsers are not familiar with TypeScript, so you must compile TypeScript files into JavaScript before deploying them. To do this, you will need to install **TypeScript compiler (tsc)**, the TypeScript compiler.

Installing TypeScript

To install TypeScript, follow the next steps:

1. Click Start | **All Programs** | **Windows System** | **Command Prompt**
2. Write the following command and press *Enter*:

```
npm install typescript -g
```

3. This will start the TypeScript installation
4. After a few seconds, the installation will end, and TypeScript will be installed on your
   machine
5. To test whether or not TypeScript is installed correctly, write the following command into Command Prompt and press *Enter*:

   ```
   tsc --version
   ```

   If the installed version is displayed, then TypeScript has been installed correctly

> If you receive an error, try to close and reopen Command Prompt and try again. If that doesn't work, try to go through the preceding steps again to reinstall TypeScript.

Google Chrome

There are several different browsers in use today — Google Chrome, Firefox, Microsoft Edge, Apple Safari, Opera, and more. The differences between them get smaller all the time, so as a user, choosing this browser or the other is not such a big deal.

However, as a developer, it is an important decision — you will need to pick the one that is most developer-friendly and has the best developer tools. Today, the Chrome **Developer Tools**, also known as Chrome DevTools, are used by many developers and provide many strong capabilities. This is why we will be using Chrome throughout this book to demonstrate and debug code samples.

> Even though Chrome is the leading browser today, do not forget to test your Web API against all major browsers before going live.

To install Google Chrome, do the following:

1. Open your browser and navigate to `https://www.google.com/chrome`
2. Click on **Download Chrome**
3. Click on **ACCEPT AND INSTALL** in the download pop-up window:

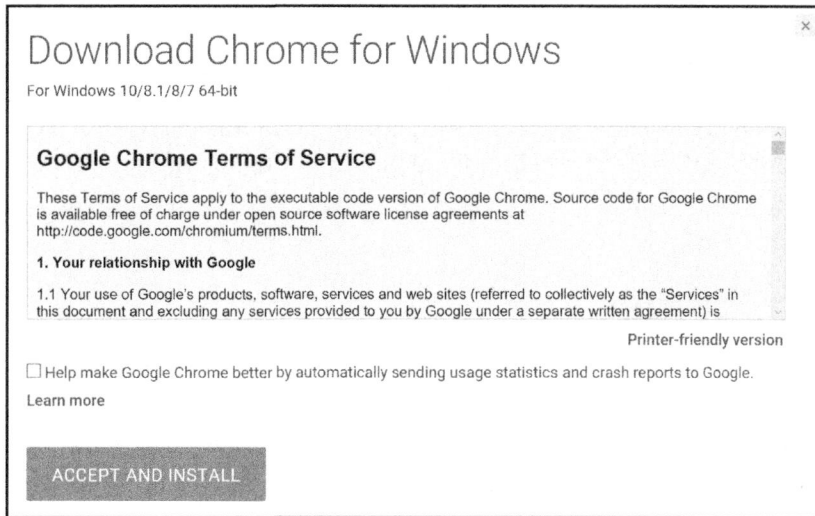

4. Run the downloaded file to start the installation process
5. The installation process will download the needed files and install Chrome
6. Once the installation is done, you will see a **Welcome to Chrome** page in the Chrome browser:

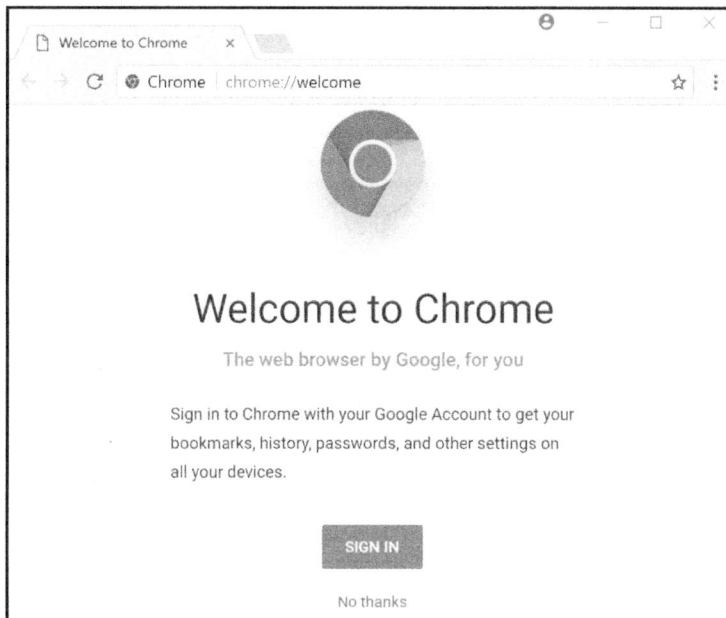

Fiddler

Fiddler is a web-debugging proxy used to test web APIs. It enables us to make sure that our backend APIs work as expected, before integrating with the client-side. We will use it in this book to test the REST services that we will be creating using the ASP.NET Core Web API.

Installing Fiddler

To install Fiddler, follow these steps:

1. Open your browser and navigate to `https://www.telerik.com/download/fiddler`
2. Fill in the required information and click the **Download** button
3. Run the downloaded file to start the installation wizard:

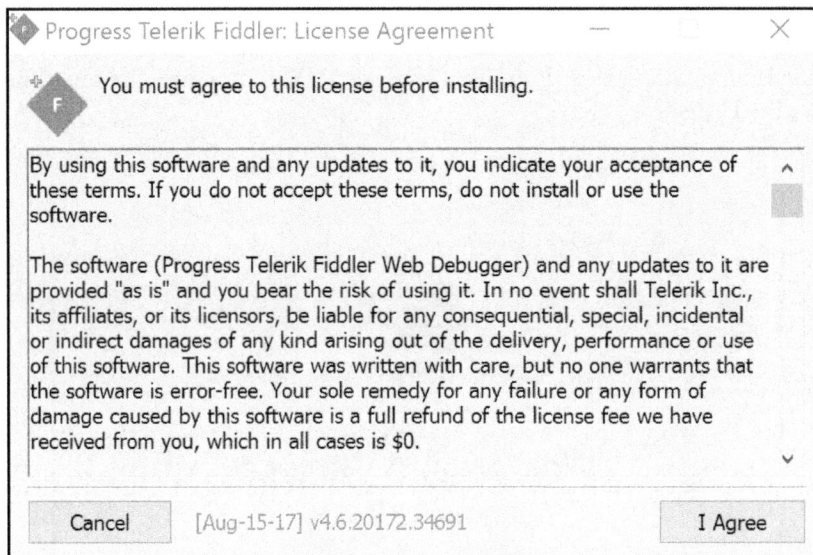

4. Move forward through the installation wizard until Fiddler is installed:

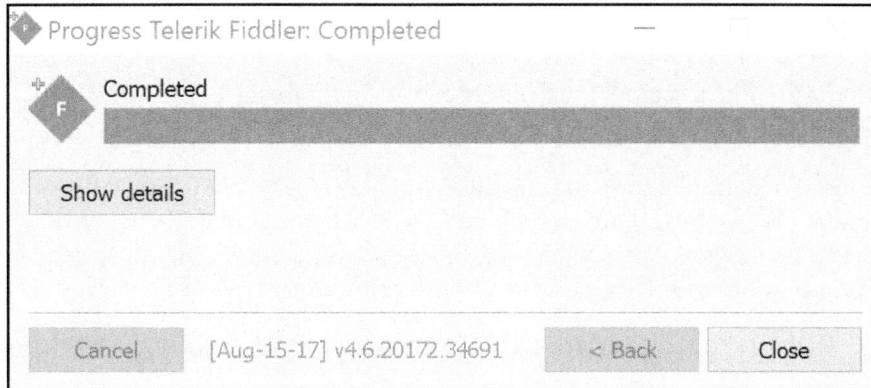

5. To test whether or not the installation succeeded, open Fiddler by clicking on Start | **All Programs** | **Fiddler 4**
6. Fiddler should open, and present you with a screen similar to the following:

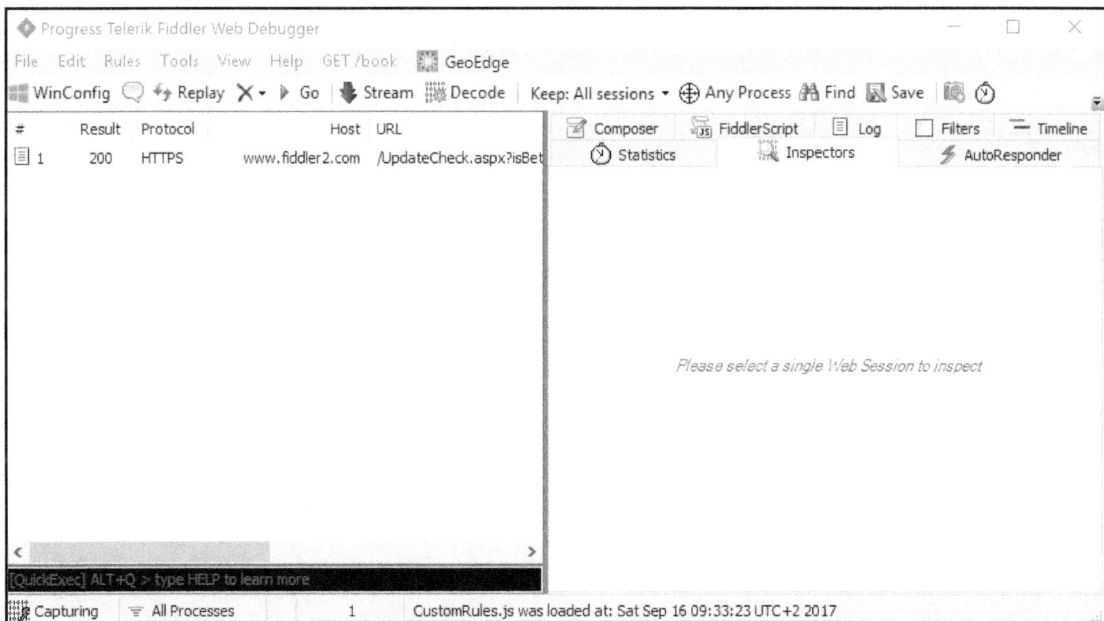

Summary

Developer tools are like a scalpel for the surgeon — without the correct one, you will work harder than needed, and risk making mistakes.

In this chapter, we learned about and installed the main tools that every full-stack developer needs. We've talked about both backend and frontend tools that will help us throughout this book. Now that everything is ready, we can continue on to deep-diving into the technologies themselves, and start building modern Web applications.

Creating a Web Application with ASP.NET Core

3

Backend development is a world full of technology. Microsoft is one of the top software companies in the world and has many years of experience in creating web development platforms. This started from Classic ASP, and continued through ASP.NET and ASP.NET MVC, to today's ASP.NET Core.

In this chapter, we will get familiar with the ASP.NET Core platform and understand how to create web servers using it. We will cover the following topics:

- ASP.NET Core overview
- Creating a new ASP.NET Core project
- The Startup class
- Serving static files
- Getting familiar with the ASP.NET Core MVC Framework

Before we begin diving into the technology, let's introduce the `GiveNTake` application— the application that we're going to develop throughout this book.

ASP.NET Core overview

ASP.NET Core is a complete redesign of the previous web framework from Microsoft, called ASP.NET. It is built to run on multiple platforms — Windows, Mac, and Linux — and is lightweight, modular, and supports modern web application development.

It has multiple advantages over ASP.NET, especially when it comes to the development of SPAs:

- Can run on any platform thanks to its foundation of .NET Core
- Completely open source
- Designed to be lightweight and fast
- Built to be modular from the very beginning
- Can run from IIS, self-hosted, or any other web server

.NET Core

ASP.NET Core is built on .NET Core, which is Microsoft's cross-platform CLR implementation. This enables ASP.NET Core and other frameworks to run smoothly on operating systems other than Windows. It was rewritten from scratch to support modern backend development, unlike the full .NET Framework, which was developed to support any coding scenario. .NET Core and the .NET Framework can coexist, even on the same project, and no plans to change this have been announced by Microsoft to this date.

.NET Core, like the full .NET Framework, implements the .NET Standard Library—if you're familiar with the .NET Framework, you will feel at home quickly. A big difference with .NET Core is the fact it does not rely on assemblies or the **Global Assembly Cache (GAC)**. However, all needed libraries are used as packages that are retrieved from NuGet, the .NET package manager. For example, if you need to use System.IO, you can get it from NuGet as a separate library, without the need to add and load the entire System assembly.

In addition, .NET Core comes with the .NET Core **Command-Line Interface (CLI)**, a utility that enables developers and IDEs to execute .NET Core commands on any platform. Commands for things such as creating a new project, adding packages, building, or publishing the solution can all be done via the .NET Core CLI. For example, creating a new ASP.NET Core application is as simple as executing the following line on the Command Prompt:

```
dotnet new web
```

This enables endless automation scenarios, as well as a new wave of brand new cross platform .NET IDEs. We will cover the .NET Core CLI in more depth throughout this book.

Open source

.NET Core and ASP.NET Core are completely open source. .NET Core is a part of the .NET Foundation that can be found on GitHub at `https://github.com/dotnet`, and is open to contributions.

Its main repositories are as follows:

- `coreclr`: This is the cross-platform **Common Language Runtime (CLR)**. It is the virtual machine that runs every .NET-based application.
- `corefx`: This repository contains the **Base Class Library (BCL)** and the **Framework Class Library (FCL)**.

ASP.NET Core has its own repositories on GitHub at `https://github.com/aspnet`. It is also open for contributions from the community.

Its main repositories are as follows:

- `MVC`: The ASP.NET MVC source code
- `EntityFrameworkCore`: The Entity Framework Core project source code
- `DependencyInjection`: ASP.NET Core dependency injection infrastructure implementation

If you're interested in reading the source code or contributing to the development efforts, visit these GitHub pages to learn how.

Lightweight and fast

ASP.NET Core was built to be lightweight and fast. Recent benchmarks prove that the hard work has paid off—ASP.NET Core is now a strong contender in web framework public benchmarks, such as TechEmpower's, and it has outperformed other major web frameworks. Needless to say, it's shown enormous improvements over its predecessor, ASP.NET 4.6.

Modular

ASP.NET Core is a modular framework. This is made available by the ASP.NET Core middleware components. ASP.NET Core handles requests and responses via a set of operations that are completed by something called the *request pipeline*. This pipeline comes predefined with specific components, but, when needed, developers can remove components, add different built-in ones, or write their own.

Other components of the ASP.NET Core Framework that are not a part of the request pipeline, such as the dependency injection service, can also be replaced within the `Startup` class.

Host anywhere

ASP.NET Core can be hosted on any web server including IIS, NGINX, APACHE, or even self-hosted as a console application. This is made possible by the brand new Kestrel server.

Kestrel is a web server that comes bundled with ASP.NET Core project templates. It has been developed as part of the ASP.NET Core project and is basically a new web server. It is capable of running ASP.NET Core web applications and supports HTTPS and WebSockets. However, it does not support all of the functionality of a full-blown web server, like IIS or NGINX do, which is why it is not recommended for use as a web server for the production of a web application.

The way to go would be to use Kestrel as a reverse proxy for a production-ready web server. Further details on that process can be found in `Chapter 16`, *Taking Advantage of Cloud Services*.

Creating an ASP.NET Core application

Every ASP.NET Core application starts with creating a new project. This new project can start empty or with a predefined template.

We will start by creating an empty project. To do so, follow these steps:

1. Open Visual Studio and go to **File** | **New** | **Project**..., as shown in the following screenshot:

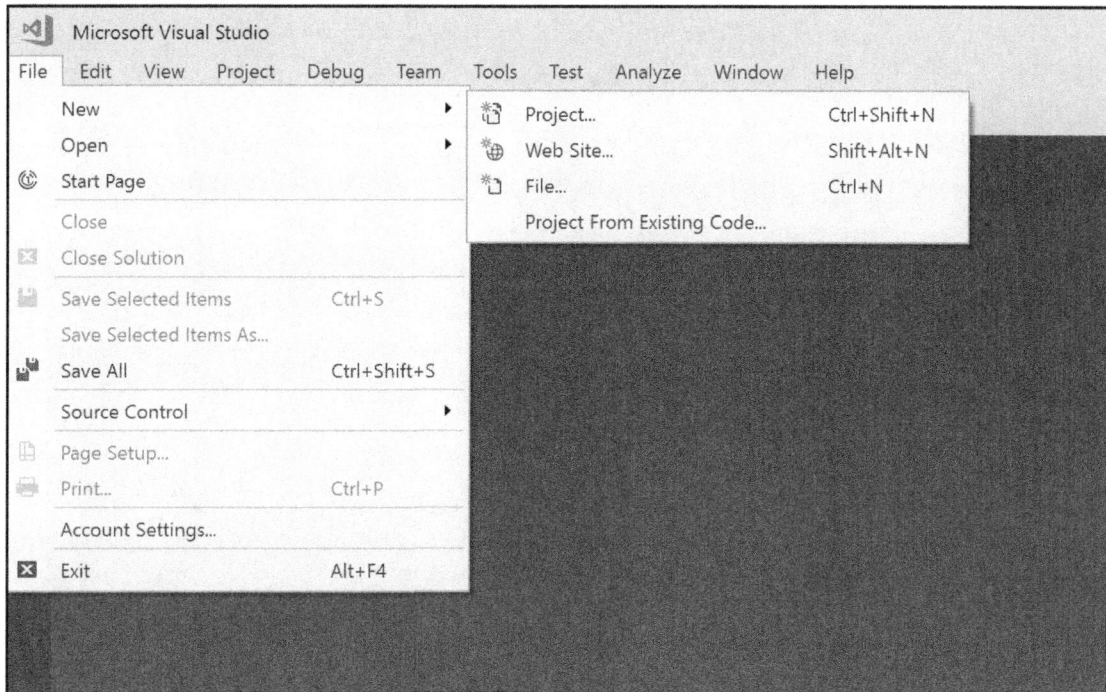

2. In the **New Project** dialog, navigate through the list on the left to **Visual C#** | **Web**, then choose **ASP.NET Core Web Application**, fill in the application name as `GiveNTake`, choose your desired location, and click **OK**:

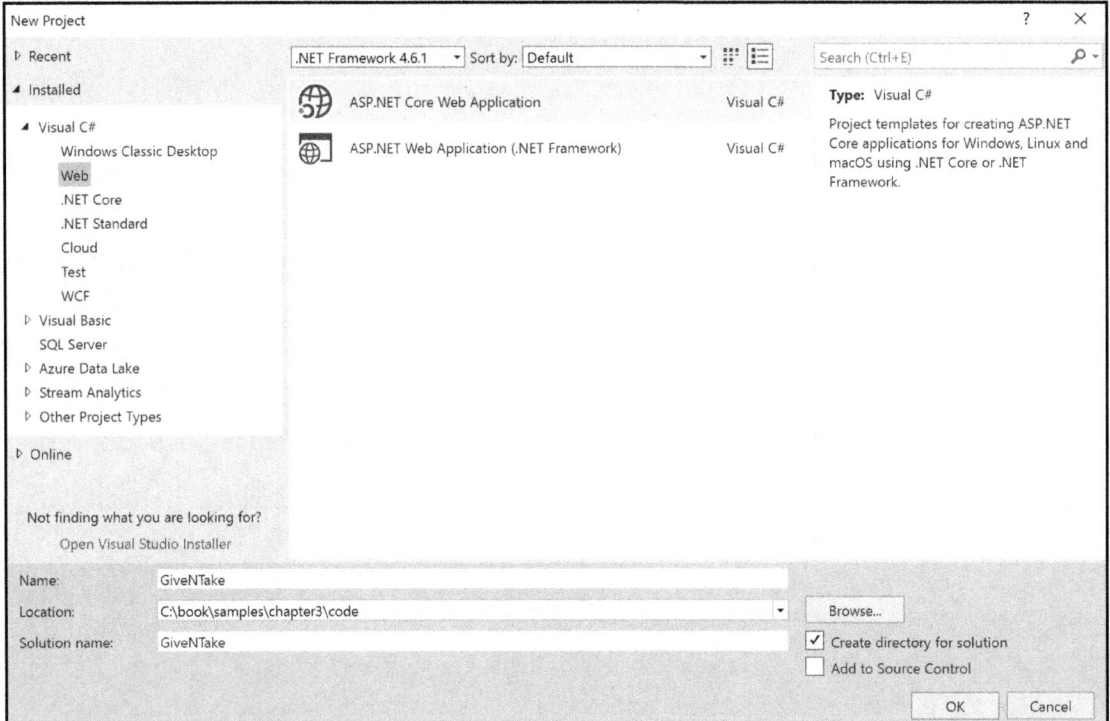

3. The **New ASP.NET Core Web Application- GiveNTake** dialog opens. Choose **Empty** from the list and click **OK** to create the project. Make sure that you choose **ASP.NET Core 2.0** from the version list:

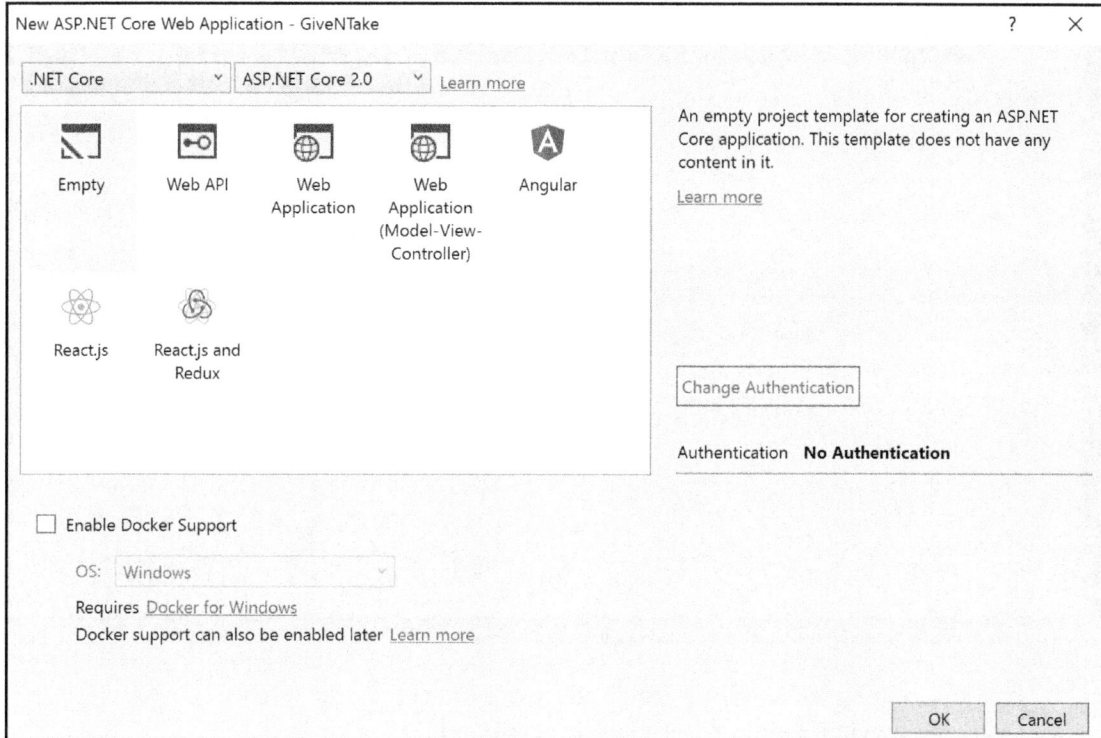

4. After a few moments, your web application will be ready, and should look something like the following:

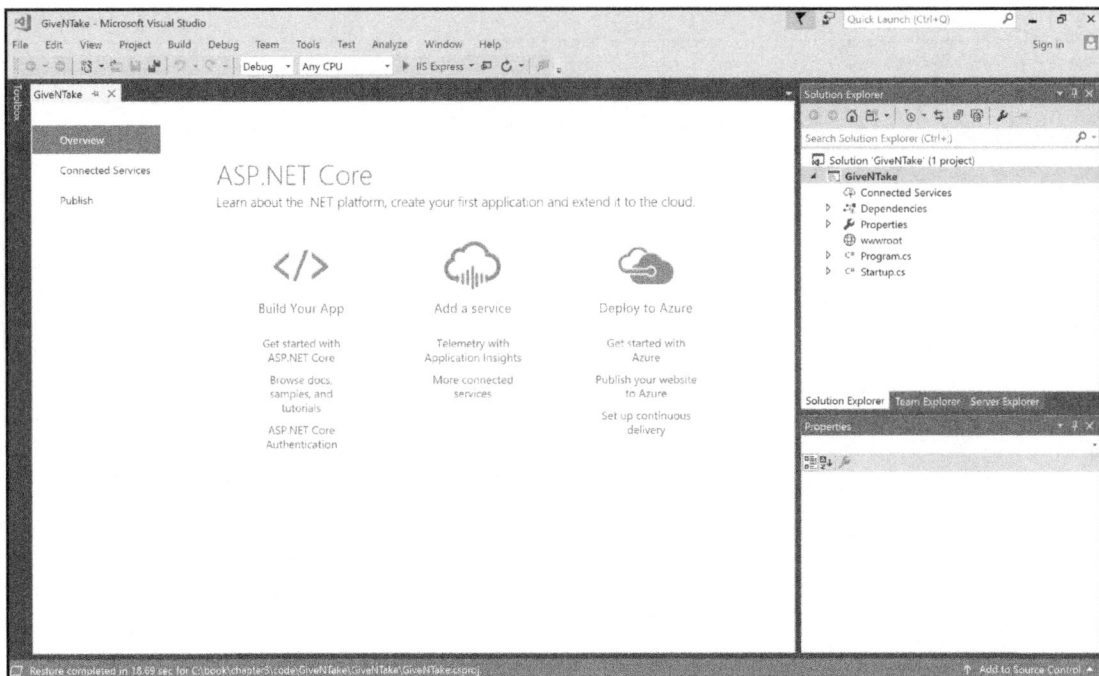

> Creating a new empty ASP.NET Core project via the .NET CLI utility is done via the `dotnet new web` command.

Default files in an ASP.NET Core project

You have probably noticed by now that your *empty* project is not entirely empty, and does, in fact, include a couple of files:

- `Program.cs`: This is the entry point of the application. It loads configuration, initiates the logging framework, and more.
- `Startup.cs`: This is run when the web project starts. It configures the application services and requests pipeline components.
- The `wwwroot` folder: This folder is where all of the static assets of the application will be stored.

Predefined project templates

ASP.NET Core comes with a few predefined project templates that you can use to create your application. These templates already include the needed packages, a recommended folder structure, initial configuration, and some sample files.

The available project templates are as follows:

- **Empty**: An empty ASP.NET Core project template, containing only the most critical initialization code files.
- **Web API**: A project template containing a sample web API class and configuration.
- **Web Application**: A project template containing a sample Razor Pages-based application.
- **Web Application (MVC)**: A project template containing a sample MVC-based application.
- **Angular**: A project template containing sample ASP.NET Core backend code, ready for frontend implementation using Angular and TypeScript. This template includes the needed dependencies from NuGet and NPM, and a preconfigured webpack.
- **React.js**: This is the same as the Angular template, just with React dependencies and sample code.
- **React.js and Redux**: This is the same as the React.js template, only this time, it uses the Redux framework on top of React.js.

In addition to the built-in project templates, you can find more project templates that have been created and maintained by the community on the Visual Studio marketplace at `https://marketplace.visualstudio.com`, on NuGet, or on GitHub.

The Startup class

The `Startup` class is initialized and executed right after the web application starts. It is located under the project root folder in the `Startup.cs` file. This is where the application services and request pipeline components can be configured.

The `Startup` class contains two methods:

- `ConfigureServices`: This is where services will be added to the project. For example, this is where logging or authentication services are added.
- `Configure`: This is where services and request pipeline components are configured. For example, the settings for the authentication and logging services will be set here.

Code execution order

The `Startup` class is executed only once during an application's lifespan, right after the web server has loaded the ASP.NET Core application.

The following screenshot shows the order of execution of the different methods in the classes involved in ASP.NET Core initialization:

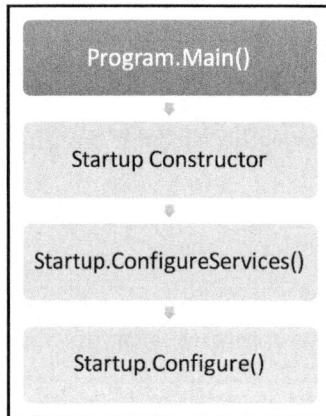

> The `Startup` class is not the place to put any code other than initialization and configuration code.

Different startups for different environments

Applications run in different environments, such as development, staging, and deployment:

- **Development environment**: Where developers run their freshly written code; this is usually their own machine.
- **Staging environment**: An environment similar to the production environment, but not open to the public. Used to test the application on similar conditions as the production environment.
- **Production environment**: Where the application runs publicly, usually on the cloud or a hosting company.

Every environment has a different set of configurations — for example, in development, logging will be set to *verbose* mode, meaning that all logs should be written, while in production, logging will be set to *warning* mode, so only warnings and errors will be logged.

ASP.NET Core supports supplying different `Startup` classes for each environment. To do this, you can create different classes with names following the convention of `Startup{Environment Name}`. For example, `StartupDevelopment` will run under the development environment and `StatupProduction` will run under the production environment.

The current environment is set via the `ASPNETCORE_ENVIRONMENT` environment variable, which you can change based on the environment you run on - Development, Testing, Production and so on.

Changing the Startup class name

The name of the `Startup` class is a convention of ASP.NET Core applications. It is recommended to leave it as it is to make the code clearer for colleagues. However, there are a few situations where you are required to use a different name for the `Startup` class—for example, when `Startup` is already a class in your application but is responsible for an entirely different task than initializing ASP.NET Core.

On such occasions, open the `Program` class file, located in the root folder under `Program.cs`, and locate the `CreateWebHostBuilder` method. It should look similar to the following:

```
public static IWebHostBuilder CreateWebHostBuiler(string[] args) =>
    WebHost.CreateDefaultBuilder(args)
        .UseStartup<Startup>();
```

In order to point ASP.NET Core to a different class name, for example, to `CustomStartup`, change the `UseStartup<Startup>()` line to `UseStartup<CustomStartup>`:

```
public static IWebHostBuilder CreateWebHostBuiler(string[] args) =>
    WebHost.CreateDefaultBuilder(args)
        .UseStartup<Startup>();
```

> If you're using different `Startup` classes for each environment, changing the name will affect the suffix. For example, instead of `StartupDevelopment`, ASP.NET Core will look for a `CustomStartupDevelopment` class.

Serving static files

In web applications, static files are files that are located on the web server and are served to the end user as is, without any manipulation. HTML, CSS, JavaScript, image, font, and video files are all included in the definition of static files.

These files are crucial to SPAs, since the entire frontend code is based on static HTML, CSS, and JavaScript files.

The content root and web root folders

ASP.NET Core defines two types of folders:

- `Content root`: This is the root directory of the application. Any files outside this directory will not take part in the frontend application.
- `Web root`: This is where static files are located.

By default, the content root is the root folder of the application, and the web root is the `<content root>/wwwroot` folder.

The `web root` folder is not exposed to the end user by default. Making it available to end users is described later in this chapter, under *Setting the server to serve static files.*

In large applications, the content root path might need to be changed. To do so, open the `Program.cs` file, locate the `CreateWebHostBuilder` static method, and add the following marked line to it:

```
WebHost.CreateDefaultBuilder(args)
    .UseContentRoot(Path.Combine(Directory.GetCurrentDirectory(),
     "/client"))
    .UseStartup<Startup>()
    .Build();
```

In this example, we're setting the path of the content root folder to `<project root>/client`.

In addition, the `wwwroot` folder name might not fit all scenarios. In order to change it, open the `Program.cs` file, find the `BuildWebHost`, and change it as follows:

```
WebHost.CreateDefaultBuilder(args)
        .UseContentRoot(Directory.GetCurrentDirectory())
        .UseWebRoot("assets")
        .UseStartup<Startup>()
        .Build();
```

The highlighted line changes the web root path to `<content root>/assets`.

Setting the server to serve static files

ASP.NET Core, by default, doesn't serve static files to end users. Even though the content root and web root paths have default values, you have to explicitly indicate that static files should be served. To do so, open the `Startup.cs` file, locate the `Configure` method, and add the following line:

```
app.UseStaticFiles();
```

Once this is placed in the right location, the ASP.NET Core platform will serve static files from the web root folder.

Make sure that the web root folder itself is not part of the URL. The following table demonstrates the physical file location and the matching URL, assuming that the default web root path, `wwwroot`, hasn't been changed:

Physical file location	URL
`wwwroot/images/logo.png`	`http://example.com/images/logo.png`
`wwwroot/css/main.css`	`http://example.com/css/main.css`
`wwwroot/readme.txt`	`http://example.com/readme.txt`

In addition to the `Web root` folder, it is possible to serve static files that reside in other directories. In order to do so, you need to pass parameters to the `UseStaticFiles` method. For example, the following code sample sets the `assets` folder as a static file folder under the `/assets` URL:

```
app.UseStaticFiles(new StaticFileOptions()
{
    FileProvider = new PhysicalFileProvider(
        Path.Combine(Directory.GetCurrentDirectory(), "assets")),
    RequestPath = new PathString("/assets")
});
```

To add multiple static file paths, call the `UseStaticFiles` method multiple times. For example, the following piece of code sets the default `Web root` as a static file folder, as well as two other folders, `images` and `videos`:

```
app.UseStaticFiles(); // web root

app.UseStaticFiles(new StaticFileOptions()
{
    FileProvider = new PhysicalFileProvider(
            Path.Combine(Directory.GetCurrentDirectory(), "images")),
    RequestPath = new PathString("/images")
});

app.UseStaticFiles(new StaticFileOptions()
{
    FileProvider = new PhysicalFileProvider(
            Path.Combine(Directory.GetCurrentDirectory(), "videos")),
    RequestPath = new PathString("/videos")
});
```

> If possible, try to avoid using static folders other than `wwwroot`. The `wwwroot` is the standard static directory in ASP.NET Core, and other developers who dive into your code will have an easier time understanding it if you stick to common practices.

Serving default documents

The frontend of modern web applications consists mostly of static files. Therefore, pointing the server to the client directory and instructing it to serve its entire content as static files is a common practice. In such situations, you will also want to send the user the main application file, such as `index.html`, when they navigate to the static folder. These files are called *default documents*.

Defining default documents for a static folder is done via the `UseDefaultFiles` method. Within the `Startup.cs` file, locate the `Configure` method and add the following marked line:

```
app.UseDefaultFiles();
app.UseStaticFiles();
```

> `UseDefaultFiles` must be used before the `UseStaticFiles` call. If they are called in the opposite order, `UseDefaultFiles` will not have any affect.

The `UseDefaultFiles` method instructs ASP.NET Core to look for the following files once a URL that directs to a static folder has been detected:

- `default.htm`
- `default.html`
- `index.htm`
- `index.html`

These files will be looked for in that order. Once a filename matching one of these names is found, it will be served to the end user.

To change the filenames that `UseDefaultFiles` searches for, create and set a `DefaultFilesOptions` object and pass it to the method. For example, the following code changes the default filename collection to look for the `main.htm` and `main.html` files, instead of the predefined filenames:

```
DefaultFilesOptions options = new DefaultFilesOptions();
options.DefaultFileNames.Clear();
options.DefaultFileNames.Add("main.htm");
options.DefaultFileNames.Add("main.html");
app.UseDefaultFiles(options);
```

Configuring the available MIME types

ASP.Net Core serves static files that are of a known MIME type. A MIME type is an identifier of the type of content that a specific file holds. For example, HTML files have a MIME type of `text/html`, and JPEG image files have a MIME type of `image/jpeg`.

When a web server serves a file, it attaches its MIME type to the response as an HTTP header named `content-type`. The browser then, in turn, uses this MIME type to decide on how to interpret the file.

ASP.NET Core recognizes almost 400 mime types automatically. When it runs into an unrecognized file, it will not serve it to the end user and instead return a 404 — Not Found response. This behavior improves the security of your web application and works in the majority of use cases.

However, sometimes, your application needs to send files to end users that are not recognized by default by ASP.NET Core; for example, `.exe` files, which are Windows' executable file format. The following code instructs ASP.NET Core to use the `application/vnd.microsoft.portable-executable` MIME type for these types of files:

```
FileExtensionContentTypeProvider provider = new
FileExtensionContentTypeProvider();
provider.Mappings[".exe"] = "application/vnd.microsoft.portable-
executable";

StaticFileOptions staticFileOptions = new StaticFileOptions()
{
    ContentTypeProvider = provider
};

app.UseStaticFiles(staticFileOptions);
```

Using this technique, you can also change existing MIME types to fit your needs, or remove MIME types that you do not want to be served. For example, the following code changes `.ts` files to be recognized as TypeScript files, instead of the video file MIME type defined by ASP.NET Core. This will be needed later in this book when we start using TypeScript:

```
FileExtensionContentTypeProvider provider = new
FileExtensionContentTypeProvider();

provider.Mappings[".ts"] = "application/x-typescript";
StaticFileOptions staticFileOptions = new StaticFileOptions()
{
    ContentTypeProvider = provider
```

```
};

app.UseStaticFiles(staticFileOptions);
```

Getting familiar with the ASP.NET Core MVC framework

ASP.NET Core MVC is a web development framework for developing traditional web applications. It is based on the MVC architectural pattern that separates the code into three layers: models, views, and controllers.

The MVC pattern

The MVC pattern divides the application into three separated layers — models, views, and controllers — each with different responsibilities:

- **Models**: Responsible for data, retrieving it from data storage, and passing it on throughout the other layers of the application.
- **Views**: Responsible for generating the output of the application, mainly in HTML documents.
- **Controllers**: The glue between all the application layers. Controllers react on user requests, ask for data from the model layer, and pass the needed information to the view to generate an output.

Additionally, ASP.NET Core MVC applications rely on another component: the request router. This component is responsible for understanding the request target, usually by its URL, and executing the matching controller.

The execution flow is described in the following diagram:

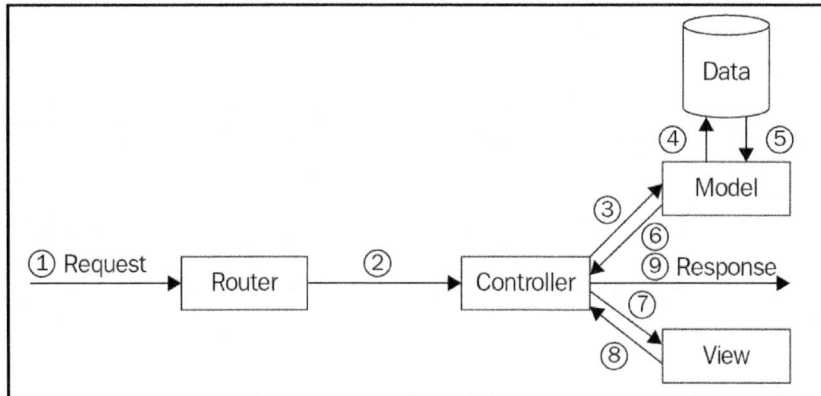

The following is a description of the preceding diagram:

1. A request is received from the end user.
2. The router decides on the relevant controller to handle the request based on the request properties. The matching controller method is then executed.
3. The controller method, in turn, asks for needed data from the model layer.
4. The model layer communicates with the data storage.
5. The model layer retrieves the requested data.
6. The data is returned to the controller, which then sends it to the view.
7. The view dynamically generates the output based on the data.
8. The generated view is returned to the controller.
9. The controller responds to the user with the generated output.

MVC in SPAs

ASP.NET Core MVC is a sophisticated web application development framework with many features. Using it to create web applications means that every user action—form submission, page navigation, page click — will generate a request to the server that will generate an updated HTML for the end user. Modern web applications, however, rely on client-side code to do most of these tasks.

This modern reality means that ASP.NET Core MVC usage has changed. From being the main technology for creating views and handling user actions, it has transformed into a supporting foundation for frontend JavaScript-based code. Its major responsibility currently is running the application API, which will be discussed in `Chapter 4`, *Building REST APIs with ASP.NET Core Web API*.

We will go through the basics of ASP.NET Core MVC that we need to know as full-stack developers, but we will not dive into all of the many different features of this vast backend framework.

Adding MVC to ASP.NET Core

ASP.NET MVC Core does not work by default in ASP.NET Core applications. You must enable it within the code before using it. To do so, follow these steps:

1. Open the `Startup.cs` file.
2. Locate the `ConfigureServices` method and add the highlighted line to it:

```
public void ConfigureServices(IServiceCollection services)
{
    services.AddMvc();
}
```

This tells ASP.NET Core to add MVC to the available services. Pay attention — this is not enough for MVC to work, since it needs to be configured first.

3. Locate the `Configure` method and add the highlighted code to it:

```
public void Configure(IApplicationBuilder app, IHostingEnvironment env)
{
    app.UseStaticFiles();

    app.UseMvcWithDefaultRoute();
}
```

This instructs ASP.NET Core to use the service we added in the `ConfigureServices` method. In addition, it has a basic configuration for the MVC router. We will discuss ASP.NET Core MVC routing later in this chapter in the *Routing* section.

By now, you should have ASP.NET MVC configured and ready to run. To see it in action, continue to the next section, *Controllers*.

Controllers

Controllers are responsible for the workflow of the application. They retrieve user requests, work with the model, and then choose the view to render.

Controllers in ASP.NET Core MVC are C# classes that reside under the `Controllers` directory and inherit from `Microsoft.AspNetCore.Mvc.Controller`. Controller classes must match one of the following rules as well:

- The class name ends with `Controller`, for example, `UsersController`
- The class inherits from a class whose name ends with `Controller`
- The class is decorated with the `[Controller]` or `[ApiController]` attribute

Public methods inside controller classes are also called *actions*. Each action handles a different request from end users and generates output. Usually, a controller class gathers multiple actions that relate to the same logical operation, such as login, or application entities such as users.

In SPAs, from the server's point of view, there is only a single page in the application. Therefore, for SPAs, we do not need more than a single controller with a single action that serves the main application page and lets the frontend code take charge.

To create the controller, follow these steps:

1. Right-click on the application name in **Solution Explorer** and choose **Add | New Folder**:

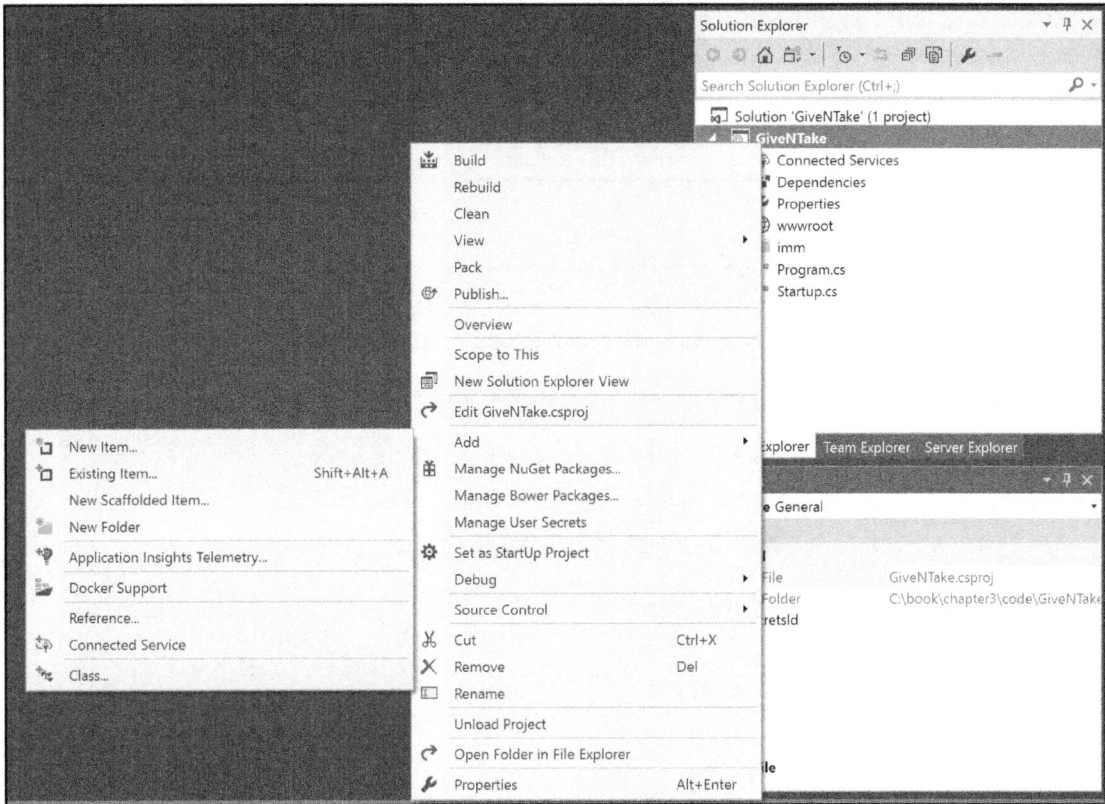

2. Set the folder name to `Controllers`.
3. Right-click on the newly created `Controllers` folder and choose **Add |**
   Controller....
4. If the `Add Dependencies` dialog pops up, choose `Minimal Dependencies` and
   click **Add**:

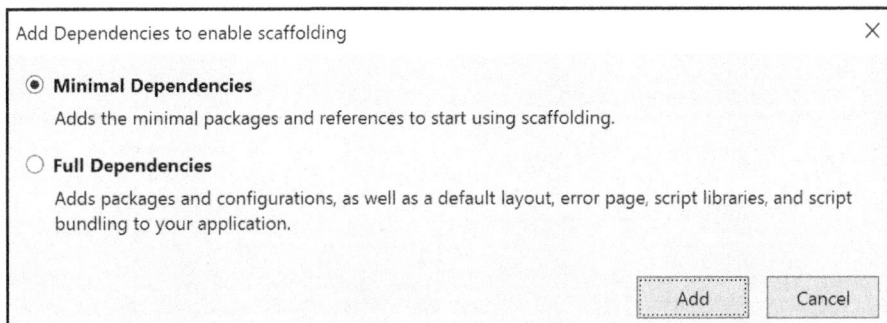

You will have to perform *step 3* once more after dependencies have been installed successfully.

5. In the list of available templates, choose MVC Controller — Empty:

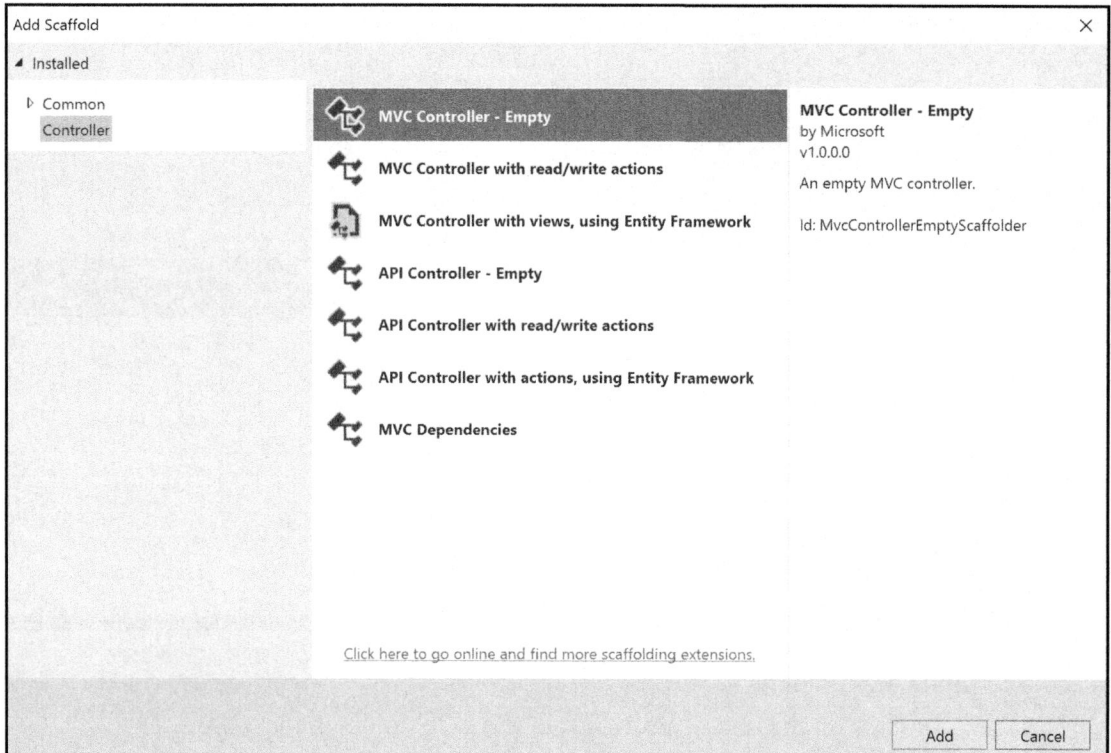

6. Set the name as HomeController and click **Add**.

The controller is now ready and should look similar to the following:

```
namespace GiveNTake.Controllers
{
    public class HomeController : Controller
    {
        public IActionResult Index()
        {
            return View();
        }
    }
}
```

This controller has a single action method called `Index`. This is the naming convention for the default action of a controller. For example, if a controller is responsible for operations related to a `User` entity, then the `Index` action will generate an output with the list of users in the system.

The `return View();` line tells ASP.NET Core MVC to generate a view using the default MVC naming convention. These will be discussed in the next section, *Views*.

For now, change the `return View();` line to `return Content("Hello from MVC!");`. This will tell MVC to return a simple `Hello from MVC!` string to the end user. The `Index` method should look similar to the following after the change:

```
public IActionResult Index()
{
    return Content("Hello from MVC!");
}
```

ASP.NET MVC is ready to run — follow these steps to build and run the application:

1. Click on **Build** | **Build Solution**, or use the keyboard shortcut *Ctrl + Shift + B*:

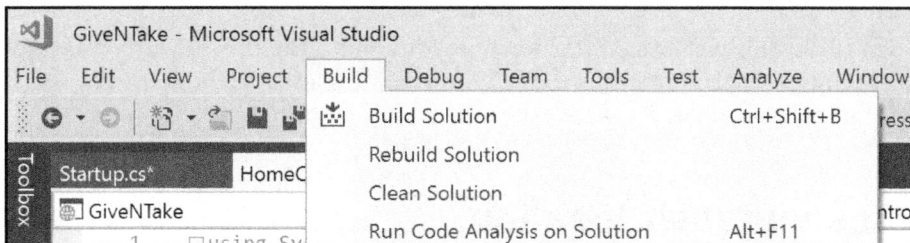

2. Once the build ends successfully, click on the Play button on the toolbar, or click *F5*:

3. The default browser should open and look like the following screenshot:

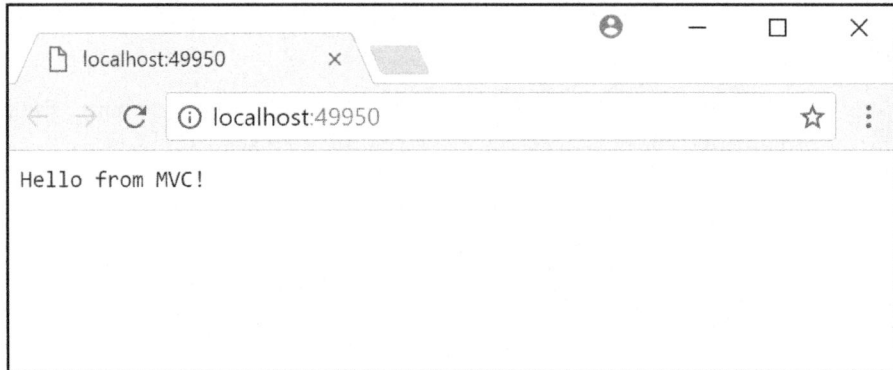

Now that we have an operating ASP.NET Core MVC application, we can continue and fit it to our needs.

Views

The views in MVC applications are responsible for generating the output for a request, containing mainly HTML content. ASP.NET Core MVC views are built with a special markup language named *Razor*—a mix of static HTML and dynamic C# code.

View files and their location

View files are saved with the extension .cshtml, which implies that these are files containing both HTML markup and C# code.

They are located within subfolders under the Views folder. By convention, each subfolder matches a single controller. For example, if the project has a controller named HomeController, then the views of this controller will reside inside the Views/Home folder.

The view's filename correlates to the controller action for which it generates the output. We saw in the previous section that the controller action ended with this line:

```
return View();
```

This line tells ASP.NET Core MVC to look for a file named `<current action name>.cshtml` under `Views/<controller name>`. For example, if the controller is named `HomeController` and the action is named `Index`, then the view file will be `Views/Home/Index.cshtml`.

> The view file lookup process can be modified to look for other view names, search in different directories, and more. These capabilities are not needed for most SPA applications, and therefore, are not within the context of this book.

Creating a view

To create a view, we first need to create the matching folder if it doesn't already exist, and then create the file. Follow these steps to accomplish that:

1. On **Solution Explorer**, right-click on the project name and choose **Add** | **New Folder**.
2. Set the name as `Views` and click *Enter*.
3. Right-click on the newly created `Views` directory and, again, choose **Add** | **New Folder**.
4. Set the new folder name as `Home` and click *Enter*.
5. Right-click on the new `Home` folder and choose **Add** | **View...**.

On the **Add View** dialog, do the following:

1. Set the **View name** as `Index`.
2. Choose **Empty (without model)** on the **Template** field.
3. Uncheck the **Use a layout page** checkbox.

4. Click **Add**:

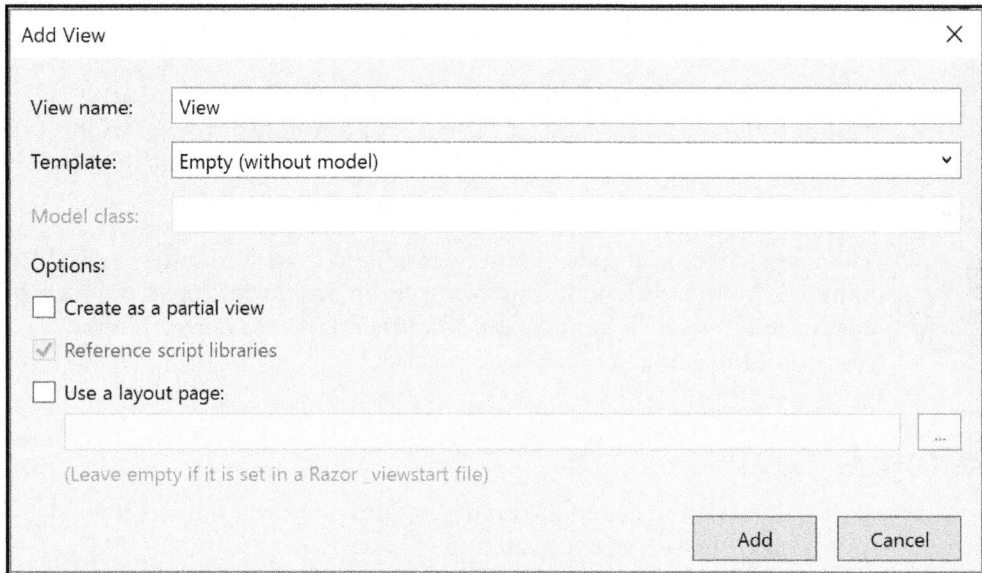

5. The new view has now been scaffolded for you.
6. Find the `<body></body>` tags and change them to `<body>I'm a fullstack developer!</body>`.

Now that we have the view ready, we need to instruct the controller action to show the view:

1. Open the `HomeController` class, which is in the `Controllers/HomeController.cs` file.
2. Find the following line:

```
return Content("Hello from MVC!");
```

Replace it with this line:

```
return View();
```

3. Run the application (press *F5*, or go to **Debug** | **Start Debugging**).
4. The browser should open and look similar to the following screenshot:

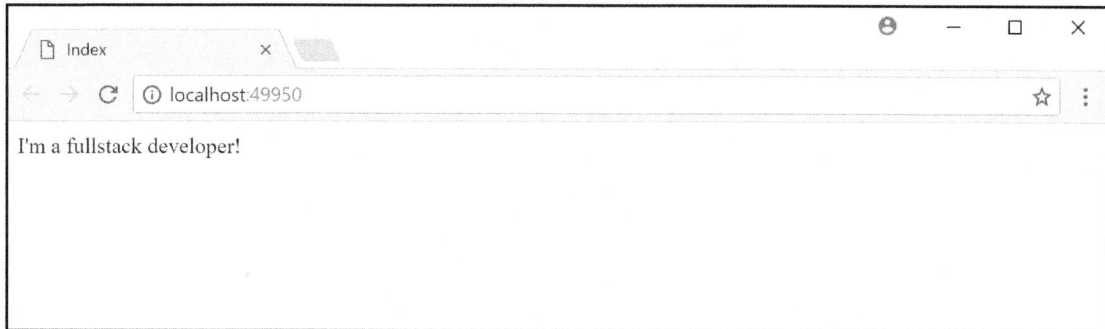

5. Congratulations! You have a working ASP.NET Core MVC view!

For now, this fits all of our SPA needs. We will dive into the HTML and view aspects more deeply when we discuss Angular in the next part of this book.

Routing

Routing is the travel guide of incoming requests — it is responsible for passing requests to their matching controller actions. The matching is done by the request URL; for example, we can instruct ASP.NET MVC Core to run the `Index` action on the `Home` controller whenever a request for the URL `/hello` gets to the server.

Adding routes

ASP.NET MVC routes are configured and added during application startup. There are two ways to add routes: within the `UseMvc` method on the Startup class, or by using route attributes.

Adding routes via UseMvc

Adding routes via the `UseMvc` method, also known as the conventional way of adding MVC routes, is a way of defining all routes in a central location.

The `UseMvc` method can be found within the `Startup.cs` file within the `Configure` method, which we talked about earlier in this chapter. At the moment, the following line will be present:

```
app.UseMvcWithDefaultRoute();
```

This tells ASP.NET Core MVC to create a default route that interprets incoming request URLs according to the MVC convention. Let's change this to its explicit equivalent:

```
app.UseMvc(routes =>
{
    routes.MapRoute(
        name: "default",
        template: "{controller=Home}/{action=Index}/{id?}");
});
```

In the preceding code snippet, we are using the conventional route creation technique to create the default route. Let's divide this code into its smaller pieces.

The `UseMvc` method retrieves a single parameter, which is a callback for configuring routes:

```
app.UseMvc(routes => {
    // ... route configuration ...
}
```

The `routes` parameter that is passed into the callback is of the `IRouteBuilder` type, which contains different methods for configuring routes. We will look at the most commonly used one, `MapRoute`.

The `MapRoute` method gets a few parameters, the basic ones of which are the route name and its URL pattern:

```
routes.MapRoute(
    name: "default",
    template: "{controller=Home}/{action=Index}/{id?}");
```

The route name does not affect URL matching. It becomes handy in different scenarios where you need to create a URL within code based on a route. Route names must be unique throughout the application, otherwise an exception will be thrown on application startup.

The route template is the URL pattern for the route. This pattern will be used by the ASP.NET Core MVC router when matching incoming request URLs to routes. It can contain default values as well.

In the preceding code block, the "`{controller=Home}/{action=Index}/{id?}`" template stores a few techniques.

Firstly, the stripped down version of this template will be `"{controller}/{action}"`, which tells ASP.NET Core MVC that the first part of an incoming request URL matches a `controller` name, such as `Home`, and the second part matches an `action` name, such as `Index`. Therefore, a request to `http://example.com/Home/Index` will end up executing the `Index` action method within the `HomeController` class. The `controller` and `action` elements within URL templates are called tokens.

Secondly, the `{token=value}` syntax defines a default value in case the URL is missing it. In our case, `{controller=Home}/{action=Index}` means that if the incoming URL is `http://example.com`, then ASP.NET Core MVC will execute the `Index` method within the `HomeController` class. If the incoming URL is `http://example.com/Users`, the `Index` method within the `UsersController` will be executed.

Thirdly, the last part of the template is `{id?}`—this tells the router that a parameter will optionally be added to the URL. Once that happens, this parameter will be sent to the matching action as a method parameter. For example, if the incoming URL is `http://example.com/Users/Edit/5`, the `Edit` method within the `UsersController` class will be executed and `5` will be sent to it as a parameter. The question mark (?) at the end means that this is an optional parameter—if we remove it, then URLs will be required to contain an ID at the end, or the route will not match.

This route is the default route for ASP.NET Core MVC because it catches all URLs that match the MVC convention of `controller/action/id`. We can also add more specific routes that do not necessarily follow this convention and set the matching controller and action method via the `defaults` parameter. For example, the following route will result in requests for `http://example.com/hello` being directed to the `Index` method of the `HomeController`:

```
routes.MapRoute(
    name: "hello",
    template: "hello",
    defaults: new { controller = "Home", action = "Index" });
```

Make sure that routes specified within `UseMvc` are matched by their order of definition. To do this, it is necessary to define the more specific routes before the less specific ones. For example, taking our previous code block, the full `UseMvc` code looks as follows:

```
app.UseMvc(routes =>
{
    routes.MapRoute(
        name: "hello",
        template: "hello",
        defaults: new { controller = "Home", action = "Index" });
    routes.MapRoute(
        name: "default",
        template: "{controller=Home}/{action=Index}/{id?}");
});
```

Conventional routing makes it easier to find out all the routes in the system and enables sophisticated route patterns, but also makes it harder to maintain as the application gets bigger. This is, usually, the preferred technique for ASP.NET Core MVC applications.

Adding routes via route attributes

Adding routes via route attributes is a way of defining the route for every controller action as an attribute on top of controller action methods.

Within the controller class (in our case, `HomeController`), add the `Route` attribute before the `Index` method:

```
[Route("Home/Index")]
public IActionResult Index()
{
    return View();
}
```

This instructs ASP.NET Core MVC to pass requests to the `Index` method whenever the URL looks like `http://example.com/Home/Index`. As patterns are not supported in attribute routing, if we want to make the `Index` method of `HomeController` the default of the application, then we need to add multiple `Route` attribute calls on top of the `Index` method:

```
[Route("")]
[Route("Home")]
[Route("Home/Index")]
public IActionResult Index()
{
    return View();
}
```

Attribute routing makes it easier to add new routes and keep them up-to-date with name changes or architectural code changes, but it doesn't support complicated patterns and makes it harder to see the full route list of the application. Attribute routing is, in most cases, the preferred way for ASP.NET Core web APIs.

Routing in SPAs

In SPAs, the complexity needed from ASP.NET Core MVC routing is low, because routing will mostly be taken care of by the frontend code. On the ASP.NET Core MVC end, we will use routing to support client-side routing capabilities.

For this, we will take advantage of conventional routing and set up two catch-all routes, as follows:

```
app.UseMvc(routes =>
{
    routes.MapRoute(
            name: "default",
            template: "{controller=Home}/{action=Index}/{id?}");

    routes.MapSpaFallbackRoute(
        name: "spa-fallback",
        defaults: new { controller = "Home", action = "Index" });
});
```

The first default route was discussed earlier in this section. This will enable all incoming requests to be directed to the Index method of the HomeController.

The second route uses the MapSpaFallbackRoute method, instead of the common MapRoute method. The difference between these methods is a small but important one: the MapSpaFallbackRoute method registers a route just like MapRoute does, but whenever a route matches its template and has a file extension at the end, the URL will be treated as a static file request and will return the file as is, without executing an action method. For example, a call to http://example.com/users will execute the Index method within the UsersController class. A call to http://example.com/images/user.png will return a file named user.png from a folder named images.

This capability is extremely important for SPAs that request many static files from the server, such as images, videos, HTML pages, JavaScript files, CSS files, and more.

These two routes enable everything that is needed for the frontend of the SPA to operate correctly. The first route enables using different MVC controllers, which is sometimes needed in large SPAs, and the second route enables the use of routing on the client-side and the serving of static files when requested.

Summary

ASP.NET Core MVC is a vast backend framework that provides countless capabilities for creating web applications. In modern web applications, the importance of backend frameworks has moved from being the center of every action in the application, to being responsible for the application data and serving the frontend code to the end user quickly and securely.

In this chapter, we went through the main features of ASP.NET Core MVC that enable it to serve successfully as the backend of modern SPAs. In the next chapter, we will be diving into creating REST APIs with ASP.NET Core MVC—an essential part of every web application today.

4
Building REST APIs with ASP.NET Core Web API

REST is an architectural style for implementing communication between the application client and server over HTTP. RESTful APIs use HTTP verbs (POST, GET, PUT, DELETE, and so on) to dictate the operation to be performed (Create, Read, Update, Delete) by the server on the domain entity. The REST style has become the de facto standard for creating services in modern application development. This makes it easy to use and consume services in any technology and on any platform, such as web frontends, desktop applications, or other web services.

In this chapter, you'll learn how to create RESTful APIs using ASP.NET Core. We will cover the following topics:

- An overview of REST APIs with the ASP.NET Core API
- Inspecting and debugging your API with Postman and Fiddler
- Defining routing rules in your API
- Binding data into model types and validating them
- Generating a response for different types

We'll first start with an overview of how REST APIs are implemented in ASP.NET Core.

Overview — REST APIs with ASP.NET Core API

In Chapter 3, *Creating a Web Server with ASP.NET Core*, you saw how to create a basic ASP.NET Core MVC application that can be broken down into three layers: models, controllers, and views. RESTful APIs in ASP.NET Core work very similarly; the only difference is that, instead of returning responses as visual views, the API response is a payload of data (usually in JSON format). The data returned from the API is later consumed by clients, such as Angular-based applications that can render the data as views, or by headless clients that have no UI and simply process data. (More information on headless clients can be found at https://en.wikipedia.org/wiki/Headless_software.) For example, consider a background process that periodically sends notifications to a user about their account status:

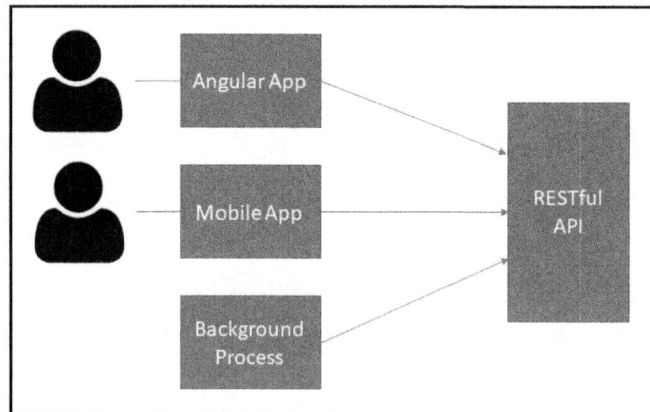

Before ASP.NET Core, Microsoft created an explicit distinction between ASP.NET MVC and the ASP.NET Web API. The former was used to create web applications with views that are generated by the server, while the former was used to create services that contain only logic and can be consumed by any client. Over time, the distinction between the two frameworks caused duplication of code and added a burden on the developers who needed to learn and master two technologies. ASP.NET Core unified the two frameworks into the ASP.NET Core MVC suite, and made it simpler to create web applications, with or without visual responses.

Let's start with a simple API that will be the foundation for our GiveNTake application.

Creating a simple API

The `GiveNTake` application allows the user to see a catalog of available products. For this to be possible, our server needs to include a specific API method that the client application can call and get back the collection of available products.

We will define the structure of the product entity in `Chapter 5`, *Persisting Data with Entity Framework*. For now, we will treat the product as a simple string in the format of `[Product ID] - [Product Name]`:

1. Open the `GiveNTake` project you created in `Chapter 3`, *Creating a Web Application with ASP.NET Core*, and add a new controller class to the `Controllers` folder. Right-click on the newly created `Controllers` folder and choose **Add | Controller**.
2. In the list of available templates, choose **API Controller - Empty** and click **Add**:

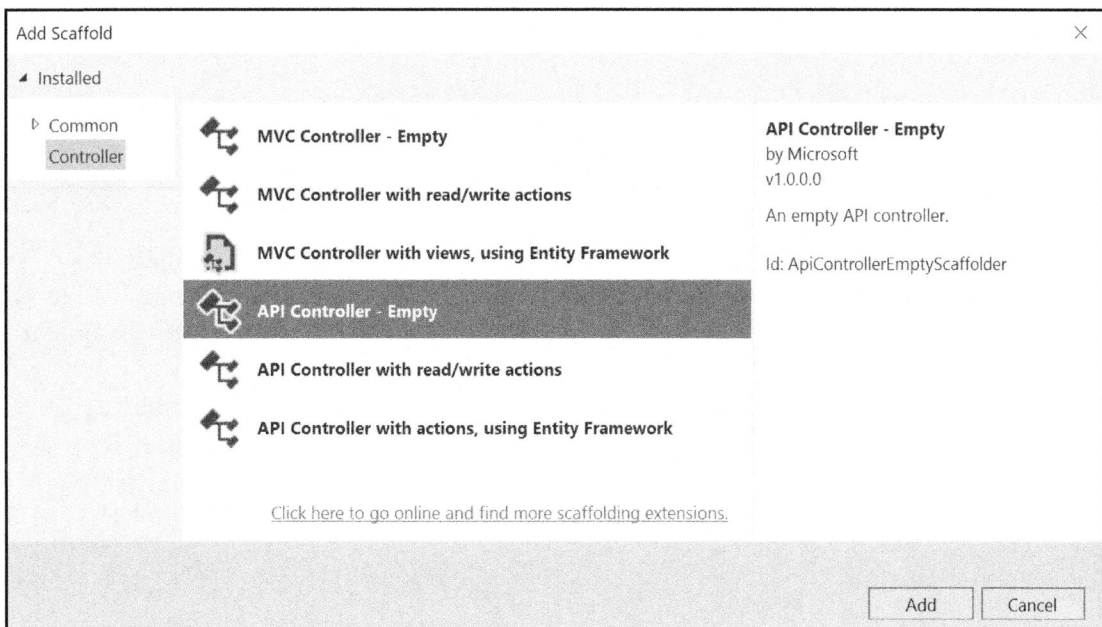

3. Set the name to `ProductsController` and click **Add**.
4. Add the following method to the generated controller:

```
public string[] GetProducts()
{
    return new[]
```

```
        {
            "1 - Microwave",
            "2 - Washing Machine",
            "3 - Mirror"
        };
    }
```

5. Your controller should look like this:

```
[Route("api/Products")]
[ApiController]
public class ProductsController : Controller
{
    public string[] GetProducts()
    {
        return new[]
        {
            "1 - Microwave",
            "2 - Washing Machine",
            "3 - Mirror"
        };
    }
}
```

Congratulations! You have completed coding your first API method. The `GetProducts` method returns the collection of the available products.

To see it in action, build and run your project. This will open a browser with the base address of your ASP.NET application. Add the `/api/Products` string to the base address in the browser's address bar and execute it. You should see the collection of strings appear on the screen like so:

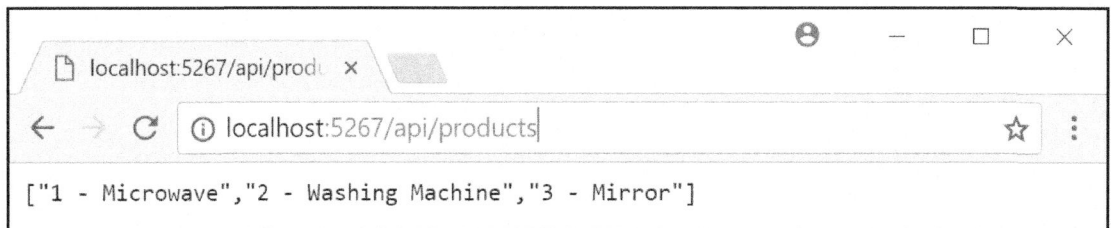

Inspecting your APIs using Fiddler and Postman

Using your browser to execute your APIs is nice enough for simple APIs that retrieve data, but as you go along and extend your APIs, you'll soon find that you need other powerful tools to test and debug what you develop. There are many tools that let you inspect and debug your APIs, but I have chosen to teach you about *Fiddler* and *Postman* because they are both simple and powerful.

Fiddler

Fiddler is a free web debugging tool that works as a proxy, logging all HTTP(S) traffic that is executed by processes in your computer. Fiddler allows you to inspect the traffic to see that exact HTTP request that was sent and the exact HTTP response that was returned. You can also use other advanced features, such as setting breakpoints and overriding the data that is sent or received.

To install Fiddler, navigate to `https://www.telerik.com/fiddler` and click the **Free download** button. Save and run the installer:

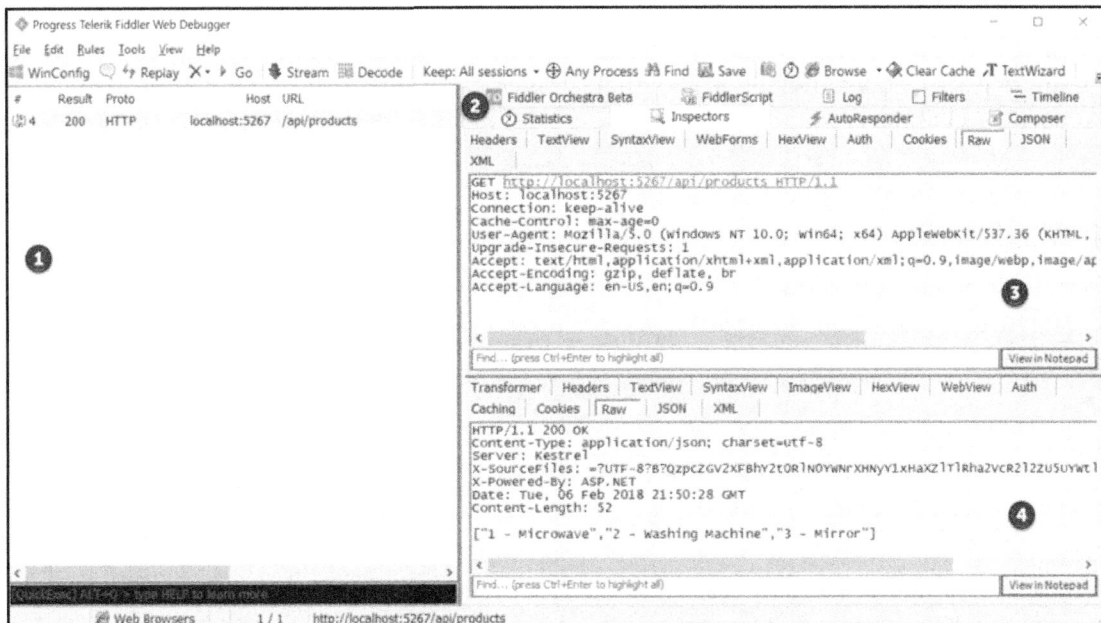

The Fiddler main screen is built from these main parts:

- **Sessions list**: Shows the HTTP(S) requests that were sent from processes in your machine
- **Fiddler tabs**: Contains different tools for inspecting and controlling sessions
- **Request inspector**: When the **Inspectors** tab and inner **Raw** tab are selected, this section shows the request as it was sent over-the-wire
- **Response inspector**: When the **Inspectors** tab and inner **Raw** tab are selected, this section shows the response as it was sent over-the-wire

Immediately after you run Fiddler, it starts collecting the HTTP sessions that are performed in your machine. If you refresh the browser that you used to navigate to the `/api/Products` API you created, you should see this session in Fiddler's Sessions List, as shown in the preceding screenshot.

> If you run a .NET application that sends HTTP requests to an address in your localhost, you won't see the session appear in Fiddler. Changing the address to `localhost.fiddler` will force the request to be captured by Fiddler.

Fiddler is a great tool for debugging the requests and responses that are made in your application, but it means that you need to have a client that sends those requests. Many times when debugging and experimenting with APIs, you want to create HTTP requests manually and inspect them. You can accomplish this task with Fiddler's **Composer** tab, but I want to teach you about another tool that is much more suitable for these scenarios—Postman.

Postman

Postman is an HTTP client that simplifies the testing of web services and RESTful APIs. Postman allows you to easily construct HTTP requests, send them, and inspect them.

Download Postman from `https://www.getpostman.com/`, and then install and run it:

1. On the introduction screen, click on the **Request** option:

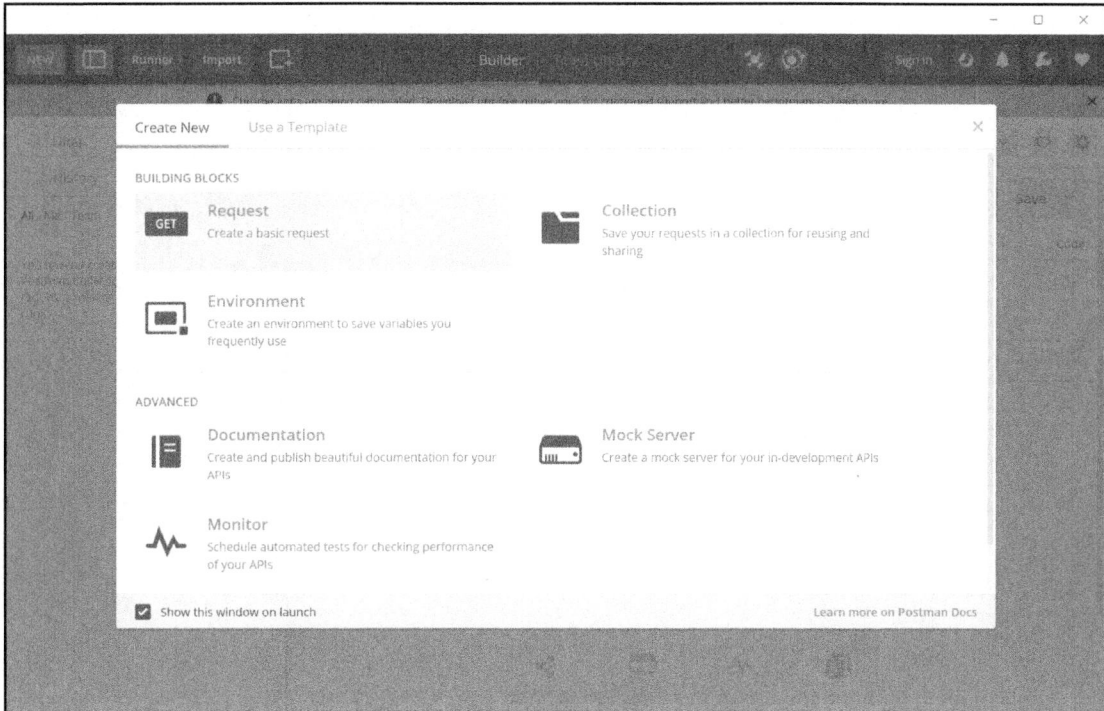

2. Enter `GetProducts` in the **Request name** field, and then type `GiveNTake` into the collection section and create a new collection. Press **Save** to create the new request:

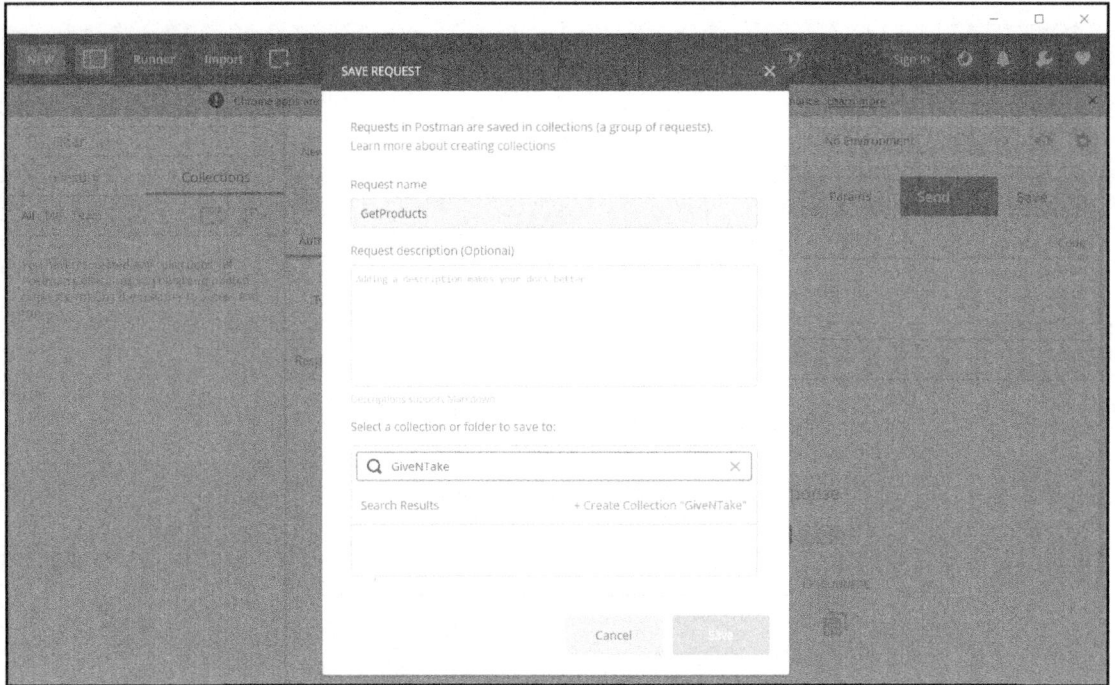

3. Enter the full URL of the `GetProducts` API (for example, `http://localhost:5267/api/products`) in the URL field:

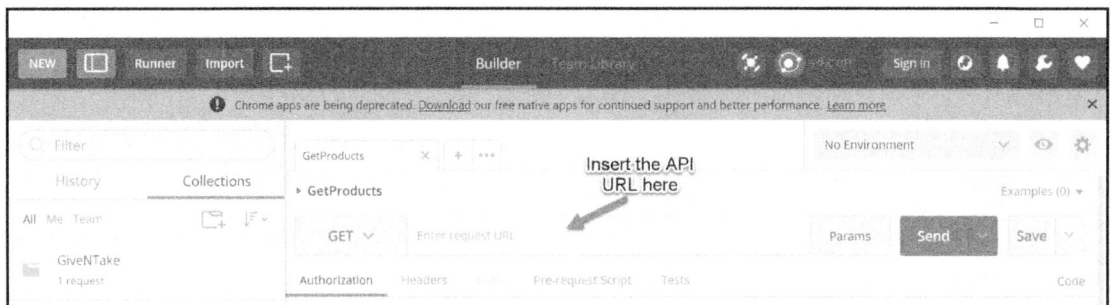

4. Make sure that the HTTP Verb is set to **GET** and click on the **Send** button.

5. After a few moments, you should see the response that was received from your service, and you can now inspect the status code, response body, and headers:

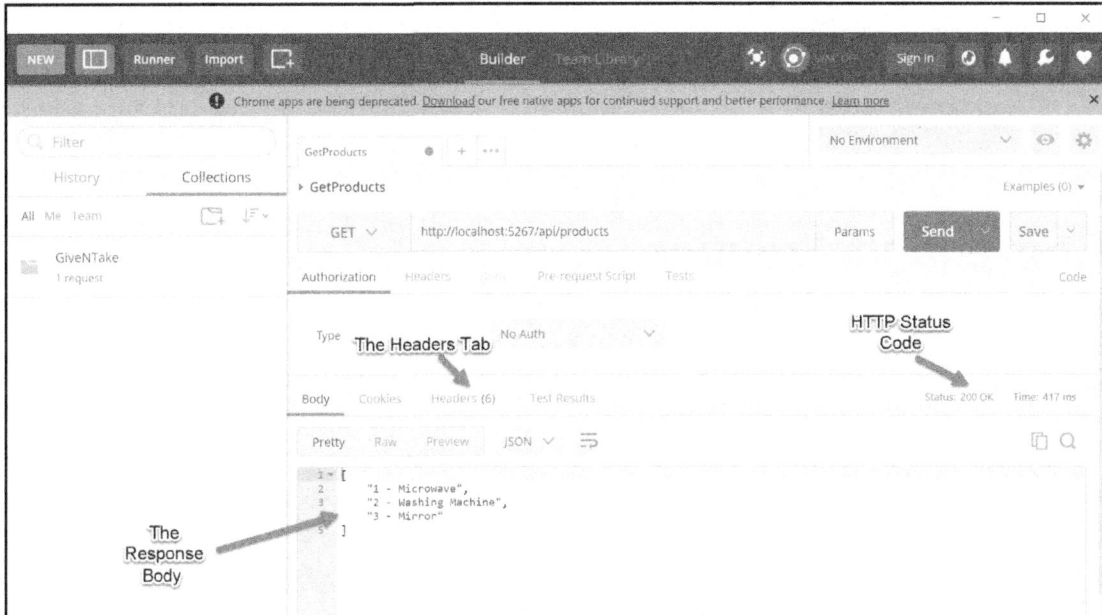

You will find *Postman* to be an indispensable development tool while you develop your APIs, and we will use it many times as we go deeper into ASP.NET Core in this book.

At this point, you might be wondering, how come the GetProducts method was invoked when we navigated to /api/Products? To answer this question, we need to talk about how ASP.NET Core routes requests into controllers and actions.

Routing

Routing in ASP.NET Core is the process of mapping incoming requests to application logic that resides in controllers and methods.

ASP.NET Core maps the incoming request based on the *routes* that you configure in your application, and for each *route*, you can set specific configurations, such as default values, message handlers, constraints, and so on.

There are a few ways of controlling the routing in an ASP.NET Core application, but in this chapter, we will concentrate on the two most common ways:

- **Conventional routing**: The route is determined based on conventions that are defined in *route templates* that, at runtime, will map requests to controllers and actions (methods).
- **Attribute-based routing**: The route is determined based on attributes that you set on your controllers and methods. These will define the mapping to the controller's actions.

Conventional routing

In the conventional routing style, during application startup, you define route *templates* that will be queried each time an incoming request is received in order to make a URL matching. This process will eventually map to a controller and a method inside it. If no route is found for the incoming request, an HTTP error of 404 (Not Found) will be returned to the caller.

When you called `AddMvc` inside the `ConfigureServices` method and the `UseMvcWithDefaultRoute` method inside the `Configure` method in your startup class, at the same time, behind the scenes, the MVC framework added a route handler and set the route to the default template, which looks like this:

```
"{controller=Home}/{action=Index}/{id?}"
```

This template defines that for every request that is received, the request pipeline will attempt to break its URL so that the first part will be mapped to the controller name, the second part (the one after the /) will be mapped to the method inside the controller, and the third part, if it exists, will be used as a *route parameter* (enclosed in curly braces { }) to map to a parameter with the `id` method.

When ASP.NET Core searches for a controller, it takes the controller part from the template and concatenates it with the suffix controller. This means that, instead of using a URL in the form of `/ExampleController/SomeAction`, you can just write `/Example/SomeAction`.

Defining a new route template

To define route templates in your application, the easiest way is to use the `UseMvc` method, instead of `UseMvcWithDefaultRoute` inside the `Configure` method in your startup class. This method allows you to define the routes you want in your application. For example, in the `GiveNTake` application, if we want our application to support not only the default route, but also expose the RESTful API with an `api` prefix (that is, URLs in the form of `/api/[controller]/[action]`), then this is how we need to change our `Configure` method:

```
public void Configure(IApplicationBuilder app, IHostingEnvironment env)
{
    ...

    app.UseMvc(routes =>
    {
        routes
            .MapRoute(name: "default", template:
"{controller=Home}/{action=Index}/{id?}")
            .MapRoute(name: "api", template:
"api/{controller}/{action}/{id?}");
    });

}
```

The `MapRoute` method is how you can define routes for your application, and you can call it multiple times to set multiple route templates.

To test the route you just configured, add a new empty class in the `Controllers` folder and name it `MessagesController`. Paste the following code to the file you created. It should look something like the following:

```
using Microsoft.AspNetCore.Mvc;

namespace GiveNTake.Controllers
{
    public class MessagesController : Controller
    {
        public string[] My()
        {
            return new[]
            {
                "Is the Microwave working?",
                "Where can i pick the washing machine from?",
            };
        }
```

```
        public string Details(int id)
        {
            return $"{id} - Is the Microwave working?";
        }
    }
}
```

Run the project and navigate your browser to
`http://localhost:{port}/api/messages/my`.

Your browser should display a page similar to this:

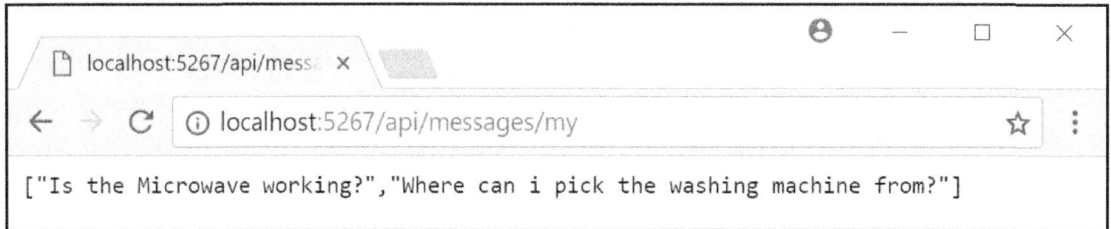

The `MapRoute` methods allow you to control the route in a more advanced way. Here is the
full `MapRoute` signature, but it has overloads that make some of the parameters optional:

```
IRouteBuilder MapRoute(this IRouteBuilder routeBuilder,
    string name,
    string template,
    object defaults,
    object constraints,
    object dataTokens)
```

These parameters operate as follows:

- `name`: Each route should be given a unique name that identifies it. The name
  doesn't affect the routing procedure, but it can be very useful when there are
  route failures, and ASP.NET Core notifies you on issues with the routes.
- `template`: This is the core of the route. This defines the URL structure and the
  tokens that should be mapped to the controller, actions, and parameters.
- `defaults`: This defines the default values for the different tokens in case they are
  missing in the request URL.
- `constraints`: This parameter covers individual constraint rules for the tokens in
  the route that determine if the value is acceptable for that token in that route.

- `data token`: These are additional values that are associated with the route. They won't affect the matching process, but when the route is determined, the values will be added to the `RouteData.DataTokens` collection property of the controller and can be used in its logic.

Here is an improved Version of our API route definition that sets the default value for the controller to `Messages`, the action to `My`, and also sets a constraint on the `id` parameter to allow only integers:

```
MapRoute(
    name: "api",
    template: "api/{controller}/{action}/{id?}",
    defaults: new { Controller = "Messages", action="My" },
    constraints: new { id = new IntRouteConstraint() });
```

`defaults` and `constraints` can also be set inside the template itself, so the preceding API definition we created is identical to this one:

```
MapRoute(
    name: "api",
    template: "api/{controller=Messages}/{action=My}/{id:int?}");
```

Conventional routing is a simple mechanism that is usually suited to small-scale APIs. But as your APIs grow, you will soon find that you need a more fine-grained approach for defining your routes, and if that's the case, it's better to use attribute-based routing.

Attribute-based routing

Attribute-based routing allows you to control the exact route that each controller and action takes part in by using the attributes that decorate your controllers and methods. I recommend that you use this approach for most of your APIs, since it will make your code more explicit and reduce routing errors that might be introduced as you add more controllers and actions.

At the beginning of this chapter, we created the `ProductsController`, which looked like this:

```
[Route("api/Products")]
[ApiController]
public class ProductsController : Controller
{
    ...
}
```

The `RouteAttribute` attribute that decorates the `ProductController` contains the URL template that maps to this controller. In this case, every request with a URL prefixed with `/api/products/` will be routed to this controller. You can use the `RouteAttribute` attribute on controllers and on methods, but for methods, it's recommended to use the `Http[Verb]Attribute` attribute, where `[Verb]` is one of the standard HTTP verbs (`Get`, `Post`, `Put`, `Delete`, and so on).

The `Http[Verb]Attribute` and `RouteAttribute` attributes can be assigned multiple times to define multiple routes, and are hierarchical, which means that they support route inheritance. This means that if you configured a route on your controller, the routes you define on the methods will extend it.

For example, here is how you can configure that the `ProductsController.GetProducts` method will be mapped to a `HttpGet` request to the URL `/api/products/all`, in addition to the URL `/api/products`:

```
[HttpGet]
[HttpGet("all")]
public string[] GetProducts()
{
    ...
}
```

> If the `Http[Verb]Attribute` that you set on a method contains a string that begins with `/`, then it won't be combined with the route defined in the controller, and will instead define a route of its own.

Parameterizing the route template

Attribute-based routing supports a few predefined tokens that are placed in square brackets (`[` and `]`), and will be replaced at runtime with their corresponding value:

- `[controller]`: This will be replaced with the controller name.
- `[action]`: This will be replaced with the method name.
- `[area]`: If your application supports areas, this will be replaced with the area in which the controller resides. Area functionality is not covered in this book, but for more information, you can refer to https://docs.microsoft.com/en-us/aspnet/core/mvc/controllers/areas.

For example, instead of writing `ProductsController` explicitly in the `RouteAttribute`, we can write it like this:

```
[Route("api/[controller]")]
[ApiController]
public class ProductsController : Controller
{
    ...
}
```

Tokens within curly braces (`{ }`) define route parameters that will be bound to the method parameters if the route is matched.

For example, suppose you wish to expose an API to search for products, based on a keyword, in the form of a `GET` request to a URL formatted as `/api/products/search/keyword`. This is how you can write it:

```
[HttpGet("search/{keyword}")]
public string[] SearchProducts(string keyword)
{
    ...
}
```

Just like with conventional routing, you can define default values and constraints on the route parameters.

Default values

Default values are defined by placing an equals sign next to the route parameter. Note that placing default values on the method parameters (not in the root template) will not work, as the routing pipeline is unable to find a match by looking at optional parameters.

For example, the `GiveNTake` application allows the user to search for products by specifying a category and a sub-category; however, the sub-category is optional, and if it is omitted, the default `subcategory` will be `all`. The following code snippet shows you how to define these rules:

```
[HttpGet("searchcategory/{category}/{subcategory=all}/")]
public string[] SearchByProducts(string category, string subcategory)
{
    return new[]
    {
        $"Category: {category}, Subcategory: {subcategory}"
    };
}
```

Run the application and navigate to
`http://localhost:[port]/api/products/searchcategory/furniture/kitchen`,
and then to `http://localhost:[port]/api/products/searchcategory/furniture`.

For the first URL, you should see results similar to the following:

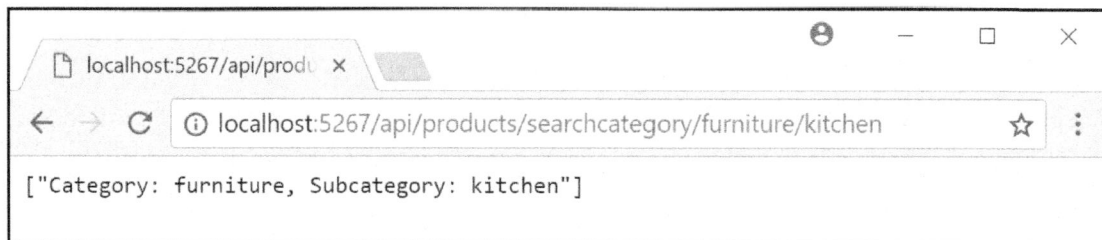

And the second URL should produce an output like this:

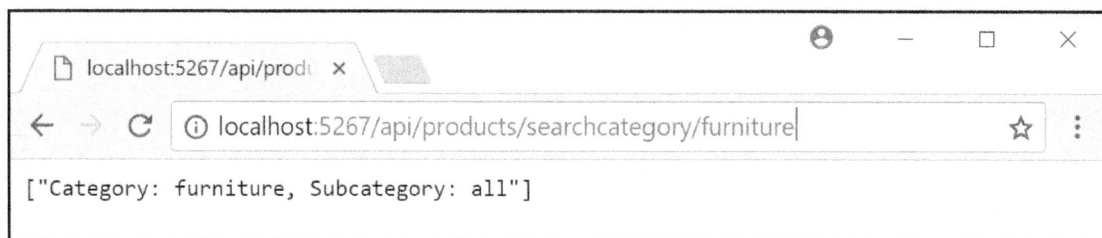

Constraints

Inline constraints inside the routing attributes are used by placing a colon with the constraint name `:constraint-name` after the route parameter name, where *constraint-name* is a constraint that you define by creating a class that implements the `IRouteConstraint` interface, or simply by using one of the built-in constraints specified in the ASP.NET documentation, available at `https://docs.microsoft.com/en-us/aspnet/core/fundamentals/routing?highlight=routing#route-constraint-reference`.

The following example shows how we can add a `search` method to our `ProductsController` that searches by the date that the product was posted online. The URL for this action must constrain the date parameter to `datetime` formats only; therefore, we will use the `datetime` constraint like this:

```
[HttpGet("search/{date:datetime}/{keyword}/")]
public string[] Search(string date, string keyword)
{
```

```
    return new[]
    {
        $"Date: {date}, keyword: {keyword}"
    };
}
```

The routing infrastructure in ASP.NET Core is very sophisticated, and there are plenty more features out of the scope of this book that therefore aren't covered. For more details about the routing capabilities in ASP.NET Core, refer to the documentation at `https://docs.microsoft.com/en-us/aspnet/core/fundamentals/routing`.

The model

The M in MVC means model, but what does a model really mean? The simplest definition is that model refers to the application problem-domain entities and their behavior, where behavior can be implemented in the entities themselves, or in a dedicated service class.

Classes that contain only properties with no logic are called **Plain Old CLR Objects (POCO)** classes. These are the type of classes that work best when received as input or returned as output from your APIs. It will save you many headaches if you stick to POCO classes in the external surface of your APIs. This will also keep you from making mistakes, namely exposing sensitive information such as your database structure, as your APIs grow. On the internals of your APIs, you can use any type of classes that you like, and in Chapter 5, *Persisting Data with Entity Framework*, you will learn how to use the **Entity Framework (EF)** core to work with classes that map to database tables and allow you to store data and query it.

Model binding

The data that is carried with an HTTP request that is mapped to parameters that you define in your method's, signature in a process called **Model binding**. The HTTP request can contain data inside the various parts that compose it:

- Route tokens
- Query strings
- Message body
- Request headers

ASP.NET Core's model binding defines the rules of how to map each value to its correct method parameter.

We already saw how to bind route tokens to method parameters in the *Routing* section of this chapter, so we won't repeat ourselves, and will instead concentrate on the other types of bindings.

Query strings

A query string is data that's sent as part of the URL that is not suitable for use as part of the hierarchical structure of the URL (where / separates between different levels of the hierarchy). Typically, the query string is the part that comes after the question mark in the URL and uses the & sign to separate between the different values. For example, the GiveNTake application allows the user to search for products in a specific location, and to constraint the search only to products that have an image attached to them. This API is exposed through a URL in the following format:

```
/api/products/searchcategory/category/subcategory?location=XXX&imageonly=true
```

ASP.NET Core automatically matches any value in the query string to a method parameter with the same name (this value is case-insensitive); therefore, the method in the controller is implemented like this:

```
[HttpGet("searchcategory/{category}/{subcategory=all}/")]
public string[] SearchByProducts(string category,string subcategory, string location="all", bool imageOnly=false )
{
    return new[]
    {
        $"Category: {category}, Subcategory: {subcategory}, Location: {location}, Only with Images: {imageOnly}"
    };
}
```

Run the application and navigate to http://localhost:[port]/api/products/searchcategory/furniture/kitchen?location=center&imageonly=true.

Your browser should show a result similar to this:

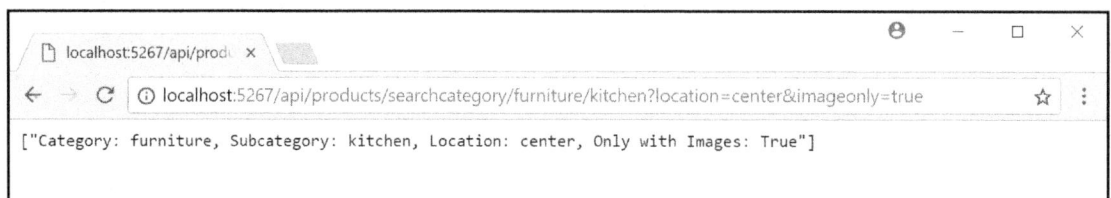

By default, simple types are automatically mapped from the request query string to method parameters with the same name. If needed, you can force ASP.NET Core to map a method parameter to a query string value with a different name by using the `[FromQuery("name")]` attribute. The `[FromQuery]` attribute also allows you to force the binding to a complex type.

Message body

HTTP allows the sender to send a message body with the request. This is useful not only for sending complex structures but also for hiding information since unlike the URL, the message body can be encrypted (for example, when using **HTTP Secure** (**HTTPS**). Not every HTTP request type can send a message body; for example, adding a message body to a `GET` request is usually not supported by server frameworks, and here, ASP.NET Core is no exception.

When a request with a message body is sent to a server, it should contain the `Content-Type` header with the message body type as one of the standard MIME types. ASP.NET Core uses the content type value to determine which formatter to use in order to deserialize the message body to a method parameter. The default formatter is `JsonInputFormatter`, which is based on the popular package Json.NET, but other formatters exist for other types.

ASP.NET Core uses the `[FromBody]` attribute to mark the method parameter that should be bound to the request's message body.

Here is how you can add an API that will let users add a new product to the `GiveNTake` application, and then test it:

1. Create a new folder is your solution with the name `Model`.
2. Create a new class in the `Model` folder, called `NewRequestDTO`, and paste the following code into your new class:

```
public class NewProductDTO
{
    public string Name { get; set; }
    public string Category { get; set; }
    public string Subcategory { get; set; }
}
```

The `NewProductDTO` is a POCO class that will be filled with the values supplied in the request body. **Data Transfer Object (DTO)** is a common name for a type that you expose from your APIs. We usually add the DTO postfix to differentiate classes you use only in the API layer and classes that are used in the business logic:

1. Add the `AddNewProduct` method to your `ProductsController`. For now, this method will receive the `NewProductDTO` and return it:

```
[HttpPost("")]
public ActionResult<NewProductDTO> AddNewProduct([FromBody]
NewProductDTO newProduct)
{
    return Ok(newProduct);
}
```

> We used the `[HttpPost]` attribute with an empty string. This means that the `AddNewProduct` method will be invoked by `POST` requests that are sent to the `Controller` route, in this case, `/api/products`. The method received a single parameter of the `NewProductDTO` type, and the `[FromBody]` attribute signals the ASP.NET Core pipeline to bind this parameter to the request body. Don't worry if you don't understand what the meaning of the `ActionResult` return type and the use of the `Ok(...)` method is yet — we will talk about them in the next section.

2. Build and run the application.
3. Open Postman and create a new `POST` request to the following URL: `/api/products`.
4. Select the Body inner tab and the raw option.
5. Change the content type from **Text** to **JSON (application/json)**. Fill the request body with the following JSON:

```
{
  "Name" : "New Product",
  "Category" : "Appliances",
  "Subcategory" : "Microwaves"
}
```

6. Postman should now look like this:

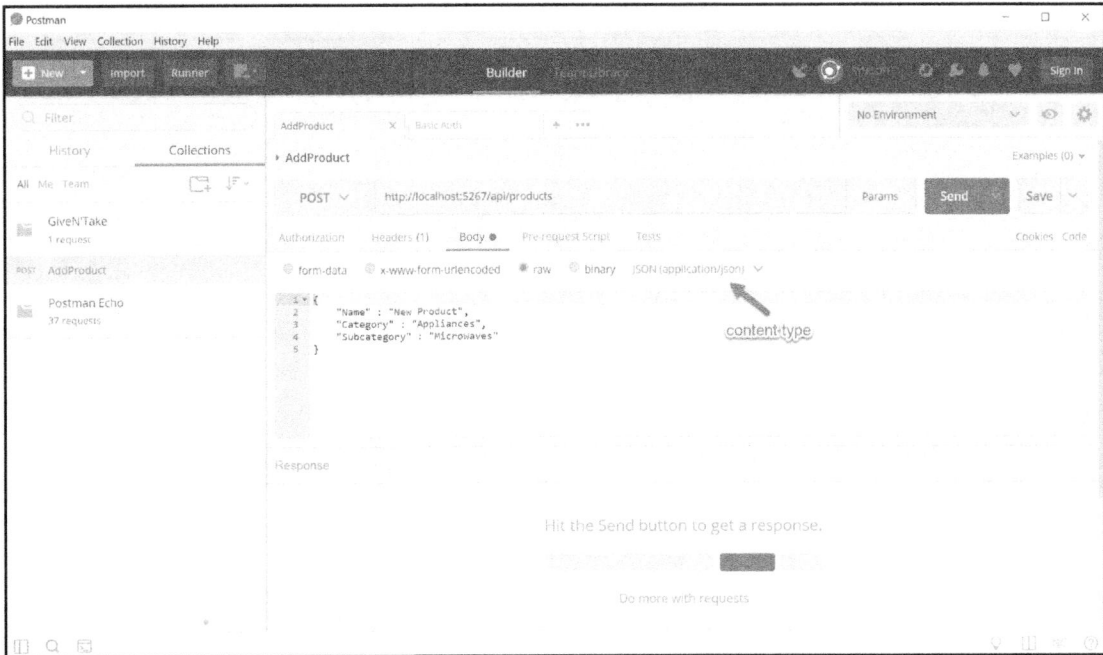

7. Click on the **Send** button, and look at the result at the bottom of the Postman window. It should reflect the same values that you sent in the request, like this:

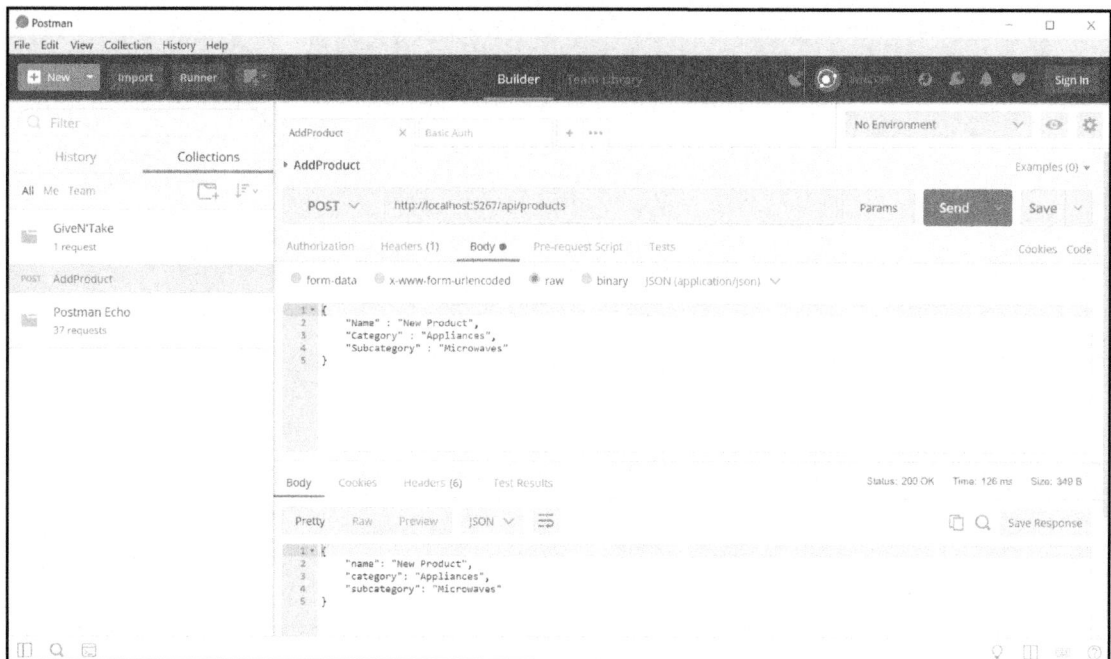

Header values

Header values can be bound to parameters in your method by placing the `[FromHeader("Header Name")]` attribute on the bounded parameter and stating the name of the header you wish to bind to.

Model validation

Model validation is ASP.NET Core's ability to run validation rules on the input that your methods receive. The easiest way to define these validation rules is by using validation attributes that are part of the `System.ComponentModel.DataAnnotations` Namespace (`https://docs.microsoft.com/en-us/dotnet/api/system.componentmodel.dataannotations?view=netframework-4.7.2`), but you can define custom validations by inheriting from the `ValidationAttribute` base class. For sophisticated validation rules, I recommend that you use the popular `FluentValidation` library, available at `https://github.com/JeremySkinner/FluentValidation`.

There are plenty of built-in validation attributes, but here is a short list of some the most popular ones:

- [Required]: Specifies that a data field value is required
- [Range]: Specifies the allowed numeric range in a data field value
- [MinLength]: Specifies the minimum length that a data field will accept
- [MaxLength]: Specifies the maximum length that a data field will accept
- [EmailAddress]: Specifies that the value of a string field must be in an email address format

For example, the following code block shows how you can define that the NewProductDTO must be set with a value in its Name property of at least 3 characters, and no more than 50:

```
public class NewProductDTO
{
    [Required]
    [MinLength(3)]
    [MaxLength(50)]
    public string Name { get; set; }
    public string Category { get; set; }
    public string Subcategory { get; set; }
}
```

Once your validation attributes are positioned, ASP.NET Core will run a validation check automatically when a request is received and the values will be bound to your method parameters. Then, you can inspect the validation result and error messages by using the controller's ModelState property, which is of type ModelStateDictionary. The ModelStateDictionary type represents the state of the attempt to bind values from the HTTP request to the method parameters. It's a dictionary where the key is the name of the parameter and the value is a valid entry. You can use the IsValid property to assert that the request fulfills the required validation rules, like this:

```
[HttpPost("")]
public ActionResult<NewProductDTO> AddNewProduct([FromBody] NewProductDTO
newProduct)
{
    if (!ModelState.IsValid)
    {
        return BadRequest(ModelState);
    }
    return Ok(newProduct);
}
```

In the `GiveNTake` application, we make sure that the details of the new product fulfill the rules we defined, and if not, we send a `BadRequest` (400 HTTP status code). The controller's `BadRequest` method accepts the `ModelStateDictionary` and adds the error message to the HTTP response.

> **TIP**
>
> Starting from ASP.NET Core 2.1, validation checks are done automatically when you decorate your controller with the `[ApiController]` attribute, and the `BadRequest` response is returned if the validation fails.

Run the application and use Postman to send two `POST` requests to the `/api/products` URL, one with an empty body, and one with the following JSON:

```
{
  "Name" : "",
  "Category" : "Appliances",
  "Subcategory" : "Microwaves"
}
```

You should see the following response:

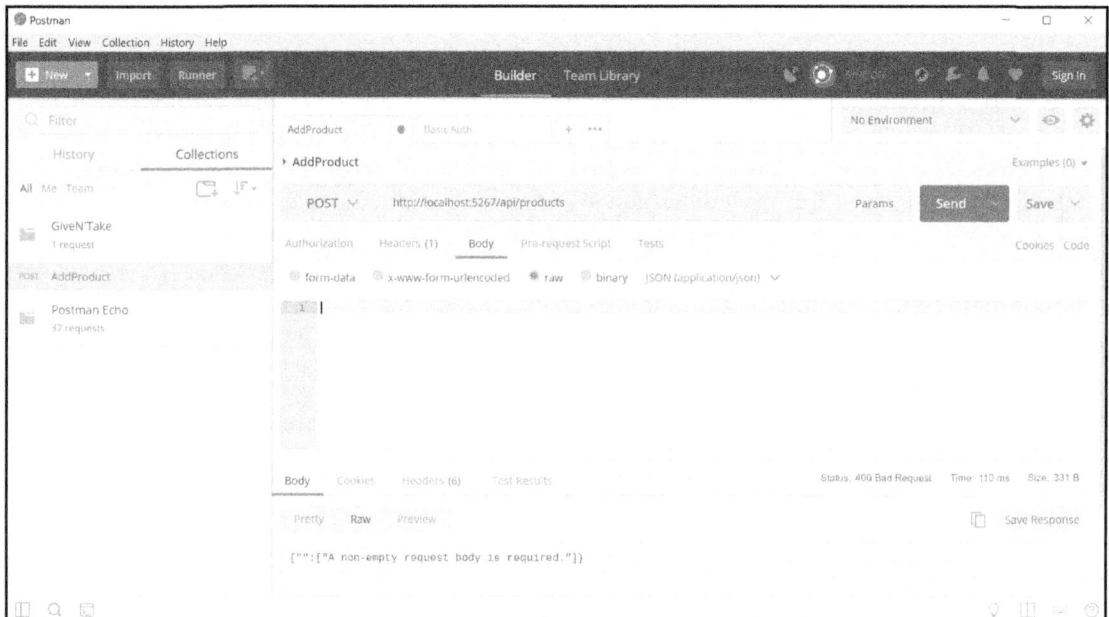

And:

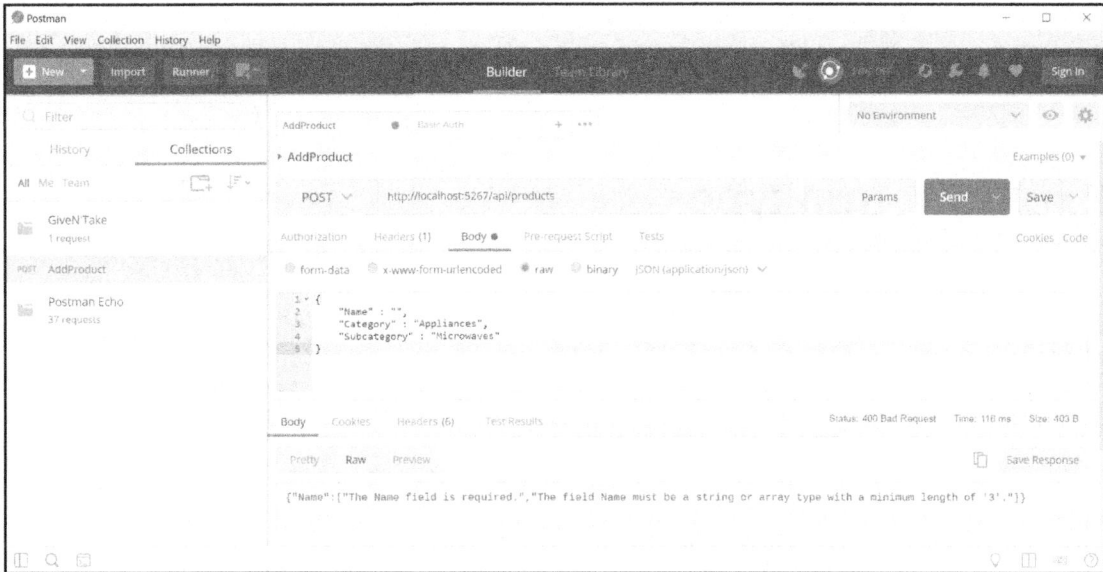

Generating a response of different types

So far, all the of action methods we have created returned simple response types, such as `string` or arrays, but the HTTP standard has no concept of method signature and return type. Instead, it defines the format of a valid HTTP response. This is how a simple HTTP response might look:

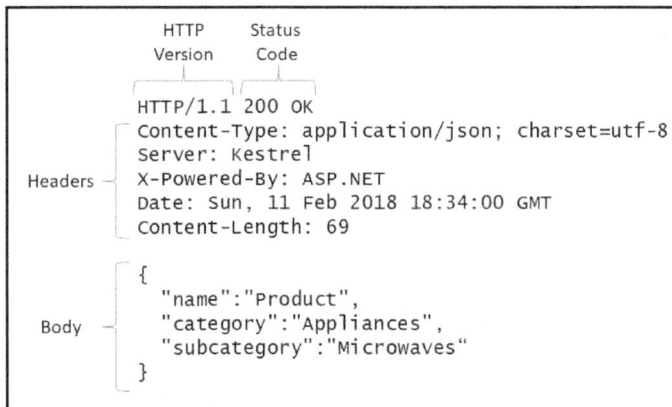

As you can see, the HTTP response includes **Status Code**, **Headers**, and **Body**. Each of these parts allows you to communicate pieces of information to the client, and ASP.NET Core provides the glue that converts the results of your action methods into those parts of the HTTP response, regardless of whether they are executed successfully, or completed with a failure.

Explicit return type

The simplest form of an action method is the one where the return type is a predefined .NET type, such as primitives or classes you have created. When the method returns a value, the ASP.NET Core pipeline create a success response (with the status code 200 OK) and serializes the value with a formatter that is suitable to the content type that the client requested (via the `Accept` header in the HTTP request) or with the configured default formatter (the JSON formatter, unless configured otherwise).

Although returning an explicit predefined type is the simplest way to create actions, it's also the most restricted way. My recommendation is not to use this method, and instead, configure all of your actions to return `ActionResult<T>` or `IActionResult`.

IActionResult and ActionResult<T>

The `IActionResult` interface defines the contract `<indexentry content="HTTP response:ActionResult">` for action method responses. The default implementation of the interface is provided by the `ActionResult` and `ActionResult<T>` types, but ASP.NET Core provides many derived response types that you can use to fully control the HTTP response that will be generated. Here is a short list of some of them:

- `EmptyResult`: Generates an HTTP response with a success status code (200 OK) and an empty body.
- `ObjectResult`: Generates a response with a body, where the body is a serialization of an object you provide. The object is serialized to the content type that was requested by the client.
- `BadRequestResult`: Generates a response with a `BadRequst` status code (400) that signals to the client that the given request is invalid.
- `ViewResult`: Allows you to render a view, from a `cshtml` file, for example, and return the result (as HTML) to the client.

- `FileResult`: Generates a response that contains file data. There are derived classes for various file reading formats.
- `RedirectResult`: Generates a response with a temporary redirect (302) or permanent redirect status code (301) that contains the URL to navigate to.

Starting from ASP.NET Core 2.1, the `ActionResult<T>` type can be used as the return type of a controller action to make it explicit what the type of the body will be in a successful response, while still allowing for the return of other response types if needed.

> When an action with an explicit predefined return type returns its result, ASP.NET Core wraps the returned value in an `ObjectResult` instance.

For example, if `GiveNTake` receives a request to add a product with invalid request data, we send the client a `BadRequestResult`, and if the request was valid, we echo the request data with an `ObjectResult`, like this:

```
[HttpPost("")]
public ActionResult<NewProductDTO> AddNewProduct([FromBody] NewProductDTO
newProduct)
{
    if (!ModelState.IsValid)
    {
        return new BadRequestResult();//(ModelState);
    }
    return newProduct;
}
```

Asynchronous actions

ASP.NET Core supports asynchronous actions that are implemented with the `async-await` pattern. If the method action return type is `Task` or `Task<T>`, ASP.NET Core will await the `Task`, and once completed, the result will be sent back to the client.

For example, here is an asynchronous version of the `AddNewProduct` action that adds a short delay (for demonstration purposes) and awaits it:

```
[HttpPost("")]
public async Task<ActionResult<NewProductDTO>> AddNewProduct([FromBody]
NewProductDTO newProduct)
{
    await Task.Delay(1000);
```

```
    if (!ModelState.IsValid)
    {
        return new BadRequestResult();//(ModelState);
    }
    return new ObjectResult(newProduct);
}
```

Controller response helper methods

The ASP.NET Core `ControllerBase` base class, from which all the controllers inherit, provides a few `helper` methods for creating responses instead of manually creating and setting instances of `IActionResult` derived types. Here is a short list of some of the popular ones:

- `Ok(...)`: Creates an `OkResult` object with or without content
- `StatusCode(int statusCode)`: Creates a response with a given status code
- `BadRequest(...)`: Creates a `BadRequestObjectResult` with a 400 status code and a body

For a complete list, refer to the `ControllerBase` documentation, available at `https://docs.microsoft.com/en-us/dotnet/api/microsoft.aspnetcore.mvc.controllerbase?view=aspnetcore-2.0#Methods`.

Summary

ASP.NET Core provides the necessary infrastructure you need to create powerful RESTful APIs. In this chapter you learned how to create controllers and actions that respond to HTTP requests, and return HTTP responses that you control.

I've introduced two popular tools: Fiddler and Postman, and you'll find them very useful when you create and debug your API applications. You've seen how to configure the routing in your application in two ways — conventional and attribute-based — and how to map values in the request's URL to parameters.

You've learned what the meaning of the M, MVC is, and how to bind the data from the request to the model classes.

You've also seen how easy it is to define validation rules on your model types, and how ASP.NET Core automatically validates these rules. We've also covered the different possibilities that you have for generating responses from your action methods, and shown some `helper` methods that the controller base class provides to assist you with generating the response types. In `Chapter 5`, *Persisting Data with Entity Framework*, we'll explain how you can work with a database to store and query your application state.

5
Persisting Data with Entity Framework

Many applications rely on databases to store and query data. Even though there are many types of databases, including graph, key-value stores, document, relational, and so on, in this book, we will use the good old relational database (also known as RDBMS). Relational databases are the oldest and most popular type of databases, and although they may not be the best solution for every type of use case, they most certainly do a very good job in most types of applications, and they have a very mature ecosystem and set of tools. Relational databases rely on the **Standard Query Language (SQL)** to both define the structure and query the data of the database, and for you to use it from within a C# (or any other language) application, you have to learn the language and keep the queries as strings inside your application so that you can send them to the remote database through a designated database client. Developers like to work rapidly and seamlessly with the technologies they use, and this led to the foundations of a new approach to working with databases—**Object-Relational Mappers (O/RM)**. Simply put, O/RM is a technique where you write your code with simple objects that represent your data model and, behind the scenes, every operation you make is translated into SQL and the results are mapped back to your objects.

EF Core is the O/RM of choice when developing an ASP.NET Core application. In this chapter, I will show how you can use it to store data in and retrieve data from your web applications.

In this chapter, you'll learn how to store and query data in a relational database using the EF Core. The following topics will be covered in this chapter:

- Entity framework core overview
- Managing the data model using migrations
- Querying data
- Saving data
- Transactions

Installing Entity Framework Core

EF Core is a powerful, open source, cross-platform, extensible O/RM framework, based on the mature non-cross-platform version called EF. EF Core will make it easy for you to work with databases from any .NET applications, and will be the engine responsible for the way we persist and query data in this book.

To use EF Core, install the EF Core NuGet package through the Package Manager Console with this command:

```
Install-Package Microsoft.EntityFrameworkCore
```

> When using ASP.NET Core from a .NET Core project, a special meta-package with the name `Microsoft.AspNetCore.App` is installed to your project by default. This package references all the ASP.NET NuGet packages (including EF Core) and will only deploy them with your application if they are used.

Creating your data model

An application data model defines the entities and their relationships that the application logic uses to do its job. The `GiveNTake` application allows people to share things they no longer need (we called them sellers, even though they give away their products for free) with people who are interested in receiving free items. The data model of our application is composed of the following entities:

- **User**: A `GiveNTake` user is a seller or a buyer who wishes to work with the published products.
- **Product**: An item that a seller wishes to give away in a specific location.
- **Category**: Products belong to a specific category. In our model, there are two levels, a category and subcategory.
- **City**: Specific locations in which items are traded.
- **ProductMedia**: Each product can have a collection of media files (images, videos, and so on).
- **Message**: User communication about products is done through the sending and receiving of messages.

Refer to the following diagram for more information:

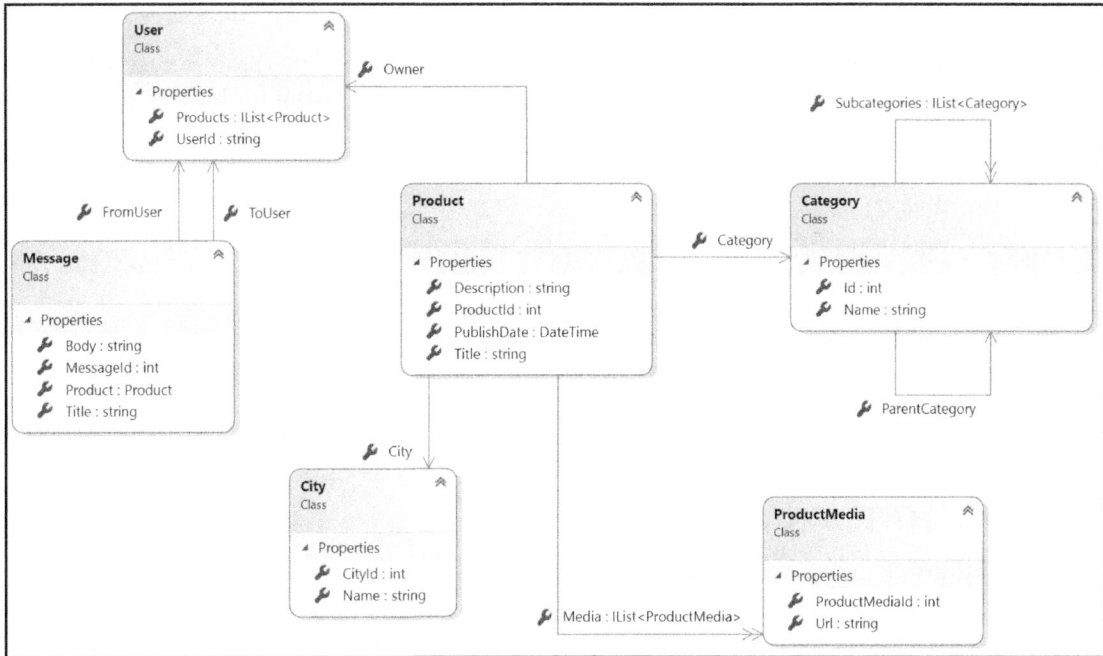

Defining the entities

Entities in EF Core are POCO classes, which means that you don't need to inherit from any base class to use them as your data model. Here is how the Product entity is defined:

```
public class Product
{
    // Primary key
    public int ProductId { get; set; }

    // Value propertis
    public User Owner { get; set; }
    public string Title { get; set; }
    public string Description { get; set; }

    // Navigation properties - represents relationships
    public Category Category { get; set; }
    public City City { get; set; }
    public IList<ProductMedia> Media { get; set; }
    public DateTime PublishDate { get; set; }
```

```
}
```

I divided the class into three sections:

- **Primary key**: Each entity must have a unique identity, called the *Primary Key*, which is composed from one or more values. By default, EF Core will set the value for the primary key (if it's a simple single value) when saving a new object.
- **Value properties**: Properties that contain simple values, such as primitives and enums.
- **Navigation properties**: Properties that make references to other entities or a collection of entities. These represent the relationships between the entities.

All the other entities we have in our GiveNTake app are defined in a similar way, and EF Core will map them to tables, columns, constraints, and other database objects, based on conventions and the explicit rules we can define.

The DbContext

EF Core configures the model and interacts with the database through a class that derives from the Microsoft.EntityFrameworkCore.DbContext base class.

The DbContext base class builds your model based on the entities you include in it, either by defining properties of the DbSet<TEntity> type, or another entity if is being used by an already included entity.

Here is how the GiveNTake DbContext looks:

```
public class GiveNTakeContext : DbContext
{
    . . .

    public DbSet<Product> Products { get; set; }
    public DbSet<Message> Messages { get; set; }
    public DbSet<Category> Categories { get; set; }
    public DbSet<City> Cities { get; set; }
    public DbSet<User> Users { get; set; }
    . . .
}
```

For each entity we wish to include in our model, we added a DbSet property that will allow us to query and persist the entity.

Configuring the model mapping

EF Core uses conventions to map your entities into database objects, but you can also configure the mapping explicitly in two ways:

- **Data Annotations**: Defines each type and property map to the database by using attributes
- **Fluent API**: The model is defined by overriding the `DbContext` `OnModelCreating` method and using a `ModelBuilder` class to define the mapping

In this book, we'll mainly use the EF Core conventions, but when there's a need to fine-tune the mapping, it will be done with the Fluent API.

Here are the default EF Core conventions that are used by our model:

- Table names take the plural form of the entity name. For example, `Products` is the table name for the `Product` entity.
- Column names are the same as the property name.
- Primary keys are named in the format of `[EntityName]Id`, for example, `ProductId`.
- Properties that reference an entity, or a collection of entities, create a relationship between the entities in the form of foreign key constraints.

This list covers almost everything you'd need to create a model, however, there are times where you'll need make adjustments. For example, in the GiveNTake application, a category can be a parent category, or a subcategory of another parent category. This means that there are two relationships between the category entity and itself:

```
public class Category
{
    public int Id { get; set; }
    public string Name { get; set; }
    public IList<Category> Subcategories { get; set; }
    public Category ParentCategory { get; set; }
}
```

EF Core is not able to understand what the relationships mean and if they are required or not. To help it, we'll define the relationships explicitly in the `DbContext.OnModelCreating()` method:

```
protected override void OnModelCreating(ModelBuilder modelBuilder)
{
    modelBuilder.Entity<Category>()
        .HasOne(sub => sub.ParentCategory)
        .WithMany(c => c.Subcategories)
        .IsRequired(false);

    modelBuilder.Entity<Product>()
        .HasOne(p => p.Category)
        .WithMany()
        .IsRequired();

    . . .
}
```

The `ModelBuilder` class is the access point for the EF Core Fluent API. The Fluent API gives you an API for shaping the entities, relationships, constraints, and conventions of your model.

Configuring the database connection with DbContextOptions<TContext>

When `DbContext` is created, it needs to be configured so that it knows <indexentry content="DbContext:database connection configuration with DbContextOptions"> which database to connect to, and with which database provider. The recommended way for passing the connection information to `DbContext` is by using the `DbContextOptions<TContext>` type (where `TContext` is the `DbContext` type that the options apply to).

You can create `DbContextOptions` inside the `OnConfiguring` method of your `DbContext` class itself, but this approach is more difficult to maintain. Instead, I recommend setting `DbContextOptions` in your application startup and injecting it into your `DbContext` class.

> ASP.NET Core makes heavy use of Dependency Injection (more information is available at `https://docs.microsoft.com/en-us/aspnet/core/fundamentals/dependency-injection`). In this technique, you register the types and instance that your application uses inside an object called a Dependency Injection Container. When resolving instances from the container, it will take care of injecting the dependencies needed by the class you asked to resolve.

These are the steps needed to work with `DbContextOptions`:

1. Add a constructor to your `DbContext` class that accepts the `DbContextOptions` instance and passes it to its base class:

   ```
   public GiveNTakeContext(DbContextOptions<GiveNTakeContext>
   options)
       : base(options)
   { }
   ```

2. Register the `DbContext` class in the `ConfigureServices` method of your startup class and pass it the necessary connection string:

   ```
   public void ConfigureServices(IServiceCollection services)
   {
       ...
       services.AddDbContext<GiveNTakeContext>(options =>
   options.UseSqlServer(Configuration.GetConnectionString("GiveNTa
   keDB")));
   }
   ```

3. Add the connection string to your application settings file (`appsettings.json`). If the file doesn't exist in your project, right-click the project, click **Add New Item**, and select **ASP.NET Configuration File**:

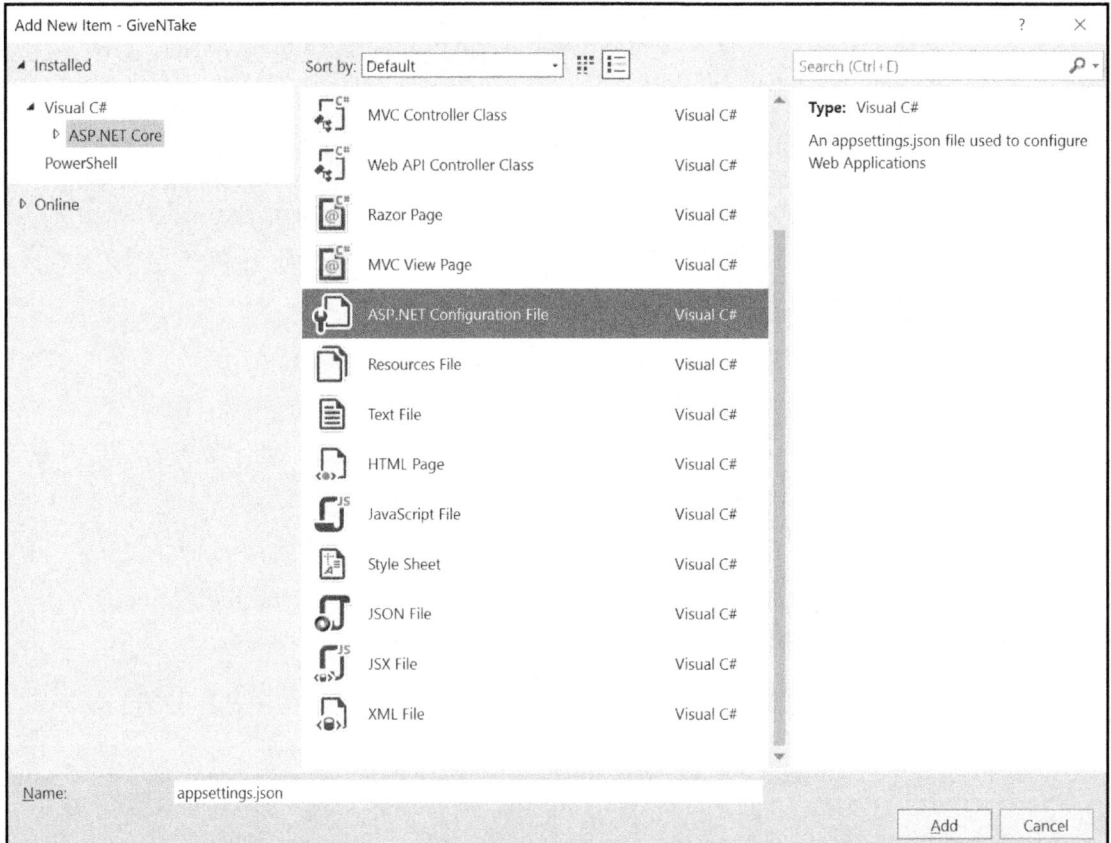

4. The newly added file should include a default connection string value. Change the database name to a meaningful name, such as `GiveNTake`:

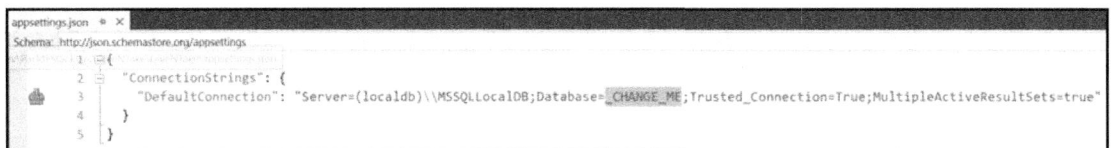

The registration code you inserted in your <indexentry
content="DbContext:database connection configuration with
DbContextOptions"> startup class not only set the DbContextOptions instance; it also
registered the DbContext type to the application's Dependency Injection Container. Now,
if you add a DbContext (such as GiveNTakeContext) parameter to your controller's
constructor, ASP.NET Core will inject its instance to the controller, when it is created, by a
request that is routed to it:

```
[Route("api/[controller]")]
public class ProductsController : Controller
{
    public ProductsController(GiveNTakeContext context)
    {
        _context = context;
    }
    ...
}
```

However, if you try to run the application now and navigate to an action in
ProductsController, you will get an exception. This is because we haven't told EF Core
to create the database for us. To create and manage the database from your code, you need
to use EF Core Migrations.

Creating a database with EF Core migrations

EF Core allows you to create and modify the database and its schema from your code. To
enable this feature, EF Core maintains the database structure, and the changes between
each schema version, in classes that are generated by the EF Core Tools. After an instance of
your DbContext is created, you can instruct it to migrate to the newest schema version.

To enable EF Core migrations in your application, you need to install the EF Core Tools by
adding the Microsoft.EntityFrameworkCore.Tools NuGet package if it's not already
installed (if you're using the Microsoft.AspNetCore.All meta-package, then you
already have it installed).

Creating a new migration

Every time your model changes, you need to add a new migration to your project. Follow these steps to learn how to do this::

1. Open the Package Manager Console (**Tools | NuGet Package Manager | Package Manager Console**).

2. Type and run the following command:

```
Add-Migration [Migration Name] -p [Project Name]
```

3. The initial migration in the `GiveNTake` application was created as follows:

```
Add-Migration InitialMigration -p GiveNTake
```

After the command is complete, a new file will be added to your project under a folder with the name `Migrations`. The file is named in the `[Creation Time]_[Migration Name]` format, for example, `20180219101736_InitialMigration.cs`.

This file contains a class that derives from `Microsoft.EntityFrameworkCore.Migrations.Migration` and contains two methods:

- `Up(MigrationBuilder migrationBuilder)`: Contains the operations needed to apply the migration. The operations are applied through the `migrationBuilder` methods.
- `Down(MigrationBuilder migrationBuilder)`: Contains the operation needed to revert the migration.

Besides the migration file, EF Core generates a file with a name in the `[DbContextName]ModelSnapshot` format. This file contains a snapshot of the model that will help EF Core to detect changes that were made in your model without connecting to the database.

Now that you have a migration file (or files) ready, I'll explain how you can add code that will run the migrations automatically on startup (if needed).

Adding automatic migrations

EF Core migration files encapsulate all the steps needed to reach a database structure that conforms to your code models, but in order to apply those steps to your database, there are a few different paths that you can take:

- Generate an SQL script and execute it in your database
- Run the external `dotnet migrate` command from the terminal
- Add automatic migration capability to your application code.

All of the mentioned methods are good, but I will concentrate on the third option because it's the most developer-friendly and allows you to move fast as you add new features.

The `DatabaseFacade` object, held by the `DbContext` and exposed by the `Database` property, contains the `Migrate` method that runs the migration process for you. To use this method, we need to get hold of the `DbContext` object and run the migration on the earliest phase of our application. The best location to do so is in your `Program` class, right before the `WebHost` is run.

Change your `Program.Main` method to the following code snippet:

```
public static void Main(string[] args)
{
    var host = CreateWebHostBuilder(args).Build();
    using (var scope = host.Services.CreateScope())
    {
        var services = scope.ServiceProvider;
        var context = services.GetService<GiveNTakeContext>();
        try
        {
            context.Database.Migrate();
        }
        catch (Exception ex)
        {
            // Error handling
        }
    }
    host.Run();
}
```

The preceding code creates the `WebHost` (described in `Chapter 3`, *Creating a Web Application with ASP.NET Core*) and afterwards uses the ASP.NET Core Dependency Injection capabilities to create a scoped region to resolve the `GiveNTakeContext` object and call its `Migrate` method. The `CreateScope` method creates a disposable `IServiceScope` that control the lifetime of the resolved objects. Once disposed, all the scoped objects will be disposed as well.

Now, build and run your application. The `GiveNTake` database will be automatically created.

Connecting to the database

Follow these steps to add the GiveN'Take database to Visual Studio so that we can work on it there:

1. Open the **SQL Server Object Explorer** view in Visual Studio (**View** | **SQL Server Object Explorer**):

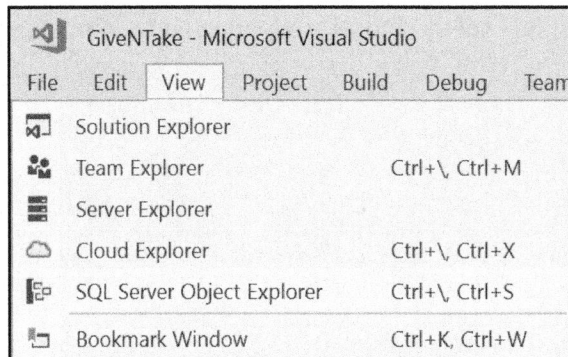

2. Right-click on the SQL Server node inside the opened view and select **Add SQL Server.**

3. In the **Connect** screen that has opened, select the database you wish to connect to, in our case, **MSSQLLocalDB**. Make sure that **Authentication** is set to **Windows Authentication** and click on **Connect**:

You should now see the `GiveNTake` database and be able to explore its schema and run queries if needed:

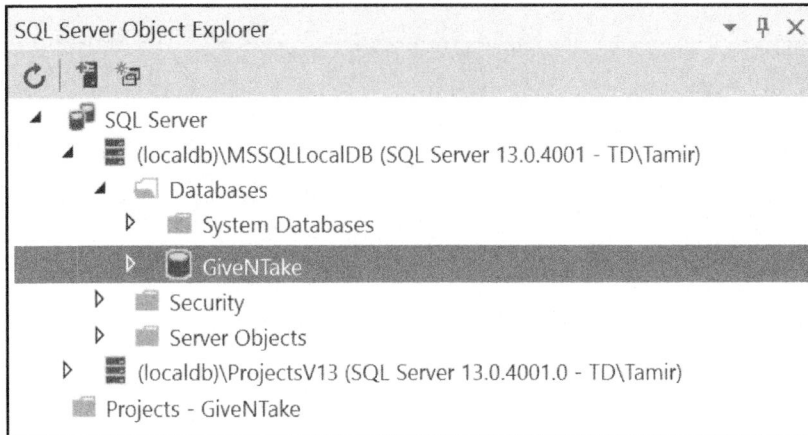

Adding seed data

After the database has been created or migrated to a new schema, the new tables will be empty. Many times, you will need to add initial data that your application relies on. For example, the categories and locations in the `GiveNTake` application are predefined, and so we would like to add them when the database is created.

To add the initial values, we must add a new method to the `GiveNTakeContext` (usually named `SeedData()`) and execute it after the migration has finished:

```
public void SeedData()
{
    if (!Categories.Any())
    {
        var appliances=new Category()
        {
            Name = "Appliances",
            Subcategories = new List<Category>()
            {
                new Category(){Name = "Microwaves"}
            }
        };
        Categories.Add(appliances);
        ...
        SaveChanges();
    }
```

```
        if (!Cities.Any())
        {
            Cities.AddRange(
                new City{Name = "New York"},
                new City{Name = "Seattle"},
                new City{Name = "San Francisco"});
            SaveChanges();
        }


    }
```

Now, we just call it from the `Program.Main` method:

```
public static void Main(string[] args)
{
    var host = CreateWebHostBuilder(args).Build();
    using (var scope = host.Services.CreateScope())
    {
        var services = scope.ServiceProvider;
        var context = services.GetService<GiveNTakeContext>();
        try
        {
            context.Database.Migrate();
            context.SeedData();
        }
        catch (Exception ex)
        {
            // Error handling
        }
    }
}
```

You have now completed all the necessary steps for creating and connecting to a database with EF Core, and supporting automatic migrations. Next, you'll learn how to save and query the data in your database.

Saving data

The `DbContext` class provided by EF Core is designed to work as a **Unit Of Work** (https://martinfowler.com/eaaCatalog/unitOfWork.html) that stores and tracks all the objects in the model. As a Unit Of Work, `DbContext` lets you add an object for tracking, and then we set the `EntityState` parameter of the object so that `DbContext` can perform the correct database operation (`INSERT`, `UPDATE`, or `DELETE`) when needed—that is, when calling the `Save()` or `SaveAsync()` methods.

When defining your instance of DbContext, you added properties of the DbContext type for each entity you wanted your model to include. The DbContext is a special type of collection that is aware of the EntityState objects, and lets you control them with simple methods such as Add() or Remove().

> EF Core scans the graph objects that are being pointed to by the object you add to it and automatically adds the referenced objects if needed.

Here is an example of how products are added in the GiveNTake application:

```
//ProductsController.cs
[HttpPost("")]
public async Task<IActionResult> AddNewProduct([FromBody] NewProductDTO
newProduct)
{
    if (!ModelState.IsValid)
    {
        return BadRequest(ModelState);
    }
    Category category = GetProduct(newpProduct.Category,
newProduct.Subcategory);
    City city = GetCity(newProduct.City);
    User owner = await _context.Users.FindAsync("seller1@seller.com"),
    var product = new Product()
    {
        owner = owner,
        Category = category,
        Title = newProduct.Name,
        Description = newProduct.Description,
        City = city,
        PublishDate = DateTime.UtcNow
    };
    _context.Products.Add(product);
    await _context.SaveChangesAsync();
    return CreatedAtAction(
        nameof(GetProduct),
        new { id = product.ProductId },
        ...);
}
```

The method does some validation checks and then fetches some related entities (we will see how to create entity relationships later in this chapter). Then, a new instance of the `Product` entity is created. At this stage, the object is *detached* from `DbContext`, which means EF Core doesn't know of its existence. The `_context.Products.Add(product)` call attaches the new product to `DbContext` so that it will be tracked. Since we used the `Add()` method, the entity state is now added, and therefore, the call to `_context.SaveChangesAsync()` generates an `INSERT` statement.

> In RESTful APIs, when an action creates a new resource, it should return the 201 (Created) status code and a header with the URI to the new resource location. ASP.NET Core makes it easy to create the standard response by using the `CreatedAtAction()` method, which accepts the action name, parameters, and the response data to return.

Updating and deleting objects

EF Core tracks objects' states through the `ChangeTracker` type. Every object that is retrieved from the database is automatically tracked by the `ChangeTracker`, and every change that is made on it changes the object's `EntityState` to `Modified`. If a retrieved object is removed from `DbSet` (or if an object that contains it is removed), EF Core will change the `EntityState` value to `Deleted`.

When EF Core `SaveChanges` is executed, it scans the tracked objects, and if they are modified or deleted, EF Core generates an `UPDATE` statement with the relevant modifications that are needed, and a `DELETE` statement for the deleted objects. Here is a code snippet that shows how to update a product and then delete it:

```
var product = await _context.Products.FindAsync(id);
product.Title = "I've changed";
await _context.SaveChangesAsync(); // The entity is updated in the DB
_context.Products.Remove(product);
await _context.SaveChangesAsync(); // The entity is deleted from the DB
```

> If you defined the relationships between your entities and enabled Cascade Delete (explicitly or implicitly), then when the principal object is removed from the `DbSet`, it will cause the dependent object to be removed as well.

After data is stored in your database, it's natural that the next thing will be to create queries to retrieve it. Luckily, we don't need to learn SQL to query the data; instead, we can use the EF Core Querying API.

Querying data

If you've ever used **Language Integrated Query (LINQ)** before, you'll feel right at home with EF Core. The `DbSet` collection, which we've used to manipulate objects' states, implements the `IQueryable` interface that defines many querying operators that are later transformed into SQL statements by the database provider you've used.

For example, the `GiveNTake` application allows the user to search for products that were published on a specific date. Here is a shortened version of how it is done:

```
[HttpGet("search/{date:datetime}/{keyword}/")]
public async Task<IActionResult> Search(DateTime date, string keyword)
{
    var products = await _context.Products
        .Where(p => p.Title.Contains(keyword))
        .Where(p => p.PublishDate.Date == date.Date)
        .ToListAsync();

    // returning a response with the found products
}
```

The `Where` operator creates a filter on the `IQueryable<Product>` that the `Products` `DbSet` collection implements. LINQ has a composable and deferred execution model, where each operator adds another layer on the result returned from the previous operator, but the query itself won't be queried unless explicitly told so. Whenever an iteration is made on the result of the query, or when any completion operator is used, the query is executed and the results are returned to the applications. This includes running a `foreach` statement, using a conversion operator, such as `ToListAsync()`, or an operator such `Count()`, which returns the amount of results.

> Any input used inside your queries will be wrapped inside an SQL parameter and *will not* be blindly concatenated to the query. This will ensure that you're more protected from SQL injection attacks.

There are many LINQ operators you can use in your queries—more than this book can cover. However, I summarized some of what I believe are the most useful ones in this table:

Operator	Description
Select	Transforms the input object of the source type to another object of the result type (which can be the same as the source) by running a given selector function.
Where	Filters the dataset by running a provided predicate on each item.
Take	Returns the specified number of items from the start of the result set.

Skip	Skips the specified number of items from the start of the result set.
GroupBy	Groups the items in the result set by a key that is specified by a provided key selector function.
SingleOrDefault	Returns the single item that the query results contains, or the default value if the results are empty. If more than one item exists in the results, an exception will be thrown.
FirstOrDefault	Returns the first item from the query results, or the default value if the results are empty.
Count	Returns the amount of items in the query result.

Loading related entities

A relational database is named so because it makes the relationship between entities (Tables) a first-class citizen and gives means to validate and query those relationships (that is, foreign key constraints and joins).

The power of EF Core as an O/RM is that it bridges the world of object-oriented class associations and the world of relational database joins. It does so by treating the class properties that reference another entity (or a collection of entities) as a Navigation Property. With a *Navigation Property*, each operation you do on the property will generate the equivalent SQL join statement. For example, GiveNTake allows its users to search for products in a specific category. This is what it looks like:

```
var products = await _context.Products
    .Where(p => p.Category.ParentCategory.Name == category)
    .ToListAsync();
```

The preceding code uses the Where operator to filter the products, but it doesn't check the product's simple values. Instead, it checks the parent category to which the products category belongs, all by simply using the navigation properties. If you're curious what SQL was used behind the scenes, here is the generated SQL statement that this code produces, which shows how the EF Core engine intelligently generates two JOIN clauses:

```
SELECT [p].[ProductId], [p].[CategoryId], [p].[CityId], [p].[Description],
[p].[OwnerUserId], [p].[PublishDate], [p].[Title]
FROM [Products] AS [p]
INNER JOIN [Categories] AS [p.Category] ON [p].[CategoryId] =
[p.Category].[Id]
LEFT JOIN [Categories] AS [p.Category.ParentCategory] ON
[p.Category].[ParentCategoryId] =
[p.Category.ParentCategory].[Id]
WHERE [p.Category.ParentCategory].[Name] = @__category_0
```

Running queries that use the navigation properties will do everything as expected on the database side, but the result that you get might be confusing because you might expect the objects that the navigation properties refer to be included as well, but you'll find them missing. Before EF Core, Entity Framework included a feature called Lazy Loading, where a referenced object would be loaded from the database automatically the first time you used the navigation property; however, EF Core doesn't include this feature at the time of writing this book. Instead, you must explicitly tell EF Core to load related entities before you execute your query by using the `Include` and `ThenInclude` operators. For example, if you wish the query we used in the preceding code to include the category and subcategory of the products it retrieves, this is how you'll write it:

```
var products = await _context.Products
    .Include(product => product.Category)
    .ThenInclude(category => category.ParentCategory);
    .Where(p => p.Category.ParentCategory.Name == category)
    .ToListAsync();
```

This query will result in the products and will include all the categories that are referenced by them (note that if a category is referenced by multiple products, it will only be retrieved once, and the same object will be used by all products).

> `Include` will work only if the type of the result that the query retrieved is the same as the type that the `Include` was applied on, so if you use the `Select` operator in your query, the `Include` might not work.

Creating conditional queries with the IQueryable deferred execution

The deferred execution model that `IQueryable` provides can be very handy when you have an API that can search by using different parameters, where some of them are optional. For example, the `GiveNTake` application allows users to narrow the search to a specific city and to a specific subcategory, but, if wanted, the user can decide to search in all cities and all categories. Here is how you can build such a dynamic query:

```
IQueryable<Product> productsQuery = _context.Products
    .Include(p => p.Category)
    .ThenInclude(c => c.ParentCategory);

if (location != "all")
{
    productsQuery = productsQuery.Where(p => p.City.Name == location);
```

```
}
if (subcategory != "all")
{
    productsQuery = productsQuery.Where(p => p.Category.Name ==
subcategory)
        .Where(p => p.Category.ParentCategory.Name == category);
}
else
{
    productsQuery = productsQuery.Where(p =>
    p.Category.ParentCategory.Name == category);
}
var products = await productsQuery.ToListAsync();
```

For now, you can ignore the instances of `Include` and `ThenInclude` that were used in the preceding code block—we will talk about them shortly.

The preceding code starts by taking `Products DbSet` as an `IQueryable` object—this virtually gives access to the entire products dataset. Then, the code checks if the user specified a certain subcategory and a specific city; if they did, then the code adds another filter (by using the `Where` operator) to the query. It's important to note that this was all possible due to the fact that the `Where` operator doesn't change the type of the `IQueryable` result type (that is, `Product`). Some operators do change the type of the results, for example, the `Select` operator allows you to transform the retrieved types. The following code snippet shows an example of how you can retrieve the products titles from your database, without the rest of the product properties:

```
var products = await productsQuery.Select(p => p.Title).ToListAsync();
```

Mapping the API results to DTOs

The entities definitions that we've used to work with EF Core are designed to give the best results when working with the database; however, they are not designed to be transferable over the wire. There are a few reasons why you wouldn't want to use the same classes that are mapped to your database tables and when sending results from your APIs:

- **Security**: Your domain model classes might include various properties that you wouldn't want to expose to your clients. For example, personal information or user roles.
- **Loose coupling**: Over time, you might need to change the data model; many times, these changes shouldn't be reflected in changes to your API, but sharing the same data types will force you to.

- **Controllable structure**: The way entities are mapped to the database may include relationships that are not always simple for clients to use. Many times, it's easier for clients to work with a flattened structure.
- **Size**: The API response goes over the wire, and therefore, we wish to make it as lean as possible for better performance.

There might be other reasons, but the conclusion should be the same—don't use your data model entities in your APIs responses; instead, use a designated DTO.

DTOs are simple POCO classes that meet your API's purpose. For example, the ProductDTO class flattens the category and subcategory and includes just the name, while the City and Media items are included as DTOs:

```
public class ProductDTO
{
    public int ProductId { get; set; }
    public OwnerDTO Owner { get; set; }
    public string Title { get; set; }
    public string Description { get; set;
    public string Category { get; set; }
    public string Subcategory { get; set; }
    public CityDTO City { get; set; }
    public MediaDTO[] Media { get; set; }
}
```

Once you have the DTO definition in place, you'll need to write the code, the map, and the original entity into the DTO. However, writing mapping code is cumbersome (and boring), so instead, I'll teach how to make it automatic with AutoMapper.

Mapping entities to DTOs with AutoMapper

AutoMapper (http://automapper.org/) is an object-to-object mapper that use conventions and configurations to reduce the amount of code you need to write. To use AutoMapper, you need to install the AutoMapper NuGet package and then configure the mapping you wish to support. After the mappings are configured, you need to create an instance of the mapper and use it to run mappings.

Since such mappings are stateless and exist across your application, I usually define them inside the static constructor of the classes that need them (in our case, the `Controller`), and then use the mapper throughout application lifetime, but if the mappings are shareable between classes, then you can create a shared class to host those mappings. For example, in the `ProductsController` object, this is how I configured the mappings and created the mapper:

```
private static readonly IMapper _productsMapper;

static ProductsController()
{
    var config = new MapperConfiguration(cfg =>
    {
        cfg.CreateMap<Product, ProductDTO>()
            .ForMember(dto => dto.City, opt => opt.MapFrom(product =>
product.City))
            .ForMember(dto => dto.Category, opt => opt.MapFrom(product =>
product.Category.ParentCategory.Name))
            .ForMember(dto => dto.Subcategory, opt => opt.MapFrom(product
=> product.Category.Name));

        cfg.CreateMap<City, CityDTO>()
            .ForMember(dto => dto.Id, opt => opt.MapFrom(city =>
city.CityId));

        // Other mappings
    });
    _productsMapper = config.CreateMapper();
}
```

You'll note from the preceding code block that I didn't need to define the mapping between every property to the destination property. `AutoMapper` has a set of conventions it uses, and, by default, will map properties with the same name.

Now, we can use the mapper we created and stored in the `_productsMapper` member when the user navigates to a specific product:

```
[HttpGet("{id}", Name = nameof(GetProduct))]
public async Task<ActionResult<ProductDTO>> GetProduct(int id)
{
    var product = await _context.Products
        .Include(p => p.Category)
        .ThenInclude(c => c.ParentCategory)
        .SingleOrDefaultAsync(p => p.ProductId == id);
    if (product == null)
    {
        return NotFound();
```

```
    }
    return Ok(_productsMapper.Map<ProductDTO>(product));
}
```

`AutoMapper` can also map a collection of objects to a collection of DTOs automatically. For example, this is how we return the results of the user's product search:

```
[HttpGet("search/{keyword}")]
public async Task<ActionResult<ProductDTO[]>> SearchProducts(string
keyword)
{
    List<Product> products = await _context.Products
        .Include(p => p.Category)
        .ThenInclude(c => c.ParentCategory)
        .Where(p => p.Title.Contains(keyword))
        .ToListAsync();

    return Ok(_productsMapper.Map<ProductDTO[]>(products));
}
```

There are many more options that `AutoMapper` allows you to use to save you the burden of writing repeatable mapping code. You can find more details in the official documentation at `http://docs.automapper.org/en/stable/`.

Summary

Storing and retrieving data is an essential part of most web applications, and you can choose all kinds of databases to work with. EF Core is an O/RM that lets you write classes and LINQ queries, and those will be mapped to the database tables and to SQL statements without you needing to leave the comfort of the C# language. In this chapter, I explained how to work with EF Core and how you can use the `DbContext` base class to create a bridge between your classes, the database, and the conventional mapping it uses. You've seen how to store data and how to retrieve it with various LINQ operators. You also added automatic migrations to your application, which allows the database to be created and migrated to newer versions automatically without the need to run scripts in the database server itself.

I explained why you shouldn't use the same types of your data model when you return responses from your APIs, and instead, use DTOs. To make development easier, I introduced `AutoMapper` and showed you how easy it is to create reusable mappings, instead of writing repeatable mapping code.

In the next chapter, you'll learn how to make your APIs more secure, and how to control access to API actions for authorized users.

Securing the Backend Server

6

Web applications that are accessible to the public internet are exposed to many types of attacks. It's almost every day that you hear about some sensitive information being leaked or a website that was not accessible due to cyber attacks. You should consider your application security a high priority, as you do not want to be on the list of insecure websites; otherwise, users will stay away from your site.

In this chapter, you'll learn the infrastructure that ASP.NET Core provides to secure your application and the means to authenticate and authorize your users so that they will be able to do only what you permit them to. You'll look at the following topics:

- Authentication and authorization
- Adding ASP.NET identity management
- Using JWT tokens
- Claim-based and role-based authorization
- Enabling Cross-Origin Resource Sharing

Authenticating and authorizing application users

Many web applications allow users to perform certain operations *only* if they are registered, and some applications will only allow paid users to view certain content that is not available to non-paying users. Also, as a user, you expect that your personal profile will be editable only by you, and not by other users, unless they are the site administrators. All the scenarios I have detailed here are examples of authentication and authorization.

Authentication is the act of knowing *who* the user is and verifying their identity, while authorization is the act of allowing or preventing users from performing actions based on their privileges.

The security technique for authentication that we will use in this book is called *token-based authentication*. This technique involves generating a security token (a hashed string) when the user logs in, and carrying this token with each request the client makes to the server. This technique is highly used in Web APIs and is both secure and simple to use.

For authorization, we are using *claim-based authorization,* where each user is assigned with claims (key-value pairs) based on their role and/or security policy, and the actions are then checked if they are authorized for the user, based on their assigned claims.

The infrastructure for user identities and authentication in ASP.NET Core is contained in the `Microsoft.Extensions.Identity.Core` NuGet package and all the related classes reside in the `Microsoft.Extensions.Identity` namespace.

Adding identity management entities to your data model

When working with user identities, your database and applications data model usually contain entities such as User, Roles, Claims, Tokens, and so on, so the first step will be to add the necessary entities to the application data model, but luckily we don't need to add them manually. Instead, the `Microsoft.Extensions.Identity` infrastructure defines base classes that we can use. Here are the steps that you need to perform to add all the identity-related entities to your application:

1. Create or modify the `User` entity in your application and make it derive from the `IdentityUser` class. Note that if you already have a User entity, you have to remove the primary key property because `IdentityUser` already contains it within the name `Id`.
2. Modify your application's `DbContext` to derive from `IdentityDbContext<User>`. Note that if you had a property with the name Users, you'll need to remove it because `IdentityDbContext` already defines it.
3. Create a new migration (as explained in `Chapter 5`, *Persisting Data with Entity Framework*).

Run the application and make sure that the migration is completed successfully, then review the database in the **Server Object Explorer (SQL)**. You should see a few tables that were added, all prefixed with **AspNet**:

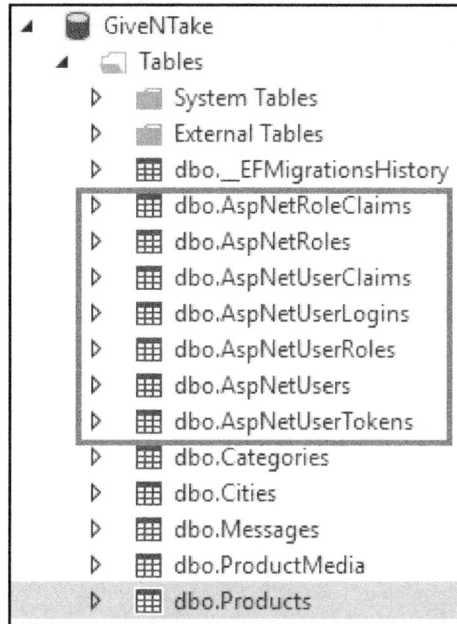

The `IdentityUser` base class brings a few properties that are used by the identity management infrastructure. However, you can add any properties you want to the derived class.

Now, you have the necessary data entities in your application, and though possible, it's not recommended that you work with them directly and insert, update, delete, or query them directly. The recommended approach is that you use the types that are provided with the identity infrastructure, such as `UserManger`, `SignInManager`, and others to get access to the operations you want to perform. To allow for the usage of those types, we first need to make our ASP.NET Core application aware of them and enable the identity infrastructure capabilities. Afterwards, I will show how you how to register users, sign them in, and query them.

Enabling the identity infrastructure

Authentication and authorization affect the way that the ASP.NET Core request pipeline is defined. Your Web API needs to check each request to see if it is authenticated, and then see if the requested action is authorized for the authenticated user. If any of these steps fail, we want the API to respond with a meaningful response. To make the necessary modifications to the Web API pipeline, we need to enable the identity infrastructure in the application's startup class. Here are the steps we perform to enable identities in the `GiveNTake` application:

1. Add the following lines to the `ConfigureService` method:

```
services.AddIdentity<User, IdentityRole>()
    .AddEntityFrameworkStores<GiveNTakeContext>()
    .AddDefaultTokenProviders();
```

These lines configure the application to recognize that User identities are defined by the `User` entity, roles are defined by the `IdentityRole` entity (part of the `Microsoft.Extensions.Identity` package), and that `GiveNTakeContext` is the `DbContext` class that holds all the identity data.

2. Add the following statement to the `Configure` method:

```
app.UseAuthentication();
```

This code will add the authentication middleware to the pipeline and enable authentication capabilities.

At this point, you have an backend application that is aware of authentication, but we still need to configure the authentication technique we want to use. ASP.NET Core supports all of the standard and common ways of authentication, such as cookie-based authentication, token-based authentication, Windows Authentication, OAuth, and so on. In this book, we are using a token-based authentication system with JWT tokens, but you can later add other authentication types or providers. For more details, see the Microsoft identity authentication documentation, available at `https://docs.microsoft.com/en-us/aspnet/core/security/authentication/social/`.

Enabling token-based authentication with JSON Web Token

One of the most used authentication mechanisms is a token-based authentication system. With this technique, each time the user logs in, a token is generated and sent back in the response. The token is a hashed and signed value that can later be validated by the server to ensure its authenticity. After the client receives the token, it sends it back with each request (as a header), and the server will extract the user details from the token (if it's valid). Using tokens gives you a few benefits:

- **Secure**: Because the value is signed (and sometimes even ciphered), the server can be sure that the values are valid. Another added benefit in the security aspect is that, unlike with cookie-based authentication, the server is not exposed to **Cross-Site Request Forgery (CSRF)** attacks.
- **Stateless**: Because the client is the one who holds the token, there's no need to store session-like data in the server. Being stateless makes your server more robust and scalable.
- **Cross-origin**: Because the token is just a value, it can be transferred and used from any type of client, even if it's located in a different domain.
- **Performance**: Because the token can contain data that can later be extracted and reused, it reduces the round trips to the datastore, and therefore improves performance.

The most used standard for token-based authentication is JWT (`https://jwt.io/introduction/`), which allows for the representation of claims securely, and sharing them between two parties.

JWT tokens are composed from three parts that are encoded in *Base64* and separated by a dot (`.`):

`{Header}.{Payload}.{Signature}`

- Header: Holds the token type and the hashing algorithm (such as *HMAC SHA256*).
- Payload: Contains claims, which are the encapsulated user data (basically, key-value pairs) and metadata such as the issuer of the token, the token expiration time, issued time, and so forth.
- Signature: A cryptographic value that is calculated by taking the `{Header}.{Payload}` part and creating a hash with the hashing algorithm specified in the header, and with a secret to which we will refer to as the *signing-key*.

Since the JWTs are encoded, they are not human-readable, so a nice web tool to know of is the JWT Debugger, which you can find at `https://jwt.io/`. After you get hold of a JWT, you can paste it into the tool and see the contained information.

For example, here is a JWT I created in the `GiveNTake` application, when the user `user@giventake.com` signed in:

The text in this image is not important. The purpose of this image is to give an idea of what the decoded JWT looks like.

To use JWTs in your application, you need to add
the `Microsoft.AspNetCore.Authentication.JwtBearer` NuGet package and then
enable it in the `ConfigureServices` method of your `Startup` class:

```
services.AddAuthentication(option =>
    {
        option.DefaultAuthenticateScheme =
JwtBearerDefaults.AuthenticationScheme;
        option.DefaultChallengeScheme =
JwtBearerDefaults.AuthenticationScheme;
    })
    .AddJwtBearer(jwtOptions =>
    {
        jwtOptions.TokenValidationParameters = new
TokenValidationParameters()
        {
            ValidateActor = true,
            ValidateAudience = true,
            ValidateLifetime = true,
            ValidIssuer = Configuration["JWTConfiguration:Issuer"],
            ValidAudience = Configuration["JWTConfiguration:Audience"],
            IssuerSigningKey = new
SymmetricSecurityKey(Encoding.UTF8.GetBytes(Configuration["JWTConfiguration
:SigningKey"]))
        };
    });
```

Note that I've used values that come from the application configuration. Open the
`appsettings.json` file of your application and add a `JWTConfiguration` section, as
shown here:

```
{
  "ConnectionStrings": {
    ...
  },
  "JWTConfiguration": {
    "Issuer": "Issuer",
    "Audience": "audience",
    "SigningKey": "my long enough key for authentication",
    "TokenExpirationDays": 7
  }
}
```

In the JWT example here, I configured the signing key by using `SymmetricSecurityKey` and retrieving the key from the configuration. In a production environment, it's not secure to store your keys in the configuration—instead, you should use a certificate (`Microsoft.IdentityModel.Tokens.X509SecurityKey`) or a security store such as Azure Key Vault (see `Chapter 16`, *Taking Advantage of Cloud Services*).

Now that the authentication capabilities are enabled, we can start using these capabilities in the application. First, I'll explain the end-to-end authentication and authorization flow that the user will have with the system.

The authentication and authorization flow

Before we start to delve into the code, I want to present a short overview of the end-to-end authentication and authorization flow the user will have with the web application we are building.

Here is a sequence diagram that shows the entire flow:

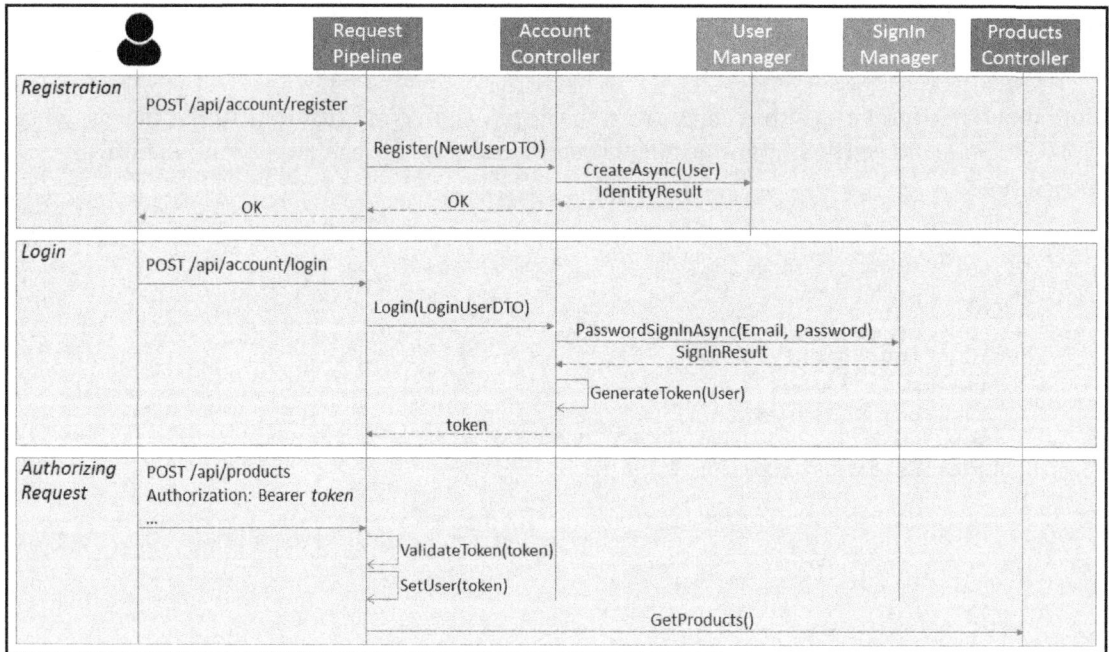

I've added a new controller whose responsibility is to deal with all the user account operations, such as registration, login, and so on. The `AccountController` uses the `UserManager` and `SignInManager` classes from the ASP.NET Core identity infrastructure. These classes encapsulate all the sensitive user management operations and create the necessary separation between our code and the `IdentityDbContext`.
The flow is separated into three parts:

1. **Registration**: The user registers to the application with a username (an email address, in our case) and password. The system validates the details, ensures that the username is not taken, and saves the information in a secured manner.
2. **Login**: The user signs in to the system with the username and password. The system then validates the details and returns a JWT that includes the user claims.
3. **Authorizing request**: With each request, the user agent (the browser, for example) sends the token in the authorization header. The system decodes and validates the token, then sets the user in the identity infrastructure. The system uses the User claims to run the authorization code, and if authorized, the request is fulfilled.

With the flow in place, we can start to implement the pieces the flow is made of.

Creating a user registration API

It goes without saying that, in order to authenticate and authorize users, we need to provide some mechanism to register them to our application. ASP.NET Core makes this task easy by providing utility classes that we can use to make sure that user registration is secure.

Open (or create, if needed) the `AccountController` and add to the constructor the following dependencies:

- `UserManager<User>`: Provides the APIs for managing users in a persistence store
- `SignInManager<User>`: Provides the APIs for user logins
- `IConfiguration`: Provides the access point for the application configuration

Store each dependency in a class member. Your class should look similar to this:

```
[Produces("application/json")]
[Route("api/Account")]
public class AccountController : Controller
{
```

```
        private readonly UserManager<User> _userManager;
        private readonly SignInManager<User> _signInManager;
        private readonly IConfiguration _configuration;

        public AccountController(UserManager<User> userManager,
            SignInManager<User> signInManager,
            IConfiguration configuration)
        {
            _userManager = userManager;
            _signInManager = signInManager;
            _configuration = configuration;
        }
    }
```

To register a user, the backend application exposes an action in the URL
/api/account/register, which should be called with a POST HTTP request, and
receives the user's email address, password, and a password confirmation.

Add a new class to your DTO folder and name it RegisterUserDTO. This class will be the
input of our registration action:

```
    public class RegisterUserDTO
    {
        [Required]
        [EmailAddress]
        public string Email { get; set; }

        [Required]
        [StringLength(100, MinimumLength = 6)]
        [DataType(DataType.Password)]
        public string Password { get; set; }

        [DataType(DataType.Password)]
        [Compare("Password", ErrorMessage = "The password and confirmation
password do not match.")]
        public string ConfirmPassword { get; set; }
    }
```

I've set validation attributes on the class properties so that we can easily validate the user
request.

Now, add the following method to your `AccountController`:

```
[AllowAnonymous]
[HttpPost("register")]
public async Task<IActionResult> Register([FromBody] RegisterUserDTO
registration)
{
    if (!ModelState.IsValid) { return BadRequest(ModelState); }

    User newUser = new User
    {
        Email = registration.Email,
        UserName = registration.Email,
        Id = registration.Email,
    };
    IdentityResult result = await _userManager.CreateAsync(newUser,
registration.Password);
    if (!result.Succeeded)
    {
        foreach (var error in result.Errors)
        {
            ModelState.AddModelError(error.Code, error.Description);
        }
        return BadRequest(ModelState);
    }

    return Ok();
}
```

The method starts by validating the user input by checking if the `ModelState` is valid. Then, a new `User` object is created and added through the `UserManager`. One of the things that the `UserManager` does for you is save the user's password in a secure way by hashing it. Cryptographic code is complex and it is easy to do it wrong, so I always recommend using a library that was created by people who are experts in the subject, just as the identity package was.

The `CreateAsync` method returns an `IdentityResult` output that contains information on whether or not the operation succeeded, and the collection of errors if it failed. In the case of failure, I add the errors to the `ModelState` and return a `BadRequest` result to the user.

Run the application and register a new user by sending an HTTP POST request with Postman, as shown here:

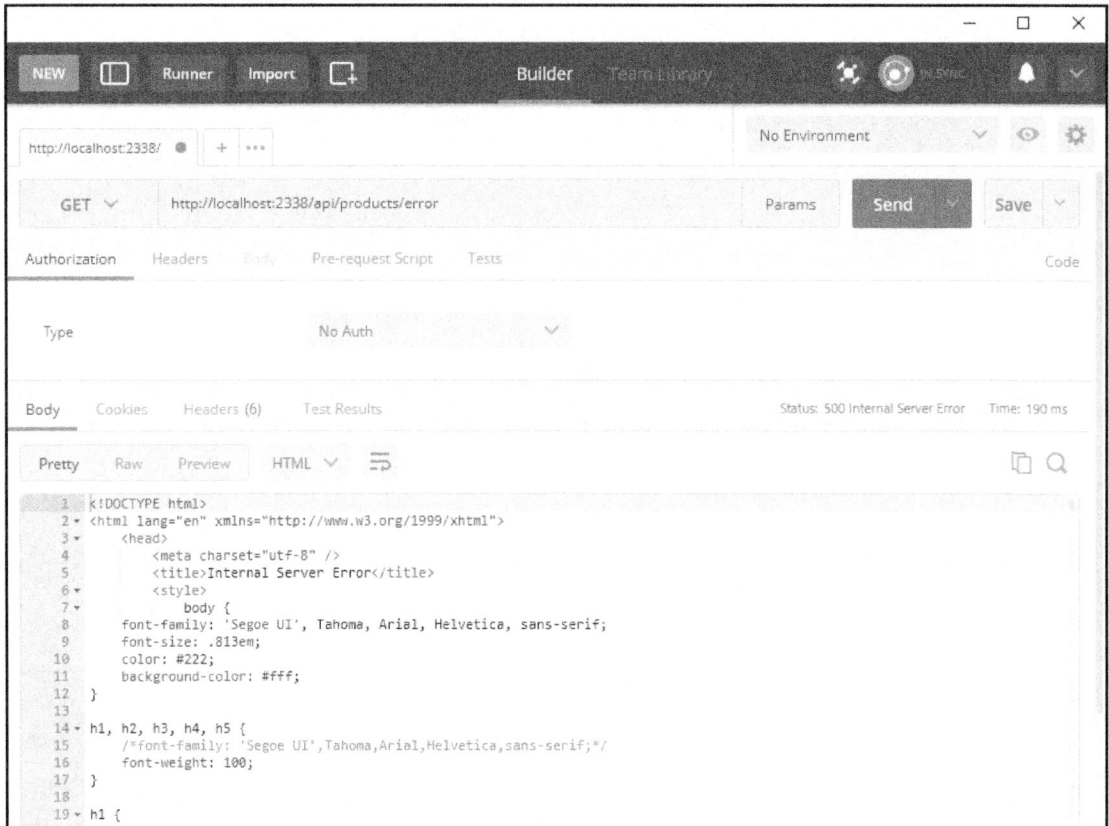

The text in this image is not important; you may get different values. The purpose of this image is to show you what the structure of the request and response should look like in Postman.

You have now successfully registered a new user to your system, and now, we can add login functionality to the application.

Implementing the login functionality and generating a JWT

The `GiveNTake` application allows anonymous users to access and use some of the APIs, such as product search and product display. But other operations, such as sending and reading messages, are only allowed to registered users, which means that users will have to go through an authentication phase where the application will validate their credentials, such as their username and password, and give them the access token in the form of a JWT. Afterwards, the token will be validated with each request and the user details will be extracted.

Adding login functionality to the `GiveNTake` application is done like this:

1. First, let's define the user login input, that is, their email and password, as a `DTO` that can be received in the HTTP request body:

    ```
    public class LoginUserDTO
    {
        public string Password { get; set; }
        public string Email { get; set; }
    }
    ```

2. Now, continue with defining the successful login response — the JWT — as a `DTO` that will be returned in the HTTP response body:

    ```
    public class SuccessfulLoginResult
    {
        public string Token { get; set; }
    }
    ```

3. Now, add a `login` endpoint by adding the following method to the `AccountController` (note that we will define the JWT generation method afterwards):

    ```
    [AllowAnonymous]
    [HttpPost("login")]
    public async Task<ActionResult<SuccessfulLoginResult>>
    Login([FromBody] LoginUserDTO login)
    {
        SignInResult result = await
        _signInManager.PasswordSignInAsync(login.Email,
    login.Password,
            isPersistent: false, lockoutOnFailure: false);
        if (!result.Succeeded)
        {
    ```

```
            return Unauthorized();
        }

        User user = await
_userManager.FindByEmailAsync(login.Email);
        JwtSecurityToken token = await GenerateTokenAsync(user);
        //defined
        string serializedToken = new
        JwtSecurityTokenHandler().WriteToken(token); //serialize
the
        token
        return Ok(new SuccessfulLoginResult() { Token =
serializedToken
        });
    }
```

The Login method accepts the user input and signs the user in with the help of the SignInManager, which securely validates that the password is correct for the specified username, and responds with an UnauthorizedResult (status code 401) if not. Afterwards, the user's details are fetched from the database and the JWT generated and returned to the user.

4. Now, define the JWT generation method that will create a JWT token with an expiration period:

```
private async Task<JwtSecurityToken> GenerateTokenAsync(User
user)
{
    var claims = new List<Claim>();

    // Loading the user Claims

    var expirationDays = _configuration.GetValue<int>
    ("JWTConfiguration:TokenExpirationDays");
    var siginingKey =
    Encoding.UTF8.GetBytes(_configuration.GetValue<string>
    ("JWTConfiguration:SigningKey"));
    var token = new JwtSecurityToken
    (
        issuer: _configuration.GetValue<string>
        ("JWTConfiguration:Issuer"),
        audience: _configuration.GetValue<string>
        ("JWTConfiguration:Audience"),
        claims: claims,
        expires:
        DateTime.UtcNow.Add(TimeSpan.FromDays(expirationDays)),
        notBefore: DateTime.UtcNow,
```

```
        signingCredentials: new SigningCredentials(new
        SymmetricSecurityKey(siginingKey),
            SecurityAlgorithms.HmacSha256)
    );

    return token;
}
```

The GenerateTokenAsync method accepts the user as input and creates a JwtSecurityToken instance that is configured with issuer, audience, and signingKey that are loaded from the application configuration. The created JWT is set to be valid from the creation time and to expire after the period of time specified in the application configuration. For now, I have left the claims collection empty, but soon, we will fill them with claims that describe the user and their permissions.

5. Run the application and send an HTTP POST request to the endpoint at http://localhost:[port]/api/account/login with the username and password, as shown here:

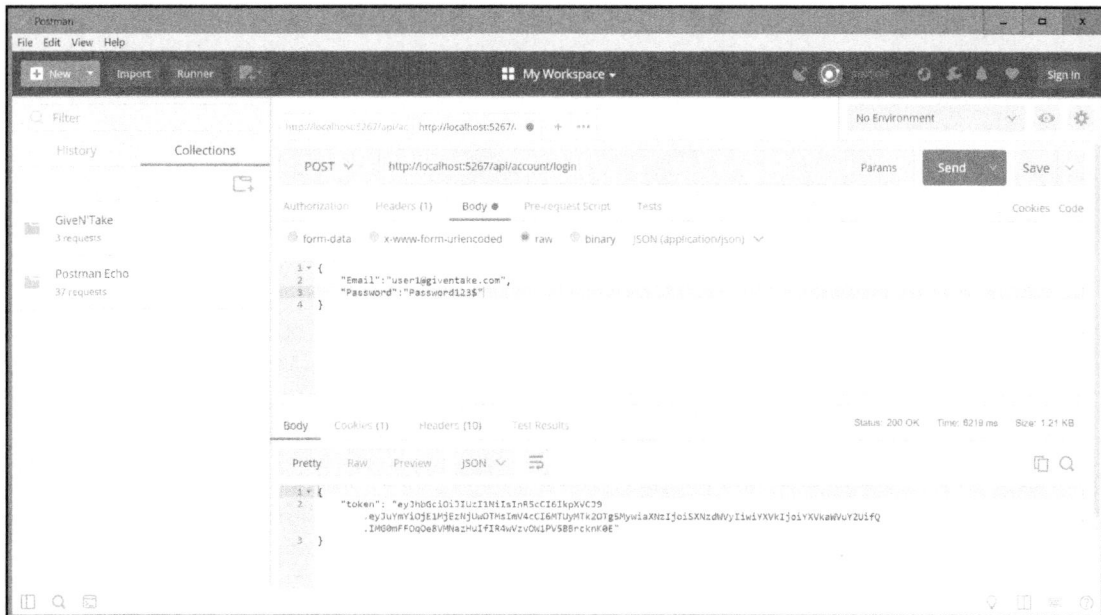

The text in this image is not important; you may get different values. The purpose of this image is to show you what the structure of the request and response should look like in Postman.

Adding user claims

The JWT we created has an empty payload so far and carries no meaningful information. And even though it's enough to make sure that the user has been authenticated by simply validating that the token was signed by the server key, we wouldn't be able to know anything about the authenticated user.

Claims allow us to add key-values pairs that we can later retrieve from the token. For example, the GiveNTake application adds the user email as a claim, and then uses it to retrieve the User entity from the database when needed.

Here is how the GenerateTokenAsync method can be modified to include all the user claims:

```
private async Task<JwtSecurityToken> GenerateTokenAsync(User user)
{
    var claims = new List<Claim>()
    {
        new Claim(JwtRegisteredClaimNames.Sub, user.UserName),
        new Claim(JwtRegisteredClaimNames.Jti, Guid.NewGuid().ToString()),
        new Claim(ClaimTypes.NameIdentifier, user.Id),
        new Claim(ClaimTypes.Name, user.UserName),
    };

    var token = new JwtSecurityToken
    (
        claims: claims,

        //... the rest of initalization
    );

    return token;
}
```

The JWT RFC document (https://tools.ietf.org/html/rfc7519) specifies a set of standard claims that can be included inside the JWT, such as the Subject (sub) and JWT ID (jit), and there are other claim types, such as name identifier, that are parts of the SAML standard. For your convenience, the JwtRegisteredClaimNames and ClaimTypes static classes contain static members that allow you to easily add those claims to your token. Beside the standard claim types, you can added whatever key-value pairs you wish.

If you run the application again and successfully log in, you should see that the token is considerably bigger than it was before:

The text in this image is not important: you may get different values. The purpose of this image is to show you what the structure of the request and response should look like in Postman.

> 💡 **TIP**
>
> You can debug the JWT and see its claims by pasting it to the JWT debugger, available at `http://jwt.io`.

Save the token so that we can use it later.

To test your token, let's add an API that will allow the client application to retrieve the logged-in user's email address. Add the following method to your `AccountController`:

```
[Authorize]
[HttpGet("Email")]
public ActionResult<string> GetEmail()
{
    return Ok(User.Identity.Name);
}
```

The `Authorize` attribute is the way we specify to the request pipeline that this method can only be used by authenticated users. When a request is received from an authenticated user (which means that a valid token is included with it), the authentication middleware extracts the user information and initializes the controller's `User` property, which is of the `System.Security.Claims.ClaimsPrincipal` type, that implements the `System.Security.Principal.IPrincipal` interface. The identity property of the `IPrincipal` interface allows you to retrieve the identity of the user, including their username, which is the user's email address in our case.

> You can use `[Authorize]` on the method level as well as on the controller class level. When the controller is decorated with the `[Authorize]` attribute, the authorization check will be applied on all the API actions contained in the class.

Create a new HTTP GET request in Postman to the URL `http://localhost:{port}/api/account/email`. Add a new Authorization header to your request and set it to `Bearer [token value]`, like this:

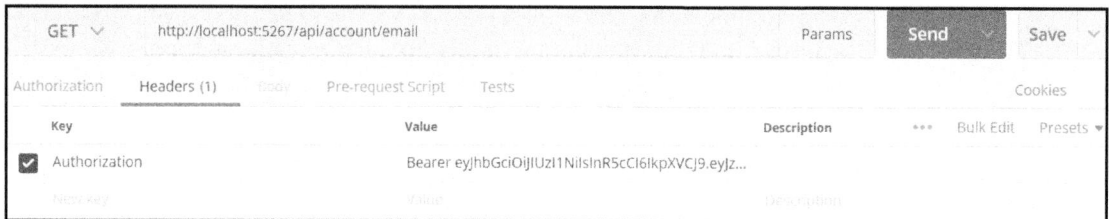

GET ⌄	http://localhost:5267/api/account/email		Params	Send ⌄	Save ⌄
Authorization	Headers (1)	Body Pre-request Script Tests			Cookies
Key		Value	Description	••• Bulk Edit	Presets ▾
☑ Authorization		Bearer eyJhbGciOiJIUzI1NiIsInR5cCI6IkpXVCJ9.eyJz...			
New key		Value	Description		

Execute the request and you'll see that the user email address has been returned:

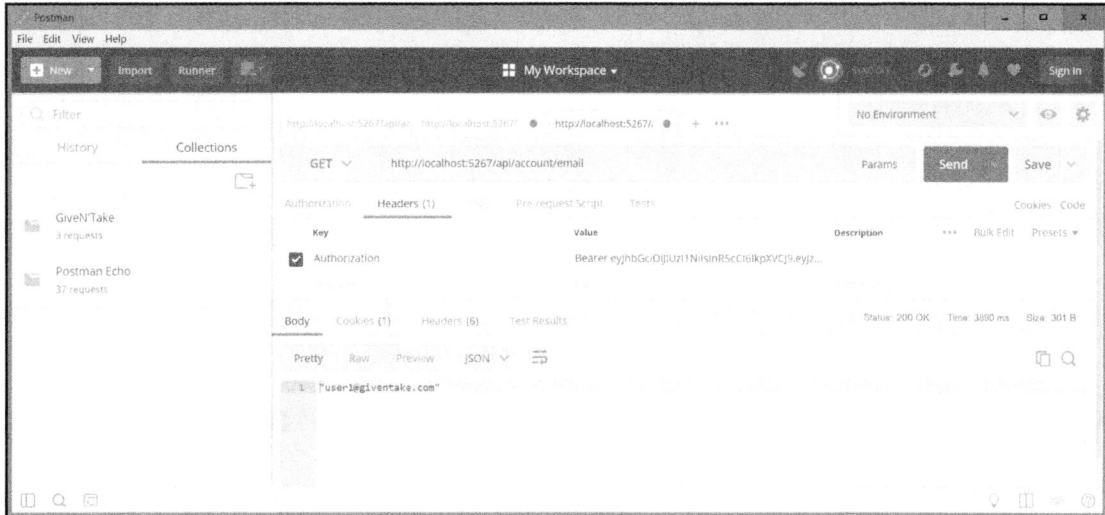

The text in this image is not important; you may get different values. The purpose of this image is to show you what the structure of the request and response should look like in Postman.

> *Bearer* is the authentication schema associated with the JWT. By specifying *Bearer* in the authorization header, we made it possible for the backend to understand that a JWT was sent, and therefore, the JWT middleware will be activated in the request pipeline.

With this technique, we can now make the necessary adjustment to make sure that added products are registered under their seller:

```
[Authorize]
[HttpPost("")]
public async Task<ActionResult<ProductDTO>> AddNewProduct([FromBody]
NewProductDTO newProduct)
{
    // ...

    var user = await _context.Users.FindAsync(User.Identity.Name);
    var product = new Product()
    {
        Owner = user,
        Category = category,
        Title = newProduct.Title,
        Description = newProduct.Description,
        City = city,
```

```
        PublishDate = DateTime.UtcNow
    };
    _context.Products.Add(product);
    await _context.SaveChangesAsync();
    return CreatedAtAction(
        nameof(GetProduct),
        new { id = product.ProductId },
        _productsMapper.Map<ProductDTO>(product));
}
```

The `AddNewProduct` method is now decorated with the `Authorize` attribute to make sure that only authenticated users can call it. This method loads the `User` entity by the ID that is encapsulated in the current user identity.

Configuring your backend to always require authentication

It's much more secure to work in a whitelist approach where the default behavior of your application is to require all actions, and only allow anonymous access to APIs that explicitly allow it.

To set the implicit authentication requirement, we need to add an authentication filter to the request pipeline that is defined by the MVC infrastructure. This can be done by modifying the way we added MVC in the `ConfigureServices` method, as shown in the following code snippet:

```
// requires: using Microsoft.AspNetCore.Authorization;
// using Microsoft.AspNetCore.Mvc.Authorization;
services.AddMvc(config =>
{
    var policy = new AuthorizationPolicyBuilder()
        .RequireAuthenticatedUser()
        .Build();
    config.Filters.Add(new AuthorizeFilter(policy));
});
```

The preceding code configures the request pipeline to include an authorization filter that is configured with a policy that requires the user to be authenticated in order to use any action that is not explicitly marked for anonymous access.

Configuring an action to allow anonymous access

The `GiveNTake` application is configured to require an authenticated user for all its actions, but some of the actions should be accessible for guests (anonymous users). This is easy to achieve by placing the `[Anonymous]` attribute before the method or controller. For example, the `GiveNTake` application allows any user to search for products:

```
[AllowAnonymous]
[HttpGet("searchcategory/{category}/{subcategory=all}/")]
public async Task<ActionResult<ProductDTO[]>> SearchByCategory(string
category, string subcategory, string location = "all",
    bool imageOnly = false)
{
  ...
}
```

Congratulations! You now have a complete authentication flow—the next step in our journey will be adding authorization and making sure that only authorized users can perform sensitive operations.

Controlling access to APIs with authorization

One of the key ways to secure your application is to only allow sensitive operations to be executed by users who are authorized to perform them.

There is more than one way to perform authorization in your application: you can check each user against a whitelist; you can check if the user is part of a group (or role) that is allowed to use the functionality in question; or you can run sophisticated logic that makes sure that the user has the necessary access clearance. In this chapter, I'm going to teach you the two most broadly used techniques in the industry:

- **Claim-based authorization**: Each user is given a set of claims that can later be retrieved and checked. The claims include both personal attributes (such as the user's birth date), metadata (the registration time), and other pieces of information, such as the user permission set.
- **Role-based authorization**: Users are grouped together into meaningful permission groups that define the application roles. Each user is assigned to one or more roles, and the application can later check if a user can access a resource or perform an operation, based on the role(s) the user has.

Previously in this chapter, you learned how to add claims to the user token; now, I'll show you how you can retrieve the claim value and use it to authorize users.

Adding claims that can be used for authorization

JWT allows you to set whatever key-value you wish as a claim. We can leverage this fact to store user permissions so that we can later retrieve them and use them for authorization. The ASP.NET Core authorization infrastructure provides us with an easy way to add claims to the user and store them in the database by giving us the `AddClaimsAsync` method that's provided by the `UserManager` class. For example, I modified the `GiveNTake` user registration logic to add the registration date as a claim:

```
[AllowAnonymous]
[HttpPost("register")]
public async Task<IActionResult> Register([FromBody] RegisterUserDTO
registration)
{
    ...

    user = await _userManager.FindByEmailAsync(registration.Email);
    await _userManager.AddClaimAsync(user,
        new Claim("registration-date", DateTime.UtcNow.ToString("yy-MM-
dd")));

    ...
}
```

The user registration date is now stored in the database as a claim, and when the user logs in, we will load it (and all other claims) by using the `UserManager GetClaimsAsync` method and adding it to the generated token:

```
private async Task<JwtSecurityToken> GenerateTokenAsync(User user)
{
    var claims = new List<Claim>() { ... };

    var userClaims = await _userManager.GetClaimsAsync(user);
    claims.AddRange(userClaims);
    var token = new JwtSecurityToken
    (
        claims: claims,
        ...
    );

    return token;
}
```

Now, when running the application and sending an HTTP POST request to the login API, the returned token includes the registration date claim.

Authorizing users by their role

Many times, users of your application will be assigned roles to define their allowed behavior in the application. For example, your application administrators will likely see areas of the application that other users won't be allowed to see, and will be able to perform administrative tasks such as adding categories.

To add authorization that is based on roles, we don't need to change the claims infrastructure that we have used so far. Instead, we will use the standard role claim and add it for each role a user possesses.

ASP.NET Core provides the RoleManager<TRole> class that resides in the Microsoft.AspNetCore.Identity namespace. RoleManager provides an API for managing the roles that exist in your application and the way they are made persistent in the database.

Here are the steps I took to add roles support to the GiveNTake application:

1. I've added the following code, as part of the application's DbContext, to add the Administrator role if it doesn't yet exist:

```
public async Task SeedRolesAsync(RoleManager<IdentityRole>
roleManager)
{
    if (!await roleManager.RoleExistsAsync("Admin"))
    {
        var admin = new IdentityRole("Admin");
        await roleManager.CreateAsync(admin);
    }
}
```

2. When the application starts, I execute the SeedRolesAsync method in the same way as I've shown in Chapter 5, *Persisting Data with Entity Framework*, when I added the initial data to the application data model:

```
public static void Main(string[] args)
{
    var host = BuildWebHost(args);
    using (var scope = host.Services.CreateScope())
    {
        var services = scope.ServiceProvider;
```

```
            var context = services.GetService<GiveNTakeContext>();
            var roleManager =
            services.GetService<RoleManager<IdentityRole>>();
            try
            {
                context.Database.Migrate();
                context.SeedData();
                context.SeedRolesAsync(roleManager).Wait();
            }
            catch (Exception ex)
            {
                var logger =
                services.GetRequiredService<ILogger<Program>>();
                logger.LogError(ex, "An error occurred while
seeding
                the GiveNTake Database.");
                throw;
            }
        }

        host.Run();
    }
```

3. Now that we have an admin role in place, we need to assign it to users. For the sake of demonstration purposes, I've added the following logic to the `GiveNTake` registration method, where users with an email that contains the word `"admin"` will be added as administrators:

```
public async Task<IActionResult> Register([FromBody]
RegisterUserDTO registration)
{
    ...

    user = await
_userManager.FindByEmailAsync(registration.Email);
    if (registration.Email.Contains("admin"))
    {
        await _userManager.AddToRoleAsync(user, "Admin");
    }

    ...

}
```

4. When the user logs in to the application, I add the role as a claim to the JWT:

```
var roles = await _userManager.GetRolesAsync(user);
foreach (var role in roles)
{
    claims.Add(new Claim(ClaimTypes.Role, role));
}
```

5. The final step is to check that a user has the required role in order to use the controller actions. This is done by the required role in the `Authorization` attribute:

```
[Authorize(Roles = "Admin")]
[HttpPost("categories")]
public Task<ActionResult> AddCategory([FromBody] NewCategoryDTO
newCategory)
{
    ...
}
```

Roles can be very handy for creating separation inside your application, but there are times when you need a more powerful mechanism to determine if a user can or can't use some functionality by performing more complex logic. In cases where the authorization needs to include more logic, the ASP.NET Core Authorization Policies should be your preferred choice.

Creating an authorization policy

ASP.NET Core provides a strong and extensible infrastructure for creating authorization rules and policies. In an attempt to keep this chapter as simple and clear as possible, I will show you the most straightforward way to create an authorization rule that will only allow users that have been registered for more than a year to add categories.

To add authorization policies, use the `AddAuthorization` extension method inside the `ConfigureServices` method, and add a policy by specifying its name and the logic it should perform:

```
services.AddAuthorization(options =>
    options.AddPolicy("ExpereincedUser", (AuthorizationPolicyBuilder
policy) =>{ /* policy logic */}));
```

For our case, where we need to check that the authenticated user has more than one year of experience, we need to extract the registration date claim and then parse its value to a DateTime format that we could check. AuthorizationPolicyBuilder includes a few methods that can help you check for simple conditions:

- RequireRole: Checks that the current user has a specified role
- RequireClaim: Checks that the current user has a certain claim, and that its value is part of the allowed group of values
- RequireUserName: Checks that the current user has the specified username
- RequireAssertion: Allows you to define a complex logic condition

Since our ExperiencedUser policy requires checking not only that the user has the registration date claim, but also that its value is from more than a year ago, we are going to use the RequireAssertion method, like so:

```
policy.RequireAssertion(context =>
{
    var registrationClaimValue =
context.User.Claims.SingleOrDefault(c=>c.Type == "registration-
date")?.Value;
    if (DateTime.TryParseExact(registrationClaimValue, "yy-MM-
dd",CultureInfo.InvariantCulture, DateTimeStyles.AdjustToUniversal,out var
registrationTime))
    {
        return registrationTime.AddYears(1) < DateTime.UtcNow;
    }
    return false;
})
```

The preceding code extracts the registration date claim, and then tries to parse it and checks if its value is of a date earlier than a year ago.

To apply the policy to a controller action, you just need to specify the policy name in the Authorize attribute that decorates the method or class, as shown here:

```
[Authorize(Policy = "ExperiencedUser")]
[HttpPost("categories")]
public Task<ActionResult> AddCategory([FromBody] NewCategoryDTO
newCategory)
{
    ...
}
```

Enabling Cross-Origin Resource Sharing

The Enabling **Cross-Origin Resource Sharing** (CORS) standard allows a web server to relax the same-origin policy that prevents a browser from sending API requests to domains other than that of the web application. Browsers enforce the same-origin policy to protect their users from many kinds of attacks that attempt to send data to other sites.

In ASP.NET Core, it's very easy to configure the domains that are allowed to use your API, and the type of HTTP methods they can use.

First, add the CORS middleware by adding these lines to the `ConfigureServices` method in your `Startup` class:

```
public void ConfigureServices(IServiceCollection services)
{
    service.AddCors()
}
```

Than, configure the CORS policy in your `Startup.Configure` method. For example, the following code shows how you can configure your web application to allow requests from any domain with any HTTP method, and with any headers:

```
public void Configure(IApplicationBuilder app, IHostingEnvironment env)
{
    ...
    app.UseCors(b =>
    {
        b.AllowAnyHeader();
        b.AllowAnyOrigin();
        b.AllowAnyMethod();
    });
    ...
}
```

Summary

In this chapter, you've learned how to add a security layer to your backend server, which allows you to authenticate users and authorize their actions. Application security is a big and important topic, which, if done incorrectly, can expose your application data and your users' privacy to attacks and leakage. Authentication and authorization can help you make sure that users can only do what you have approved. ASP.NET Core provides the identity infrastructure, which takes advantage of the EF Core `DbContext` and adds necessary entities to your data model. After you enabled the identity infrastructure, I showed you how to add authentication and generate a JWT that holds the user's claims. Afterwards, you saw how to use these claims to create authorization rules and policies. Our journey to secure the backend is not complete yet. In `Chapter 14`, *Moving Your Solution to the Cloud*, I'll teach you how to add more protection layers.

In the next chapter, we'll take a break from adding features to the application, and concentrate on ways in which we can improve application maintainability and development productivity with useful techniques for diagnosing, troubleshooting, and debugging application errors.

Troubleshooting and Debugging

No software product is perfect, and the harsh truth is that no matter how much effort you put into designing and testing your code, there is always a very good chance that you missed some edge case that will cause your application to fail. If you can't win the game, you need to change the rules. Instead, make sure that, even if your application fails with an error, it will know how to recover and give you as much information as it can so that you can reproduce the scenario and solve the problem.

In this chapter, you will learn how you can protect your API from unhandled exceptions, and how you can return meaningful error responses to your API client that will later allow you to decipher what the problem was. You will also learn how to add logging and diagnostics to your code, so that problem investigation will become easier.

In this chapter, we will cover the following topics:

- Adding logging to your application
- Enabling diagnostics with Application Insights
- Responding gracefully in cases of errors and exceptions
- Making your APIs discoverable, and self-documenting with the OpenAPI standard (Swagger)

Adding logging to your application

Running applications in production can be very complex. A lot of things might happen when your application is in the wild, things that you don't expect, or that slipped your QA process, such as edge cases or events in the data center that affect your application. Besides these cases, there are times when you want to investigate the correct flow of work and get insights about how a certain feature is used, or if it is used at all. Your best friend in the aforementioned cases is the log. Logging in ASP.NET Core is now a first-class citizen, and a logging framework, middleware, and abstraction layer are included out-of-the-box, so it's much easier to work with different logging packages and providers.

The `Microsoft.Extensions.Logging` package, which is referenced by the `Microsoft.AspNetCore.App` meta-package, contains the building blocks of the logging infrastructure. The following list explains what the main classes are in the logging infrastructure:

- `ILogger` and `ILogger<T>`: These are abstractions for the type used to perform the logging. The generic parameter is meant to be the type by which the logger is used—this type will be the category name of the log events.
- `ILoggerProvider`: This is an abstraction for a type that can create instances of `ILogger` for a specific target (such as a file or console window). There can be more than one provider in your application.
- `ILoggerFactory`: This is an abstraction for the type, used to configure the logging and create instances of `ILogger` from a given `ILoggerProvider`.

By using these building block types, you can write log events that describe different scenarios that happen in your application.

Writing a log message from the controller

The logging infrastructure is already registered in the built-in dependency injection container, so all you need to do to get access to the logger is to add it as a parameter in your controller constructor so that it will be injected when the controller is created. For example, this is how the logger is injected into the GiveNTake ProductsController:

```
using Microsoft.Extensions.Logging;

[Authorize]
[Route("api/[controller]")]
public class ProductsController : Controller
{
```

```
    ...
    private readonly ILogger<ProductsController> _logger;


    public ProductsController(GiveNTakeContext context,
ILogger<ProductsController> logger)
    {
        _logger = logger;
        ...
    }
    ...
}
```

Whenever you need to write a log event, you need to use one of the `ILogger Log[Level]` methods, where level can be `Trace`, `Debug`, `Information`, `Warning`, `Error`, or `Critical`. These methods are extension methods to the `ILogger` interface that simply wrap the call to the generic `Log` method.

For example, the action for searching by category validates that the client provided a value for the category parameter, and if not, responds with a `BadRequest`. It will be helpful for us to write a log event of a warning so that we can later check why the user request has failed:

```
[AllowAnonymous]
[HttpGet("searchcategory/{category}/{subcategory=all}/")]
public async Task<ActionResult<ProductDTO[]>> SearchByCategory(string
category,
    string subcategory,
    string location = "all",
    bool imageOnly = false)
{
    if (string.IsNullOrEmpty(category))
    {
        _logger.LogWarning("An empty category was sent from the client.
SubCategory: '{SubCategory}', Location: '{Location}'", subcategory,
location);
        return BadRequest();
    }
    ...
}
```

The logging method has a few overloads (that vary based on the level) and their signature looks roughly like what's shown in the following screenshot:

```
(this ILogger logger, EventId eventId, Exception exception, string message, params object[] args):void
```

The parameters in the preceding screenshot are defined as follows:

- `eventId` (optional): A value (usually an integer) that represents a logical event in the application. This can be helpful for grouping various messages that belong to the same logical context.
- `exception` (optional): The exception that represents the error that is being logged.
- `message`: The message to be logged. It can contain placeholders for formatted arguments in the form `{argument}`. The arguments are placed based on position, and not on content.
- `args`: A collection of arguments placed inside the formatted message to be delivered to the logging provider for storage.

> You might be surprised that the string format doesn't use argument placeholders with numbers in them (argument location) in the `args` collection. The reason for that is that the `Microsoft.Extensions.Logging` package is built around the concept of semantic logging, also known as structured logging. In semantic logging, the log keeps not only the formatted message but also the key (the content inside the curly brackets) and value of each argument. If the argument is a complex type, the entire object is stored. Because each argument is stored, the system can index it, which allows us to create sophisticated queries.

Run the application and perform a request to the `SearchByCategory` action without passing a category to see the log message in the output window:

You can see that, besides the log event that you've written in the controller, other logs are written from other areas in the request pipeline. As useful as they may be, they can be distracting, and therefore, it's worthwhile to have the ability to filter log events by certain conditions.

Filtering log messages

Different execution modes of your application can require different levels of logging. For example, in development mode, you might want to see log events from all application areas, no matter what level they are from. While in production, you probably want to see only log events with warnings and errors that are produced by your application logic, and not from the ASP.NET infrastructure. Luckily, the ASP.NET logging framework makes it very easy to configure a filter with the `application` settings file.

To set the minimum level of the log messages you allow, open the `appsettings.json` file and add the `Logging` element, like this:

```
{
  ...
  "Logging": {
    "LogLevel": {
      "Default": "Warning"
    }
  }
}
```

In the preceding example, we set the minimum allowed level to `Warning`, which means that only events with a level of `Warning`, `Error`, and `Fatal` will be allowed to be written.

You can also set different filter rules for different categories. For example, you may wish to see all logs that you produce in your application logic, but filter out any log event that comes from the ASP.NET Core pipeline, that is, logs that originate from classes that are part of the `Microsoft.AspNetCore` namespace. Because each logger category is defined to be the class's full name to which the logger belongs, this task is easily accomplished like this:

```
{
  ...
  "Logging": {
    "LogLevel": {
      "Default": "Debug",
      "Microsoft.AspNetCore": "Warning"
    }
  }
}
```

In the preceding example, I set a specific rule for logs in the
`Microsoft.AspNetCore` category, so only log events with a `Warning` level and above will
allowed to be written, while other events will be written if they have a level of at least
`Debug`.

Log providers

Log providers are the bridge between the application code that write logs and the output
medium to which the logs will be written. There are a few providers that offer out-of-the-
box solutions, such as `Console`, `Debug`, `EventSource`, and more that you can find
at `https://docs.microsoft.com/en-us/aspnet/core/fundamentals/logging/?view=`
`aspnetcore-2.1#built-in-logging-providers`. There are also third-party providers, such
as `serilog` (`https://github.com/serilog/serilog-aspnetcore`) and `NLog` (`https://`
`github.com/NLog/NLog.Extensions.Logging`), that give more control about the logging
configuration and destinations.

By default, the ASP.NET Core logging framework sets the logging providers to `Debug` (the
output debug window) and `Console` (the `stdout` and `stderr` streams). The default
implementation is similar to what we could have written manually in the creation of the
`WebHostBuilder` in the `Program` class:

```
public class Program
{
    ...

    public static IWebHostBuilder CreateWebHostBuiler(string[] args) =>
        WebHost.CreateDefaultBuilder(args)
            .ConfigureLogging(cfg =>
            {
                cfg.AddConsole();
                cfg.AddDebug();
            })
            .UseStartup<Startup>();
}
```

Provider-specific configuration and filters

Each logging provider can be configured independently. For example, if you wish to enable all logs in the `Debug` output, but want to filter the `Console` output to only display `Warning` and above, here is how you can configure it in the `appsettings.json` file:

```
{
   ...
   "Logging": {
     "Debug": {
       "LogLevel": {
         "Default": "Information"
       }
     },
     "Console": {
       "LogLevel": {
         "Default": "Warning"
       }
     },
     "LogLevel": {
       "Default": "Debug",
       "Microsoft.AspNetCore": "Warning"
     }
   }
}
```

The `Console` and `Debug` providers are helpful when running locally, but in production, you need a more powerful provider that can also store the logs that are coming from all of your services (and their instances) in a centralized way to allow querying of them at a later time. There are a few options you can choose from for centralized logging, such as *Loggly*, *Logz.io*, *Application Insights*, and so forth, each with their own set of features and pricing models. In this book, we'll use Application Insights, because it's both powerful and easy to integrate with the ASP.NET Core application.

Enabling diagnostics with Application Insights

Application Insights is an analytics platform that monitors the use of applications and provides insights on their performance and behavior. Application Insights has rich diagnostics capabilities and can be used to query logs and metrics that are sent to it. Application Insights is hosted in Microsoft Azure, but allows you to work with it locally and use its features from inside Visual Studio.

To use Application Insights in your application, follow these steps:

1. Right-click the project in the **Solution Explorer**.
2. Click on **Add** | **Application Insights Telemetry...**:

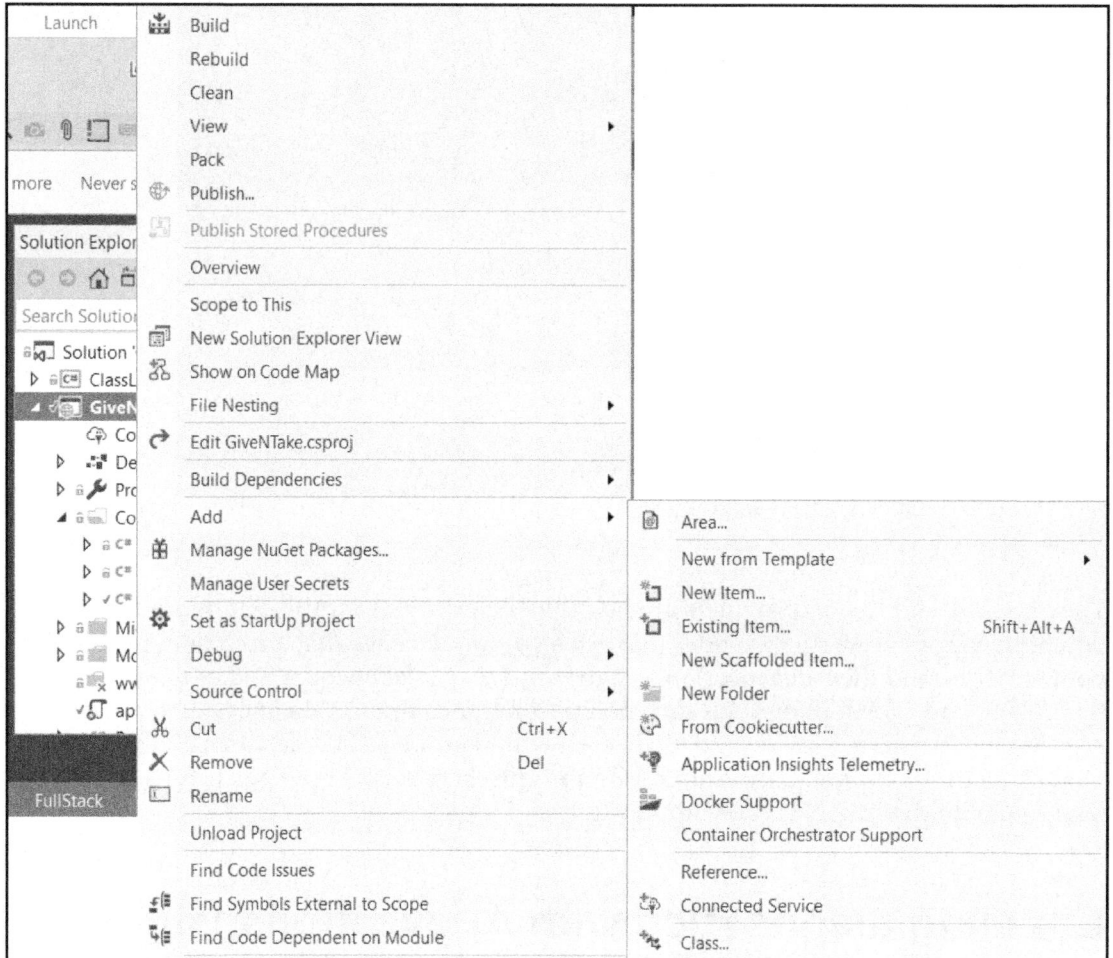

Launch		Build			
		Rebuild			
		Clean			
		View	▶		
more	Never s	Pack			
		Publish...			
Solution Explor		Publish Stored Procedures			
		Overview			
Search Solution		Scope to This			
Solution		New Solution Explorer View			
ClassL		Show on Code Map			
GiveN		File Nesting	▶		
Co		Edit GiveNTake.csproj			
De		Build Dependencies	▶		
Pro		Add	▶	Area...	
Co		Manage NuGet Packages...		New from Template	▶
C		Manage User Secrets		New Item...	
C		Set as StartUp Project		Existing Item...	Shift+Alt+A
Mi		Debug	▶	New Scaffolded Item...	
Mc		Source Control	▶	New Folder	
ww		Cut	Ctrl+X	From Cookiecutter...	
ap		Remove	Del	Application Insights Telemetry...	
FullStack		Rename		Docker Support	
		Unload Project		Container Orchestrator Support	
		Find Code Issues		Reference...	
		Find Symbols External to Scope		Connected Service	
		Find Code Dependent on Module		Class...	

3. In the **Application Insights Configuration** window that was opened, click on the **Get Started** button:

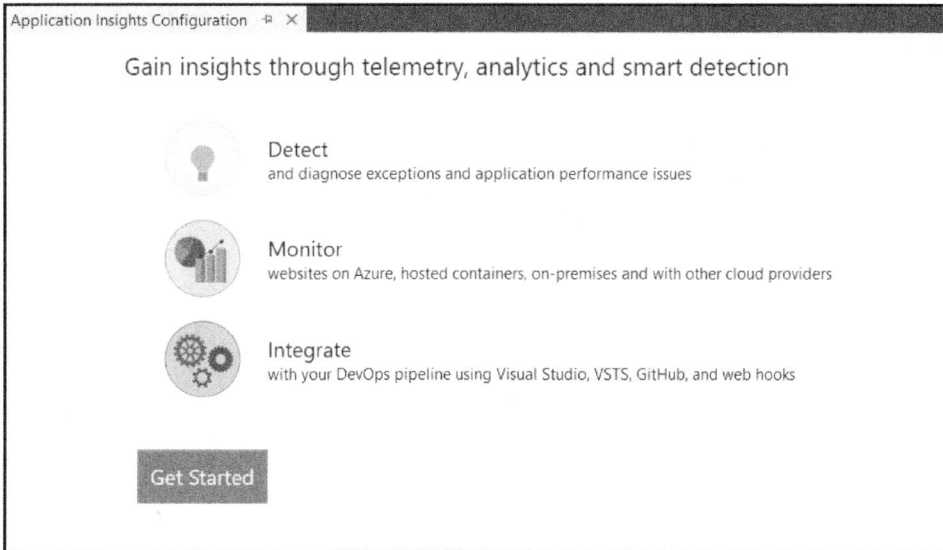

4. At this point, we will use Application Insights locally. Scroll down to the bottom and click on the link to set Application Insights to local mode:

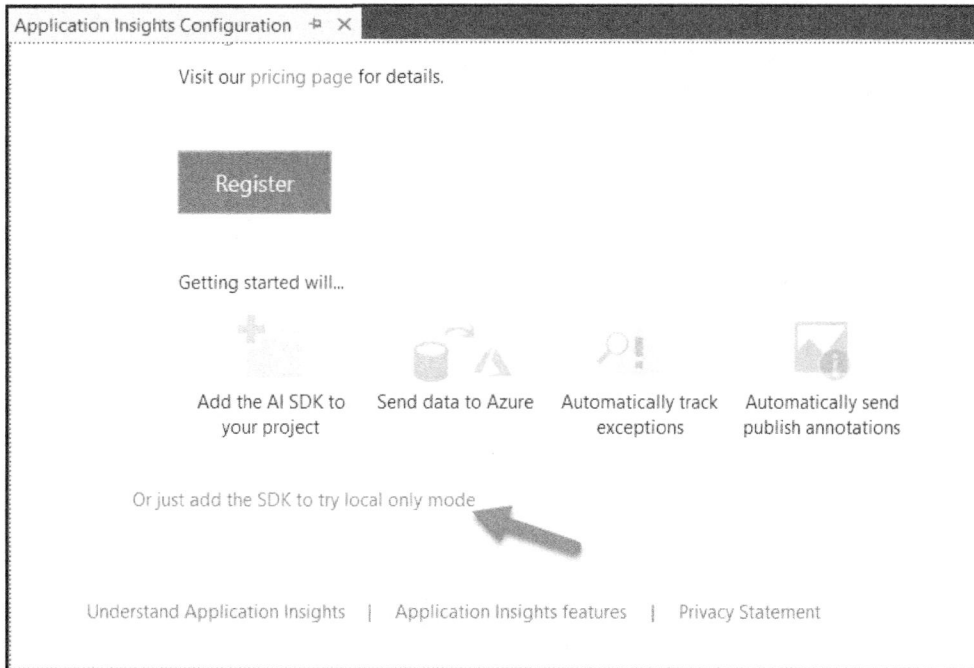

After completing these steps, you should see that the Application Insights packages were added to your project references, and the addition of Application Insights in the creation of the `WebHostBuilder` in the `Program.cs` file:

```
public static IWebHostBuilder CreateWebHostBuiler(string[] args) =>
    WebHost.CreateDefaultBuilder(args)
        .UseApplicationInsights()
        .UseStartup<Startup>();
```

To configure the log level for Application Insights, you can use the following snippet in the `appsettings.json` file:

```
"Application Insights": {
    "LogLevel": {
        "Default": "Debug"
    }
}
```

5. Add the Application Insights logger to the ASP.NET Logger Factory by modifying your `Startup.Configure()` method, like this:

```
public void Configure(IApplicationBuilder app,
IHostingEnvironment env,
    ILoggerFactory loggerFactory)
{
    var appInsightsLogLevel =
        Configuration.GetValue<LogLevel>("Logging:Application
Insights:LogLevel:Default", );
    loggerFactory.AddApplicationInsights(app.ApplicationServices, ap
pInsightsLogLevel);

    // Rest of code
}
```

At the time of writing this block, the Application Insights logger doesn't reflect the log level in the `appsettings.json` file automatically and instead uses a default level of `Warning`. The preceding code overcomes this limitation by reading the log level from the configuration property. Note that if the log level doesn't exist in the configuration file, the default log level will be `Trace`.

To configure the log level for Application Insights, you can use the following snippet in the `appsettings.json` file:

```
"Application Insights": {
    "LogLevel": {
        "Default": "Debug"
    }
}
```

6. Run the application and send some requests to it, and you should see the Application Insights button in the Visual Studio toolbar:

7. Clicking on this button will open the **Application Insights Search** window, which will display all the log events in the current debug session:

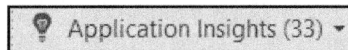

Through this window, you can search and filter log events, and drill down to specific events to see all the data arguments that were sent with each event.

> In Chapter 14, *Moving Your Solution to the Cloud*, you will create the Application Insights service on Azure and connect your application to it so that you can run the same search and analytics in your production environment.

Responding gracefully in the event of errors and exceptions

In a classic application development, where the caller of your method runs in the same process as your logic, it's obvious that when an error occurs, the code will either throw an exception or return an error code of some type.

In a Web API application, we strive to get the same semantic, only that the caller doesn't run in the same process, and therefore, the error response should be serialized on the wire. HTTP already provides the notion of status code, which allows you to communicate to the caller if the request was processed successfully or not. Unfortunately, in many cases, this is not enough, and the users of your API are unable to understand exactly what the problem is by only looking at a single generic status code. Instead, it's better to provide a standard error object with finer details.

Adding a correlation identifier to responses

Not all application errors will result in an error response — there are times when the application logic has a bug that results in a successful response but with the wrong values. In those cases, you need to have some way to correlate between the response the user received and the log events in your system. This is the purpose of the correlation identifier (or CorrelationID).

The CorrelationID is a value that you create when a request is received, which you use whenever you write a log event. When the request handling is done, you attach the CorrelationID to the response, usually as a header, to allow the user to communicate it back to you if needed. You can even enhance this technique and send the CorrelationID to other services your API consumes, so later, when investigating an issue, you can rebuild the entire flow that the logical transaction went through.

Application Insights already generates a unique Operation ID for each request, so we can leverage this value and send it as a header in the response. The typical header name for a correlation identifier is X-Correlation-ID.

To add a header for each response, we need to intercept the request pipeline and implement some middleware that will inject the header when the response is being written.

Here is a simple implementation of such a piece of middleware:

```
public class CorrelationIdHeaderMiddleware
{
    private const string CorrelationHeaderKey = "X-Correlation-ID";

    private readonly RequestDelegate _next;

    public CorrelationIdHeaderMiddleware(RequestDelegate next)
    {
        _next = next;
    }

    public async Task Invoke(HttpContext context)
    {
        // Retrieve the current Application Insight Telemetry object for
the request
        var requestTelemetry = context.Features.Get<RequestTelemetry>();

        // Register to be notified when the headers are written to the
response
        context.Response.OnStarting(_ =>
        {
            // Add the Correlation ID header when the response is being
written
            context.Response.Headers.Add(CorrelationHeaderKey, new[] {
requestTelemetry.Id });
            return Task.CompletedTask;
        }, null);

        // Continue the execution pipeline
        await _next(context);
    }
}
```

With the implementation of the middleware ready, you need to add it to your application. To make it easier and more readable, I created an extension method that sets the middleware to the ASP.NET Application Builder:

```
public static class CorrelationIdMiddlewareExtensions
{
    public static void UseCorrelationIdHeader(this IApplicationBuilder app)
    {
        app.UseMiddleware<CorrelationIdHeaderMiddleware>();
    }
}
```

Finally, you need to use the extension method when configuring the application in the Startup class:

```
public class Startup
{
    ...
    public void Configure(IApplicationBuilder app, IHostingEnvironment env)
    {
        ...
        // Each response will now include a 'X-Correlation-ID' header
        app.UseCorrelationIdHeader();

        ...
    }
}
```

Now, whenever you make a request to the API, the response will include the X-Correlation-ID header that holds the same value as the Operation ID that Application Insights uses when writing the logging events.

For example, here is the response I received after using the search API without providing a category name:

Having the `CorrelationID` allows me to go through the logs I have in my **Application Insights Search** and see what happened with this request. For brevity, I filtered the messages that are marked `Debug` level:

The developer exception page

The MVC middleware of ASP.NET Core comes with a built-in developer exception page that is aimed at providing meaningful information while you're in development mode. When you created your ASP.NET Core project, Visual Studio automatically generated the code that enables the usage of the developer exception page inside the `Configure` method of the `Startup` class:

```
if (env.IsDevelopment())
{
    app.UseDeveloperExceptionPage();
}
```

> How does ASP.NET Core determine that you are in development mode? ASP.NET uses an environment variable by the name of `ASPNETCORE_ENVIRONMENT`. If its value is Development, then the `IsDevelopment` method returns `true`. You can control the value of the `ASPNETCORE_ENVIRONMENT` environment variable for each of the profiles you run the application in through the **Debug** tab in the project properties screen:

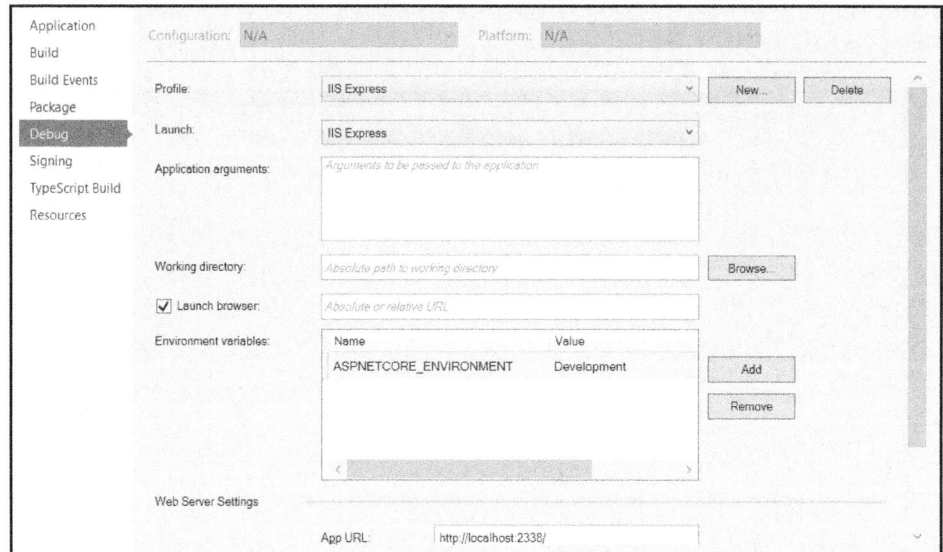

Ultimately, these configurations are saved in the `launchSettings.json` file, located under the `Properties` folder of your project, so alternatively, you can edit this file and get the same effect.

To test the developer exception page, I've added a new action in the `ProdcutsController` class that simply throws an exception to simulate an unhandled exception situation:

```
[AllowAnonymous]
[HttpGet("error")]
public ActionResult ThrowError()
{
    throw new InvalidOperationException("This is an example of unhandled
exception");
}
```

Run the application and navigate your browser to `http://localhost:{port}/api/products/error`. You should see a page similar to this:

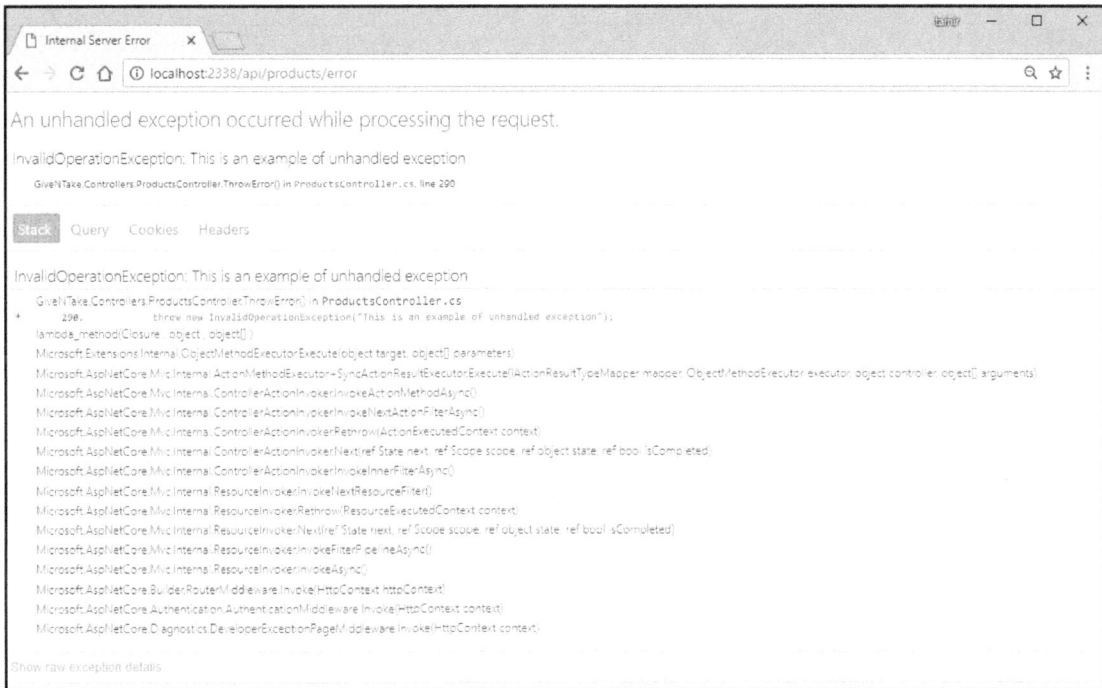

The text in this image is not important. The purpose of this image is to show what an error page will look like when it occurs.

The page includes the stack trace and the message of the thrown exception, as well as the request details, such as the query string, cookies, and headers that were sent.

As useful to the developer as this may be, it's unpractical for usage when dealing with Web APIs, because the caller of the API is not a browser that can render an HTML output. For example, here is the response that Postman shows after sending the request to the `error` action:

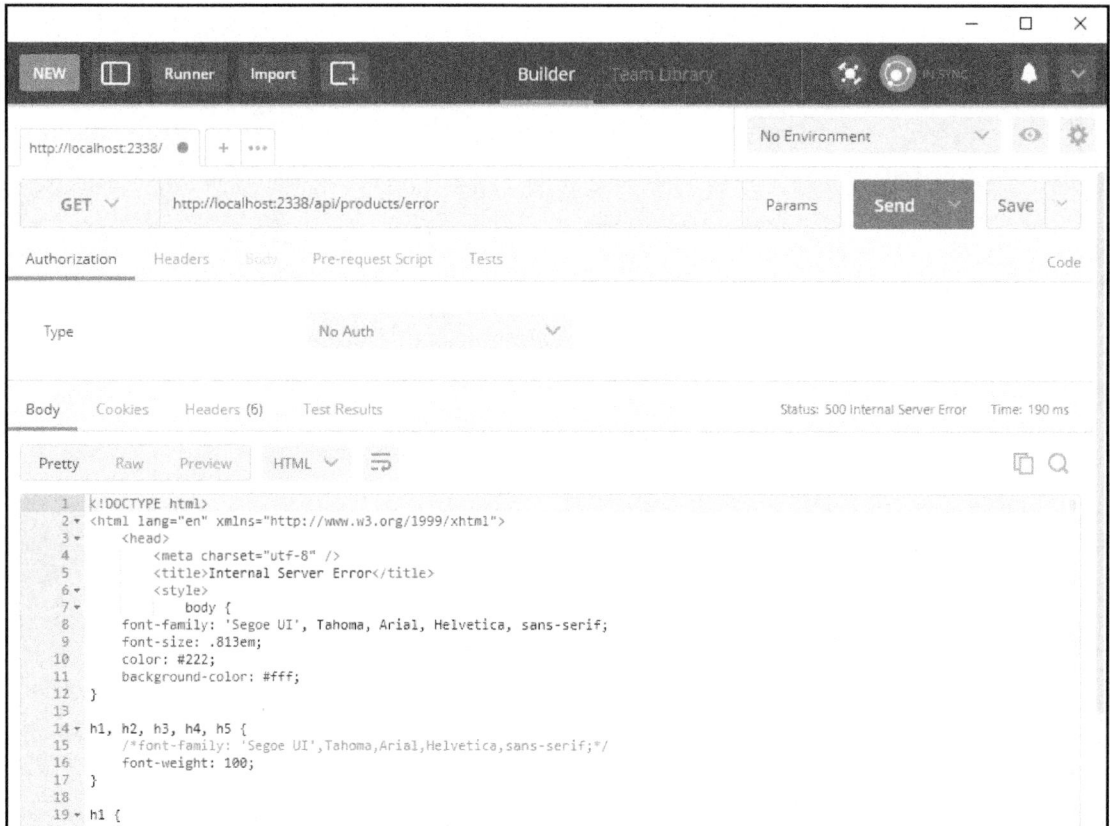

Developers, including yourself, will have a hard time deciphering the content, and even if you manage to do so, the application that talks with your API can receive those errors in runtime and won't be able to extract the needed information to write to a log or explain to you what the problem was.

The bottom line is that, when developing a Web API, you should avoid usage of the developer exception page, and add another mechanism to deal with unhandled exceptions.

Adding a global exception handler

When an unhandled exception is thrown from a controller action, ASP.NET Core responds to the caller with the status code 500 (**Internal Server Error**). For the client, this status code means that something bad happened on the server but doesn't offer any meaningful information that the user can provide to the API support team (such as the request/correlation identifier).

To overcome this, we need to add a global exception handler — a piece of code that can intercept the calls made to the request pipeline and catch exceptions that were thrown. There is more than one way to add a global exception handler, but I believe the easiest way is by adding an `Exception Filter` that will be added to the MVC pipeline.

To create an `Exception Filter`, you need to implement the `Microsoft.AspNetCore.Mvc.Filters.IExceptionFilter` interface and provide an implementation of the `OnException()` method that will be called whenever there's an unhandled exception.

The following implementation intercepts the unhandled exception and creates an object with details about the error. If the application is in development mode, the exception details are returned as well:

```
public class GlobalExceptionFilter : IExceptionFilter
{
    private readonly IHostingEnvironment env;
    private readonly ILogger<GlobalExceptionFilter> _logger;

    public GlobalExceptionFilter(IHostingEnvironment env,
ILogger<GlobalExceptionFilter> logger)
    {
        this.env = env;
        this._logger = logger;
    }

    public void OnException(ExceptionContext context)
    {
        _logger.LogError(new EventId(context.Exception.HResult),
            context.Exception,
            context.Exception.Message);

        var errorDetails = new ErrorDetails()
        {
            Instance = context.HttpContext.Request.Path,
            Status = StatusCodes.Status500InternalServerError,
            Detail = "Please refer to the errors property for additional
```

```
details.",
        Errors =
        {
            {"ServerError", new[] {"An unexpected error ocurred."}}
        },
    };

    if (env.IsDevelopment())
    {
        errorDetails.Exception = context.Exception;
    }

    context.Result = new ObjectResult(errorDetails)
    {
        StatusCode = StatusCodes.Status500InternalServerError
    };
    context.HttpContext.Response.StatusCode =
(int)HttpStatusCode.InternalServerError;

    context.ExceptionHandled = true;
}
private class ErrorDetails : ValidationProblemDetails
{
    public Exception Exception { get; set; }
}
}
```

The `ErrorDetails` type is the DTO I'm using for returning the error details in the response. It derives from
the `Microsoft.AspNetCore.Mvc.ValidationProblemDetails` class that implements
the RFC 7807 standard (`https://tools.ietf.org/html/rfc7807`), a standardized format
for carrying machine-readable details of errors in HTTP responses.

> **TIP**
> In your application, you can extend the `GlobalExceptionFilter` so that if
> an application-specific exception is caught, it will change the error message
> appropriately.

To add `GlobalExceptionFilter` to the request pipeline, you need to register it in the
`Startup` class as part of the MVC services inside the `ConfigureServices` method:

```
public void ConfigureServices(IServiceCollection services)
{
    services.AddMvc(config =>
    {
        ...
```

```
        config.Filters.Add<GlobalExceptionFilter>();
    });
    ...
}
```

Now, when sending a request that generates an error, we get, in response, a structured format to work with:

Making your APIs discoverable and self-documenting with the OpenAPI standard (Swagger)

When discussing Web APIs, you need to consider that the users that will interact with your API are developers, and not the end users of the product. The developers that use your API can use it in a variety of clients that can be written in various programming languages and technologies. Even though you created a REST API that uses standards such as HTTP and JSON, there are still things that are not standardized, such as the date-time format you use, numbers accuracy, and so on. Besides this, developers who want to use your API need a way to find out which data structures your API works with; what the URL structure is; what type of errors are returned from each action; and so forth. Then, the developer needs to put these definitions into code that can talk with your API, which can be a daunting task, especially when the API can change over time. You might even want to automate this task. To mitigate all the issues I've listed, the industry sought a standard specification that could be used to define the structure of an API in both a human and machine-readable way, which allows for the generation of documentation, client code, and UIs for interacting with the API in an automated way. This specification is known as OpenAPI (formerly, Swagger), and more information can be found at `https://github.com/OAI/OpenAPI-Specification`.

OpenAPI is a JSON document (usually with the name `swagger.json`) that contains metadata on the API (such as versions) and the description of each endpoint it exposes. The following example shows a reduced version of the `GiveNTake` API:

```
{
    "swagger": "2.0",
    "info": {
        "version": "v1",
        "title": "GiveNTake.API"
    },
    "paths": {
        "/api/Account/register": {
            "post": {
                "tags": [
                    "Account"
                ],
                "operationId": "ApiAccountRegisterPost",
                "consumes": [
                    "application/json-patch+json",
                    "application/json",
                    "text/json",
                    "application/*+json"
```

```
                ],
                "produces": [],
                "parameters": [
                    {
                        "name": "registration",
                        "in": "body",
                        "required": false,
                        "schema": {
                            "$ref": "#/definitions/RegisterUserDTO"
                        }
                    }
                ],
                "responses": {
                    "200": {
                        "description": "Success"
                    }
                }
            }
        },
        ...
    },
    "definitions": {
        "RegisterUserDTO": {
            "required": [
                "email",
                "password"
            ],
            "type": "object",
            "properties": {
                "email": {
                    "type": "string"
                },
                "password": {
                    "format": "password",
                    "maxLength": 100,
                    "minLength": 6,
                    "type": "string"
                },
                "confirmPassword": {
                    "format": "password",
                    "type": "string"
                }
            }
        },
        ...
    },
    "securityDefinitions": {
        "Bearer": {
```

```
            "name": "Authorization",
            "in": "header",
            "type": "apiKey"
      }
    },
    "security": [
        {
            "Bearer": []
        }
    ]
}
```

Swagger (`https://swagger.io/`) is not only the former name of the specification; it's also a set of open source tools that help in designing, validating, visualizing, and transforming the OpenAPI file and the REST API it represents.

Generating a Swagger file from the ASP.NET Core application

To generate the Swagger file automatically in your project, I recommend using the popular `Swashbuckle` (`https://github.com/domaindrivendev/Swashbuckle.AspNetCore`) NuGet package.

`Swashbuckle` uses the metadata of your API to build the OpenAPI file. The metadata is automatically created by ASP.NET Core, based on the routing attributes, and the method's signature of the action in your controllers.

To use `Swashbuckle`, do the following:

1. Install the `Swashbuckle.AspNetCore` NuGet package.
2. Register the Swagger generator in the `ConfigureServices` method of your `Startup` class. In the registration process, specify the details of the API and its Version (note that you can define more than one Swagger document):

```
services.AddSwaggerGen(c =>
{
    c.SwaggerDoc("v1", new Info { Title = "GiveNTake.API", Version
    = "v1" });
});
```

3. Enable the Swagger middleware by adding the following line in the `Configure` method of your `Startup` class:

```
public void Configure(IApplicationBuilder app, IHostingEnvironment
env)
{
    ...
    app.UseSwagger();
}
```

At this point, the Swagger file will be available when running the application and navigating to `http://localhost:[port]/swagger/v1/swagger.json`. The `v1` in the URL might be different for you if you set a different version identifier in the Swagger generator registration.

4. Add the security definition in the Swagger generator registration to make it explicit that the actions in your API require the `Authorization` header with a `Bearer` value:

```
services.AddSwaggerGen(c =>
{
    c.SwaggerDoc("v1", new Info { Title = "GiveNTake.API",
     Version
    = "v1" });
    c.AddSecurityDefinition("Bearer", new ApiKeyScheme
    {
        Name = "Authorization",
        In = "header",
    });
    c.AddSecurityRequirement(new Dictionary<string,
    IEnumerable<string>>
    {
        { "Bearer", new string[] { } }
    });
});
```

Adding the Swagger UI to your application

Downloading the Swagger file and reading it can be a complex task for human beings. For us, it's much easier to see a visualization of the API in a nice, automatically generated UI, where we could easily see if the API is what we expect it to be.

Part of the `Swashbuckle` package you installed contains the Swagger UI, which is one of tools in the Swagger toolkit. To use it, add the following lines to the `Configure` method in the `Startup` class and specify the relative URL of the Swagger file in your API:

```
app.UseSwaggerUI(c =>
{
    c.SwaggerEndpoint("/swagger/v1/swagger.json", "GiveNTake.API");
});
```

Run the application and browse to `http://localhost:[port]/swagger`. You should see a page similar to this:

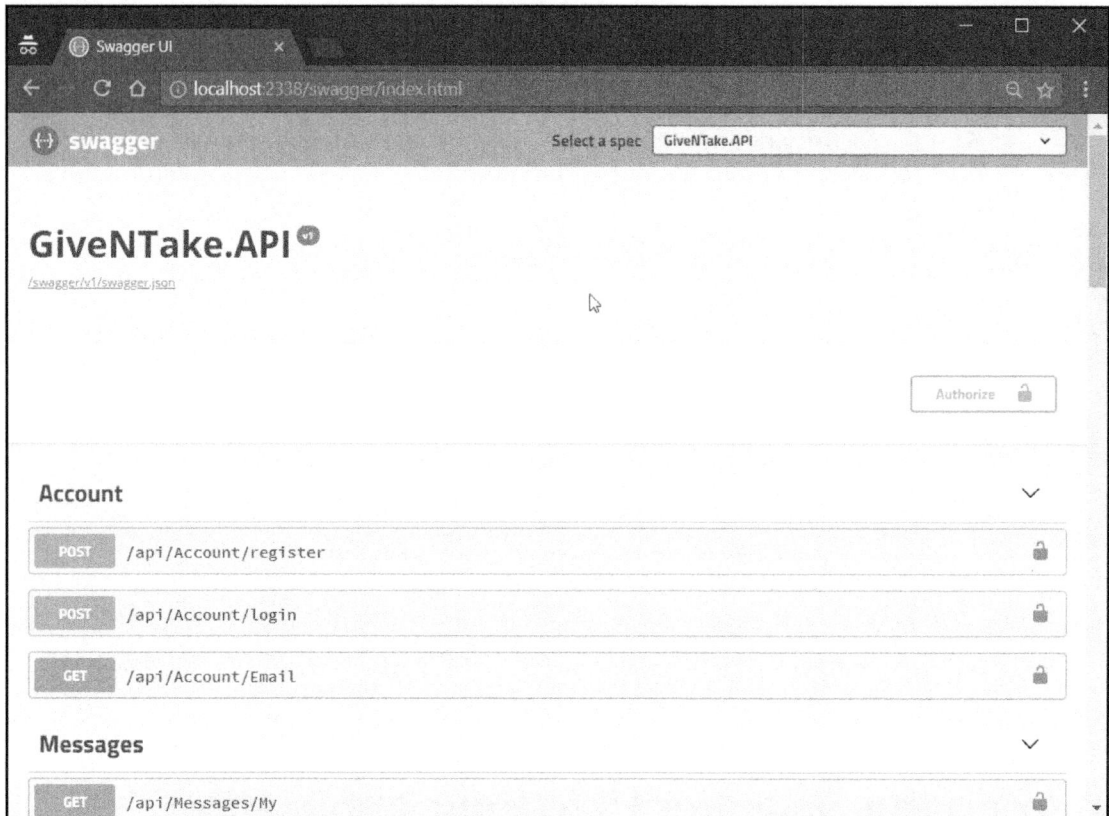

The UI is separated into sections that conform to the controllers in your application. For each controller section, you'll find the actions and can drill into them to see their definitions and test them.

Sending a request through the Swagger UI

You can test each of the actions listed in the Swagger UI by clicking on the action name and clicking the **Try it out** button, as shown here:

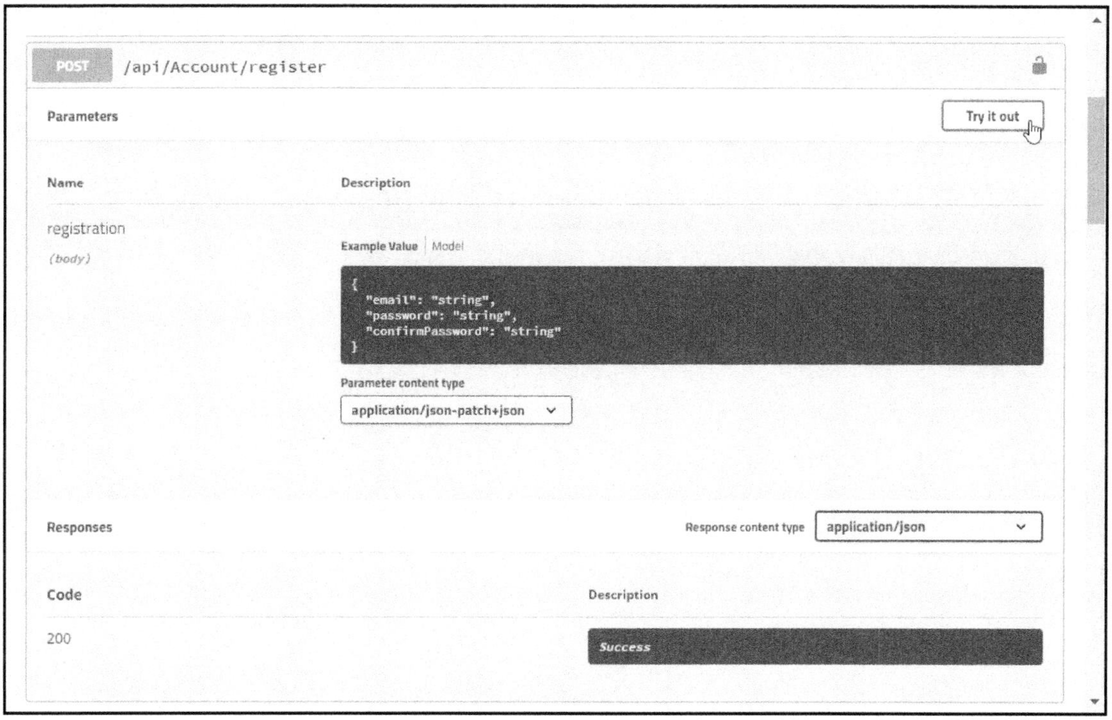

If there are any parameters, they will be open for editing. This includes the body of the request, where you can set the values of the data contract. When you're done filling in the values, you can click on the **Execute** button:

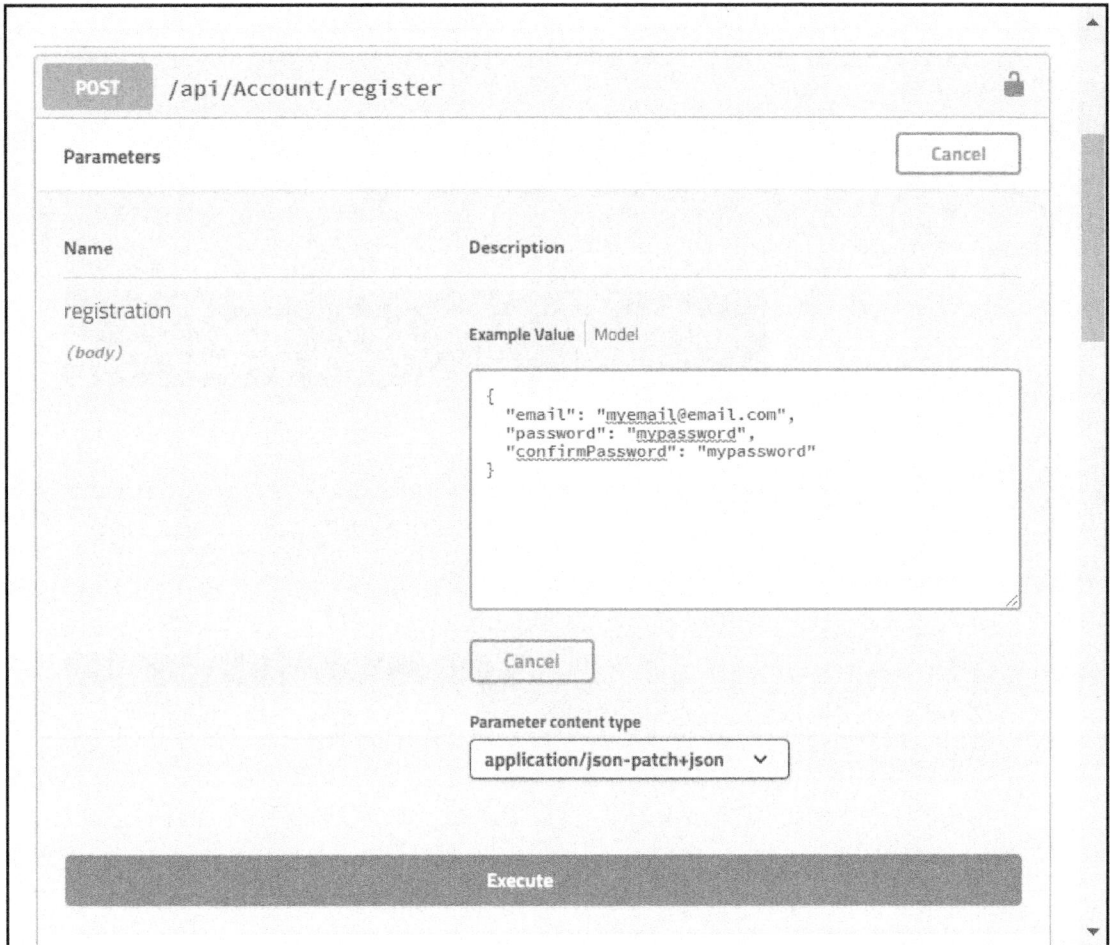

```
POST    /api/Account/register                                    🔓

Parameters                                                [ Cancel ]

Name                          Description

registration
                              Example Value | Model
(body)
                              {
                                "email": "myemail@email.com",
                                "password": "mypassword",
                                "confirmPassword": "mypassword"
                              }




                              [ Cancel ]

                              Parameter content type

                              [ application/json-patch+json    ∨ ]


                              Execute
```

After executing the request, the response will be shown together with the status code, headers, and body:

The Swagger UI is a handy tool to let developers explore your API. I found it to be a precious tool when having a team that needs to interact with the API.

> If you don't wish the Swagger file or the Swagger UI to be available outside of development mode, then you can surround the code that enables it in the `Configure` method with an
> `if(env.IsDevelopement()){...}` block.

Generating client code from a Swagger file

Users of your API will have to create code that can interact with it. To make it easier for them, you can provide an SDK that contains a reusable client code that fits the schema of your API. By providing the SDK, you can add client-side logic, such as validations and transformations, that can reduce the load from your API and help the developers that use your API to write their applications faster and with reduced errors.

Swagger provides two nice tools that can help you generate the client code (or at least the stubs in it) from the OpenAPI definition file:

- **Swagger Editor**: A web editor that allows the editing of OpenAPI/Swagger definitions, visualizing them, and generating code from them.
- **Swagger Codegen**: A template-driven engine to generate documentation, API clients, and server stubs in different languages by parsing your OpenAPI/Swagger definition. This is usually used as a CLI tool that can be incorporated and then generate the client build automatically.

Swagger editor

The Swagger Editor (`https://swagger.io/tools/swagger-editor/`) is a web application that you can use to edit OpenAPI definition files. You can run the web application on-premises, or you can use an online sample version at `https://editor.swagger.io`.

The Swagger Editor allows you to open a Swagger file from your computer or an external API. I downloaded the `swagger.json` file from the `GiveNTake` API and imported it into the **Swagger Editor**, as shown here:

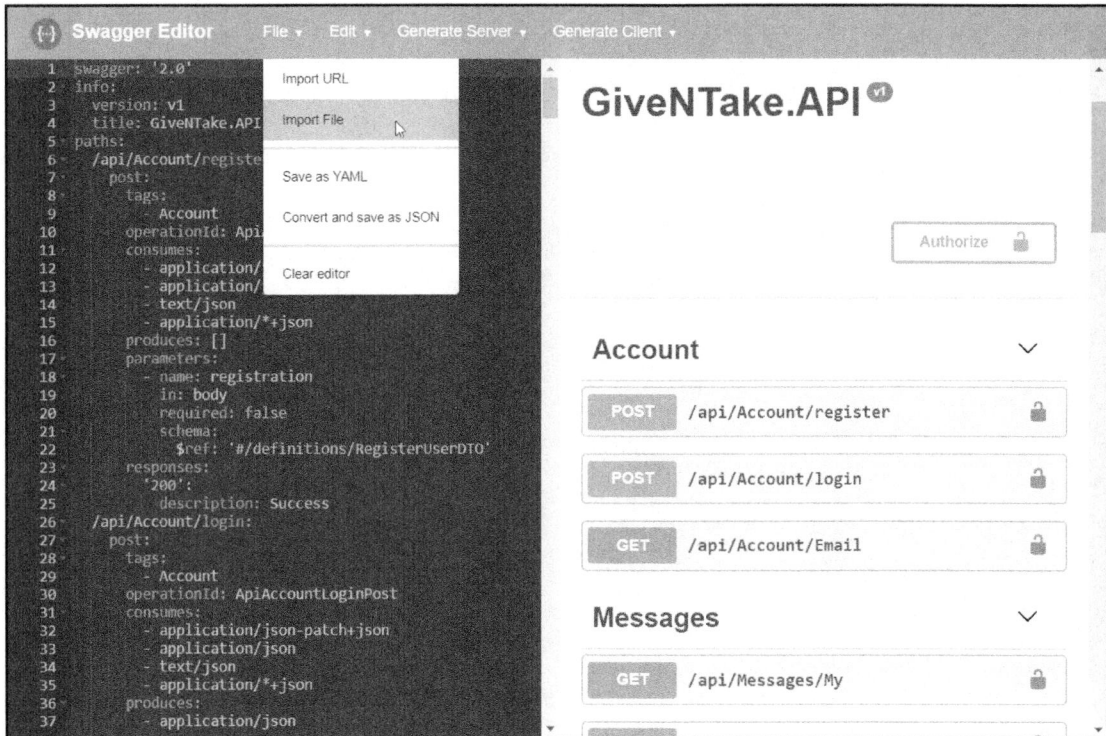

With the OpenAPI definitions loaded, you can click on the **Generate Client** menu item to select the language you wish to generate for the client:

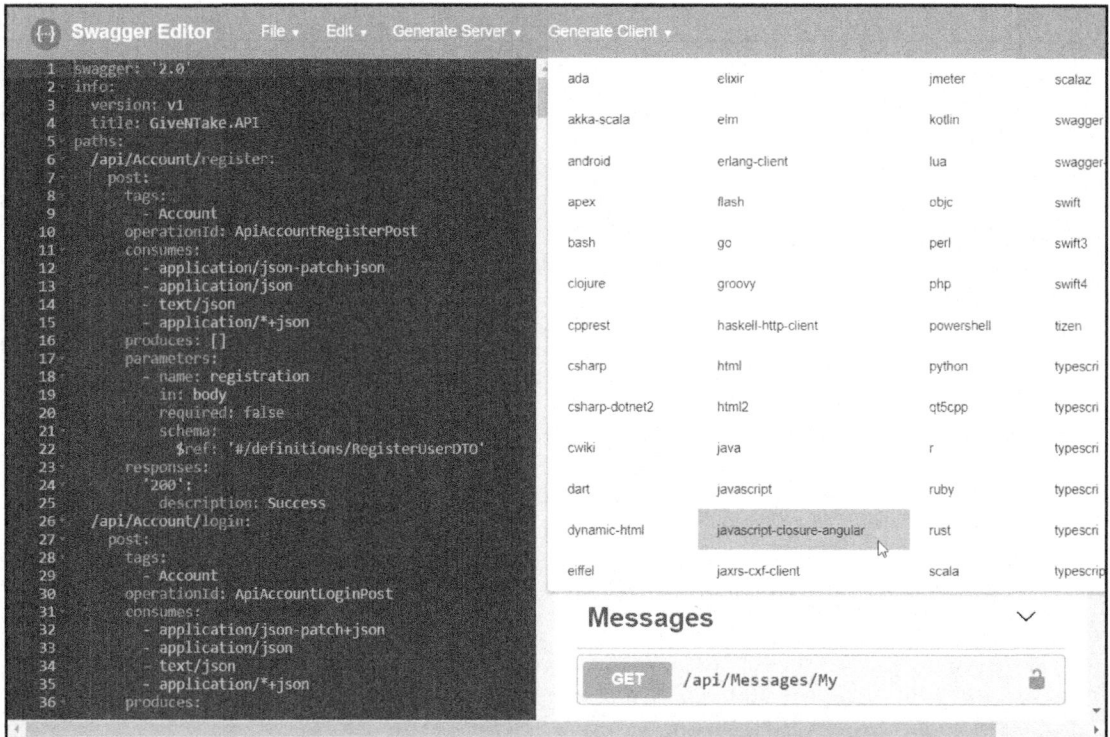

After code generation is complete, a ZIP file will be downloaded to your machine containing the code that you can now use in your application.

Summary

In this chapter, we covered some of the tools and techniques that you can use to make it easier for you and the users of your API, who are developers themselves, to find and diagnose errors in your application.

Logging is one of the most helpful things you have in case of a problem. Often, it is the only way for you to find out what happened when the error occurred. The new logging framework that ASP.NET Core introduced is integrated very nicely with the ASP.NET Core request pipeline, and using it in your application code is straightforward. There are many logging providers that you can use, and I've shown you how you can use Application Insights, which provides a nice search window inside Visual Studio, along with other diagnostic utilities that can be used when running in production.

Because the users of your API are developers themselves, you need to make sure that they can consume the errors from your application and deal with them gracefully. I've shown you how to add a global exception filter so that error responses can be standardized in your application. Finally, you've learned what the OpenAPI specifications are, and how to automatically generate the Swagger file and Swagger UI in your application, so that developers can later use it to experiment with the API and generate client code from it.

8
Getting Started with Frontend Web Development

From standard textual websites with minimal interaction to complete and immersive smart client apps, frontend web development has evolved tremendously throughout the last two decades. Web development, due to its immense growth and versatility, has become one of the most popular and in-demand fields today.

In this chapter, you'll learn the importance and relevance of the web development field while covering some of its background as well as its current state. Additionally, this chapter covers the basic principles and pillars of frontend web development.

We will focus on the following topics:

- The relevance of the web development field
- The pillars of the web — HTML, CSS, and JavaScript
- Key progress and future development
- App illustrations, which you build throughout this book
- jQuery app development

First, let's start with an overview of the web development field and recognize its true power and great relevance for today.

Getting started with frontend web development

It's important to acknowledge the relevance of web development, and not only specifically to frontend development. Today, nearly every kind of software we build can be developed using web technologies, and target virtually every platform.

It's amazing how JavaScript has penetrated the industry and, it has certainly been a game changer ever since. Using web technologies, you can write complete backend systems, including microservices and serverless architecture styles, while using your preferred protocols and patterns, such as REST, GraphQL, and WebSockets. It doesn't stop there either: web technologies are relevant for IoT, VR, OpenGL, and even databases!

MongoDb supports implementing stored procedures using JavaScript.

Focusing on frontend web development, what is a web app really?

When people hear the term *web apps*, they usually think about apps that run in the browser. However, that has not been the case for a long time now. Web technologies enable you to target multiple platforms such as desktop and mobile, and possibly even share a code base between these platforms.

Web development is one of the most popular and in-demand fields today, but how did that come to be?

Historically, in the desktop era, before the age of smartphones, people primarily used their desktop machines to use applications and browse the web, as those were simpler times. Later, the explosion of devices took place. Smart devices emerged onto the market and were widely used. Nowadays, people have numerous devices, and not just one; everyone is connected — all the time, everywhere.

Typically, businesses want to build software and reach as many users as possible, which usually implies targeting multiple platforms. Building platform-specific software is not a simple task. It has vast implications for time and cost, as this entails managing, testing, and developing practically separate products. Truthfully, not every business can really afford that, and few actually do it.

This turn of events has created a critical situation in the field of software development. The industry was in a dire need of an open platform that would allow them to build software at scale and meet all those platforms in a somewhat manageable way and within an affordable budget. At the time, the web showed great promise to fill in the gap. Nearly every device has a browser, and that was certainly a good starting point. Ever since, web development technologies and tooling have been evolving at a fast pace with great innovation, and the field keeps on gaining more popularity and demand.

Consequently, the web is one of the most versatile and dynamic fields today. Web developers have a tendency to be early adopters. Combine this with massive growth and you get exciting innovation. Additionally, the web community is keen on open source software, leading to great collaboration and contribution. Evidently, this is an exciting time to be a web developer. You have the ability to leverage the same skill set and become a true full-stack developer while enjoying cutting-edge innovation and massive collaboration.

Throughout this book, you learn how to build web apps using popular modern frameworks such as Angular, React, and Vue. Regardless of which framework you choose, when it comes to web apps, it still all boils down to the basic principles of the web: HTML, CSS, and JavaScript, as shown in the following diagram:

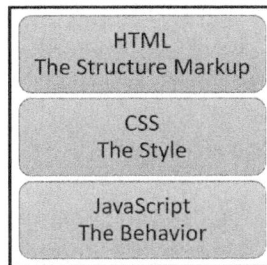

Next, let's cover these technologies, as these are the pillars of web apps, even though the expectation is that you are already familiar with, and have the experience to some extent with, these technologies.

HTML

HTML became a public phenomenon in the early 1990s. Originally, HTML was created to describe the structure and content of textual documents with basic functionality, such as links and simple forms.

HTML is an XML-like markup, and is essentially the display language of browsers. Every browser-based app, at its very core, returns structured HTML to the browser. The browser then parses the HTML and generates the HTML DOM, and then finally renders it to the screen.

Essentially, HTML is comprised of structural and semantic elements that instruct the browser of the structure and content. The following is a simple example of HTML:

```
<!doctype html>
<html>
  <head>
```

```
    <title>Hello HTML!</title>
  </head>
  <body>
    Welcome to HTML!
  </body>
</html>
```

The current HTML version is 5.2, which was published in December 2017. With HTML 5, it advanced to include more elements, including native media and extended forms of support.

While HTML hasn't progressed in a major way in recent years, it is not going away. First, as noted, it is the display language of browsers, but that's not all. Actually, many other tools support HTML in various ways, with the ability to view as well as generate it. HTML is still one of the most interoperable and cross-platform display languages today.

CSS

CSS is the style language for HTML; together they comprise the presentation layer of web applications. The standard usage of CSS is by defining selectors in which you can specify style properties and their desired values.
The following is a simple example of basic CSS:

```
#menu {
  width: 100%;
  background-color: 'black';
  color: 'white';
}
```

The preceding selector matches an element with its id attribute set to menu and sets multiple style properties to the matching elements. Obviously, there's much more to CSS selectors, including advanced usages, such as matching by class and element, as well as using pseudo-classes. CSS has a specific priority system in which the browsers know how to apply multiple styles that match the same element.

CSS has had many issues compared to modern styling technologies. First, the fact that it styles HTML, a markup language that was built originally to represent textual documents, has made it often extremely difficult to style modern apps with it. A popular example of this is the notorious vertical alignment, which is a somewhat basic need for modern apps, and in early versions of CSS it was certainly difficult to control.

CSS 3 has divided the CSS specification into separate modules, in which each can advance independently. Fortunately, different modules have made productive progress, and even new ones have emerged, such as CSS Variables, Flexbox, and CSS Grid. Those types of advancements have certainly made life easier when styling apps with CSS. Referencing the previous example, the vertical alignment difficulty has become history.

CSS is not yet without problems. The concepts of hierarchy, extensions, and mixins are not yet part of CSS. Therefore, reusability is very much compromised in plain CSS. Consequently, additional technologies have surfaced to assist with such concerns, known as CSS preprocessors, such as SASS, SCSS, and Less. When CSS does introduce built-in support for hierarchy and mixins, along with its CSS variables and `calc` function, these CSS preprocessors may no longer be needed. Furthermore, there is another popular pattern called *CSS in JS*. Its basic idea is to treat CSS as actual code: you write it in actual JavaScript and manage it accordingly.

Lastly, CSS specification doesn't instruct general conventions on how to manage selectors to achieve predictable standard, encapsulation, and reuse. For that purpose, several styling architecture styles have emerged, the most popular of which are BEM and SMACSS.

In conclusion, CSS and its ecosystem are extremely rich. However, it still has a long way to go before it becomes a complete off-the-shelf styling solution, or becomes a silver bullet for that matter.

JavaScript

JavaScript, ever since its first standardized version as **ECMAScript** (**ES**) in 1997, has been the key coding language for web technologies. Today, JavaScript can run virtually everywhere, making it a practical choice for cross-platform development and reuse of the same skill set. As its name implies, JavaScript is a scripting language. It is parsed and interpreted during runtime, and only then is it executed by the relevant platform.

Another matter of JavaScript that causes controversy is its dynamic type system. JavaScript, as with most languages, does have a type system. Although a type is not specified while declaring a variable, variables have the type of the last value assigned to it. Consequently, this also means variables in JavaScript can change types dynamically.

JavaScript is considered a functional language, meaning functions in JavaScript are first class citizens, and a function is just another object like anything else. You can pass functions as parameters, usually referred to as callbacks, return functions, and even instantiate them.

For many years, JavaScript hasn't had a steady and rapid update pace. At the time web apps started to grow steadily, the version was ES5, which was released in 2009. During this time, JavaScript developers suffered mostly around encapsulation. Even though there were good practices to achieve proper encapsulation, many JavaScript developers were not aware of or keen on doing so. Then, with JavaScript ES6 (aka ES2015), JavaScript made a great leap forward. With this release, JavaScript developers enjoyed the addition of class-based object-oriented programming, modules, destructuring, generators, and more.

It's important to note that object-oriented-like programming was still possible even in ES5. The inheritance model of JavaScript is based on a prototype system wherein every object has a prototype that you can manipulate, and even extend an existing one. Actually, the built-in class-based programming that ships with ES6 is basically a syntactic sugar over the same underlying prototype system.

JavaScript, due to its dynamic nature, lacks static typing in what is usually referred to as being a strongly typed language. This can certainly present difficulties, especially in cases of large teams, changes of personnel, a big code base, and the use of external libraries. Thankfully, other languages have surfaced in order to improve this situation; currently leading the field are TypeScript and Flow. In addition to static typing, such languages provide additional benefits such as faster updates, experimental features, configurable project-specific adjustments, external type definitions, and more.

Notable progress and future development

The web development field keeps evolving rapidly, from minor frameworks to complete platforms and tooling support. In particular, there are two advancements that have been growing into maturity for quite some time now:

- Web components
- WebAssembly

Although these two have been in the works for a while now, support has been spreading widely more recently as many browsers and frameworks are starting to adopt them.

Web components

Web components are a declared standard of features that allow developers to extend the HTML structure with new elements, as well as encapsulate styles and behavior. One of the main reasons developers choose a modern component-based framework is to have the ability to decompose their app into smaller units, namely components.

Web components are comprised of key features that enable this scenario:

- Custom elements enable extending HTML with new elements.
- Shadow DOMs allow encapsulation of DOM and styles.
- HTML import supports external sources.
- HTML templates let you construct repeatable structures at will.

The fact that such capability is now met as standard can be quite revolutionary. Now one can develop such components using basic HTML, CSS, and JavaScript. The beautiful thing behind it is that it's really a standard, meaning others can use these components in any other app and any other framework they might be using.

This is certainly a good start in the right direction; however, that does not really accommodate every need to shift developers from choosing modern component frameworks. Those frameworks still provide a handful of benefits, such as data binding, component interaction, optimized rendering, and some sort of change detection or reconciliation. To emphasize, you can actually use modern frameworks to build standard web components. If you're interested in that, you can read further about Stencil, Angular Elements, and Vue CLI Web Components Build Target.

WebAssembly

By default, the behavior language for browsers has always been JavaScript; unfortunately, a key caveat is the fact that it's an interpreted language that incurs the performance penalty. Wouldn't it be great if browsers supported some binary code format instead? Definitely! That's **WebAssembly (Wasm)**. The idea is that developers can now use higher-level languages, for instance, C++, Rust, C#, Java, and compile those to Wasm standardized binary format.

The benefit is not just performance as it creates new opportunities to do cross-platform development across multiple technologies. Wasm is importable in JavaScript, hence we might consider using it as a bridge between these technologies. Additionally, browsers are not the only platform that can execute Wasm; server-side platforms can do that too, which means it can be used for server-side processes such as server-side rendering, headless computing, and so on. With Wasm, developers can actually develop complete browser-based apps and not use JavaScript. There are already several technologies that take advantage of this, for example, Xamarin, and Blazor.

The Everyday Market app

Let's get you familiar with the app you're going to build throughout this book. Fortunately, you have implemented a REST API as part of previous chapters, so let's build on top of that. The REST API provides state and functionality for a basic exchange system in which people can purchase and sell items.

The Everyday Market app is the frontend web app that uses this REST API.

It consists of three key areas:

- Homepage with product listings
- Product page
- New product page

The following are the wireframes that illustrate the concept of the app.

Homepage with product listings

The following is the home page of the app. As you can see, the following functionality is implied:

- The user sees a list of available products filtered by a category.
- The user can click a product card to view its details.
- The user can add a new product that they wish to sell:

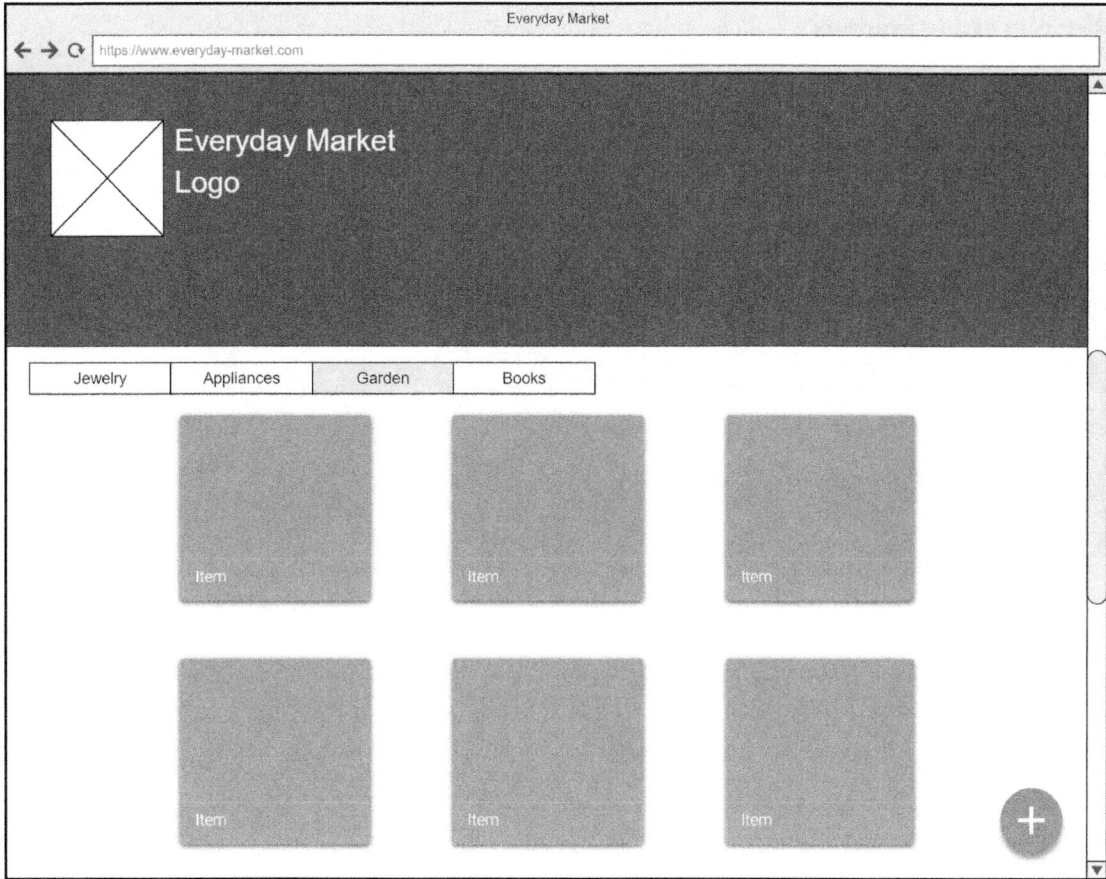

Everyday Market

https://www.everyday-market.com

Everyday Market
Logo

| Jewelry | Appliances | Garden | Books |

Item

Item

Item

Item

Item

Item

Product page

The following is the product page, which includes the product details, such as title, description, and so on. It is shown after the user selects a product in the home page:

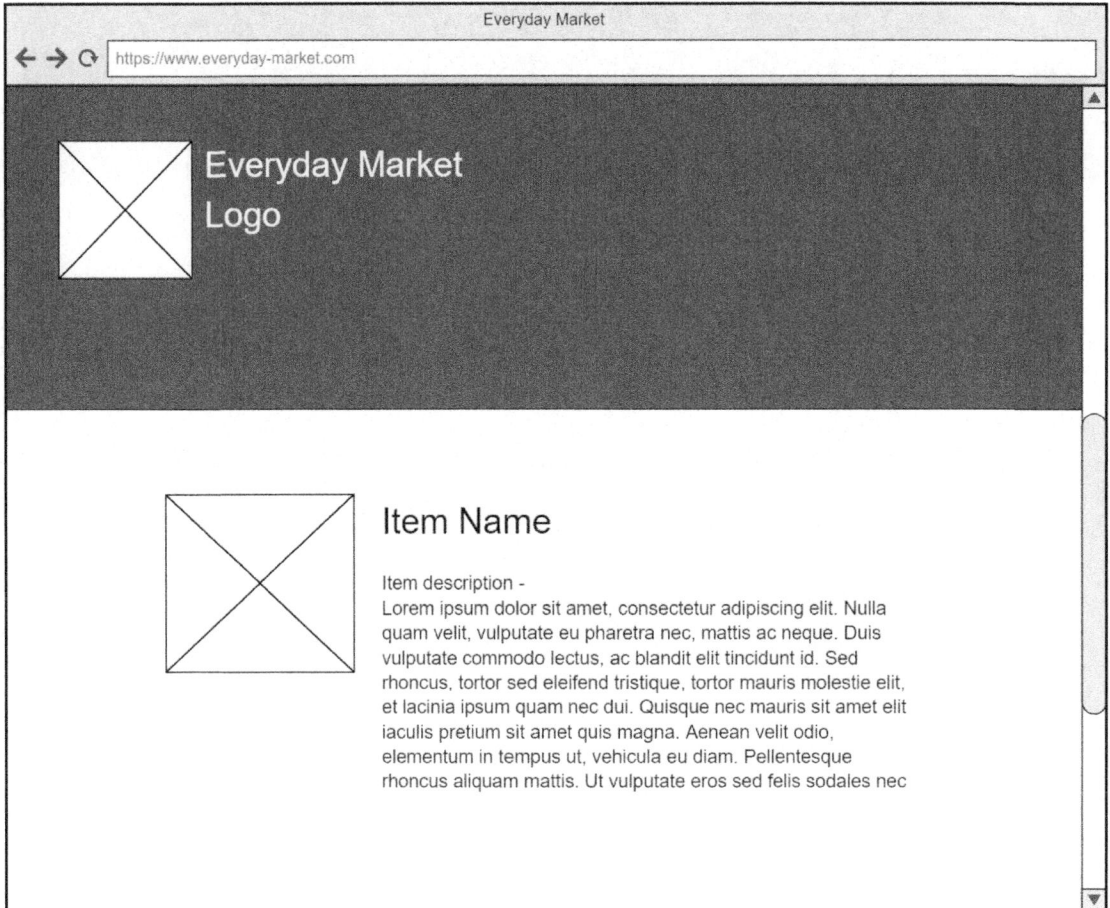

New product page

The following is the new product page shown when the user chooses to sell a new product. The page includes a basic form into which the user is required to populate fields and submit it:

Everyday Market

← → ↻ https://www.everyday-market.com

Everyday Market
Logo

Sell an item

Name   Enter item name...

Category   Books ▼

Description Multi-line
             textarea

             Save

> You can find all the code of Everyday Market at `https://github.com/`
> `azuker/frontend-web-dev`.

jQuery

Now that you are familiar with the app, let's see how to implement the home page of the app using jQuery. The assumption is that you are already experienced with jQuery, thus the purpose isn't to teach it, but rather to illustrate a standard implementation with what was considered the best framework for web developers for quite some time.

jQuery is a JavaScript library that enables developers to build multi-browser web apps that require some sort of client-side logic and manipulations. When jQuery entered the field, it certainly caused a great buzz. With it, developers could support various browsers quite easily. Moreover, standard and mundane client-side tasks that previously required some time to code have become a breeze with jQuery.

Breaking down jQuery, its key feature areas are the following:

- DOM selectors and manipulation fluent API
- Events
- Ajax and asynchrony
- Effects

Furthermore, jQuery is extensible through plugins. Actually, the ecosystem of plugins for jQuery is astonishing in size, there's nearly everything you're ever going to need to build modern apps.

Why do we need anything else then?

jQuery has certainly given us a lot, but it is not yet a productive framework that enables us to decompose our app into a real reusable and encapsulated components structure. Additionally, modern frameworks provide us with additional benefits such as optimized HTML DOM updates, data binding, and more.

Next, let's build the main functionality of the Everyday Market app homepage using jQuery.

Everyday Market homepage using jQuery

In the glory days when jQuery ruled the field, developers used JavaScript ES5. Following this notion, the sample code demonstrated here, for the most part, is written in ES5 too.

Initial layout

To begin with, let's create the initial layout of the page:

1. Create a file called `index.html` and write the following HTML:

```html
<html>
  <head>
    <title>Everyday Market</title>
    <link rel="stylesheet" type="text/css" href="app.css">
    <link rel="stylesheet" type="text/css"
href="http://code.jquery.com/ui/1.12.1/themes/base/jquery-ui.min.cs
s">
    <script src="https://code.jquery.com/jquery-3.3.1.min.js">
    </script>
    <script
src="https://code.jquery.com/ui/1.12.1/jquery-ui.min.js"></script>
  </head>
  <body>
    <header class="app-header app-bg">
      <div class="maxHeight flex flex-align-items--center">
        <img src="images/logo.png" class="app-logo" />
        <span class="app-slogan">Shop 'till you Drop</span>
      </div>
    </header>
    <div class="app-main">
    </div>
  </body>
</html>
```

2. Create a file named `app.css` and add the relevant CSS:

```css
html {
    box-sizing: border-box;
    font-size: 62.5%; /* =10px */
}

*, *:before, *:after {
    box-sizing: inherit;
}
```

```
html, body {
    margin: 0;
    padding: 0;
    width: 100%;
    height: 100%;
}

body {
    font-size: 1.4rem;
}

.hidden {
    display: none !important;
}

.app-header {
    height: 100px;
    border-bottom: 1px solid black;
}

.app-header::after {
    content: "";
    height: 100px;
    opacity: 0.5;
    background: url('images/herobg.jpg');
    background-position: center;
    background-repeat: no-repeat;
    background-size: cover;
    position: absolute;
    top: 0;
    left: 0;
    bottom: 0;
    right: 0;
    z-index: -1;
  }

.app-logo {
    height: 80px;
    margin-left: 50px;
}

.app-slogan {
    font-family: 'Comic Sans MS', 'Comic Sans', cursive;
    font-weight: bold;
    margin-left: 5px;
}

.app-main {
```

```
        padding-top: 10px;
        background-color: rgb(236,236,236);
        height: calc(100% - 100px);
        width: 100%;
        position: relative;
        top: 0; lefT:0;
    }

    .clear-fix {
        clear: both;
        float: none;
    }

    .maxHeight {
        height: 100%;
    }

    .flex {
        display: flex;
    }

    .flex-justify-content--center {
        justify-content: center;
    }

    .flex-align-items--center {
        align-items: center;
    }
```

If you look closely, both the HTML and CSS reference two images: `logo.png` and
`herobg.jpg`.

To see these images, make sure to place these files in a folder named `images` located where
the HTML and CSS files are.

You can now view the HTML page in your browser and see the basic layout of the page, it
should look similar to this:

REST API access

After creating the initial layout, let's implement the API access layer by encapsulating it in its own dedicated file and namespace:

1. Create a file named `api.js` and implement the REST API query calls:

```
'use-strict';

(function (window) {
  const ns = window.api = window.api || {};
  // EDIT the URL with the the address of your REST API -
  const baseUrl = 'http://localhost:55564/api';

  // build the URL for a REST API call and include the
parameters
  function getApiAction(action, parameters = null) {
    const p = (!parameters || parameters.length === 0)
      ? ''
      : `/${Object.values(parameters).join('/')}`;
    return `${baseUrl}/${action}${p}`;
  }

  // iterate through products returned from REST API and set
the primary image accordingly for each product
  function visitProducts(products, callback) {
    products.forEach(p => {
      if (p.media && p.media.length > 0) {
        p.primaryImage = p.media[0].url;
      }
    });

    if (callback) callback(products);
  }
  // expose a function to load products from the REST API as
part of the namespace object
  ns.getProducts = function (category, callback) {
    return $.getJSON(getApiAction('products/searchcategory',
category),
      data => visitProducts(data, callback));
  }

  // expose a function to load categories from the REST API as
part of the namespace object
  ns.getCategories = function (callback) {
    return $.getJSON(getApiAction('products/categories'),
callback);
  }
```

```
}) (window);
```

2. Edit the `baseUrl` constant with the base URL of your hosted REST API:

```
// EDIT the URL with the the address of your REST API -
const baseUrl = 'http://localhost:55564/api';
```

Menu item template

Before you query for categories, let's use a basic template approach for dynamically adding category menu items. There are a number of ways to do templating; in this instance, you use a simple regex string formatting approach:

1. Add the HTML template for the dynamically added category menu items to `index.html`:

```html
<script type="text/template" data-template="menu-item">
  <li
    class="${className}"
    categoryName="${name}"
  >
    ${name}
  </li>
</script>
```

2. Add the relevant CSS to `app.css`:

```css
#menu {
    border: 0;
    padding-left: 10px;
}

.ui-menu:after {
    content: "";
    display: block;
    visibility: hidden;
    line-height: 0;
    height: 0;
}

.ui-menu .ui-menu-item {
    display: inline-block;
    float: left;
    width: auto;
}
```

```css
.ui-menu {
    margin: 0;
    padding: 0;
}

.ui-menu-item {
    border: 1px solid black;
    padding: 2px 5px 2px 5px;
}

.ui-menu-item:hover {
    background-color: lightgray;
}

.menu-selected {
    background-color: bisque;
}
```

Category menu items query

You are now ready to add the horizontal menu and query for the categories list:

1. Add the HTML in bold to index.html:

```html
<div class="app-main">
  <div>
    <ul id="menu"></ul>
  </div>
</div>
```

2. Create a file named app.js, then implement a categories query and execute it when the app loads:

```js
const templatesCache = {};

function render(props) {
  return function(tok, i) { return (i % 2) ? props[tok] : tok;
};
}

// a basic templating approach that uses regex for formatting
specified props into the relevant placeholders in the template
function renderTemplate(templateName, props) {
  let template = templatesCache[templateName];
  if (!template) {
    // reserve templates in cache for future quicker access
    template = $(`script[data-
```

```
    template="${templateName}"]`).text()
      .split(/\$\{(.+?)\}/g);
    templatesCache[templateName] = template;
  }

  // map every placeholder to a matching specified prop and
build the finalized HTML
  return template.map(render(props)).join('');
}

function loadCategories(callback) {
  const menu = $('#menu');

  window.api.getCategories(items => {
    items[0].className = 'menu-selected';
    menu.append(items.map(item => renderTemplate('menu-item',
item)));

    if (callback) callback();
  });
}

function setupAppMenu() {
  $('#menu').menu({items: "li"});
  $('#menu > li').click(e => {
    $('#menu > li').removeClass('menu-selected');
    $(e.currentTarget).toggleClass('menu-selected');
  });
}

function bootstrapApp() {
  loadCategories(setupAppMenu);
}

$(bootstrapApp);
```

3. Add references to the relevant scripts in `index.html`:

```
...
  <script src="api.js"></script>
  <script src="app.js"></script>
</body>
```

You can now view the page and see the menu and populated categories in action, it should look similar to this -

Product item template

Before you query for products, let's use a basic template approach for dynamically adding product cards:

1. Add the HTML template for the dynamically added product cards to `index.html`:

```
<script type="text/template" data-template="product-item">
  <div class="item-card">
  <div class="item-card-content-container">
  <img class="item-card-content-container-img"
  src="${primaryImage}" />
  <span class="item-card-content-container-title">${title}
  </span>
  <span class="item-card-content-container-
  text">${description}</span>
  </div>
  </div>
</script>
```

2. Add the relevant CSS to `app.css`:

```
.item-card {
    box-shadow: 0 4px 8px 0 rgba(0,0,0,0.2);
    transition: 0.3s;
    background-color: white;
    width: 280px;
    height: 200px;
    float: left;
    margin: 10;
}
```

```
.item-card:hover {
    box-shadow: 0 8px 16px 0 rgba(0,0,0,0.2);
}

.item-card-content-container {
    padding: 2px 16px;
    display: flex;
    height: 100%;
    flex-direction: column;
    align-items: center;
    justify-content: center;
    cursor: hand;
}

.item-card-content-container-img {
  display: block;
  max-width: 80px;
  max-height: 80px;
  width: auto;
  height: auto;
  text-align: center;
}

.item-card-content-container-title {
    display: block;
    font-size: 1.6rem;
}

.item-card-content-container-text {
    word-wrap: normal;
    font-size: 1.2rem;
    overflow: hidden;
}
```

Product cards query

You are now ready to query for products from the REST API and display them in the page:

1. Add the HTML in bold to `index.html`:

```
<div class="app-main">
  <div>
    <ul id="menu"></ul>
  </div>
  <div id="productsContainer" class="clear-fix"></div>
  <div class="clear-fix"></div>
</div>
```

2. Implement a products query and execute it when a category changes by adding the code in bold to `app.js`:

```
function syncProducts() {
  const productsContainer = $('#productsContainer');
  const category = $('#menu > li').filter('.menu-
    selected').attr('categoryName');

  productsContainer.empty();
  window.api.getProducts(category, items => {
    productsContainer.append(
      items.map(item => renderTemplate('product-item', item)));
  });
}

function setupAppMenu() {
  $('#menu').menu({items: "li"});
  $('#menu > li').click(e => {
    $('#menu > li').removeClass('menu-selected');
    $(e.currentTarget).toggleClass('menu-selected');
    syncProducts();
  });

  syncProducts();
}
```

Busy indicator

Let's complete our page by adding a simple busy indicator spinner:

1. Add the HTML in bold to `index.html`:

```
<div id="productsContainer" class="clear-fix"></div>
<div class="clear-fix"></div>
<div id="wait" class="loader-container hidden">
  <div class="loader"></div>
</div>
```

2. Add the relevant CSS to `app.css`:

```
.loader-container {
    position: absolute;
    left: 0; right: 0; top: 0; bottom: 0;
    background-color: azure;
    opacity: 0.5;
    display: flex;
    align-items: center;
```

```
        justify-content: center;
    }

    .loader {
        border: 16px solid #f3f3f3;
        border-top: 16px solid #3498db;
        border-radius: 50%;
        width: 80px;
        height: 80px;
        animation: spin 2s linear infinite;
    }

    @keyframes spin {
        0% { transform: rotate(0deg); }
        100% { transform: rotate(360deg); }
    }
```

3. Implement spinner activation in `app.js` by adding the JavaScript in bold:

```
function hideBusyIndicator() {
  $('#wait').addClass('hidden');
}

function showBusyIndicator() {
  $('#wait').removeClass('hidden');
}

function syncProducts() {
  const productsContainer = $('#productsContainer');
  const category = $('#menu > li').filter('.menu-
selected').attr('categoryName');

  productsContainer.empty();
  showBusyIndicator();

  window.api.getProducts(category, items => {
    productsContainer.append(
      items.map(item => renderTemplate('product-item', item)));
    hideBusyIndicator();
  });
}

function loadCategories(callback) {
  const menu = $('#menu');
  showBusyIndicator();

  window.api.getCategories(items => {
    items[0].className = 'menu-selected';
```

```
      menu.append(items.map(item => renderTemplate('menu-item',
item)));
    hideBusyIndicator();

    if (callback) callback();
  });
}
```

Congratulations! You have just finished implementing the app's home page. You can now view the complete result in the browser and see it in action, it should look similar to this -

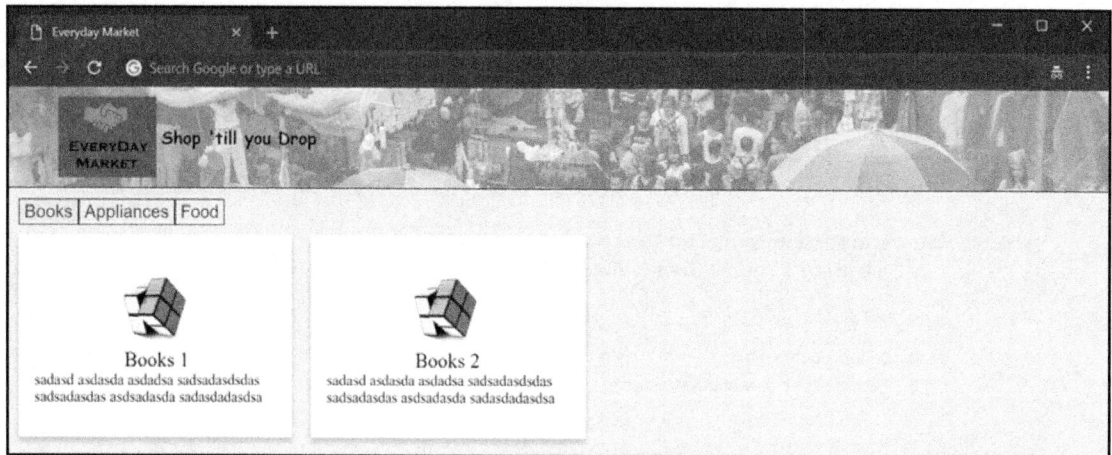

Summary

Web development has taken its place as one of the most open platforms and in-demand fields today. Using web technologies, one can leverage the same skill set to build software targeting nearly every platform, be that microservices, serverless, desktop, mobile, browser, or IoT.

In this chapter, we reviewed some background and current development in the realm of the web while focusing on the cornerstones of web technologies — HTML, CSS, and JavaScript. Additionally, we illustrated the Everyday Market app built throughout the book, and finished with a practical example of how one would implement a portion of that using jQuery.

Now that we have these fundamentals covered, we can begin the journey into modern frameworks and technologies in frontend web development. Next, we focus on TypeScript.

Getting Started with TypeScript 9

JavaScript, being a flexible scripting language along with its dynamic type system, can become harder to maintain the more a project scales up and as the team's staff changes. There are many tools and languages that can assist with this situation, one of which is TypeScript.

In this chapter, you'll become a TypeScript programmer as we cover its fundamentals:

- TypeScript compiler
- Types
- Interfaces
- Classes
- Modules
- Decorators

First, let's start with an overview of TypeScript.

TypeScript

Back in the day when JavaScript ES5 was the active version, writing JavaScript code that adhered to encapsulation and modularity was not a trivial task. Things such as prototypes, namespaces, and self-executing functions could certainly improve your code; unfortunately, many JavaScript developers did not invest the necessary effort to improve the manageability of their code using those constructs.

Consequently, new technologies surfaced to help with this matter; a popular example relevant at that time was CoffeeScript. Then, JavaScript ES6 was released. ES6, with its great added features, such as modules, classes, and more specific variable scoping, basically overturned CoffeeScript and similar alternatives at that time.

Evidently, JavaScript is still missing a key feature, and that is type information. JavaScript's dynamic type system is a strong feature at times; unfortunately, the manageability and reusability of existing code suffers due to this fact. For that key purpose, every large-scale project should examine the use of tools that compensate the situation; those leading the field now are TypeScript and Flow.

TypeScript, an open source scripting language, is developed and maintained by Microsoft. Its killer feature is bringing static typing to JavaScript-based systems and allowing you to annotate the code with type information. Additionally, it supports augmenting existing JavaScript code with external type information, similar to the header files pattern, as it's commonly known in C++.

TypeScript is a superset of JavaScript, that meaning it has seamless integration with JavaScript, and makes JavaScript developers feel right at home. Being a JavaScript developer makes you a TypeScript developer as well since JavaScript code is actually valid TypeScript. Importantly, this makes the gradual upgrade of existing JavaScript code fairly easy.

Another example of how great TypeScript is is the fact that Angular, a framework built by Google, adopts it extensively, and is actually implemented in TypeScript internally.

The TypeScript compiler

TypeScript is a superset of JavaScript, yet browsers and other platforms don't recognize it, nor are they able to execute it. For that purpose, TypeScript is processed by the TypeScript compiler, which transpiles your TypeScript code to JavaScript. Then, you can run the transpiled code basically everywhere JavaScript is supported.

The `tsc` is available as an `npm` package that you can install globally. Open your favorite terminal and install it using the following command:

```
npm install -g typescript
```

Afterwards, you can use the command `tsc` to execute the `tsc`:

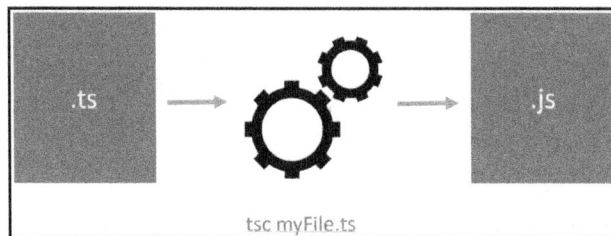

tsc myFile.ts

TypeScript files have a .ts file extension; this is where you write your TypeScript code. When needed, you use the TypeScript compiler to transpile your TypeScript code, which creates the JavaScript implementation of the code; you do that by executing the following command:

```
tsc <typescript_filename>
```

Types

One of the key features of TypeScript is bringing static typing to JavaScript. In TypeScript, you annotate your code with type information; every declaration can be defined with its associated typing.

In the declaration, you do that by adding a colon following the type. For example, the following statement defines a variable of type number:

```
const productsCount: number;
```

Annotating your code with type information enables validation. The TypeScript compiler should throw errors if you try to do anything that is not supported by the specified type, thus productivity and discoverability benefit substantially through type safety. Additionally, with proper tooling support, you get IntelliSense support and automatic code completion.

TypeScript supports a handful of types to reflect most constructs in JavaScript. We will cover these next, starting with basic types.

Basic types

TypeScript supports a handful of built-in types; the following are examples of the most common ones:

```
const fullName: string = "John Doe";
const age: number = 6;
const isDone: boolean = false;
const d: Date = new Date();
const canBeAnything: any = 6;
```

As you can see, TypeScript supports basic primitive types such as string, number, boolean, and date.

Another thing to notice is the type `any`. The `any` type is a valid TypeScript type that indicates that the declaration can be of any given type and all operations on it should be allowed and considered safe.

Arrays

TypeScript arrays can be written in one of two ways. You can specify the item type followed by square brackets or you can use the generic `Array` type as follows:

```
const list: number[] = [1, 2, 3];
const list: Array<number> = [1, 2, 3];
```

Enums

Enums allow you to specify named values that correspond to numeric or string values. If you don't manually set the associated corresponding value, the named values in the enum are numbered, starting at 0 by default. Enums are extremely useful, and are commonly used to represent a set of predefined options or lookup values.

In TypeScript, you define enums by using the `enum` keyword as follows:

```
enum Color {Red, Green, Blue}
const c: Color = Color.Red;
```

Objects

In JavaScript, objects contain key/value pairs that form the shape of the object. TypeScript supports object types as well, very similar to how you write plain JavaScript objects.

Consider the following plain JavaScript object:

```
const obj = {
   x: 5,
   y: 6
}
```

In the preceding code, `obj` is a plain object defined with two keys, `x` and `y`, both with number values.

To define an object type in TypeScript, you use a similar format — curly braces to represent an object, inside the keys, and their type information:

```
{ x:number, y:number }
```

Together, this is how you associate a type to an object:

```
const obj: { x:number, y:number } = {
    x: 5,
    y: 6
}
```

In the preceding code, the `obj` object is initialized the same as before, only now along with its type information, which is marked in bold.

Functions

Functions have type information as well. Functions are comprised of parameters and a return value:

```
function buildName(firstName: string, lastName: string): string {
    return firstName + " " + lastName;
}
```

Each parameter is annotated with its type, and then the return value's type is added at the end of the function signature.

Unlike JavaScript, TypeScript enforces calls to functions to adhere to the defined signature. For example, if you try to call the function with anything other than two string parameters, the TypeScript compiler will not allow it.

You can define more flexible function signatures if you like. TypeScript supports defining optional parameters by using the question mark symbol, ?:

```
function buildName(firstName: string, lastName: string, title?: string):
string {
    return title + " " + firstName + " " + lastName;
}

const name = buildName('John', 'Doe'); // valid call
```

The preceding function can now be called with either 2 or 3 string parameters.

> Everything in JavaScript is still supported, of course. You can still use ES6 default parameter values and rest parameters as well.

Type inference

Until now, the illustrated code included the type information in the same statement where the actual value assignment took place. TypeScript supports type inference, meaning that it tries to resolve the relevant type information if you don't specify any.

Let's look at some examples:

```
const count = 2;
```

In the preceding simple example, TypeScript is smart enough to realize that the type of count is a number without you having to explicitly specify that:

```
function sum(x1: number, x2: number) {
        return x1 + x2;
}

const mySum = sum(1, 2);
```

The preceding example demonstrates the power of type inference in TypeScript. If you pay close attention, the code doesn't specify the return value type of the sum function. TypeScript evaluates the code and determines that the return type is number in this case. As a result, the type of the variable mySum is also a number.

Type inference is an extremely useful feature since it saves us the incredible time that would be otherwise spent in adding endless type information.

Type casting

Having the code statically typed leads to type safety. TypeScript does not let you perform actions that are not considered safe and supported.

In the following example, the `loadProducts` function is defined with a return value of type any, thus the type of `products` is inferred as any:

```
function loadProducts(): any {
    return [{name: 'Book1'}, {name: 'Book2'}];
}

const products = loadProducts(); // products is of type 'any'
```

In some cases, you may actually know the expected type. You can instruct TypeScript of the type by using a cast. Typecasting in TypeScript is supported by using the as an operator or the use of angle brackets, as follows:

```
const products = loadProducts() as {name: string}[];
const products = <{name: string}[]>loadProducts();
```

Using the preceding cast, you have full support and recognition by TypeScript that `products` is now an array of objects with a `name` key.

Type aliasing

TypeScript supports defining new types via type aliases. You can use type aliases to reuse type information in multiple declarations, for example:

```
type person = {name: string};
let employee: person;
let contact: person;
```

Given the preceding example, the code defines a type alias named `person` as an object with a `name` key of type `string`. Afterwards, the rest of the code can reference this type where needed.

Type aliases are somewhat similar to interfaces (covered next), but can name primitives, unions, and tuples. Unlike interfaces, type aliases cannot be extended or implemented from, and so interfaces are generally preferred.

> Unions and intersections allow you to construct a type from multiple existing types, while tuples express arrays with a fixed number of known elements. You can read more about these at https://www.typescriptlang.org/docs/handbook/basic-types.html and https://www.typescriptlang.org/docs/handbook/advanced-types.html.

Interfaces

Interfaces allow you to construct the shape of certain implementation. Interfaces should not really be a new concept to you considering your background in .NET, and in TypeScript it is very much the same.

Interfaces are defined using the keyword `interface`, as follows:

```
enum Operand {
    Sum, Subtract, Multiply, Divide
}

interface Calculable {
    left: number;
    right: number;
    operand: Operand;
}
```

Furthermore, interfaces support optional members and read-only properties, too:

```
interface Calculable {
    readonly left: number;
    readonly right: number;
    operand?: Operand;
}
```

In the preceding example, the `Calculable` interface has two `readonly` properties, `left` and `right`, as well as an optional `operand` property. Read-only declarations can only be set when first initialized or inside the constructor of the owning class.

Like other interface-supporting languages, you can code a certain hierarchy of interfaces by extending them.

Extending interfaces

Just like in .NET, interfaces can extend one another:

```
interface Serializable {
    serialize(): string;
}

interface PersistedCalculable extends Calculable, Serializable {
    shouldSaveInHistory: boolean;
}
```

In the preceding example, the `PersistedCalculable` interface extends two interfaces. In addition to its own members, it includes all the members defined in the extended interfaces, `Calculable` and `Serializable`.

Classes

Like interfaces, classes should not be a new concept to you due to your background in .NET. Classes enable you to define state and behavior in a single unit while promoting encapsulation and reuse. TypeScript supports classes and they look very much like ES6 classes. The following is a simple example of a `Calculator` class with a single `sum` function:

```
class Calculator {
        sum(left: number, right: number): number {
                return left + right;
        }
}

const calc = new Calculator();
console.log(calc.sum(2,3));
```

Access modifiers

Similar to .NET, TypeScript allows you to define access modifiers to class members. This is a great feature as it expands your ability to author well-designed, encapsulated, and safer code. In JavaScript, for example, a common convention to represent private and internal code is to use an underscore (_) prefix, which should no longer be needed.

TypeScript classes support multiple access modifiers – private, protected, and public (default):

- **Private**: Members are accessible from within the instance of the same class
- **Public**: Members are accessible everywhere
- **Protected**: Members are accessible from within the instance of the same or a derived class

Consider the following example:

```
class SumCalculator {
    protected history: Calculable[] = [];
```

```
        constructor(private saveHistory: boolean) { }

    sum(left: number, right: number): number {
        return this.calcCore(left, right);
    }

    private calcCore(left: number, right: number): number {
        if (this.saveHistory) this.history.push({left, right});
        return left + right;
    }
}

const calc = new SumCalculator();
console.log(calc.sum(2,3));
```

If you look closely, the preceding example defines an access modifier for the constructor argument `saveHistory`. TypeScript supports this special construct to ease a very common need. More often than not, constructor arguments are simply being set to instance fields, and that is exactly the effect in place.

If you add an access modifier or read-only to a constructor argument, TypeScript sets an instance field with the same name to the value of the argument automatically for you.

For example, both of the following statements are equivalent:

```
class SumCalculator {
    private saveHistory: boolean;
    constructor(saveHistory: boolean) {
        this.saveHistory = saveHistory;
    }
}

class SumCalculator {
    constructor(private saveHistory: boolean) {}
}
```

Members

In JavaScript ES6, classes support different types of members, such as methods and properties. TypeScript enriches that by bringing fields, read-only fields, and static members. Consider the following example:

```
class SumCalculator {
    static readonly supportedOperand = Operand.Sum;

    private _history: Calculable[] = [];
```

```
    get history() { return this._history; }
    set history(value: Calculable[]) {
        this._history = value || [];
    }

    constructor(private readonly logPrefix: string) { }

    logHistory() {
        console.log(
            `${this.logPrefix}: current history length:
${this.history.length}`);
    }
}

console.log(SumCalculator.supportedOperand);
const calc = new SumCalculator('MyApp');
calc.history = [{left: 2, right: 3}];
calc.logHistory();
```

In the preceding code, you can see different usages of properties, static, and read-only members:

- `supportedOperand` is a static and a read-only member. Static, just like in C#, means that the member is allocated and accessed at the class-level and not per class instance, that is, `SumCalculator.supportedOperand`.
- `history` is a property with a `getter` and a `setter` on top of the private `_history` field. In the setter, it makes sure that the history is not set to null.
- `logPrefix` is a constructor argument that is set as a private and a `readonly` field, thanks to the support of TypeScript for such shorthand techniques.

Class inheritance and interface implementation

Just like in .NET, TypeScript classes can inherit from only one class, but can implement as many interfaces as desired.

Inheritance is defined by using the `extends` keyword, while interface implementation uses the `implements` keyword, as follows:

```
interface Calculator {
    calc(left: number, right: number): number;
}

interface Printable {
    print();
```

```
    }

    class HistoryCalculator {
        protected history = [];
        protected logHistory() {
            console.log(`current history length: ${this.history.length}`);
        }
    }

    class SumCalculator extends HistoryCalculator implements Calculator,
    Printable {
        calc(left: number, right: number): number {
            this.history.push({left, right});
            return left + right;
        }

        print() {
            this.logHistory();
        }
    }

    const calc = new SumCalculator();
    console.log(calc.calc(2,3));
    calc.print();
```

In the preceding example, two interfaces are defined: `Calculator` with a `calc` function and `Printable` with a `print` function.

Then, a class called `HistoryCalculator` is defined that states that other calculator classes can derive from and get this specific history implementation.

Then, we have the class called `SumCalculator`, which inherits from `HistoryCalculator` and implements the two interfaces.
As you can see, `SumCalculator` is required to implement the declared members of the interfaces and is able to use the derived state and behavior from `HistoryCalculator`.

Modules

TypeScript modules are quite similar to ES6 modules, so you should be familiar with their construct already. Modules enable encapsulation and reuse, and allow dependency order resolution.

The scope of TypeScript modules are bound to files. Every file is a module and its internal declarations should not conflict with anything external. When a module desires to expose a declaration, such as a function, class, and even a constant, you can use the export keyword. On the other hand, if a module needs an exported member from another module, the import keyword is used.

Moreover, the TypeScript compiler supports generating TypeScript modules out to several formats, for example, CommonJS, ES6, and more. This means that you can use TypeScript with different module loaders, including Node.js and Webpack.

Just like ES6, TypeScript modules support default, named, and wildcard import and export statements. Consider the following exported utility functions that have been implemented in the log.ts file:

```
// log.ts

export default function(o: any) { console.log(o); }

export function logArray(o: any[]) {
    console.log(`Array (length: ${o.length}`, o);
}

function appLog(o: any) { console.log('MyApp Log Entry', o); }
export { appLog };
```

When another file needs to use these functions, it looks like this:

```
// app.ts

import log, { logArray as logA, appLog } from './log';
import * as logUtils from './log';

log(5);
logA([2, 3]);
appLog(4);
logUtils.default(5);
logUtils.logArray([2, 3]);
logUtils.appLog(5);
```

As you can see, the format is identical to standard ES6 modules.

Decorators

Decorators are a stage 2 proposal feature for JavaScript and are available as an experimental feature of TypeScript. Decorators, at their core, are just functions. Such functions can be used on different kinds of declarations, such as classes and their members, as well as parameters.

Decorators can emit metadata that can be inspected later by other code or processes, enabling a meta-programming style. Considering your background in .NET, you can think about TypeScript decorators as .NET attributes. Unlike .NET attributes, though, decorator functions can actually manipulate the decorated code.

Decorators are considered a somewhat advanced feature of TypeScript and there's much to learn in that regard. The depth of this feature is not in the scope of this chapter yet, so it is important that you get you familiar with it since Angular uses it quite extensively.

The following is an example of a simple class decorator that logs to the console every time a decorated class is instantiated:

```
function logClassInit(target: any) {
    // preserve a reference to the original constructor
    const original = target;

    // a class instance factory
    function construct(constructor, args) {
      const c: any = () => constructor.apply(this, args);
      c.prototype = constructor.prototype;
      return new c();
    }
    // the new constructor behavior
    const f: any = (...args) => {
      console.log("Instantiated: " + original.name);
      return construct(original, args);
    };

    // copy prototype so intanceof operator still works
    f.prototype = original.prototype;
    // return new constructor (will override original)
    return f;
}

@logClassInit
class Person {}

const p = new Person(); // logs to the console: `Instantiated: Person`
```

In the preceding example, the decorator `logClassInit` is implemented and, as you can see, it's just a function. The implementation is basically replacing the constructor with a utility one that logs to the console and then uses the original constructor.

Decorators are applied using the at sign, `@`. In the preceding code, you can see that the decorator is applied to the `Person` class by annotating it with the decorator function (`@logClassInit`). Now, whenever the code instantiates `Person`, a log is written to the console.

> Decorators are an experimental feature in TypeScript.
> To support them, you must specify the `experimentalDecorators` flag when using `tsc`:
>
> `tsc --experimentalDecorators`

Summary

TypeScript is one of the most popular scripting languages in respect to JavaScript-based code bases. At its very core, it brings static typing and assists tremendously with maintainability and productivity.

In this chapter, we covered the fundamentals of TypeScript, including types, interfaces, classes, modules, and decorators. TypeScript advances at a steady pace and shows great promise for using it in large projects. It has more features that weren't addressed in this chapter, such as generics, mapped types, abstract classes, project references, and much more.

Now that you have learned TypeScript, we can proceed and learn about modern UI frameworks, starting with Angular.

Further reading

- If you want to learn more about TypeScript, then visit the TypeScript documentation website at `https://www.typescriptlang.org/docs/`
- You can find all the client-side related code in a public online repository at `https://github.com/azuker/frontend-web-dev`

10
App Development with Angular

Web apps have evolved to become rich clients in all senses of the phrase. The development of such modern apps benefits substantially from frameworks that provide developers with a rapid and manageable means of implementation.

The era of jQuery led projects to the point where the HTML DOM was highly coupled with the code—there was simply no productive separation of concerns. Additionally, rich apps usually ended up with performance issues due to the nature of browsers' flexibility toward the DOM, and the maintainability of such projects suffered greatly over time. While there was a way to improve the implementation in this regard while using jQuery, writing real encapsulated and reusable code with optimized performance was not for the faint of heart.

In this chapter, we unravel Angular, one of the leading frameworks that help developers rapidly implement and manage apps. Throughout this chapter, we will build the *Everyday Market* app using Angular, while covering Angular's fundamentals as well. The following topics will be covered:

- Angular overview
- Angular CLI
- Modules
- Components
- Data binding
- Component interaction
- Injectable services
- HTTP
- Distribution

First, let's start with an overview of Angular.

Angular overview

Google's Angular is a massively popular MV* JavaScript framework for building complex modern applications, be that for the web, mobile, or desktop. It comes with nearly everything you need to build complicated frontend apps, including powerful templates with fast rendering, data management, HTTP services, form handling, routing, modules, and more.

Historically, Google launched the first version, toward the end of 2010, of what they were proud to present as the best framework for SPA: AngularJS. The AngularJS framework relates to the former incarnation of today's Angular, which was given version numbers of 1.*x*. Interestingly, AngularJS is still quite active and continues to be updated.

Later, Google decided that AngularJS was not on par with recent progress made in the field of web UI development. Its structure and the way it was built made it difficult to improve its performance and design to meet future standards. Therefore, Google announced that they had been working on the successor to AngularJS, which was Angular. Confusingly, readers should note that while there are similarities in the high-level building blocks, these are actually two completely separate frameworks.

By the end of 2016, Google released its new Angular framework. Angular is a vast framework that provides a complete toolset intended to allow developers to build complete modern apps. This notion alone was met with quite a bit of controversy. On one hand, there are many developers who love the fact that they're handed nearly everything they need to build apps from start to finish. On the other hand, others tend to prefer the flexibility and freedom to employ their own formulation of toolsets for different parts of their applications.

Building blocks

Angular is one of the most comprehensive SPA frameworks available, as it attempts to provide almost everything you need to implement complete apps. Due to this fact, Angular brings quite a lot to the table.

Let's review the key application building blocks:

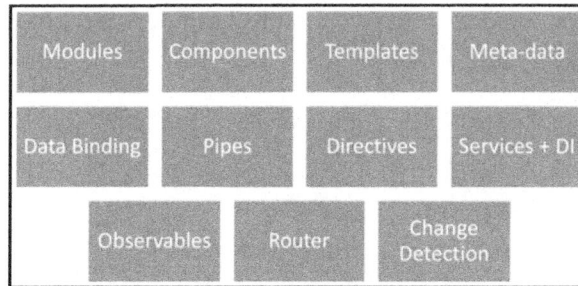

- **Modules**: Unrelated to ECMAScript or TypeScript modules, Angular modules are logical containers that encapsulate logical parts.
- **Components**: Angular enables you to decompose your app's visual tree into smaller reusable units called components.
- **Templates**: Angular adheres to MVC-style programming, meaning the view is separated from the component's logic. Views in Angular are called templates and consist mostly of plain HTML.
- **Metadata**: Angular uses metadata extensively, enabling declarative-style programming.
- **Router**: Angular Router enables you to implement client-side routing to support user-intuitive and shareable links.
- **Data binding**: Having the view and code separated can be a nuisance, as these usually need to interact with each other. To deal with this issue, enter data binding.
- **Directives**: Directives allow extending or customizing existing elements in all sorts of ways.
- **Pipes**: Pipes enable transforming values in an encapsulated and reusable way.
- **Services and dependency injection**: Angular promotes encapsulating business logic into application services. Dependency injections can be used to compose everything together.
- **Observables**: Angular enables advanced asynchronous patterns, such as observer, pub/sub, and sagas, with the use of **Reactive Extensions** (**RxJs**) and its observable APIs.
- **Change detection**: Leveraging Zone.js, Angular detects state changes and makes minimal updates to the HTML DOM to optimize app performance.

The preceding blocks are the key features you use in Angular apps. Actually, Angular is more than just an application framework as it is meant to be a real platform in the sense of providing everything you need to write, test, build, deploy, upgrade, and maintain the app. By that notion, the Angular platform adds more platform-oriented building blocks to the overall picture:

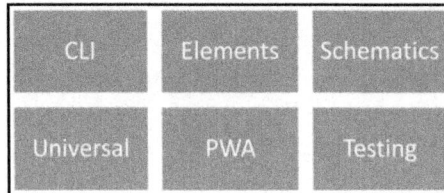

CLI	Elements	Schematics
Universal	PWA	Testing

- **Angular CLI**: A CLI tool provided by the team to assist you with starting and managing your project.
- **Elements**: Angular elements enable the implementation of components as standard web components that can improve interoperability between apps and technologies.
- **Schematics**: Angular CLI uses a schematics system to manage and execute its command system. You can use schematics to extend the command system to customize scaffolding, and even perform code alterations.
- **Universal**: Angular Universal enables isomorphic rendering in your Angular apps. In many projects, you might need to use server-side rendering, which can assist greatly with the initial time-to-render, as well as improve **search engine optimization (SEO)**.
- **Progressive web apps (PWA)**: PWA can be a quick and simple alternative to provide users a native-like mobile app experience. Angular provides a package that aims to assist developers to build their apps as PWAs.
- **Testing:** Angular provides rich support for testing all parts of your application and it is built-in as part of the tooling as well.

As you can see, there's much to learn when it comes to Angular. While many prefer the fact that much is provided out-of-the-box, others might see it as a constraint and choose an alternative instead.

Angular CLI

Angular CLI is an extremely useful tool when it comes to managing your Angular project. It provides all sorts of capabilities, such as creating projects, generating code, managing and upgrading packages, building and testing apps, and more.

Furthermore, Angular CLI-based projects are not just about the app itself. Such projects can actually contain multiple apps and libraries within, turning the project into something similar, in concept, to an actual workspace that contains multiple projects within.

Setup and common commands

Let's use Angular CLI to create and manage an Angular Everyday Market app.

First, open the Terminal or Command Prompt and install Angular CLI with the following steps:

1. Run the following command:

```
npm install -g @angular/cli
```

2. Afterward, the CLI should be installed, and you can start using it by executing the ng command.
3. Next, let's use the basic commands available as part of the CLI.

Using the Terminal, create our Everyday Market project:

1. Run the following command:

```
ng new everyday-market-ng
```

The ng new command creates new projects. When executed, it creates the folder with the specified name and scaffolds the entire project using Angular's preferred structure and recommended practices, in addition to installing the required dependencies.

Next, let's cover some more common commands in Angular CLI. In order to use these commands, make sure you enter them in the Terminal while you're located in the root folder of the project, which is everyday-market-ng.

Linting code

To lint code, execute the following in the Terminal:

Run the following command:

```
ng lint
```

The `ng lint` command runs the TypeScript linter on the source code. Linting is essentially static code analysis and assists immensely with maintaining code standards and conventions, as well as helping to find potential issues and bugs.

> You can configure the linter by specifying ruleset settings in the `tslint.json` file in the root of the project.

Running tests

To run standard tests, execute the following in the Terminal:

```
ng test
```

To run **end-to-end (e2e)** tests, execute the following in the Terminal:

```
ng e2e
```

Both of the preceding commands execute the tests that are implemented in your project. `ng test` is responsible for standard unit/integration tests. Don't be alarmed if the default tests that ship with the project template fail—they can be easily adjusted to work, although testing is not covered in this chapter.

The test-related frameworks and tooling Angular CLI-based projects are created with Jasmine, Karma, and Protractor.

There are many more built-in commands. Later in this chapter, you will use the popular `generate` command, which enables the creation of new parts in your application, such as components, services, and modules.

> **TIP**
>
> Angular CLI supports a useful help flag if you need to explore all options or get general instructions. To see it, try running the `ng serve --help` command.

Running the project

To run the project, execute the following in the Terminal:

```
ng serve
```

The `ng serve` command builds the app for development purposes, and spins up a development server to serve the app. You can now open the browser and access the app by browsing to `http://localhost:4200`.

The Terminal should appear similar to the following screenshot:

And the app itself should look something like the following:

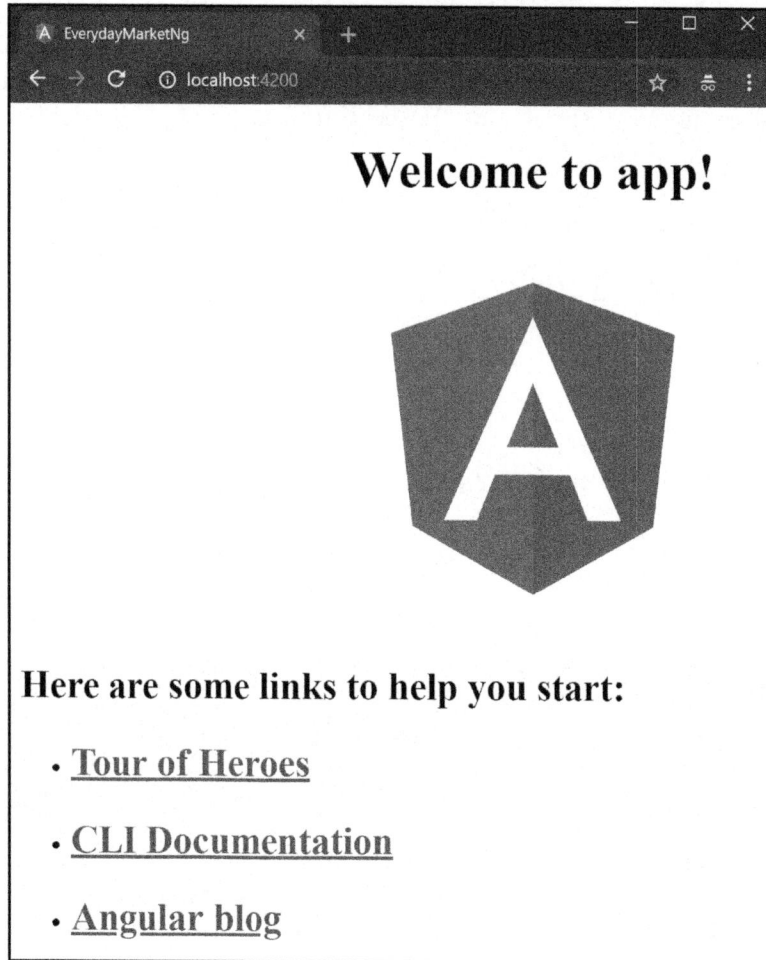

Furthermore, the development server supports hot reloading, meaning changing the code while the `serve` command is running. Hot reloading rebuilds and refreshes your app as you work, which greatly improves developer productivity.

> **TIP**
>
> Most commands have a set of additional options you can specify. For example, you can instruct the `ng serve` command to build the application for different environments, and also open a browser, by specifying the `-o` option.

Key app parts

After having used Angular CLI and its basic command set, let's review the key parts of the app you just created.

- `main.ts`: This is the main entry point, which takes care of bootstrapping the entire application:

```
platformBrowserDynamic().bootstrapModule(AppModule)
    .catch(err => console.log(err));
```

As you can see, the code uses a browser-compliant mechanism to bootstrap the specified root application module.

- `app.module.ts`: This is the root application module, which contains the app-level functional units. While modules are explained in detail in the *Modules* section, pay close attention to the fact that this module currently declares a specific component, the `AppComponent`.
- `app.component.ts`: This is the root application component that is included as part of the root application module (`AppModule`). Components are explained later in this chapter—for now, consider this as the root UI component that contains the entire app component graph within it.

Modules

If you are familiar with composite application blocks in other UI technologies, then you may notice that Angular modules are similar in that they share the notion of enabling application-level modularity.

Conceptually, Angular modules are simple containers. Every part of your application, such as components, directives, and pipes, must be registered as part of a module. You should think about modules as a set of logical containers in which you structure features and code.

There are numerous approaches to deciding how to modularize apps, and there is no single approach to this question. Many concerns can affect this decision: security, lazy loading, varied packaging, and feature encapsulation, to name a few.

You can read the Angular team's recommended modularization strategies here:
`https://angular.io/guide/module-types`

Let's review the auto-generated `AppModule` module:

```
import { BrowserModule } from '@angular/platform-browser';
import { NgModule } from '@angular/core';
import { AppComponent } from './app.component';

@NgModule({
    declarations: [AppComponent],
    imports: [BrowserModule],
    providers: [],
    bootstrap: [AppComponent]
})
export class AppModule { }
```

As you can see, Angular modules are just classes; the `@NgModule` decorator makes it an actual Angular module. The decorator receives a configuration object with the following key properties:

- `declarations`: An array of declarable. Declarable can be either components, directives, or pipes. Every declarable you wish to use must be registered in a module, meaning that a module must declare it as part of its `declarations` property.
- `imports`: An array of other modules that this module requires. A module can use other modules' exported parts by importing the module it depends on.
- `providers`: An array of providers to be incorporated into the Angular injector to support dependency injection.
- `bootstrap`: An array of root components that should be bootstrapped and mounted to the HTML DOM. Normally, an application has only one root component.
- `exports`: An array of exported declarable, and even modules. If a module's parts are to be used in other modules, then these should be specified as part of its `exports`.

Angular follows this paradigm quite extensively. Most Angular parts that you will encounter are basically just a class, annotated with a decorator from Angular, which instructs its meaning and usage.

In this chapter, you will implement the following modules as part of our Everyday Market app:

- `AppModule`: This is the root module of the application, which is automatically generated when you create a new project using Angular CLI
- `CoreModule`: This is the module that contains the core application infrastructure
- `SharedModule`: This is the module that contains common application components
- `MarketModule`: This is a feature module responsible for navigating product-related pages and information

First, create all the relevant modules using Angular CLI:

1. Open the Terminal or Command Prompt
2. Navigate to the project's root folder at `everyday-market-ng`
3. Create modules using Angular CLI's `generate` command:

```
ng generate module modules/core
ng generate module modules/shared
ng generate module modules/market
```

> Some of the CLI commands can be activated using shorthand. For example, `generate` and `module` can use the shorthand `g` and `m` respectively.

You can navigate through the created folders and see the modules that were generated. You will add functionality to these modules very soon, as you'll learn about components next.

Components

Components are a key part of every modern UI framework. The idea is simple: you decompose the application visually into smaller encapsulated and reusable units, called components.

Let's review the auto-generated `AppComponent` component:

```
import { Component } from '@angular/core';

@Component({
    selector: 'app-root',
    templateUrl: './app.component.html',
```

```
    styleUrls: ['./app.component.css']
})
export class AppComponent {
  title = 'app';
}
```

Just like modules, Angular components are classes with an `@Component` decorator. The decorator receives a configuration object with the following relevant key properties:

- `selector`: This is the `selector` element associated with the given component. This selector is used in templates where this component should be displayed. Since this is the root component, you can find the use of this selector in the `index.html` file, which indicates where the root of the application should be mounted.
- `templateUrl`: This is the relative path to the component's template. Every component must have a template, which is essentially its HTML view.
- `template`: As an alternative to `templateUrl`, you can use the template property to specify the component's template inline, and not separate it to a different file.
- `styleUrls`: An array of relative paths to the component's styles. A component can have several separate CSS files.
- `styles`: In addition to `styleUrls`, you can use the styles property to specify inline CSS as an array of strings.

> Angular follows an MVC-style architecture, in the sense that the `Component` class is the controller and the template is the view. Angular CLI supports CSS preprocessors such as LESS, SASS, and Stylus. To enable this, follow the instructions listed at `https://github.com/angular/angular-cli/wiki/stories-css-preprocessors`.

In this chapter, you're going to implement the following components in their corresponding module as mentioned in the brackets:

- `AppComponent` (`AppModule`)
- `HeaderComponent` (`SharedModule`)
- `BusyComponent` (`SharedModule`)
- `ProductsPageComponent` (`MarketModule`)
- `CategoryMenuComponent` (`MarketModule`)
- `CategoryMenuItemComponent` (`MarketModule`)
- `ProductListComponent` (`MarketModule`)
- `ProductCardComponent` (`MarketModule`)

The following diagram depicts the component hierarchy and dependency graph that you're going to implement in this chapter:

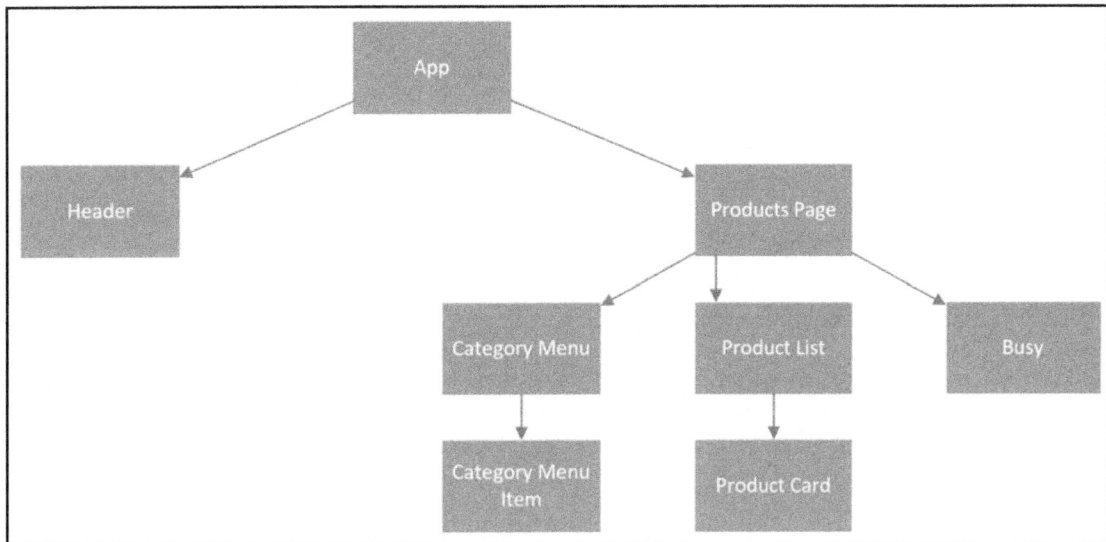

Header component

To begin with, implement the header component by following these steps:

1. Generate the component using Angular CLI by executing the following command:

```
ng generate component modules/shared/header
```

What happens behind the scenes of the generate **command?**

Generating a component via Angular CLI performs multiple changes. It creates the Component class, style, and template files by default, and registers the component with the relative module by adding the component to the modules' declarations, which in this instance is SharedModule.

In Angular, the common naming convention is kebab (dash) case, followed by a dot and the unit type (for example, component, directive, service, and so on).

2. Replace the HTML
   file /src/app/modules/shared/header/header.component.html contents
   with the following:

```
<header class="app-header app-bg">
  <div class="maxHeight flex flex-align-items--center">
    <img src="../../../../assets/logo.png" class="app-logo" />
    <span class="app-slogan">Shop 'till you Drop</span>
  </div>
</header>
```

3. Replace the CSS file
   /src/app/modules/shared/header/header.component.css contents with
   the following:

```
.app-header {
  height: 200px;
  border-bottom: 1px solid black;
}
.app-header::after {
  content: "";
  height: 200px;
  opacity: 0.5;
  background: url('../../../../assets/herobg.jpg');
  background-position: center;
  background-repeat: no-repeat;
  background-size: cover;
  position: absolute;
  top: 0;
  left: 0;
  bottom: 0;
  right: 0;
  z-index: -1;
}
.app-logo {
  height: 80px;
  margin-left: 50px;
}
.app-slogan {
  font-family: 'Comic Sans MS', 'Comic Sans', cursive;
  font-weight: bold;
  margin-left: 5px;
}
```

Usually, the shared module includes declarable that can be used elsewhere as needed. To do this, you need to specify such declarable as part of the `exports` module.

4. Add `HeaderComponent` to the module's `exports` declarable as follows:

   1. Open the `shared.module.ts` file.
   2. Add `exports` to the `@NgModule` decorator, with an array as the value.
   3. Add `HeaderComponent` to the exports array, as shown here:

```
@NgModule({
    imports: [
      CommonModule,
    ],
    declarations: [
      HeaderComponent,
    ],
    exports: [
      HeaderComponent
    ],
})
export class SharedModule { }
```

5. Use the header component in the `AppComponent` template (`app.component.html`). Replace the entire HTML file contents with the following:

```
<app-header></app-header>
```

Angular uses a prefix in the generated component selectors to prevent conflicts. The default prefix is configurable in the `angular.json` file, but you can specify the prefix as part of the `ng generate` command by using the `-p` flag.
As you can see, the app component template uses the `header` component (that is, the `app-header` selector). `HeaderComponent` is exported as part of `SharedModule`, but you still need to import `SharedModule` to use it in an app component that is part of the `AppModule`.

6. Import `SharedModule` in `AppModule` (`app.module.ts`) as follows:

```
import { SharedModule } from './modules/shared/shared.module';

@NgModule({
  declarations: [
```

```
      AppComponent,
      HeaderComponent
    ],
    imports: [
      BrowserModule,
      SharedModule,
    ],
    providers: [],
    bootstrap: [AppComponent]
  })
  export class AppModule { }
```

Global styles

Currently, the header component makes use of class names that do not exist as part of its component CSS file, as these are expected to be available globally. Angular CLI projects include a src/styles.css file for that purpose, to include application-wide styles.

Add the following CSS to src/styles.css:

```css
html {
   box-sizing: border-box;
   font-size: 62.5%;   /* =10px */
}

*, *:before, *:after {
  box-sizing: inherit;
}

html, body {
  margin: 0;
  padding: 0;
  width: 100%;
  height: 100%;
}

body {
  font-size: 1.4rem;
}

.hidden {
  display: none !important;
}

.maxHeight {
  height: 100%;
```

```
}

.maxWidth {
  width: 100%;
}

.flex {
  display: flex;
}

.flex-justify-content--center {
  justify-content: center;
}

.flex-align-items--center {
  align-items: center;
}
```

> Angular provides view encapsulation, meaning the component-specific CSS affects the specific component alone.
> By default, Angular uses an emulated Shadow DOM mechanism that takes care of style encapsulation.
> You can read more about view encapsulation in Angular at `https://angular.io/guide/component-styles`.

Assets

The header component references two images as part of the application asset: one in its CSS, and the other in its template. Angular CLI projects include a folder named `src/assets`. This folder is supposed to keep assets that you need to be included as part of the build output.

In this specific example, you need to add the missing assets.

> Add `herobg.png` and `logo.png` to the `assets` folder.

Great! You can now run the application and see the header in place. It should look similar to the following screenshot:

Category-menu-item component

Next, let's implement the products page with the categories menu and product list.

To begin with, implement the `category-menu-item` component by following these steps:

1. Generate the component using Angular CLI by running the following command:

```
ng generate component modules/market/category-menu-item
```

2. Replace the HTML file `/src/app/modules/market/category-menu-item/category-menu-item.component.html` contents with the following:

```
<div class="container">
   <span>Category Name</span>
</div>
```

3. Replace the CSS file `/src/app/modules/market/category-menu-item/category-menu-item.component.css` contents with the following:

```
.container {
   display: inline;
   padding: 5px 3px 5px 3px;
   border: 1px solid black;
   padding: 2px 5px 2px 5px;
   cursor: pointer;
}

.container:hover {
   background-color: lightgray;
}

.selected {
   background-color: bisque;
}
```

category-menu component

After completing the menu items, implement the `category-menu` component by following these steps:

1. Generate the component using Angular CLI by running the following commands:

   ```
   ng generate component modules/market/category-menu
   ```

2. Replace the HTML file `/src/app/modules/market/category-menu/category-menu.component.html` contents with the following:

   ```html
   <ul>
       <li>
         <app-category-menu-item></app-category-menu-item>
       </li>
       <li>
         <app-category-menu-item></app-category-menu-item>
       </li>
       <li>
         <app-category-menu-item></app-category-menu-item>
       </li>
   </ul>
   ```

3. Replace the CSS file `/src/app/modules/market/category-menu/category-menu.component.css` contents with the following:

   ```css
   ul, li {
       list-style: none;
       padding: 0;
       margin: 0;
       display: inline;
   }
   ```

products-page component

Next, follow these steps to implement the `products-page` component with just the menu for now:

1. Generate the component using Angular CLI by running the following:

   ```
   ng g component modules/market/products-page
   ```

2. Replace the HTML file `/src/app/modules/market/products-page/products-page.component.html` contents with the following:

```
<app-category-menu></app-category-menu>
```

3. Add `ProductsPageComponent` to the market module's exports as follows:
    1. Open the `market.module.ts` file.
    2. Add `exports` to the `@NgModule` decorator, with an array as the value.
    3. Add `ProductsPageComponent` to the exports array.

```
@NgModule({
    imports: [
      CommonModule
    ],
    declarations: [
      CategoryMenuItemComponent,
      CategoryMenuComponent,
      ProductsPageComponent,
    ],
    exports: [
      ProductsPageComponent,
    ]
})
export class MarketModule { }
```

Finally, add the products page to the root app component as follows:

4. Add the products page component to `app.component.html`:

```
<app-header></app-header>
<div class="main-area">
  <app-products-page></app-products-page>
</div>
```

5. Replace the CSS file contents in the `app.component.css` file with the following:

```
.main-area {
  margin: 10px;
}
```

6. Since `AppComponent` uses the `ProductsPageComponent`, `AppModule` now requires `MarketModule`: so let's add it as follows:

   1. Add `MarketModule` to the imports of `AppModule` by adding the following to `app.module.ts`:

```
import { MarketModule } from
'./modules/market/market.module';

@NgModule({
  declarations: [
    AppComponent,
    HeaderComponent
  ],
  imports: [
    BrowserModule,
    SharedModule,
    MarketModule,
  ],
  providers: [],
  bootstrap: [AppComponent]
})
export class AppModule { }
```

You can now run the application and see the category menu items in place. It should look similar to that in the following screenshot, only with different categories:

Currently, the menu items are defined statically with a constant name.

To complete the functionality of the category menu items, we need to do the following:

- `CategoryMenuComponent` should receive the menu items data from its `ProductsPageComponent` parent component.
- `CategoryMenuItemComponent` should receive the item name, and an indication of whether or not it is selected from its `CategoryMenuComponent` parent component.

- `CategoryMenuComponent` should manage the menu item selection by doing the following:
    1. `CategoryMenuItemComponent` should notify it when it is clicked.
    2. It should maintain the selection as part of its state.
    3. It should notify selection changes to its parent.

The following diagram visualizes the preceding detailed steps:

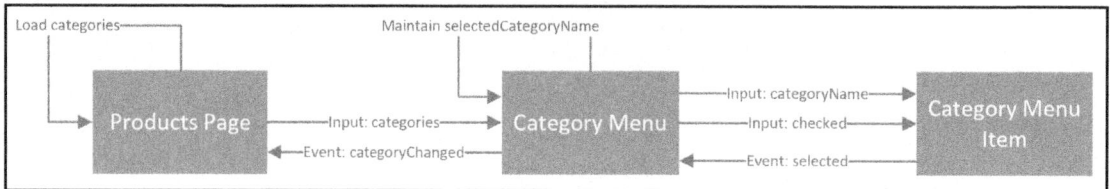

For the purpose of implementing the preceding flow, you will learn about data binding and component interaction next.

Data binding

A key feature in every modern component framework that separates the view from the component's behavior is data binding. Data binding bridges the gap between the view and the controller by enabling us to bind the view to the component's data, as well as user interactions with the view, to the component's functions.

Importantly, the template's default expression context is the controller; that is, the component instance. This means that the template can bind to every public member of the class, including fields, properties, and functions. To clarify, when *component data* is mentioned in the context of binding, it means all of the bindable members.

> The Angular team is working on replacing its current renderer with a new one called Ivy, which should bring multiple enhancements, one of which is the fact that you should be able to private members of the class as well.

Angular's data binding can be applied on components, as well as standard HTML elements, using multiple forms of binding. These include interpolation, property, event, and two-way binding.

Interpolation binding

Interpolation binding allows you to bind component data inside the template where needed. You use interpolation binding by surrounding the relevant expression with double curly braces:

```
<span>{{ name }}</span>
```

In the preceding example, the component view displays a `name` field or property from the `Component` class as the span content. When the `name` field changes in the component, so does the view.

Property binding

Property binding is used to bind an element's property to the component data. You use property binding by surrounding the property with square brackets and have the expression as a standard value assignment:

```
<app-category-menu [items]="menuItems"></app-category-menu>
```

In the preceding example, the component view binds a `menuItems` field or property in its component state to the `items` property of `app-category-menu`. When `menuItems` changes in the component, so does the bound `items` property of the child component.

Event binding

Event binding works a bit differently in the sense that it reverses the flow. These bindings are used to respond to events, and usually bind an event to a component event handler. You use event bindings by surrounding the event with parenthesis and have the handler as a standard assignment:

```
<span (click)="onSelected()">Category Name</span>
```

In the preceding example, the component view binds the click event of `span` to the component's `onSelected` function. When the user clicks the `span` area, the component's function will be executed.

Furthermore, Angular supports the notorious `$event` object as part of the event binding's statement context. In standard HTML events, `$event` represents the actual HTML event object, whereas in a component's custom events, it represents the payload that was specified when emitting the event:

```
<span (click)="onSelected($event)">Category Name</span>
```

Two-way binding

Last, but not least, is two-way binding, which is essentially a combination of event and property bindings. Not every property can be used with two-way binding, since it requires a certain convention and is used mostly in forms.

Two-way binding is used to bind an element's property to component data, in addition to updating the component data when the target element's property changes. You use two-way binding by surrounding a property with both parentheses and square brackets:

```
<input [(ngModel)]="myNameField" />
```

In the preceding example, `ngModel` is set with a two-way binding; thus, the input value is bound to the component's `nameInput` field and vice versa, so `nameInput` should change when the input value changes.

> `ngModel` is a built-in directive, as part of Angular's forms module, that supports two-way binding with common form elements. This is covered in `Chapter 11`, *Implementing Routing and Forms*, where you learn implementing forms in Angular.
> There is much more to template syntax, binding, and directives. You can read more about it at `https://angular.io/guide/template-syntax`.

Component interaction

As stated before, apps today use components to better structure the user interface. The idea is to break down the app to a set of encapsulated and reusable scoped components and avoid the primitive monolith approach.

Consequently, the user interface is built from a hierarchical component graph, comprising parent and child components. Often, this situation requires some sort of parent-child interaction control, such as the following:

- Parent needs to pass down input data to its child components
- Parent needs to respond when something occurs in a child component

Angular supports these two common scenarios using input and output.

Input

The `@Input` decorator is used when a component is supposed to receive data passed down from its parent. When a field or property is set as input, the parent can specify the value via standard assignment.

Let's use input in the category menu-related components:

1. Create the relevant model representations:
    1. Create a folder at `src/app/model`.
    2. Create a file, `category.ts`, in the new `model` folder, with the following content:

       ```
       export interface Category {
         name: string;
       }
       ```

2. Use the re-export strategy to aggregate all model representations by creating a file called `index.ts` in the model folder with the following content:

   ```
   export * from './category';
   ```

3. Open `category-menu.component.ts` and add the `categories` field as input:

   ```
   import { Component, Input } from '@angular/core';
   import { Category } from '../../../model';

   @Component({
     selector: 'app-category-menu',
     templateUrl: './category-menu.component.html',
     styleUrls: ['./category-menu.component.css']
   })
   export class CategoryMenuComponent {
     @Input() categories: Category[];
   }
   ```

4. Open the parent `products-page.component.ts` component file and initialize categories with hardcoded values:

```
import { Component, OnInit } from '@angular/core';
import { Category } from '../../../model';

@Component({
  selector: 'app-products-page',
  templateUrl: './products-page.component.html',
  styleUrls: ['./products-page.component.css']
})
export class ProductsPageComponent implements OnInit {
  categories: Category[] = [
    {name: 'Books'},
    {name: 'Appliances'},
    {name: 'Food'},
  ];

  constructor() { }

  ngOnInit() {
  }
}
```

5. In `products-page.component.html`, pass down the hardcoded categories to the child's `categories` input by using property binding:

```
<app-category-menu [categories]="categories"></app-category-menu>
```

6. The categories should now be available to the `CategoryMenuComponent` as passed-down input.

7. Before using the categories to generate the menu items, enable `CategoryMenuItemComponent` to receive the category name as input:

   1. In `category-menu-item.component.ts`, add a `categoryName` field as input:

   ```
   import { Component, Input } from '@angular/core';

   @Component({
     selector: 'app-category-menu-item',
     templateUrl: './category-menu-item.component.html',
     styleUrls: ['./category-menu-item.component.css']
   })
   export class CategoryMenuItemComponent {
     @Input() categoryName: string;
   }
   ```

8. In `category-menu-item.component.html`, bind the field `categoryName` state with interpolation binding:

   ```
   <div class="container">
     <span>{{ categoryName }}</span>
   </div>
   ```

9. Replace the entire contents of `category-menu.component.html` and bind the component's field `categories` to generate the menu items:

   ```
   <ul>
     <li *ngFor="let c of categories">
         <app-category-menu-item [categoryName]="c.name">
         </app-category-menu-item>
     </li>
   </ul>
   ```

You can now run the application and see the generated menu items generated according to the hardcoded state you initialized.

ngFor

In Angular, you can use the `ngFor` directive to generate templates from lists. Essentially, `ngFor` repeats the template's element it is applied to, along with its subtree, for every item in the bound list.

The basic format with which to use `ngFor` is shown in the following statement:

```
let <variableName> of <componentData>
```

Note that `componentData` can be either a field, a property, or a function that returns a list.

This makes `variableName` available to the context of the template associated with `ngFor` directive. This is the reason you can use `c.name` to pass it down to the child component as input.

> The asterisk you see next to `ngFor` is often used with structural directives. This a special construct with which Angular provides syntactic sugar over structural directives that modify the HTML DOM layout.
>
> You can read more about the many built-in directives in Angular at `https://angular.io/guide/template-syntax#built-in-directives`.

Output

You use the `@Output` decorator when a component is supposed to notify a parent when something occurs. For this purpose, you use `EventEmitter`, Angular's events abstraction. Then the parent component can subscribe to these events using event bindings and respond to them.

Let's use `@Output` in the category menu-related components:

1. Open `category-menu-item.component.ts`:
    1. Define an `EventEmitter` field named `selected` with an `@Output` decorator.
    2. Implement a function that emits the event with the same category name as the payload:

```
import { Component, Input, Output, EventEmitter } from
'@angular/core';

@Component({
  selector: 'app-category-menu-item',
  templateUrl: './category-menu-item.component.html',
  styleUrls: ['./category-menu-item.component.css']
})
export class CategoryMenuItemComponent {
  @Input() categoryName: string;
  @Output() selected = new EventEmitter<string>();
```

```
onSelected() {
  this.selected.emit(this.categoryName);
}
}
```

2. In `category-menu-item.component.html`, bind the click to the `onSelected` function:

```
<div class="container" (click)="onSelected()">
  <span>{{ categoryName }}</span>
</div>
```

3. In `category-menu.component.ts`, do the following:

   1. Define an `EventEmitter` field, `categoryChanged`, with an `@Output` decorator

   2. Implement a function that emits the event with the category according to the name as the event payload:

```
import { Component, Input, EventEmitter, Output } from
'@angular/core';
import { Category } from '../../../model';

@Component({
  selector: 'app-category-menu',
  templateUrl: './category-menu.component.html',
  styleUrls: ['./category-menu.component.css']
})
export class CategoryMenuComponent {
  @Input() categories: Category[];
  @Output() categoryChanged = new
EventEmitter<Category>
    ();

  onCategorySelected(categoryName: string) {
    const cat = this.categories.find(c => c.name ===
      categoryName);
    this.categoryChanged.emit(cat);
  }
}
```

4. In `category-menu.component.html`, bind to the menu items' `selected` event:

```html
<ul>
  <li *ngFor="let c of categories">
     <app-category-menu-item
       [categoryName]="c.name"
       (selected)="onCategorySelected($event)"
     >
     </app-category-menu-item>
  </li>
</ul>
```

5. In `products-page.component.ts`, implement a function to handle category changes with a simple alert message:

```typescript
import { Component, OnInit } from '@angular/core';
import { Category } from '../../../model';

@Component({
  selector: 'app-products-page',
  templateUrl: './products-page.component.html',
  styleUrls: ['./products-page.component.css']
})
export class ProductsPageComponent implements OnInit {
  categories: Category[] = [
    {name: 'Books'},
    {name: 'Appliances'},
    {name: 'Food'},
  ];
  selectedCategory: Category;

  constructor() { }

  ngOnInit() {
  }

  onCategoryChanged(category: Category) {
    this.selectedCategory = category;
    alert(category.name);
  }
}
```

6. In `products-page.component.html`, bind to the `categoryChanged` event:

```html
<app-category-menu
  [categories]="categories"
  (categoryChanged)="onCategoryChanged($event)"
></app-category-menu>
```

Congratulations! You can now run the app, and you will see the alerted message as you click on different menu items.

Injectable services

Another key building block of Angular services. Following Angular's architecture, services are supposed to encapsulate business logic and application-wide states. Additionally, services are useful to bridge between different components that aren't necessarily a direct parent and child.

As this is your first services-related task, extract the categories data to an Angular service.

First, generate the CategoriesService service, as part of the CoreModule, by executing the following command:

```
ng generate service modules/core/services/categories
```

Afterward, the service is created in a file named categories.service.ts, containing the following content:

```
import { Injectable } from '@angular/core';

@Injectable({
  providedIn: 'root'
})
export class CategoriesService {
  constructor() { }
}
```

As you can see, services in Angular are simply classes decorated with an @Injectable decorator.

Angular provides a dependency injection solution, which eases the use of services in your app. Dependency injection enables you to plug services into the Angular injector and then resolve it where needed by specifying it as part of the constructor arguments.

> There are several ways to plug a service into Angular's injector to make it available. A standard and simple way of doing that is by instructing Angular with the module that the service should be provided with as part of the @Injectable decorator.
> You can read more about it at https://angular.io/guide/dependency-injection.

Next, complete `CategoriesService` and use it to load and display the categories:

1. Implement `CategoriesService` as follows:
    1. Change the `providedIn` value so that the service is provided as part of `CoreModule`
    2. Implement a function to retrieve the categories, as follows:

```
import { Injectable } from '@angular/core';
import { CoreModule } from '../core.module';
import { Category } from '../../../model';

@Injectable({
  providedIn: CoreModule
})
export class CategoriesService {
  loadCategories(): Category[] {
    return [
      {name: 'Books'},
      {name: 'Appliances'},
      {name: 'Food'},
    ];
  }
}
```

2. Import `CoreModule` as part of the root application module in `app.module.ts`:

```
...
import { CoreModule } from './modules/core/core.module';

@NgModule({
  ...
  imports: [
    BrowserModule,
    CoreModule,
    SharedModule,
    MarketModule,
  ],
  ...
})
export class AppModule { }
```

3. Use the new service in `ProductsPageComponent` by requiring it as a dependency as part of its constructor arguments:

```
import { Component, OnInit } from '@angular/core';
import { Category } from '../../../model';
import { CategoriesService } from
'../../core/services/categories.service';

@Component({
  selector: 'app-products-page',
  templateUrl: './products-page.component.html',
  styleUrls: ['./products-page.component.css']
})
export class ProductsPageComponent implements OnInit {
  categories: Category[];
  selectedCategory: Category;

  constructor(private readonly categoriesService:
CategoriesService) { }

  ngOnInit() {
    this.categories = this.categoriesService.loadCategories();
  }

  onCategoryChanged(category: Category) {
    this.selectedCategory = category;
    alert(category.name);
  }
}
```

Congratulations! You just implemented and consumed your first service in Angular. You can now run the app and confirm that everything works—the categories should now be loaded as part of the service.

> As you can see, the use of the service is made in a function called `ngOnInit`.
>
> Angular components have a certain life cycle that you can hook into. One of these hooks is `ngOnInit`, which is executed after a component is initialized, making it a useful place to load component data.
>
> You can read more about lifecycle hooks at `https://angular.io/guide/lifecycle-hooks`.

HTTP

The categories are currently hardcoded values; however, they should be loaded from the RESTful API and through HTTP calls. Angular provides its own abstraction for HTTP, in the form of a service that you can use when necessary.

Next, let's use Angular's `HttpClient` service to load the categories from the backend RESTful API:

1. Import `HttpClientModule` into `app.module.ts` to make the `HttpClient` service available to the entire app:

   ```
   ...
   import { HttpClientModule } from '@angular/common/http';
   ...
   @NgModule({
     ...
     imports: [
       HttpClientModule,
       ...
     ],
     ...
   })
   ```

2. Use the `HttpClient` service in `CategoriesService` as follows. If the HTTP address differs in your setup, then make sure to change it accordingly:

   ```
   import { Injectable } from '@angular/core';
   import { HttpClient } from '@angular/common/http';
   import { CoreModule } from '../core.module';
   import { Category } from '../../../model';

   @Injectable({
     providedIn: CoreModule,
   })
   export class CategoriesService {
     constructor(private readonly http: HttpClient) {}

     loadCategories(): Promise<Category[]> {
       return this.http
         .get('http://localhost:55564/api/products/categories')
         .toPromise()
         .then(result => result as Category[]);
     }
   }
   ```

3. Adjust `ProductsPageComponent` to handle a promise:

```
...
ngOnInit() {
  this.categoriesService.loadCategories()
    .then(r => this.categories = r);
}
...
```

That's it! You can now run the app and see that the categories are loaded by calling the RESTful API using Angular's `HttpClient` service—just make sure that the backend API is running.

> Angular provides several tools to handle asynchrony and event pipelines, such as RxJs Observables and AsyncPipe.
> You can read more about these here:
> https://angular.io/guide/observables
> https://angular.io/guide/observables-in-angular
> https://angular.io/guide/rx-library
> https://angular.io/api/common/AsyncPipe

Armed with these tools, let's continue by implementing the product listing. The following diagram depicts the data and interaction flow you implement:

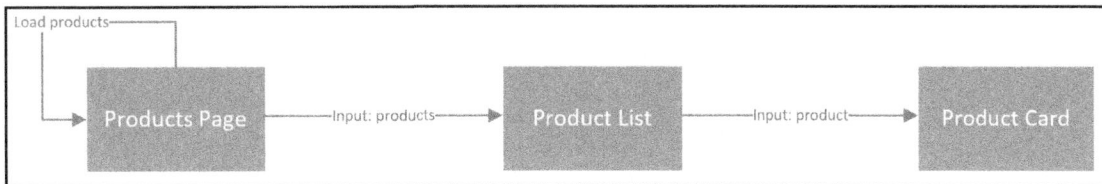

Now implement the product listing with the following steps:

1. Create the product-related model representations in the `src/app/model` folder. Start by creating a file named `product-media.ts` and write the following content:

```
export interface ProductMedia {
  url: string;
}
```

2. Re-export `ProductMedia` in the `src/app/model/index.ts` file, by using the following command:

```
export * from './product-media';
```

3. Create a file named `product.ts` and write in the following content:

```
import { ProductMedia } from '.';

export interface Product {
  title: string;
  description: string;
  media: ProductMedia[];
}
```

4. Re-export `Product` in the `src/app/model/index.ts` with the following command:

```
export * from './product';
```

5. Generate a `ProductCardComponent` component to display a product card with this command:

```
ng generate component modules/market/product-card
```

6. Edit `/src/app/modules/market/product-card/product-card.component.ts` to receive the product as input and implement a function to resolve the primary image URL, as follows:

```
import { Component, Input } from '@angular/core';
import { Product } from '../../../model';

@Component({
  selector: 'app-product-card',
  templateUrl: './product-card.component.html',
  styleUrls: ['./product-card.component.css']
})
export class ProductCardComponent {
  @Input() product: Product;

  get primaryImageSrc() {
    const hasMedia =
      this.product && this.product.media &&
this.product.media.length > 0;
    return hasMedia
      ? this.product.media[0].url
      : null;
  }
}
```

7. Replace the HTML file `/src/app/modules/market/product-card/product-card.component.html` contents with the following:

```html
<div class="item-card">
  <div class="item-card-content-container">
      <img class="item-card-content-container-img"
      [src]="primaryImageSrc" />
      <span class="item-card-content-container-title">
      {{product.title}}</span>
      <span class="item-card-content-container-text">
        {{product.description}}
      </span>
  </div>
</div>
```

8. Replace the CSS file `/src/app/modules/market/product-card/product-card.component.css` contents with the following:

```css
.item-card {
  box-shadow: 0 4px 8px 0 rgba(0,0,0,0.2);
  transition: 0.3s;
  background-color: white;
  width: 280px;
  height: 200px;
  float: left;
  margin: 10;
}

.item-card:hover {
  box-shadow: 0 8px 16px 0 rgba(0,0,0,0.2);
}

.item-card-content-container {
  padding: 2px 16px;
  display: flex;
  height: 100%;
  flex-direction: column;
  align-items: center;
  justify-content: center;
  cursor: pointer;
}

.item-card-content-container-img {
  display: block;
  max-width: 80px;
  max-height: 80px;
  width: auto;
  height: auto;
```

```
      text-align: center;
    }

    .item-card-content-container-title {
      display: block;
      font-size: 1.6rem;
    }

    .item-card-content-container-text {
      word-wrap: normal;
      font-size: 1.2rem;
      overflow: hidden;
    }
```

9. Generate `ProductListComponent` with the following command so that we can display a list of product cards:

```
ng generate component modules/market/product-list
```

10. Edit `/src/app/modules/market/product-list/product-list.component.ts` and implement the behavior to receive a product array as input, as follows:

```
import { Component, Input } from '@angular/core';
import { Product } from '../../../model';

@Component({
  selector: 'app-product-list',
  templateUrl: './product-list.component.html',
  styleUrls: ['./product-list.component.css']
})
export class ProductListComponent {
  @Input() products: Product[];
}
```

11. Replace the HTML file `/src/app/modules/market/product-list/product-list.component.html` contents with the following:

```
<div>
  <ul class="products-container">
    <li *ngFor="let p of products">
      <app-product-card [product]="p"></app-product-card>
    </li>
  </ul>
</div>
```

12. Replace the CSS file `/src/app/modules/market/product-list/product-list.component.css` contents with the following:

```
ul, li {
  list-style: none;
  padding: 0;
  margin: 0;
  display: inline;
}

.products-container {
  display: flex;
  justify-content: space-around;
  flex-wrap: wrap;
}
```

13. Generate `ProductsService` responsible for managing products-related state and actions:

```
ng generate service modules/core/services/products
```

14. Edit `/src/app/modules/core/services/products.service.ts` and implement its behavior as follows:

```
import { Injectable } from '@angular/core';
import { HttpClient } from '@angular/common/http';
import { CoreModule } from '../core.module';
import { Product } from '../../../model';

@Injectable({
 providedIn: CoreModule,
})
export class ProductsService {
 constructor(private readonly http: HttpClient) { }

 loadProducts(categoryName: string): Promise<Product[]> {
 return this.http
.get(`http://localhost:55564/api/products/searchcategory/${categoryName}`)
 .toPromise()
 .then(result => result as Product[]);
 }
}
```

15. In `ProductsPageComponent,` load products when the category is changed:

```
...
export class ProductsPageComponent implements OnInit {
  ...
  products: Product[];

  constructor(
    private readonly categoriesService: CategoriesService,
    private readonly productsService: ProductsService,
  ) { }

  ...

  onCategoryChanged(category: Category) {
    this.selectedCategory = category;
    this.productsService.loadProducts(category.name)
      .then (r => this.products = r);
  }
}
```

16. Edit `/src/app/modules/market/products-page/products-page.component.html` to render the products:

```
<app-category-menu
  [categories]="categories"
  (categoryChanged)="onCategoryChanged($event)"
></app-category-menu>

<app-product-list [products]="products"></app-product-list>
```

Next, let's show the indication for the selected category:

17. In `CategoryMenuItemComponent,` add an input to reflect whether the category is selected, and then set a class name accordingly:

```
export class CategoryMenuItemComponent {
  ...
  @Input() checked = false;
  ...
}
```

18. Edit `/src/app/modules/market/category-menu-item/category-menu-item.component.html` to set a class name according to whether the menu item is selected, as follows:

```
<div class="container" (click)="onSelected()"
[class.selected]="checked">
 <span>{{ categoryName }}</span>
</div>
```

The preceding is an example of a specialized binding in Angular: the class binding, formatted as `class.<name>`. This is a useful feature, since toggling elements' class names conditionally according to state is often needed. In this case, the `div` element is set with a `selected` class when the value of the component property `checked` is true; otherwise, `selected` is removed.

> In addition to class binding, there's also a specialized binding for styles. Alternatively, there are `NgStyle` and `NgClass` directives, which are generally preferred in cases of multiple style properties or class names.

In `CategoryMenuComponent`, maintain the selected category as follows:

```
...
export class CategoryMenuComponent {
  ...
  selectedCategoryName: string;

  onCategorySelected(categoryName: string) {
    const cat = this.categories.find(c => c.name ===
categoryName);
    this.selectedCategoryName = cat.name;
    this.categoryChanged.emit(cat);
  }
}
```

Edit `/src/app/modules/market/category-menu/category-menu.component.html` to specify the `checked` input as follows:

```
<ul>
  <li *ngFor="let c of categories">
  <app-category-menu-item
  [categoryName]="c.name"
  [checked]="c.name === selectedCategoryName"
  (selected)="onCategorySelected($event)"
  >
  </app-category-menu-item>
```

```
        </li>
    </ul>
```

Congratulations! You have just completed setting up the core functionality of this page. You can run the app and see the products when selecting a category, which should look similar to the following screenshot:

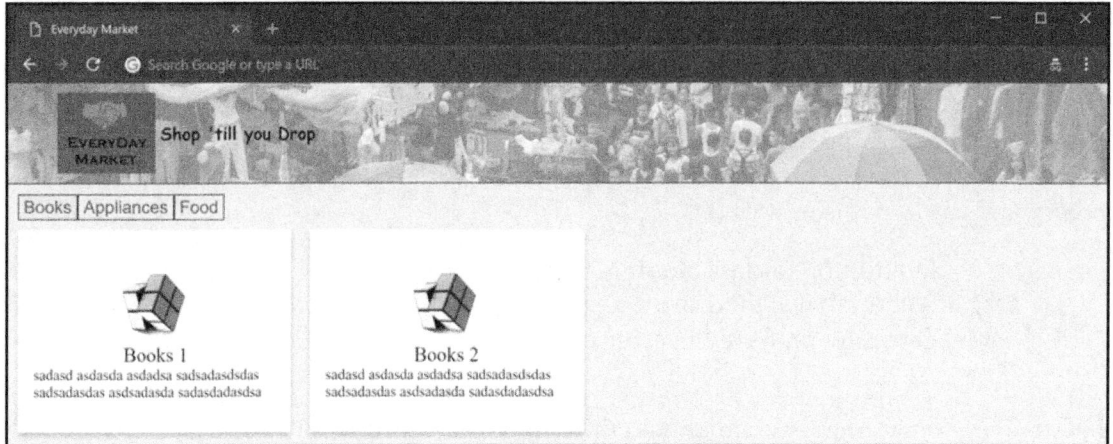

Busy indicator

As a final implementation step, let's implement a busy indicator on our page:

1. Generate a `BusyComponent` component as part of the `shared` module with the following command:

   ng generate component modules/shared/busy

2. Replace the HTML file `/src/app/modules/shared/busy/busy.component.html` contents with the following:

```
<div class="loader-container">
    <div class="loader"></div>
</div>
```

3. Replace the CSS file `/src/app/modules/shared/busy/busy.component.css` contents with the following:

```css
.loader-container {
  position: absolute;
  left: 0; right: 0; top: 0; bottom: 0;
  background-color: azure;
  opacity: 0.5;
  display: flex;
  align-items: center;
  justify-content: center;
}

.loader {
  border: 16px solid #f3f3f3;
  border-top: 16px solid #3498db;
  border-radius: 50%;
  width: 80px;
  height: 80px;
  animation: spin 2s linear infinite;
}

@keyframes spin {
  0% { transform: rotate(0deg); }
  100% { transform: rotate(360deg); }
}
```

4. Export the component in `SharedModule` as follows:

```
...
@NgModule({
  ...
  exports: [
    ...
    BusyComponent,
  ],
})
export class SharedModule { }
```

5. Import `SharedModule` into `MarketModule`:

```
...
import { SharedModule } from '../shared/shared.module';
...
@NgModule({
  imports: [
    ...
    SharedModule,
```

```
            ],
            ...
        })
        export class MarketModule { }
```

6. Include the busy component in `ProductsPageComponent` while making HTTP calls using the following code:

```
...
export class ProductsPageComponent implements OnInit {
  ...
  isBusy = false;

  ...
  async ngOnInit() {
    this.isBusy = true;

    try {
      this.categories = await
this.categoriesService.loadCategories();
    } finally {
      this.isBusy = false;
    }
  }

  async onCategoryChanged(category: Category) {
    this.selectedCategory = category;
    this.isBusy = true;

    try {
      this.products = await
this.productsService.loadProducts(category.name);
    } finally {
      this.isBusy = false;
    }
  }
}
```

That's it! You have just completed creating the busy indicator, and with that, the page functionality in this chapter is complete.

ngIf

Like `ngFor`, `ngIf` is another built-in structural directive that affects the HTML DOM layout.

When applied to an element in its basic form, as seen here, the element is mounted to the DOM when the assigned expression evaluates to `true`; otherwise, it is removed from the DOM. Therefore, the busy indicator is displayed only when the component state, `isBusy`, is `true`.

Distribution

Until now, to run the application, you've used the local development environment, along with the following command:

```
ng serve
```

For the sake of deployment, as will be covered in a later chapter, the app needs to be built for distribution purposes, meaning its finalized artifacts should be generated to be ready for deployment.

Angular CLI projects support distribution. Open the Terminal in the project folder and run the following command:

```
ng build
```

Afterward, you should see that a folder has been created, named `dist`. This folder contains the finalized artifacts of the application, which generally need to be hosted in an HTTP endpoint to become accessible.

When deploying to production, you should execute the following command:

```
ng build --prod
```

This command instructs Angular CLI to use the production configuration, as well as to enable the **Ahead-of-Time (AOT)** build process, which produces better-optimized artifacts for production purposes.

> Angular offers two ways of compilation, AOT and **Just-in-Time (JIT)**. You can read more about this at `https://angular.io/guide/aot-compiler`.

Environments

Typically, apps require environment-specific configuration. In this specific app, we have the base address of the RESTful API that should change across environments.

Angular provides a basic solution for configuration through its environments feature. Let's use environment configuration with the RESTful API base address, as follows:

1. Add the base address in the default environment configuration with the following steps:
    1. Open the `environment.ts` file in the `src/environments` folder.
    2. Add the base address configuration as follows:

    ```
    export const environment = {
      production: false,
      marketApiBaseUri: 'http://localhost:55564/api/',
    };
    ```

2. Add the base address in the production environment configuration:
    1. Open the `environment.prod.ts` file.
    2. Add the base address configuration. Currently, the code uses the same address—this should be changed later when the address of the API in the deployed environment is known:

    ```
    export const environment = {
      production: false,
      marketApiBaseUri: 'http://localhost:55564/api/',
    };
    ```

3. Use the configured `marketApiBaseUri` in `CategoriesService` as follows, replacing the previous hardcoded value, and therefore supporting different environments:

    ```
    ...
    import { environment } from
    '../../../../environments/environment';
    ...
    export class CategoriesService {
      private readonly apiUri = environment.marketApiBaseUri;

      constructor(private readonly http: HttpClient) {}

      loadCategories(): Promise<Category[]> {
        return this.http
          .get(`${this.apiUri}products/categories`)
    ```

```
      .toPromise()
      .then(result => result as Category[]);
  }
}
```

4. Use the configured `marketApiBaseUri` in `ProductsService` as follows, replacing the previous hardcoded value, and therefore supporting different environments:

```
...
import { environment } from
'../../../../environments/environment';
...
export class ProductsService {
  private readonly apiUri = environment.marketApiBaseUri;

  constructor(private readonly http: HttpClient) { }

  loadProducts(categoryName: string): Promise<Product[]> {
    return this.http
.get(`${this.apiUri}products/searchcategory/${categoryName}`)
      .toPromise()
      .then(result => result as Product[]);
  }
}
```

Congratulations! You can now set different configurations for production when you deploy the application in a later chapter by using the following command:

```
ng build --prod
```

> You can find all the client-side related code in a public GitHub repository at https://github.com/azuker/frontend-web-dev.

Summary

Angular is certainly a comprehensive framework that thrives on providing a complete platform for building modern web apps. Many projects, big and small, choose Angular to develop their apps, especially for those who find RxJs and TypeScript desirable, in addition to being willing to accept a complete toolset and align to that accordingly.

In this chapter, we unraveled Angular in great length, covering many of its key features, such as modules, components, data binding, and services.

Unfortunately, we have merely scratched the surface—there's much more to Angular that can't be covered in just a single chapter. One of these is its rich support for forms and routing, which we will cover in the next chapter.

11
Implementing Routing and Forms

Angular is a comprehensive framework. In addition to its core component features, covered in `Chapter 10`, *App Development with Angular*, Angular provides rich support for forms and routing as well.

In this chapter, you will learn about client-side routing and the template-driven forms that ship with Angular as you implement new features in our Everyday Market app. Specifically, we'll be creating a new product and displaying product details.

The following topics are covered in this chapter:

- Angular Router
- ngModel
- Form validation

Client-side routing

Most apps today use client-side routing, which helps with the following key aspects:

- App sections can be made shareable and navigable. For example, the Everyday Market app could benefit substantially if users were able to share links that display a specific product directly.
- Properly designed `routes` can make the user understand the context better. Additionally, users might find it trivial enough to even change the URL manually to get to the page or level they want.

- Client-side routing also improves usability through integration with the built-in back and forward browser buttons.
- Combined with isomorphic (server-side) rendering, client-side routing can assist greatly with **Search Engine Optimization (SEO)**.

Client-side routing is made possible due to the fact that the app can tweak the browser URL to reflect certain areas it chooses to support routing for. For many years, the use of named anchors, via the hash symbol (#), was used to implement `routes`. Thanks to the newer HTML5 history push API, app developers can tweak the URL without the hash sign, and thus apply more intuitive and readable `routes`, without having the browser refresh the app.

Angular, being the comprehensive framework that it is, brings a complete solution for client-side routing via its `RoutingModule` and Angular Router.

Using Angular Router

In Everyday Market, let's implement the following `routes`:

- `/products`: This is the default route that displays the product's listing homepage.
- `/products/new` : This displays the form to create a new product.
- `/products/:id` : This displays product details for the specified product `id`. The fact that the `id` is prefixed with a colon instructs Angular Router to treat it as a parameter and match it with the URL.

These `routes` are illustrated in the following diagram:

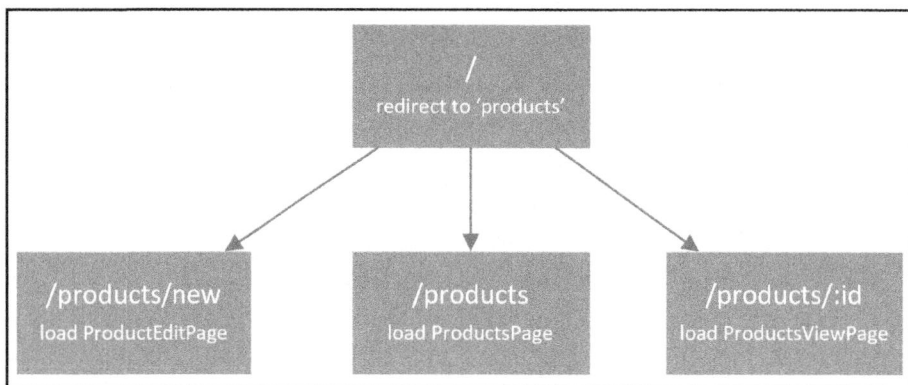

Using Angular Router, let's implement client-side routing with the following steps:

1. Create the components to be used in the new `routes` with the following command:

```
ng generate component modules/market/product-view-page

ng generate component modules/market/product-edit-page
```

2. Define the market `routes` configuration in `market.module.ts` as follows:
   1. Import `RouterModule` and `Routes` from the `@angular/router` package.
   2. Create a `routes` configuration object.
   3. Import `RouterModule` as part of `MarketModule`.
   4. You can remove the exported `ProductsPageComponent` component from `MarketModule`, since it is now part of the route configuration and `AppModule` should no longer use it directly.

The code for the preceding steps looks as follows:

```typescript
import { NgModule } from '@angular/core';
import { CommonModule } from '@angular/common';
import { RouterModule, Routes } from '@angular/router';

import { SharedModule } from '../shared/shared.module';

import { ProductsPageComponent } from './products-page/products-page.component';
import { CategoryMenuItemComponent } from './category-menu-item/category-menu-item.component';
import { CategoryMenuComponent } from './category-menu/category-menu.component';
import { ProductListComponent } from './product-list/product-list.component';
import { ProductCardComponent } from './product-card/product-card.component';
import { ProductViewPageComponent } from './product-view-page/product-view-page.component';
import { ProductEditPageComponent } from './product-edit-page/product-edit-page.component';

const routes: Routes = [
  { path: 'products', component: ProductsPageComponent },
  { path: 'products/new', component: ProductEditPageComponent },
```

```
        { path: 'products/:id', component:
ProductViewPageComponent },
];

@NgModule({
  imports: [
    CommonModule,
    SharedModule,
    RouterModule.forChild(routes),
  ],
  declarations: [
    ProductsPageComponent,
    CategoryMenuItemComponent,
    CategoryMenuComponent,
    ProductListComponent,
    ProductCardComponent,
    ProductViewPageComponent,
    ProductEditPageComponent,
  ],
})
export class MarketModule { }
```

As you can see in the preceding code, the `routes` configuration is an object of the `Routes` type, which is the array of a route configuration. The key properties for a route configuration are the following:

- `path`: This represents the URL path for which the route is considered a match.
- `component`: This defines the component that should be mounted if the route matches.
- `pathMatch`: This defines the match rule policy, which is used in `AppModule`. When set to `full`, the match policy forces a complete match.

Then you attach the route configuration while importing the `RouterModule` into the root module. `RouterModule` provides two key methods: `forRoot` and `forChild`.

The paradigm of `forRoot`/`forChild` is a common method in Angular for modules to respond differently, depending on whether they are imported in the root or child modules, which is usually related to lazy-loaded modules and associated providers.
This is considered an advanced subject and is not covered as part of this book, you can read more about it here if you like - `https://angular.io/guide/lazy-loading-ngmodules#forroot-and-forchild`, `https://angular.io/guide/singleton-services#forroot`.

To simplify, typically, the root module is the one that is bootstrapped in the `main.ts` file, which, in this case, is the `AppModule`. The `routes` you defined in the preceding code are defined as part of a different module, the `MarketModule`, which is therefore considered a child module, and the `forChild` method is used.

Now that you have the `MarketModule` routes in place, implement the default route configuration and edit the template by following the next steps:

1. Define the app `routes` configuration in `app.module.ts`:
    1. Import `RouterModule` and `Routes` from the `@angular/router` package.
    2. Create a `routes` configuration object.
    3. Import `RouterModule` as part of `AppModule`, as follows:

```
import { BrowserModule } from '@angular/platform-browser';
import { HttpClientModule } from '@angular/common/http';
import { NgModule } from '@angular/core';
import { RouterModule, Routes } from '@angular/router';

import { AppComponent } from './app.component';
import { HeaderComponent } from
'./components/header/header.component';
import { SharedModule } from
'./modules/shared/shared.module';
import { MarketModule } from
'./modules/market/market.module';
import { CoreModule } from './modules/core/core.module';

const routes: Routes = [
  { path: '', pathMatch: 'full', redirectTo: 'products' },
];

@NgModule({
  declarations: [
    AppComponent,
    HeaderComponent,
  ],
  imports: [
    HttpClientModule,
    BrowserModule,
    CoreModule,
    SharedModule,
    MarketModule,
    RouterModule.forRoot(routes),
  ],
```

```
    providers: [],
    bootstrap: [AppComponent]
})
export class AppModule { }
```

As you can see in the preceding code, the `routes` configuration includes a default `path: ''` route. A default route simply redirects the app to the relevant route, and therefore doesn't specify a component itself. Additionally, `pathMatch` is set to `full`, as otherwise, this route path would match against every URL. Then you attach the route configuration using the `RouterModule`, only this time you use `forRoot`, since this is the `AppModule`, which is bootstrapped in `main.ts` file, hence it's the root module.

2. Use `router-outlet` to instruct Angular as to where route components are to be mounted:
   1. Open `app.component.html`
   2. Replace the app products page with a `router-outlet`:

   ```html
   <app-header></app-header>
   <div class="main-area">
     <router-outlet></router-outlet>
   </div>
   ```

   Due to the fact that the app layout includes the header across all pages, you can simply mount routed components into the main area section in this case.

That's it! You can now run the app and see if it first navigates to `/products` due to the default route configuration and whether the products page is displaying correctly. To test other `routes`, you can simply change the URL manually at this point; for example, try changing `/products/new` to `/products/1`.

> Angular includes a concept of routing and routed modules. Ideally, you should encapsulate route-related concerns in separate modules. You can read more about these topics in the Angular documentation, available at `https://angular.io/guide/router` and `https://angular.io/guide/module-types`.

Implementing a routed page

Having the `routes` setup in place, implement the product details page component by following these steps:

1. Generate `ProductDetailsComponent` with the following command:

    ```
    ng generate component modules/market/product-details
    ```

2. Replace its HTML file content with the following:

    ```
    <div>
      <img [src]="primaryImageSrc" />
      <h3>{{product.title}}</h3>
      <span>{{product.description}}</span>
    </div>
    ```

3. Replace its CSS file content with the following:

    ```
    img {
      max-width: 80px;
      max-height: 80px;
    }
    ```

4. Set the class to receive a product as input with a `primaryImageSrc` getter:

    ```
    import { Component, Input } from '@angular/core';
    import { Product } from '../../../model';

    @Component({
      selector: 'app-product-details',
      templateUrl: './product-details.component.html',
      styleUrls: ['./product-details.component.css']
    })
    export class ProductDetailsComponent {
      @Input() product: Product;

      get primaryImageSrc() {
        return this.product && this.product.media &&
    this.product.media.length > 0
          ? this.product.media[0].url
          : null;
      }
    }
    ```

5. Implement product retrieval in `ProductsService` as follows:

```
...
export class ProductsService {
  ...
  loadProduct(id: number) {
    return this.http
      .get(`${this.apiUri}products/${id}`)
      .toPromise()
      .then(result => result as Product);
  }
}
```

6. Load the product according to the specified route parameter in
`ProductViewPageComponent`:

```
import { Component, OnInit } from '@angular/core';
import { ActivatedRoute } from '@angular/router';
import { ProductsService } from
'../../core/services/products.service';
import { Product } from '../../../model';

@Component({
  selector: 'app-product-view-page',
  templateUrl: './product-view-page.component.html',
  styleUrls: ['./product-view-page.component.css']
})
export class ProductViewPageComponent implements OnInit {
  product: Product;
  isBusy = false;

  constructor(
    private readonly route: ActivatedRoute,
    private readonly productsService: ProductsService,
  ) { }

  ngOnInit() {
    // should generally use the observer and subscribe.
    const productId = +this.route.snapshot.paramMap.get('id');

    this.isBusy = true;
    try {
      this.productsService.loadProduct(productId)
        .then(p => this.product = p);
    } finally {
      this.isBusy = false;
    }
  }
}
```

```
}
```

As you can see, Angular Router includes a service named `ActivatedRoute`. It is a useful service when implementing routed components as it enables responding to route parameters, navigating in code, and more.

> `ActivatedRoute` includes a parameter map as an observable, to which you can subscribe. Using this instead of the static snapshot is generally preferred, since it supports synchronizing with updates to `routes` while the component stays mounted.

7. Replace the `ProductViewPageComponent` HTML file's content with the following:

```
<div *ngIf="product">
  <app-product-details [product]="product"></app-product-
details>
  <button routerLink="/products">Back</button>
</div>
<app-busy *ngIf="isBusy"></app-busy>
```

Here, you see the use of `routerLink`, which is another directive that comes with Angular Router. It is used to perform navigation as specified directly in the templates. You set it with the desired path to which to navigate. It supports both a path and an array of segments, which we will use in an upcoming section.

8. Edit the template of `ProductCardComponent` so that it navigates to the product page:

```
<div class="item-card">
  <div class="item-card-content-container"
       [routerLink]="['/products', product.productId]">
    <img class="item-card-content-container-img"
[src]="primaryImageSrc" />
    <span class="item-card-content-container-
title">{{product.title}}</span>
    <span class="item-card-content-container-
text">{{product.description}}</span>
  </div>
</div>
```

Next, follow these steps to implement the navigation from `ProductsPageComponent` to `ProductsEditPageComponent`:

1. Generate a new button component as part of `SharedModule` with the following command:

   `ng generate component modules/shared/plus-button`

2. Replace the HTML file `/src/app/modules/shared/plus-button/plus-button.component.html` contents with the following:

   ```
   <a class="round-button">+</a>
   ```

3. Replace the CSS file `/src/app/modules/shared/plus-button/plus-button.component.css` contents with the following:

   ```
   .round-button {
     display:block;
     width:50px;
     height:50px;
     line-height:47px;
     border: 2px solid #f5f5f5;
     border-radius: 50%;
     color:#f5f5f5;
     text-align:center;
     text-decoration:none;
     background: #464646;
     box-shadow: 0 0 3px gray;
     font-size:20px;
     font-weight:bold;
     cursor: pointer;
   }

   .round-button:hover {
     background: #262626;
   }
   ```

4. Export `PlusButtonComponent` in `SharedModule`:

   ```
   ...
   @NgModule({
     ...
     exports: [
       ...
       PlusButtonComponent,
     ],
   })
   ```

```
export class SharedModule { }
```

5. Use the new component in the `ProductsPageComponent` template, position it in the bottom-right corner, and set up the navigation using `routerLink`:

```
<app-category-menu
  [categories]="categories"
  (categoryChanged)="onCategoryChanged($event)"
  ></app-category-menu>

<app-product-list [products]="products"></app-product-list>

<div class="plus-container" routerLink="/products/new">
  <app-plus-button></app-plus-button>
</div>

<app-busy *ngIf="isBusy"></app-busy>
```

6. Replace the CSS file `/src/app/modules/market/products-page/products-page.component.css` contents with the following:

```
.plus-container {
  position: fixed;
  right: 50px; bottom: 50px;
}
```

Congratulations! You have just completed implementing the product view page and wiring up the navigation, so go ahead and give it a try yourself—the product view page should look similar to this:

Implementing template-driven forms in Angular

Having finished the product details and with routing now in place, let's use Angular's rich support for forms as you go on to implement `ProductEditPageComponent`.

Angular's team understands that most apps require some level of handling forms, including the following:

- Two-way binding of HTML form elements
- Field-specific and form-wide validation
- Validation monitoring and user feedback
- Form editing trackability (for example, to determine which fields are pristine, touched, and valid)
- Binding update trigger modes (blur, change, submit, and so on)

Angular provides two key alternatives when handling forms: Reactive-style and template-driven.

The former is generally preferred in the case of nontrivial and somewhat complicated forms, while the latter is usually preferred in simple and static forms.

While there are technical differences between the two, this chapter focuses on using template-driven forms.

First, let's implement the `ProductEditPageComponent` by adding all the necessary form elements and loading the categories list that the user should choose from. To do this, follow these steps:

1. Generate `ProductFormComponent` with the following command:

```
ng generate component modules/market/product-form
```

2. Replace the HTML file `/src/app/modules/market/product-form/product-form.component.html` contents with the following:

```html
<form>
  <div>
    <label for="title">Title</label>
    <input id="title" name="title" />
  </div>
  <div>
    <label for="description">Description</label>
```

```
      <textarea id="description" name="description"></textarea>
    </div>
    <div>
      <label for="category">Category</label>
      <select id="category" name="category">
        <option value=''>Select category..</option>
        <option *ngFor="let c of categories" [value]="c.name">{{
        c.name }}</option>
      </select>
    </div>
    <div class="actions-panel">
      <button>Save</button>
      <button>Cancel</button>
    </div>
  </form>
```

3. Replace the CSS file `/src/app/modules/market/product-form/product-form.component.css` contents with the following:

```
form {
  padding: 20px;
  display: flex;
  flex-direction: column;
  width: 350px;
}

form > div {
  padding: 5px;
}

input, select, textarea {
  width: 100%;
}

textarea {
  height: 80px;
}

.actions-panel {
  margin-top: 10px;
  align-self: center;
}

.actions-panel > button:first-child {
  margin: 5px;
}
```

4. Edit file `/src/app/modules/market/product-form/product-form.component.ts` and set `categories` to be received as an input:

```
import { Component, Input } from '@angular/core';
import { Category } from '../../../model';

@Component({
  selector: 'app-product-form',
  templateUrl: './product-form.component.html',
  styleUrls: ['./product-form.component.css']
})
export class ProductFormComponent {
  @Input() categories: Category[];
}
```

5. Edit `ProductEditPage` template file `/src/app/modules/market/product-edit-page/product-edit-page.component.html` and render `ProductFormComponent` as follows:

```
<div *ngIf="categories">
  <app-product-form [categories]="categories"></app-product-form>
</div>

<app-busy *ngIf="isBusy"></app-busy>
```

6. Edit `ProductEditPage` component file `/src/app/modules/market/product-edit-page/product-edit-page.component.ts` and set `categories` to load while maintaining a busy indication state as follows:

```
import { Component, OnInit } from '@angular/core';
import { CategoriesService } from
'../../core/services/categories.service';
import { Category } from '../../../model';

@Component({
  selector: 'app-product-edit-page',
  templateUrl: './product-edit-page.component.html',
  styleUrls: ['./product-edit-page.component.css']
})
export class ProductEditPageComponent implements OnInit {
  categories: Category[];
  isBusy = false;

  constructor(
    private readonly categoriesService: CategoriesService,
```

```
) { }

ngOnInit() {
this.isBusy = true;
try {
this.categoriesService.loadCategories()
.then(o => this.categories = o);
} finally {
this.isBusy = false;
}
}
}
```

You can now run the app and click on the plus button that navigates to the editing page. It should look similar to the following:

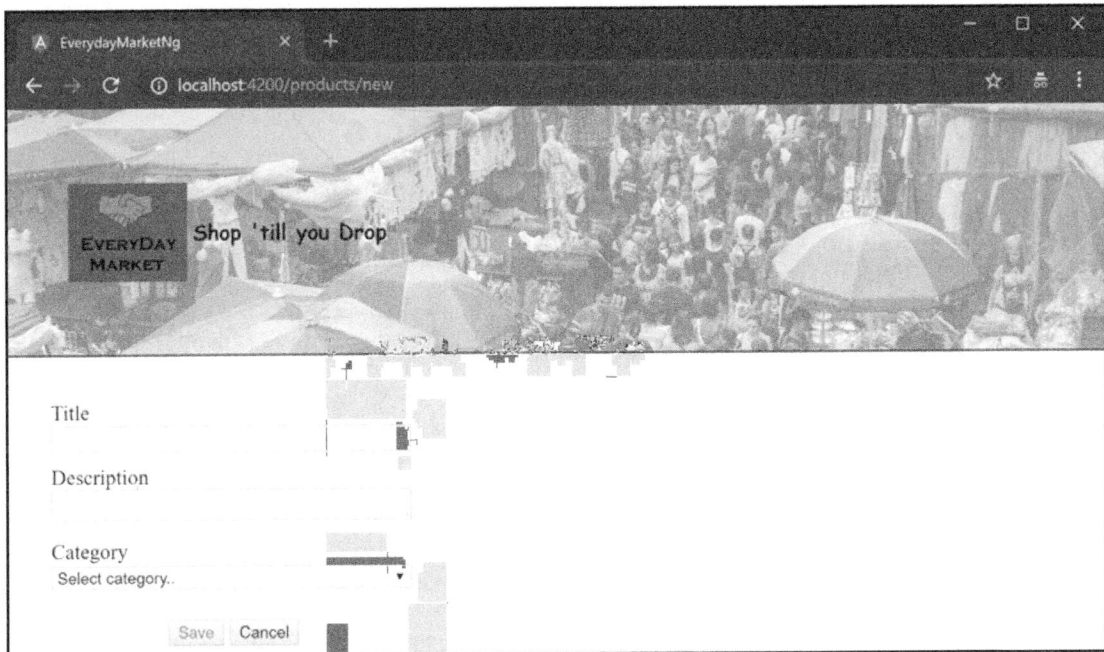

As you can see, the form is in place and currently consists of a standard HTML form.

Next, let's use Angular's template-driven forms to bind the form elements to the component state.

First, you need to import Angular's template-driven module, named `FormsModule`, into `MarketModule` as follows:

```
...
import { FormsModule } from '@angular/forms';
...

@NgModule({
  imports: [
    CommonModule,
    SharedModule,
    FormsModule,
    RouterModule.forChild(routes),
  ],
  ...
})
export class MarketModule { }
```

Using Angular's ngModel directive

Once the forms module is imported, you can start using Angular's template-driven features, and, specifically, the extremely useful `ngModel` directive.

`ngModel` is an extensible directive that includes built-in support for two-way binding between component fields or properties and standard form elements.

Let's use `ngModel` in `ProductFormComponent`:

1. Create a new model at `src/app/model/new-product.ts`:

```
export interface NewProduct {
  title: string;
  description: string;
  category: string;
}
```

2. Re-export the new model as part of the `src/app/model/index.ts` file:

```
...
export * from './new-product';
```

3. In `ProductFormComponent`, initialize a new product as a field in the component:

```
...
import { Category, NewProduct } from '../../../model';
...
export class ProductFormComponent {
  @Input() categories: Category[];

  product: NewProduct = {
    title: '',
    description: '',
    category: '',
  };
}
```

4. In the `ProductFormComponent` template, use `ngModel` to bind form elements to corresponding product data values using the two-way binding format:

```
<form>
  <div>
    <label for="title">Title</label>
    <input id="title" name="title" [(ngModel)]="product.title"
/>
  </div>
  <div>
    <label for="description">Description</label>
    <textarea id="description" name="description"
              [(ngModel)]="product.description"></textarea>
  </div>
  <div>
    <label for="category">Category</label>
    <select id="category" name="category"
[(ngModel)]="product.category">
      <option value=''>Select category..</option>
      <option *ngFor="let c of categories" [value]="c.name">{{
        c.name }}</option>
    </select>
  </div>
  <div class="actions-panel">
    <button>Save</button>
    <button>Cancel</button>
  </div>
</form>
```

With that in place, the form elements are now bound to the product data property in the component, and vice versa! This means that changing the component data synchronizes the form elements, as well as keeping the data in your component updated as the user manipulates the form.

At this moment, the product field in the component state reflects what the user populates as part of the form. Now let's implement the cancel and save functionality:

1. Implement creating a new product in ProductsService as follows:

```
...
import { Product, NewProduct } from '../../../model';
...
export class ProductsService {
  ...
  addProduct(product: NewProduct) {
    return this.http
      .post(`${this.apiUri}products/slim`, product)
      .toPromise()
      .then(result => result as Product);
  }
}
```

> The API action, in this case, should allow anonymous access. Usually, real-life apps that involve authoring data include authentication. In such cases, it mostly requires the app to send a token with each request, which is first generated by a user login.

2. Bind the click events on the following buttons in the ProductFormComponent template with the onSubmit event handler function defined in the component:

```
...
<div class="actions-panel">
  <button (click)="onSubmit(true)">Save</button>
  <button (click)="onSubmit(false)">Cancel</button>
</div>
...
```

3. Implement the submit callback in ProductFormComponent, and then emit an event to be handled by the parent component. Include the product payload in case the user chooses to save; otherwise, emit null, as shown here:

```
import { Component, Input, OnInit, Output, EventEmitter } from
'@angular/core';
...
export class ProductFormComponent implements OnInit {
```

```
@Output() productSubmit = new EventEmitter<NewProduct>();
...
onSubmit(ok) {
  this.productSubmit.emit(ok ? this.product : null);
}
}
```

4. Bind the `productSubmit` event in the `ProductEditPageComponent` template with the `onProductSubmit` event handler function defined in the component, and then pass it the payload:

```
<div *ngIf="categories">
  <app-product-form
    [categories]="categories"
    (productSubmit)="onProductSubmit($event)"
    >
  </app-product-form>
</div>

<app-busy *ngIf="isBusy"></app-busy>
```

5. Implement `onProductSubmit` in the `ProductEditPageComponent` class with the following settings:
   1. If the payload `product` is null, use Angular's location abstraction to navigate back.
   2. Otherwise, use `ProductsService` to add the product, and then navigate back:

```
...
import { Category, NewProduct } from '../../../model';
import { Location } from '@angular/common';
import { ProductsService } from
'../../core/services/products.service';
...
export class ProductEditPageComponent implements OnInit {
  ...
  constructor(
    private readonly location: Location,
    private readonly categoriesService: CategoriesService,
    private readonly productsService: ProductsService,
  ) { }
  ...
  onProductSubmit(newProduct: NewProduct) {
    if (!newProduct) {
      this.location.back();
    } else {
```

```
                    this.isBusy = true;
                    try {
                      this.productsService.addProduct(newProduct)
                        .then(o => this.location.back());
                    } finally {
                      this.isBusy = false;
                    }
                  }
                }
              }
            }
```

That's it! You can now run the app and try to create a new product. Currently, the app expects the user to enter a valid input on their own, but we will implement form validation in the next section.

> Angular provides another directive: `ngSubmit`, which you can use with event binding on the form element instead of the submit button.

Implementing form validation

Angular provides useful validation-related techniques, one of which works by using standard HTML validation attributes.

Inspecting the REST API, we can see that the following fields' validation rules should be met:

- `title`: Required, `minlength="3"`, `maxlength="50"`
- `category`: Required

Let's add the necessary HTML attributes to `product-form.component.html` to reflect these validation rules:

```
...
    <input id="title" name="title" [(ngModel)]="product.title"
      required minlength="3" maxlength="50" />
...
    <select id="category" name="category"
      [(ngModel)]="product.category" required>
      <option value=''>Select category..</option>
      <option *ngFor="let c of categories" [value]="c.name">{{ c.name
}}</option>
    </select>
  ...
```

Luckily, Angular tracks element-specific and form-wide states. Specifically, `ngModel` toggles the following class names on every element, according to its state:

- `ng-touched` / `ng-untouched`: Represents whether the element was visited at least once or not by the user
- `ng-dirty` / `ng-pristine`: Represents whether the element's value was changed or not
- `ng-valid` / `ng-invalid`: Represents whether the element's value is valid or not

To reflect elements' invalid status, add the following CSS to the `product-form.component.css` file:

```
...
.ng-invalid:not(form) {
  border-left: 5px solid #a94442;
}
```

You can now run the app, and you should see a red border visible when the elements' **Title** and **Category** fields are invalid.

Furthermore, you can use Angular's form-state monitoring to control the HTML DOM. Let's add feedback to the user, indicating error messages and disabling the submit button until the form is valid.

To do so, let's use another feature of Angular: element references.

Element references

Element references allow you to attach a variable name to elements inside the template. Then you can reference those elements throughout the template, and even in code.

You use the hash symbol (#), followed by a name of your choice. This is the associated element name, which you then use elsewhere.

The following is an example of a simple usage of element references:

```
<input #title />
<span>{{ Title length: title.value.length }}</span>
```

Moreover, element references can be set to certain directives, and `ngModel` is one of them. Combined, you get the `ngModel`, associated with the element as the element reference variable, which includes the validity state, among other things.

Now change the `ProductFormComponent` template to display error messages, and then disable the **Submit** button according to the validity state:

```html
<form #productForm="ngForm">
  <div>
    <label for="title">Title</label>
    <input id="title" name="title" [(ngModel)]="product.title"
      #title="ngModel" required minlength="3" maxlength="50" />

    <span [class.hidden]="!title.errors?.required">Title is
     required</span>
    <span [class.hidden]="!title.errors?.minlength">
      Title should be at least 3 characters long
    </span>
    <span [class.hidden]="!title.errors?.maxlength">
      Title should be less than 50 characters long
    </span>
  </div>
  <div>
    <label for="description">Description</label>
    <textarea id="description" name="description"
      [(ngModel)]="product.description"></textarea>
  </div>
  <div>
    <label for="category">Category</label>
    <select id="category" name="category" [(ngModel)]="product.category"
      #category="ngModel" required>
      <option value=''>Select category..</option>
      <option *ngFor="let c of categories" [value]="c.name">{{ c.name
        }}</option>
    </select>
    <span [class.hidden]="category.valid">Category is required</span>
  </div>
  <div class="actions-panel">
    <button (click)="onSubmit(true)" [disabled]="!productForm.form.valid">
      Save
    </button>
    <button (click)="onSubmit(false)">Cancel</button>
  </div>
</form>
```

As you can see in the preceding code, in addition to ngModel, the template uses an element reference with another directive from Angular Forms—ngForm. The element reference variable is set to the ngForm directive that tracks and monitors the form-wide validity status, which affects the submit button's disabled state.

Congratulations! You can now run the app and see the form validation function in action. It should look similar to the following screenshot:

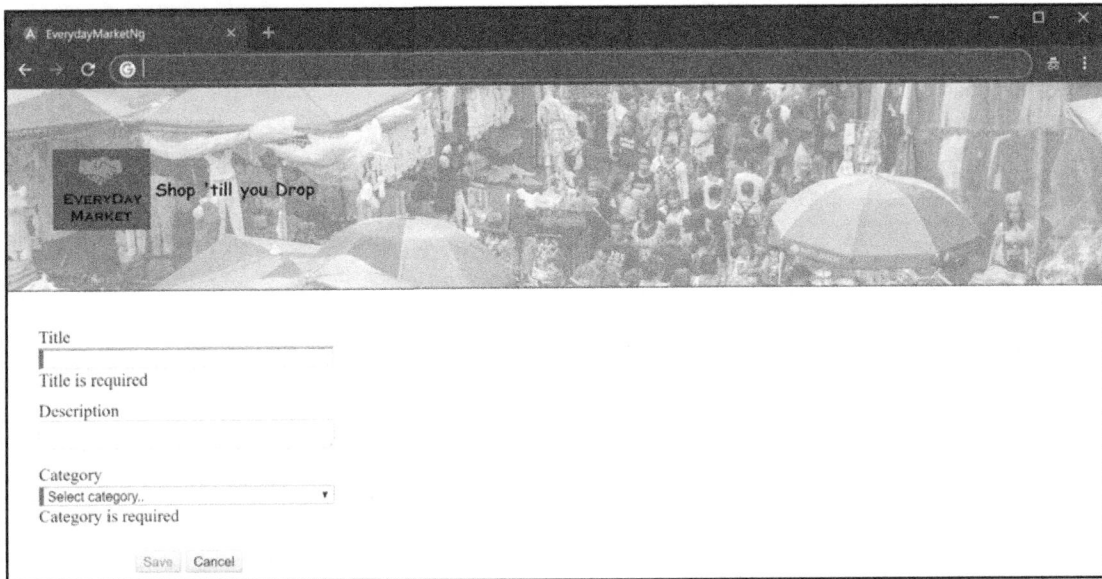

> You can read more about template-driven and reactive-style forms in the Angular documentation at `https://angular.io/guide/forms` and `https://angular.io/guide/reactive-forms`.
> You can find all the client-side related code in a public GitHub repository at `https://github.com/azuker/frontend-web-dev`.

Summary

In this chapter, you extended the Everyday Market app to better resemble a real-life implementation. As we did this, we also covered another two key features of Angular: Forms and Routing.

This concludes the chapters about Angular. While there's still an abundance of features to learn, we managed to cover much of Angular's core functionality.

Anyone who seeks to become a modern web developer can substantially benefit from knowing numerous technologies. Therefore, in Chapter 12, *App Development with React*, you will continue by learning React.

12
App Development with React

The web development field is vast in terms of open source software and community support and collaboration. As such, there are always multiple alternative frameworks for implementing the same thing, and that includes modern component frameworks to build SPA.

Now that you are familiar with Angular, it's certainly encouraged to gain familiarity with other technologies with a similar purpose. In this chapter you will learn about React, another incredibly popular SPA framework, while we cover the following topics:

- React overview
- Creating a React app
- Components
- JSX
- State and props
- Component interaction

React overview

Facebook's React, a JavaScript framework for building SPAs, is incredibly popular, and has constantly been receiving a lot of attention from the community. Additionally, React spreads out to mobile apps via React Native, as well as 3D and VR via React 360.

React was released to the public in 2013 and has revolutionized the way you build web apps. React is essentially a JavaScript-based view library, focusing on building encapsulated and reusable components, and its format was considered a novel approach at the time.

Similar to Angular, React is highly opinionated, although it focuses on a single aspect of building an app, which is the view engine, that is, components. Along with React comes JSX, enabling you to write the user interface template code combined with the logical code, but more on that later in this chapter.

Building blocks

These are the key building blocks of React:

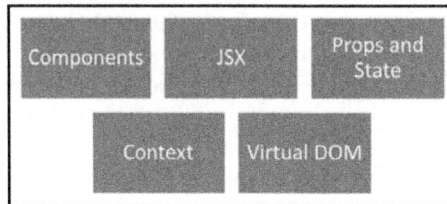

Following is the description of each block:

- **Components**: React enables you to decompose your app's visual tree into smaller reusable units called components.
- **JSX**: React's response to templates. JSX enables you to write components' template in code in a productive manner.
- **Props and state**: Props enable parent-child component interaction, while state is used by components to manage its behavior.
- **Context**: React supports a propagated context to be shared that is accessible through a visual tree that the context is applied to.
- **Virtual DOM**: Essentially a JavaScript object graph, this is composed by React every time its state changes by traversing through the application components and calling their `render` function. The Virtual DOM reflects the actual HTML DOM and is a key part of React's reconciliation process, similar to the purpose of Angular's change detection.

Compared to Angular (React being a view engine), React has much fewer building blocks since it focuses on components alone.

Creating a React app

A popular method for creating new React-based projects is using the CLI tool called **Create React App (CRA)**. Like Angular CLI, CRA enables you to create, run, and build your project; however, Angular CLI is much more comprehensive as it is intended as an integral tool as part of the Angular platform.

> **TIP**
>
> CRA supports boilerplate generation scripts. When creating a project, you can specify a boilerplate generation script. For example, there's a script for integrating TypeScript as the language of choice, as you can read here: `https://github.com/wmonk/create-react-app-typescript`.

Next, install CRA and create the `Everyday Market` project using the default boilerplate:

1. Open the terminal or Command Prompt and install CRA by executing the following:

   ```
   npm install -g create-react-app
   ```

2. Create the app project by executing the following:

   ```
   create-react-app everyday-market-react
   ```

   When the preceding command is executed, CRA creates the folder with the specified name and scaffolds the entire project using the default boilerplate script, in addition to installing the required dependencies.

   You can now open the folder in your editor and examine the scripts section in `package.json`:

   - `start`: Builds and hosts the app locally, with hot reloading in place for development purposes
   - `build`: Builds the app for distribution purposes
   - `test`: Executes a project's tests
   - `eject`: Ejects a project's build- and packaging-related configuration in cases where you need to take control

3. Continue by running the project. Open the terminal or Command Prompt and execute the following in the project folder:

   ```
   npm start
   ```

Now the development server should be running and your browser should open on the app's address.

Key app parts

CRA-based projects include the following key parts:

- `index.js`: This is the main entry point, and it takes care of bootstrapping the entire application:

```
ReactDOM.render(<App />, document.getElementById('root'));
```

- `App.js`: App is the root application component and is covered next, as you learn about React components.

Components

As described previously, React is a view engine, enabling you to decompose the app into smaller units, called components.

Let's review the auto-generated `App` component:

```
import React, { Component } from 'react';
import logo from './logo.svg';
import './App.css';

class App extends Component {
  render() {
    return (
      <div className="App">
        <header className="App-header">
          <img src={logo} className="App-logo" alt="logo" />
          <h1 className="App-title">Welcome to React</h1>
        </header>
        <p className="App-intro">
          To get started, edit <code>src/App.js</code> and save to reload.
        </p>
      </div>
    );
  }
}

export default App;
```

Before explaining class components, there are additional things to notice here:

```
import logo from './logo.svg';
import './App.css';
```

CRA-based projects use Webpack behind the scenes to build, bundle, and package your app. The default configuration supports importing static assets and CSS files directly in code. Then, those references are bundled and included as part of the build's finalized artifacts.

> Unlike Angular, React doesn't provide any built-in style encapsulation. Thus, you should determine your choice of CSS selector naming conventions or use relevant tools to avoid conflicts.

Back to components. The `App` component is a React class component. React has two types of component — class and functional. Class components are required when you need an instance-specific behavior or state, including lifecycle hooks. Otherwise, you should prefer implementing it as a functional component instead, as demonstrated later.

To create React class components, you simply write a class that extends `React.Component`. Then the minimum necessity is implementing a `render` function.

Render function

The `render` function is called by React every time its state changes as part of its reconciliation process. The `render` function is expected to return the component's visual tree. Confusingly, it isn't the real HTML DOM, but rather the component-specific slice of the final Virtual DOM.

In React, you don't respond to state changes imperatively and immediately. Instead, you manage the component state, and every time `render` is called, you simply render the entire visual tree according to the current state snapshot.

You must be asking yourself what that code is in the `App` component `render` function. That's JSX, which you will learn about in the next section.
In this chapter, you're going to implement the following components:

- `AppComponent`
- `HeaderComponent`
- `ProductsPageComponent`
- `CategoryMenuComponent`
- `CategoryMenuItemComponent`

- `ProductListComponent`
- `ProductCardComponent`
- `BusyComponent`

The following diagram depicts the component hierarchy and dependency graph you're going to implement in this chapter:

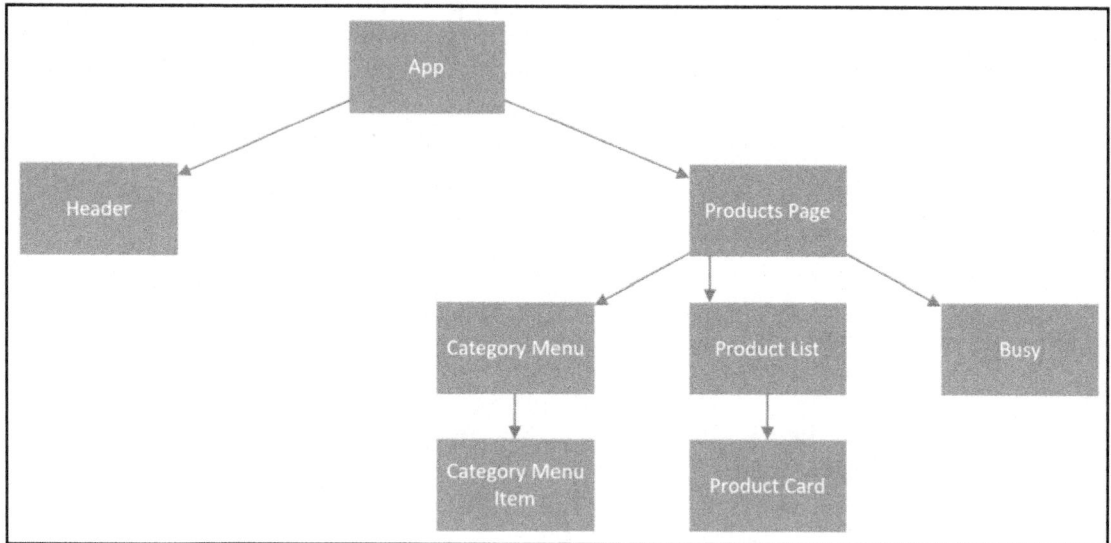

JSX

JSX is React's template **domain-specific language** (**DSL**), allowing you to write the user interface in code next to its logical code. This is the part where non-React developers often cringe, especially those used to MVC-style programming. React follows the notion that components can (and should) be hard-wired with its template. Arguably, it is indicated that this is actually more productive, since one rarely needs the same logic with completely different templates, and thus having it in one piece should be more easily maintainable.

JSX is not really mandatory. As part of the build process, JSX is compiled to plain JavaScript code behind the scenes. Therefore, it is possible to use the underlying JavaScript API to construct the Virtual DOM, rather than using JSX. Despite that, the use of JSX is certainly encouraged as it increases the speed and productivity of development, as well as the manageability of the code.

Using JSX

Basically, JSX allows you to use HTML-like syntax along with code expressions. You use HTML elements to construct the visual tree and embed code expressions enclosed inside curly braces, inline, or as an attribute value, as follows:

```
render() {
  const text = 'Hello JSX';
  const textClass = 'attention';

  return (
    <span className="{textClass}">{text}</span>
  );
}
```

Notice the use of the `className` attribute. React discourages the use of XML attributes that correspond to JavaScript-reserved keywords and recommends using the DOM property names instead. For example, `className` instead of `class` and `htmlFor` instead of `for`.

Having the user interface written in code opens up everything developers love about code. You can refactor and reuse it, just as any other code, into variables and functions:

```
getHeader(headerText) {
  return (
    <header className="App-header">
      <img src={logo} className="App-logo" alt="logo" />
      <h1 className="App-title">{headerText}</h1>
    </header>
  );
}

render() {
  const header = this.getHeader('Hello JSX');
  return (
    <div className="App">
      {header}
    </div>
  );
}
```

Header component

Now that you understand class components and JSX, implement the header component by following the next steps:

1. Create a new folder called `/src/components/common/Header`.
2. Create a new file called `/src/components/common/Header/Header.css`.
3. Write the following CSS in `Header.css`:

```css
.app-header {
  height: 200px;
  border-bottom: 1px solid black;
}

.app-header::after {
  content: "";
  height: 200px;
  opacity: 0.5;
  background: url('../../../assets/herobg.jpg');
  background-position: center;
  background-repeat: no-repeat;
  background-size: cover;
  position: absolute;
  top: 0;
  left: 0;
  bottom: 0;
  right: 0;
  z-index: -1;
}

.app-logo {
  height: 80px;
  margin-left: 50px;
}

.app-slogan {
  font-family: 'Comic Sans MS', 'Comic Sans', cursive;
  font-weight: bold;
  margin-left: 5px;
}
```

4. Create a new file called `/src/components/common/Header/Header.js`.
5. Write the following code in `Header.js`:

```js
import React from 'react';
import './Header.css';
```

```
import headerLogo from '../../../assets/logo.png';

class Header extends React.Component {
  render() {
    return (
      <header className="app-header app-bg">
        <div className="maxHeight flex flex-align-items--
          center">
          <img src={headerLogo} className="app-logo" alt="logo"
            />
          <span className="app-slogan">Shop 'till you
            Drop</span>
        </div>
      </header>
    );
  }
}

export default Header;
```

6. Create a new file called /src/components/common/index.js.
7. Re-export the header in index.js:

```
import Header from './Header/Header';

export {
  Header
};
```

Re-exporting is a useful feature that enables module aggregation and location transparency; nearly all packages you use follow this paradigm. For example, if all dependent modules import the Header component from the index module, you can then move the Header related files anywhere you like and change only the import statement in the index module.

8. Use the new Header component in App.js by replacing the content of App.js with the following:

```
import React from 'react';
import {Header} from './components/common';
import './App.css';

class App extends React.Component {
  render() {
    return (
      <div>
```

```
        <Header />
      </div>
    );
  }
}

export default App;
```

9. Replace the CSS content of `index.css` with the following:

```css
html {
  box-sizing: border-box;
  font-size: 62.5%;   /* =10px */
}
*, *:before, *:after {
  box-sizing: inherit;
}

html, body {
  margin: 0;
  padding: 0;
  width: 100%;
  height: 100%;
}

body {
  font-size: 1.4rem;
}

.hidden {
  display: none !important;
}

.maxHeight {
  height: 100%;
}

.maxWidth {
  width: 100%;
}

.flex {
  display: flex;
}

.flex-justify-content--center {
  justify-content: center;
}
```

```
.flex-align-items--center {
  align-items: center;
}
```

10. Add static image assets:
    1. Create a folder called `/src/assets`.
    2. Place the referenced images, `herobg.png` and `logo.png`, inside the folder.

That's it! You can now run the project and see the app with the header in place. It should look similar to this:

Before proceeding to the products section, let's learn about props, state, and functional components.

Props

Like other component frameworks, React supports parent-child component interaction by using props. Every component in React has an accessible `props` property, which is a key-value object containing all the data passed in from the parent component.

Consider the following example:

```
import React from 'react';

class Child extends React.Component {
  render() {
    return (
      <span>Hello {this.props.greet}</span>
    );
  }
}

export default Child;
```

The `Child` component is a simple component that renders a `span` element with some greeting text. Importantly, it uses the `props` object while rendering, meaning it expects a `text` property to be passed down from the parent. To pass down expected props, a parent component simply needs to specify those as simple HTML-like attributes, as follows:

```
import React from 'react';
import Child from './Child';

class Parent extends React.Component {
  render() {
    return (
      <div>
        <Child text='Props and State' />
      </div>
    );
  }
}

export default Parent;
```

The `props` object keys, like any plain JavaScript object, can contain any value. The parent component can pass down primitives, objects, arrays, and even functions. Additionally, the `props` object is treated as immutable and shouldn't be modified in the child component.

The other form of interaction is to allow a child to notify the parent when something occurs. While Angular uses events, React uses a callback approach. A parent component can pass down a function as a prop that the child can execute when desired. Here's an example:

```
class Child extends React.Component {
  render() {
    return (
      <div>
        <span>Hello {this.props.greet}</span>
```

```
            <button onClick={this.props.onUpdate}></button>
          </div>
        );
      }
    }

    class Parent extends React.Component {
      onUpdate = () => {
        console.log('Child triggered callback');
      };

      render() {
        return (
          <div>
            <Child text='Props and State' onUpdate={this.onUpdate} />
          </div>
        );
      }
    }
```

The parent component passes down a function named onUpdate as a prop. Then the child component uses this prop and binds it to the button's click event.

Evident from this example, there are additional things you should pay attention to:

- **Callbacks and lexical** this: Similar to dealing with standard HTML DOM events, when class instance functions are propagated or used in JSX, it might lose the context of having this set to the class instance. To ensure it remains the class instance, be sure to use arrow functions or the bind JavaScript method.

- **DOM event names JSX syntax**: React uses a specific format with DOM event names— on<Event>. It starts with the on keyword, followed by the event name with its first letter capitalized. For instance, to bind the click event, you use onClick in JSX.

Lastly, if you need a component to use fallback default values for unprovided props, you can use React's feature of default props, as follows:

```
    class Child extends React.Component {
      static defaultProps = {
        greet: 'Default text',
        onUpdate: () => {}, // do nothing
      };

      render() {
        return (
```

```
      <div>
        <span>Hello {this.props.greet}</span>
        <button onClick={this.props.onUpdate}></button>
      </div>
    );
  }
}
```

You can define a static key-value `defaultProps` property on your component to apply default prop values. React enables us to populate the `props` object with the missing unprovided keys specified in the default `props` object.

> There is a package called `prop-types` that enables defining the expected `props` for every component. This is extremely useful since it enables prop validation, eases usage, and improves code documentation.

State

Props are immutable and are controlled by the parent component. In React, every class component has a state property used for self-managed and mutable data. Like `props`, `state` is just a plain JavaScript object.

To set the default starting state, you can declare the state as a class field, thanks to Webpack, or set it in the constructor instead:

```
class Parent extends React.Component {
  state = {
    greet: 'Props and State',
  };

  onUpdate = () => {
    console.log('Child triggered callback');
  };

  render() {
    return (
      <div>
        <Child text={this.state.greet} onUpdate={this.onUpdate} />
      </div>
    );
  }
}
```

The parent component sets a `greet` key on the initialized state object with an initial value. Then the state object is used in the render method to pass down the `text` as a prop to the child component.

setState

To mutate state, you use React's `setState` method available to you as part of the `React.Component` base class. The simplest usage is to provide it with a new object, as follows:

```
onUpdate = () => {
  this.setState({
    greet: 'State Updated',
  });
};
```

Internally, `setState` merges the object you specify with the complete `state` object. Therefore, you can provide it with an object that includes only the updated portion of the entire state and not repeats of all the properties every time. More importantly, `setState` is usually asynchronous, meaning you shouldn't rely on having an updated state right after calling `setState`.

In this example, when the child component's button is clicked, `onUpdate` is executed in the parent and updates its state. Calls to `setState` trigger React's reconciliation process; therefore, the parent's component tree is re-rendered. The parent renders and passes the updated prop to the child, which should now display `Hello State Updated`.

> `setState` is significant in React, and understanding its effects and usage
> is important. You can read more about props and state here:
> https://reactjs.org/docs/components-and-props.html
> https://reactjs.org/docs/state-and-lifecycle.html

Stateless functional components

As the name implies, functional components are really just functions. If a component doesn't require any state, lifecycle hooks, or basically any class-specific behavior or state, it is preferable to implement it as a functional component. Previously, you implemented the header component as a class component. The header implements nothing but the `render` method, a definite clue that it can be a functional component instead.

Now, implement the header component as a functional component by replacing the entire content of `Header.js` with the following:

```
import React from 'react';
import './Header.css';
import headerLogo from '../../../assets/logo.png';

const Header = (props) => (
  <header className="app-header app-bg">
    <div className="maxHeight flex flex-align-items--center">
      <img src={headerLogo} className="app-logo" alt="logo" />
      <span className="app-slogan">Shop 'till you Drop</span>
    </div>
  </header>
);

export default Header;
```

Now the header component is just a pure function. In React, **Stateless Functional Components (SFC)** are functions that receive `props` populated with passed down data and return the rendered content. If you are wondering why the `import` statement of React is included, it's actually needed whenever a file uses JSX because, without it, the app fails to build.

It is generally preferred to implement functional components when possible. First, it is considered simpler and more readable. Second, the React team has future plans to better optimize the performance of such components.

CategoryMenu

Having learned about state and props, implement the categories menu, as depicted in this diagram, by following the next steps:

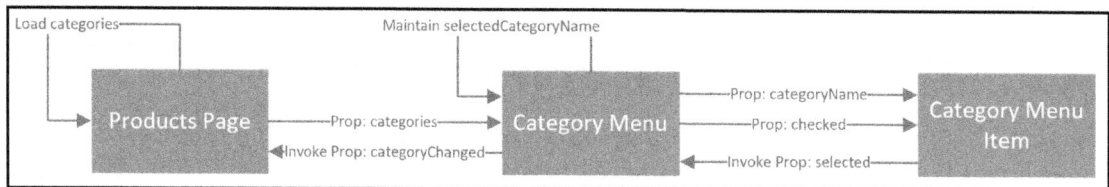

Follow these steps:

1. Create the following folders:
   - `/src/components/market`
   - `/src/components/market/CategoryMenuItem`
   - `/src/components/market/CategoryMenu`
   - `/src/components/market/ProductsPage`

2. Implement `CategoryMenuItem` component styles by creating this file and adding the following CSS styles:

   `/src/components/market/CategoryMenuItem/CategoryMenuItem.css`

   ```css
   .menu-item-container {
     display: inline;
     padding: 5px 3px 5px 3px;
     border: 1px solid black;
     padding: 2px 5px 2px 5px;
     cursor: pointer;
   }

   .menu-item-container:hover {
     background-color: lightgray;
   }

   .menu-item-selected {
     background-color: bisque;
   }
   ```

3. Implement `CategoryMenuItem` component behavior by creating this file and adding the following JavaScript code:

   `/src/components/market/CategoryMenuItem/CategoryMenuItem.js`

   ```javascript
   import React from 'react';
   import './CategoryMenuItem.css';

   function getItemClassNames(checked) {
     return 'menu-item-container' + (checked ? '
       menu-
     item-selected' : '');
   }

   const CategoryMenuItem = (props) => (
     <div
       onClick={() =>
       props.onSelected(props.categoryName)}
   ```

```
            className={getItemClassNames(props.checked)}
                >
                    <span>{props.categoryName}</span>
                </div>
            );

        export default CategoryMenuItem;
```

> **TIP**
> If you need to manage conditional class names according to state, you can use a simple and popular library called `classnames` for that purpose: https://github.com/JedWatson/classnames

4. Re-export the `CategoryMenuItem` component:
   1. Create the `/src/components/market/index.js` file and write the following:

   ```
   import CategoryMenuItem from
   './CategoryMenuItem/CategoryMenuItem';

   export {
     CategoryMenuItem,
   };
   ```

5. Implement `CategoryMenu` component styles by creating this file and adding the following CSS styles:

   /src/components/market/CategoryMenu/CategoryMenu.css

   ```
   #cat-menu, #cat-menu > li {
     list-style: none;
     padding: 0;
     margin: 0;
     display: inline;
   }
   ```

6. Implement `CategoryMenu` component behavior by creating this file and adding the following JavaScript code:

   /src/components/market/CategoryMenu/CategoryMenu.js

   ```
   import React from 'react';
   import './CategoryMenu.css';
   import {CategoryMenuItem} from '../';
   class CategoryMenu extends React.Component {
     state = {
       selectedCategoryName: null,
   ```

```
        };

onCategorySelected = (categoryName) => {
  const cat = this.props.categories.find(c =>
    c.name
  === categoryName);
  this.props.onCategoryChanged(cat);
  this.setState({selectedCategoryName:
   cat.name});
};

render() {
  return (
    <ul id="cat-menu">
      {this.props.categories.map(c => (
        <li key={c.name}>
          <CategoryMenuItem
            categoryName={c.name}
            checked={c.name ===
            this.state.selectedCategoryName}
            onSelected=
            {this.onCategorySelected}
          />
        </li>
      ))}
    </ul>
  );
}
}
export default CategoryMenu;
```

In the preceding code, the component renders the child menu items using
the map operator. This is related to list rendering, and is described in more
detail after the category menu features implementation steps.

7. Re-export the CategoryMenu component by writing the following in
/src/components/market/index.js:

```
import CategoryMenuItem from
'./CategoryMenuItem/CategoryMenuItem';
import CategoryMenu from './CategoryMenu/CategoryMenu';

export {
  CategoryMenuItem,
  CategoryMenu,
};
```

8. Implement a service for retrieving categories and products:
    1. Create a `/src/services/marketService.js` file.
    2. Write the following code:

```
const baseUrl = 'http://localhost:55564/api/';

function loadCategories() {
  return fetch(`${baseUrl}products/categories`)
    .then(r => r.json());
}

function loadProducts(categoryName) {
    return
fetch(`${baseUrl}products/searchcategory/${categoryName}`)
    .then(r => r.json());
}

export default {
  loadCategories,
};
```

9. Implement the `ProductsPage` component:
    1. Create a file called `/src/components/market/ProductsPage/ProductsPage.js`
    2. Write the following code:

```
import React from 'react';
import MarketService from
'../../../services/marketService';
import {CategoryMenu} from '../';

class ProductsPage extends React.Component {
  state = {
    categories: [],
  };

  componentDidMount() {
    MarketService.loadCategories()
      .then(o => this.setState({categories: o}));
  }

  onCategoryChanged = (category) => {
    console.log(category);
  }
```

```
    render() {
      return (
        <div>
          <CategoryMenu
            categories={this.state.categories}
            onCategoryChanged={this.onCategoryChanged}
          />
        </div>
      );
    }
}
export default ProductsPage;
```

In the preceding code snippet, the service is used in a function called
`componentDidMount`.

React components have a certain life cycle, which you can hook into. One
of these hooks is `componentDidMount`, which is executed after a
component is mounted to the DOM, making it a useful place to load
related data asynchronously.

You can read more about lifecycle hooks here:
`https://reactjs.org/docs/react-component.html`
`https://reactjs.org/docs/state-and-lifecycle.html`

10. Re-export the `ProductsPage` component by writing the following in
`/src/components/market/index.js`:

```
import CategoryMenuItem from
'./CategoryMenuItem/CategoryMenuItem';
import CategoryMenu from './CategoryMenu/CategoryMenu';
import ProductsPage from './ProductsPage/ProductsPage';

export {
  CategoryMenuItem,
  CategoryMenu,
  ProductsPage,
};
```

11. Modify the `App` component's behavior:
    1. Make it a functional component.
    2. Import and render the `ProductsPage` component:

```
import React from 'react';
import {Header} from './components/common';
import {ProductsPage} from './components/market';
import './App.css';
```

```
const App = () => (
  <div>
    <Header />
    <div className="main-area">
      <ProductsPage />
    </div>
  </div>
);

export default App;
```

12. Modify `App` component styles, replacing the entire content of its CSS file with the styles given in the following code snippet:

```
.main-area {
  margin: 10px;
}
```

Great! You can now run the app and see the category menu working and the selection tracking in place. It should look similar to this:

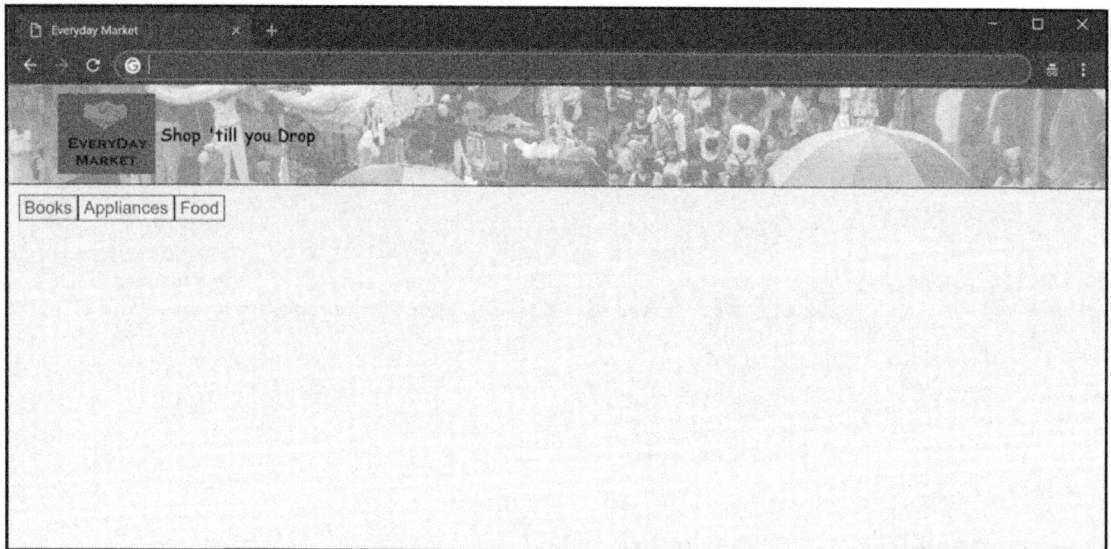

List rendering

Pay attention to the `CategoryMenu` component as it renders the child menu items from the `categories` array prop:

```
render() {
  return (
    <ul id="cat-menu">
      {this.props.categories.map(c => (
        <li key={c.name}>
          <CategoryMenuItem
            categoryName={c.name}
            checked={c.name === this.state.selectedCategoryName}
            onSelected={this.onCategorySelected}
          />
        </li>
      ))}
    </ul>
  );
}
```

In React, to render multiple children commonly through arrays, you use the `map` operator and return the rendered content for every item. In such cases, React promotes assigning a `key` prop for every item's rendered root element.

The `key` prop is a specialized prop that should represent the identity, meaning elements with the same key are considered interchangeable, which can better optimize performance if the collection changes.

> You can read more about list rendering in React here: `https://reactjs.org/docs/lists-and-keys.html`.

Product listing

Now that the category menu is complete, continue by implementing the product listing, as depicted in this diagram, by following the next steps:

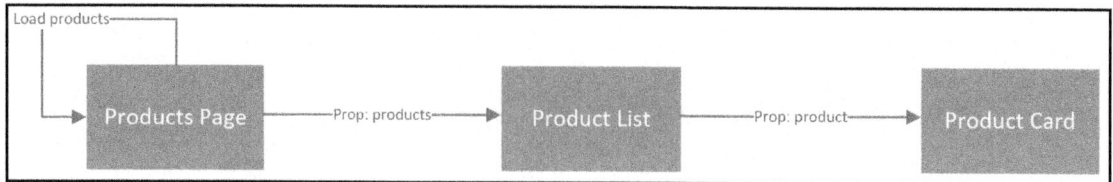

Follow the following steps:

1. Create the following folders:
    - `/src/components/market/ProductCard`
    - `/src/components/market/ProductList`

2. Implement the `ProductCard` component's behavior by creating this file and adding the following JavaScript code:

`/src/components/market/ProductCard/ProductCard.js`

```javascript
import React from 'react';
import './ProductCard.css';

function primaryImageSrc(product) {
  return product && product.media &&
  product.media.length > 0
    ? product.media[0].url
    : null;
}

const ProductCard = ({product}) => (
  <div className="item-card">
    <div className="item-card-content-
container">
      <img
        className="item-card-content-
container-
         img"
        alt="product"
        src={primaryImageSrc(product)}
      />
      <span className="item-card-content-
        container-
```

```
            title">
              {product.title}
            </span>
            <span className="item-card-content-
              container-
              text">
              {product.description}
            </span>
        </div>
      </div>
    );

    export default ProductCard;
```

3. Implement `ProductCard` component styles by creating this file and adding the following CSS styles:

/src/components/market/ProductCard/ProductCard.css

```css
.item-card {
  box-shadow: 0 4px 8px 0 rgba(0,0,0,0.2);
  transition: 0.3s;
  background-color: white;
  width: 280px;
  height: 200px;
  float: left;
  margin: 10;
}

.item-card:hover {
      box-shadow: 0 8px 16px 0 rgba(0,0,0,0.2);
}

.item-card-content-container {
  padding: 2px 16px;
  display: flex;
  height: 100%;
  flex-direction: column;
  align-items: center;
  justify-content: center;
  cursor: pointer;
}

.item-card-content-container-img {
  display: block;
  max-width: 80px;
  max-height: 80px;
  width: auto;
```

```
            height: auto;
            text-align: center;
        }

        .item-card-content-container-title {
            display: block;
            font-size: 1.6rem;
        }

        .item-card-content-container-text {
            word-wrap: normal;
            font-size: 1.2rem;
            overflow: hidden;
        }
```

4. Re-export the `ProductCard` component by writing the following in `/src/components/market/index.js`:

```
import CategoryMenu from './CategoryMenu/CategoryMenu';
import CategoryMenuItem from
'./CategoryMenuItem/CategoryMenuItem';
import ProductCard from './ProductCard/ProductCard';
import ProductsPage from './ProductsPage/ProductsPage';

export {
  CategoryMenu,
  CategoryMenuItem,
  ProductCard,
  ProductsPage,
};
```

5. Implement the `ProductList` component's behavior by creating this file and adding the following JavaScript code:

`/src/components/market/ProductList/ProductList.js`

```
import React from 'react';
import './ProductList.css';
import {ProductCard} from '..//';

const ProductList = ({products}) => (
  <div>
    <ul id="products-container">
      {products.map(p => (
        <li key={p.productId}>
          <ProductCard product={p} />
        </li>
      ))}
```

```
        </ul>
      </div>
    );

    export default ProductList;
```

6. Implement `ProductList` component styles by creating this file and adding the following CSS styles:

`/src/components/market/ProductList/ProductList.css`

```css
#products-container, #products-container > li {
  list-style: none;
  padding: 0;
  margin: 0;
  display: inline;
}

#products-container {
  display: flex;
  justify-content: space-around;
  flex-wrap: wrap;
}
```

7. Re-export the `ProductList` component, and then write the following in `/src/components/market/index.js`:

```javascript
import CategoryMenu from './CategoryMenu/CategoryMenu';
import CategoryMenuItem from
'./CategoryMenuItem/CategoryMenuItem';
import ProductCard from './ProductCard/ProductCard';
import ProductList from './ProductList/ProductList';
import ProductsPage from './ProductsPage/ProductsPage';

export {
  CategoryMenu,
  CategoryMenuItem,
  ProductCard,
  ProductList,
  ProductsPage,
};
```

8. Modify the `ProductsPage` component:
    1. Add an empty products array as the default starting state
    2. Load products when the selected category is changed
    3. Render the `ProductList` component:

```
import React from 'react';
import MarketService from
'../../../services/marketService';
import {CategoryMenu, ProductList} from '../';

class ProductsPage extends React.Component {
  state = {
    categories: [],
    products: [],
  };

  componentDidMount() {
    MarketService.loadCategories()
      .then(o => this.setState({categories: o}));
  }

  onCategoryChanged = (category) => {
    MarketService.loadProducts(category.name)
      .then(o => this.setState({products: o}));
  }

  render() {
    return (
      <div>
        <CategoryMenu
          categories={this.state.categories}
          onCategoryChanged={this.onCategoryChanged}
        />
        <ProductList products={this.state.products} />
      </div>
    );
  }
}

export default ProductsPage;
```

That's it! You have just completed implementing the product listing. Go ahead and run the app and see it in action; it should look similar to this:

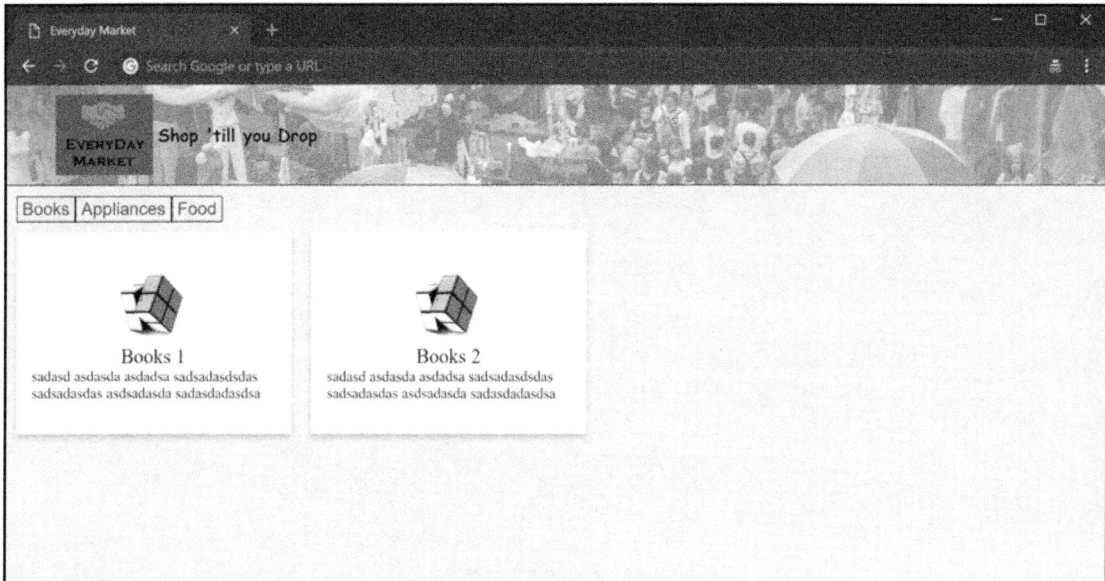

Busy indicator

Finally, implement a busy indicator in the page by following the next steps:

1. Implement the `Busy` component's behavior by creating this file and adding the following JavaScript code:

```
/src/components/common/Busy/Busy.js

import React from 'react';
import './Busy.css';

const Busy = () => (
  <div className="busy-loader-container">
    <div className="busy-loader"></div>
  </div>
);

export default Busy;
```

2. Implement `Busy` component styles by creating this file and adding the following CSS styles:

`/src/components/common/Busy/Busy.css`

```css
.busy-loader-container {
  position: absolute;
  left: 0; right: 0; top: 0; bottom: 0;
  background-color: azure;
  opacity: 0.5;
  display: flex;
  align-items: center;
  justify-content: center;
}

.busy-loader {
  border: 16px solid #f3f3f3;
  border-top: 16px solid #3498db;
  border-radius: 50%;
  width: 80px;
  height: 80px;
  animation: busy-spin 2s linear infinite;
}

@keyframes busy-spin {
  0% { transform: rotate(0deg); }
  100% { transform: rotate(360deg); }
}
```

3. Re-export the `Busy` component by writing the following in `/src/components/common/index.js`:

```js
import Header from './Header/Header';
import Busy from './Busy/Busy';

export {
  Header,
  Busy,
};
```

4. Modify the `ProductsPage` component:
   1. Add a `busy` property set to `false` as the default starting state
   2. Change to the `busy` state when loading data is initiated and completed
   3. Render the `Busy` component if the `busy` state is `true`:

```
import React from 'react';
import MarketService from
'../../../services/marketService';
import {CategoryMenu, ProductList} from '..//';
import {Busy} from '../../common';

class ProductsPage extends React.Component {
  state = {
    categories: [],
    products: [],
    busy: false,
  };

  componentDidMount() {
    this.setState({busy: true});
    this.loadCategoriesWhileBusy();
  }

  async loadCategoriesWhileBusy() {
    try {
      const categories = await
      MarketService.loadCategories();
      this.setState({
        categories,
        busy: false,
      });
    } catch (e) {
      this.setState({busy: false});
      throw e; // consider implementing actual error
      handling
    }
  }

  onCategoryChanged = (category) => {
    this.setState({busy: true});
    this.loadProductsWhileBusy(category);
  }

  async loadProductsWhileBusy(category) {
    try {
      const products = await
      MarketService.loadProducts(category.name);
```

```
                    this.setState({
                      products,
                      busy: false,
                    });
                  } catch (e) {
                    this.setState({busy: false});
                    throw e; // consider implementing actual error
                    handling
                  }
                }

              render() {
                return (
                  <div>
                    <CategoryMenu
                      categories={this.state.categories}
                      onCategoryChanged={this.onCategoryChanged}
                    />
                    <ProductList products={this.state.products} />
                    {this.state.busy && <Busy />}
                  </div>
                );
              }
            }

            export default ProductsPage;
```

Congratulations! You have just completed the busy indicator, and with that, the page's functionality, in this chapter.

Conditional rendering

Pay attention to the Busy component's render function. It includes conditional rendering, which you have not yet used in React:

```
{this.state.busy && <Busy />}
```

When this.state.busy is false, the expression resolves as false. React ignores Booleans while rendering, and hence the expression doesn't render anything in this case. Otherwise, when busy is true, the expression resolves to the busy component, which in turn renders.

Summary

React is certainly a leading SPA framework in the field. It has had a great impact on how web apps are built ever since its initial release and has been gaining popularity steadily through the years. Admittedly, React is considered a slim framework with a slighter learning curve than Angular. You do not need to invest too much time and effort in getting started, which is considered a popular comparison factor. However, it's just a view engine.

React focuses on components, and therefore React followers have created a vast number of libraries to complete React-based apps with other app development concerns such as state management, routing, server-side rendering, services, lazy loading, and more.

In this chapter, you learned about React, including components, JSX, state, props, and more. While there's still more depth to all of these, you actually know much of the core functionality at this stage.

To complete the journey of frontend web app development, let's continue to learn another popular SPA component framework: Vue.js.

App Development with Vue 13

Now that you are familiar with both React and Angular, you can advance to the final step in the web app development journey by learning another leading framework. In this chapter, you will learn to use Vue.js, a promising and rapidly growing framework, during which you will build the Everyday Market app using the following topics:

- Vue.js overview
- Vue CLI
- Components
- Data binding and events
- The component definition object

Vue.js overview

Vue.js, also known as Vue, and pronounced *view*, was created by Evan You and was released in the beginning of 2014. Originally, Evan had been working with AngularJS a lot, so many people argue that Vue very much resembles AngularJS.

Like React, it features a lightweight adoptable architecture, and thus it can be more easily embedded and integrated with existing apps and other technologies. Additionally, Vue is essentially a view engine, focusing on building components. Even when compared to React, Vue is less opinionated, and is actually more flexible in how you build components, in addition to offering supporting libraries that are maintained officially by the Vue team alongside its core Vue framework product.

Vue is constantly growing and gaining popularity quite steadily. Being a flexible framework focusing on component with support for MVC-style programming, it is often considered the middle ground in the spectrum between Angular and React.

Building blocks

The following are the key building blocks of Vue:

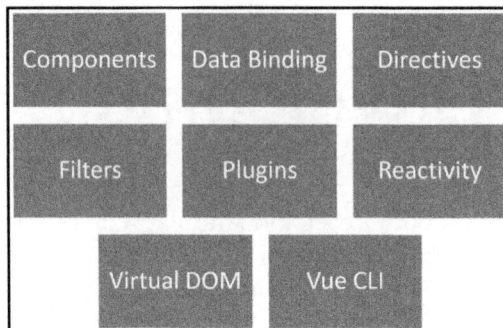

Components	Data Binding	Directives
Filters	Plugins	Reactivity
	Virtual DOM	Vue CLI

- **Components**: like other SPA frameworks, Vue enables you to decompose your app's visual tree into smaller reusable units called components.
- **Data binding**: having the view and code separated can be a nuisance as these usually need to interact, and, for that purpose, enter data binding.
- **Directives**: directives allow us to extend or customize existing elements in all sorts of ways.
- **Filters**: like Angular's pipes, filters enable us to transform values in an encapsulated and reusable way.
- **Plugins**: plugins and mixins enable you to extend and customize both global or component-specific options, states, or behavior.
- **Reactivity**: Vue uses a reactive API to determine and act when changes take place. You can leverage this via data, watches, and computed properties, and even use the underlying API directly.
- **Virtual DOM**: like React, Vue also implements the concept of virtual DOM. It is essentially a JavaScript object that reflects the actual DOM and takes part of the change detection sequence to optimize updates made to the actual HTML DOM.
- **Vue CLI**: a command-line interface tool provided to assist you with starting and managing your project.

As you can see, Vue brings with it many features, some of them comparable to Angular and some to React. Despite that, Vue alone is still a slim and lightweight framework, and programmer should learn and start to use it fairly quickly.

> If you wish to understand the differences between Vue and other
> frameworks better, Vue docs have a dedicated section just for that
> purpose:
> `https://vuejs.org/v2/guide/comparison.html`

Vue CLI

Like Angular CLI and create-react-app covered in previous chapters, Vue also brings a CLI
that you can use to create and manage your project. It is called Vue CLI. While it is not yet a
key ingredient to make Vue a complete platform like Angular's, it is still quite rich
compared to create-react-app for example.

Next, install Vue CLI and create the Everyday Market project by following the next steps:

1. Open the terminal or command prompt and install Vue CLI by executing the
   following code:

   ```
   npm install -g @vue/cli
   ```

2. Create the app project by executing the following code:

   ```
   vue create everyday-market-vue
   ```

By executing the preceding command, Vue CLI creates the folder with a specified name
and scaffolds the entire project using its default options, in addition to installing the
required dependencies.

> Vue CLI is quite extensive. You can use the `--help` flag along with every
> command to inspect the supported options and different possibilities.

You can now open the folder in your editor. So, let's examine the scripts section in
`package.json`:

- `serve`: Builds and hosts the app in a local `dev` server with hot module reload in
  place for development purposes
- `build`: Builds the app for distribution purposes
- `lint`: Executes the static-code analysis linter

Continue by running the project: open the terminal or command prompt and execute the following in the project folder :

```
npm run serve
```

Now the dev server is running. You can open the browser and navigate to the address written in the terminal to see the app running in the browser. It should look similar to this:

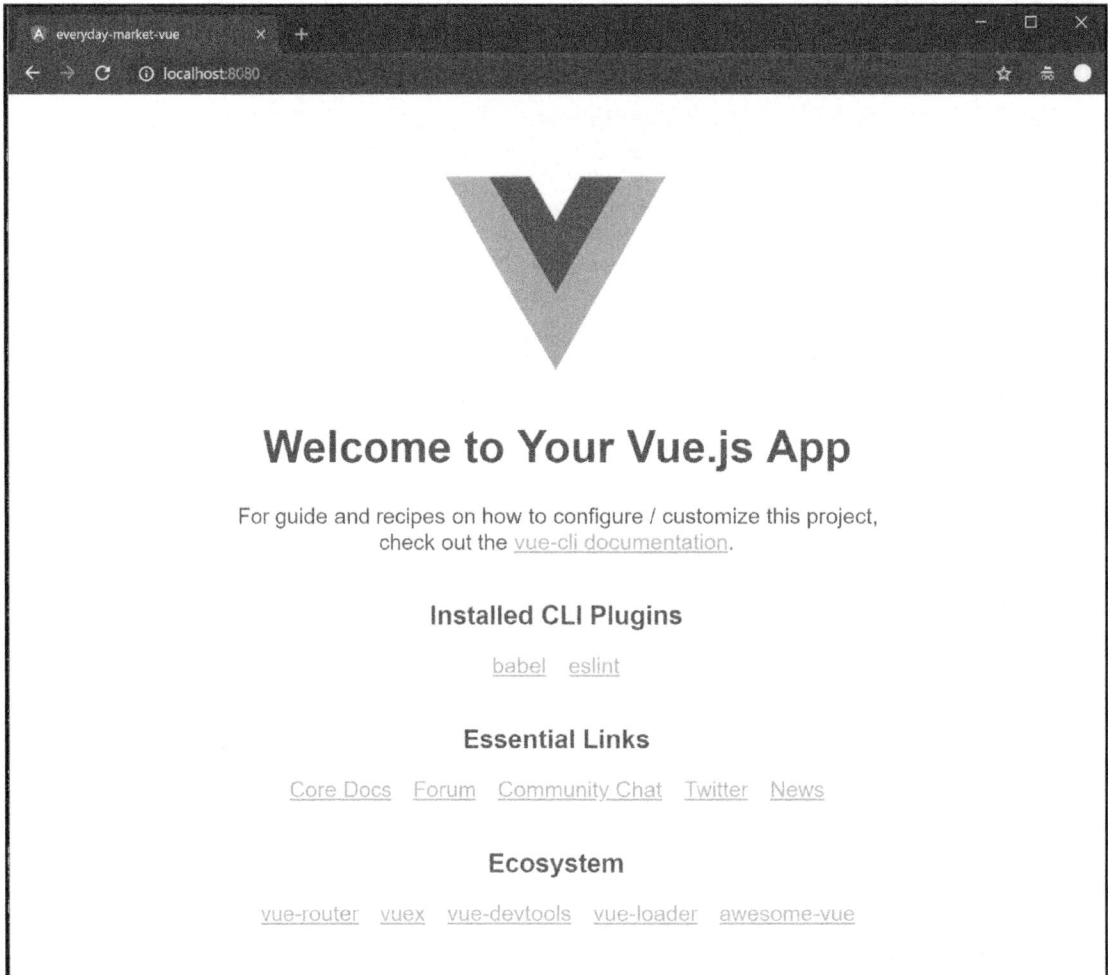

Key app parts

Vue CLI-based projects include the following key parts :

- `main.js`: This is the main entry point, which takes care of bootstrapping the entire application and mounting the root component to the HTML DOM, as shown in the following code:

```
new Vue({
  render: h => h(App)
}).$mount('#app');
```

- `App.vue`: This is the root application component, and will be studied next as you learn about Vue components.

Components

In a similar way to React, Vue focuses mainly on components. Vue is extremely flexible in how you write and register components. You can write components as plain objects, use classes and decorators, and even JSX, to name a few.

In this chapter, you will use a common form called single file components. This is very popular, especially in Vue CLI-based projects.

> You can read more about the different options of writing and registering components here:
> https://vuejs.org/v2/guide/components-registration.html
> https://vuejs.org/v2/guide/render-function.html
> https://github.com/vuejs/vue-class-component

Single file components

Let's review the auto-generated `App` component, as shown in the following example:

```
<template>
  <div id="app">
    <img alt="Vue logo" src="./assets/logo.png">
    <HelloWorld msg="Welcome to Your Vue.js App"/>
  </div>
</template>

<script>
```

```
import HelloWorld from './components/HelloWorld.vue'

export default {
  name: 'app',
  components: {
    HelloWorld
  }
}
</script>

<style>
#app {
  font-family: 'Avenir', Helvetica, Arial, sans-serif;
  -webkit-font-smoothing: antialiased;
  -moz-osx-font-smoothing: grayscale;
  text-align: center;
  color: #2c3e50;
  margin-top: 60px;
}
</style>
```

As you can see from the preceding code snippet, Vue supports using standard web constructs to compose components. Typically, single file components are written in files with a `.vue` extension and include three sections :

- `<template>`:
  This tag contains the view of the component. Similar to Angular, this is an HTML-like construct that supports additional specifications such as data-binding annotations, directives, and more.

- `<script>`:
  This tag contains the definition of the component, as well as its behavior implementation, and is exported as a plain object.
  While the object can include many properties, most of which are covered later in this chapter, here you can see a few as follows:
  - name: The component's name that other components can use to reference it in their templates.
  - components: The referenced child components this component renders. When a parent component uses child components, these child components must be recognized by Vue. While there are several ways to do that, the components property is a simple way to specify the referenced child components.

- In this example, the `App` component renders the `HelloWorld` component as part of its template, and therefore it is specified as part of the `components` property as well.

- `<style>`:
  This tag contains the component-related CSS-style definitions. By default, Vue doesn't apply any sort of style encapsulation, but you can enable that by specifying a `scoped` attribute on the style tag, as shown in the following example:

  ```
  <style scoped>
  ...
  </style>
  ```

  Specifying the `scoped` attribute instructs Vue to process the style definitions and provide style encapsulation. Often, this is the preferred approach when writing specific and encapsulated components.

  > In addition to standard components, Vue supports functional components in a similar way to React.
  > You can read more about it here: `https://vuejs.org/v2/guide/render-function.html#Functional-Components`

In this chapter, you're going to implement the following components:

- App
- Header
- ProductsPage
- CategoryMenu
- CategoryMenuItem
- ProductList
- ProductCard
- Busy

The following diagram depicts the component hierarchy and dependency graph you're going to implement in this chapter -

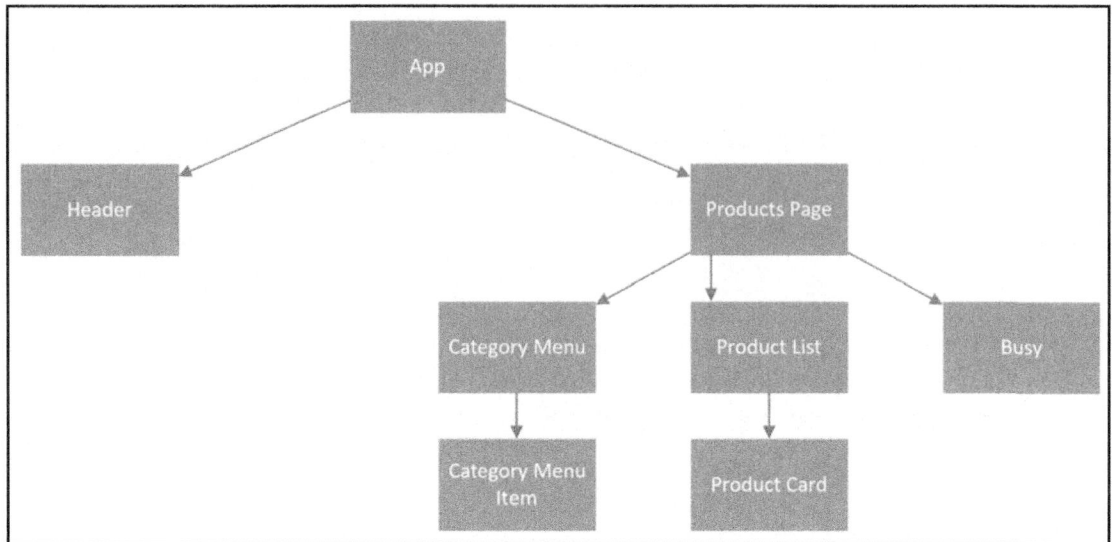

Header component

Now that you have understood the fundamentals of single file components, implement the header component by following the next steps:

1. Create a new folder `/src/components/common`
2. Create a new file `/src/components/common/Header.vue`
3. Write the following code in `Header.vue`, as shown in the following example:

```
<template>
  <header class="app-header app-bg">
    <div class="maxHeight flex flex-align-items--center">
      <img src="../../assets/logo.png" class="app-logo" />
      <span class="app-slogan">Shop 'till you Drop</span>
    </div>
  </header>
</template>

<script>
export default {
  name: 'Header',
```

```
}
</script>

<style scoped>
.app-header {
  height: 200px;
  border-bottom: 1px solid black;
}

.app-header::after {
  content: "";
  height: 200px;
  opacity: 0.5;
  background: url('../../assets/herobg.jpg');
  background-position: center;
  background-repeat: no-repeat;
  background-size: cover;
  position: absolute;
  top: 0;
  left: 0;
  bottom: 0;
  right: 0;
  z-index: -1;
}

.app-logo {
  height: 80px;
  margin-left: 50px;
}

.app-slogan {
  font-family: 'Comic Sans MS', 'Comic Sans', cursive;
  font-weight: bold;
  margin-left: 5px;
}
</style>
```

4. Use the new Header component in `App.vue` by replacing its content with the following code:

```
<template>
  <div>
    <Header />
  </div>
</template>

<script>
import Header from './components/common/Header.vue';
```

```
export default {
  name: 'app',
  components: {
    Header,
    }
  }
}
</script>
```

Global styles

While you could include the global app styles as part of the app component's non-scoped styles, Vue CLI-based projects support importing CSS files in code:

1. Create a new file `/src/styles.css`
2. Write the following CSS:

```css
html {
  box-sizing: border-box;
  font-size: 62.5%;   /* =10px */
}

*, *:before, *:after {
  box-sizing: inherit;
}

html, body {
  margin: 0;
  padding: 0;
  width: 100%;
  height: 100%;
}

body {
  font-size: 1.4rem;
}

.hidden {
  display: none !important;
}

.maxHeight {
  height: 100%;
}

.maxWidth {
  width: 100%;
```

```
}

.flex {
  display: flex;
}

.flex-justify-content--center {
  justify-content: center;
}

.flex-align-items--center {
  align-items: center;
}
```

3. Import the styles in `main.js`, as shown in the following code:

```
import Vue from 'vue';
import App from './App.vue';
import './styles.css';

Vue.config.productionTip = false;

new Vue({
  render: h => h(App)
}).$mount('#app');
```

Assets

The header component references two images in its template and style. Vue CLI-based projects include a folder named `assets`, which you can use for static assets to have it bundled and distributed with your app.

To complete the header, add `herobg.png` and `logo.png` into the `assets` folder.

Great! You can now run the application and see the header in place. It should look similar to this:

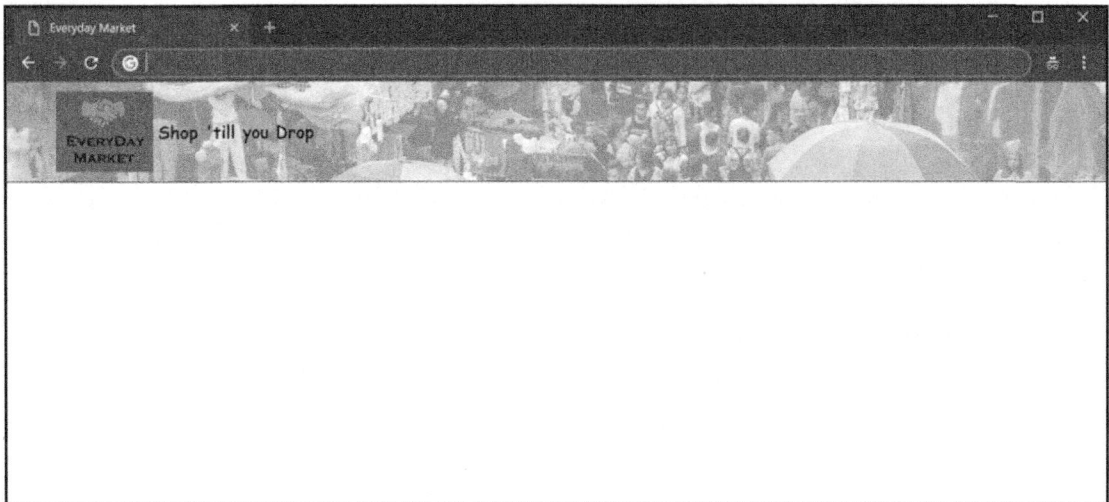

Data binding and component interaction

Like Angular, Vue supports data binding with specialized syntax in templates, and it can be applied to standard HTML elements as well as child components. Having the view and code separate can lead to much nuisance for the developer, as the two usually need to interact. For example, views need to display data managed in the component logic and the component logic needs to respond to events triggered from the template. Therefore, data binding is a key tool that eases the development immensely.

To achieve such scenarios, Vue provides several features that you can use as part of the component definition object, which you will learn about now.

Component definition object

Building Vue components in the form you witnessed now involves defining the component definition object, which is the exported object from the script block in single file components.

The component definition object supports different properties that you can use to shape the component and implement its behavior and state.
The following are the main options :

- `name`: The name of the component
- `components`: Registration of child components rendered within a certain component
- `props`: The immutable input that the component allows parent components to pass in
- `data`: The mutable state the component manages for its own behavior
- `methods`: The implemented behavior methods associated with the component
- `computed`: The set of properties that depend on the underlying reactive state
- `watch`: The set of watcher-implementations for handling reactive data changes

Props

You use props to allow a component to receive input from its parent. Props are immutable in the child component and are defined as part of the component definition object as shown in the following code:

```
<script>
export default {
  name: 'Child',
  props: {
    greet: String,
  },
}
</script>
```

In the preceding code, the `Child` component expects an input from its parent, specifically, a prop named `greet` of the type `String`.

> Props support more definitions, such as default values and validation. You can read more about it here: `https://vuejs.org/v2/guide/components-props.html`.

Interpolation binding

You can use interpolation binding, via mustache syntax like Angular, to bind the template to component data. In the following example, let's implement a child component that greets a person's name that the parent component should be passing in:

```
<template>
  <span>Hello {{ greet }}</span>
</template>

<script>
export default {
  name: 'Child',
  props: {
    greet: String,
  },
}
</script>
```

In the preceding code, the Child component binds the greet prop and writes it to the span's inner text.

Importantly, the template expression context is set to the component instance, referred to usually as the viewmodel. In this context, you should be able to access props, data, methods, and computed properties implicitly from the template.

Now, let's write the Parent component, which passes down the necessary prop as follows:

```
<template>
  <div>
    <Child greet="John Doe" />
  </div>
</template>

<script>
import Child from './Child.vue';

export default {
  name: 'Parent',
  components: {
    Child,
  },
}
</script>
```

As you can see in the preceding code, props are passed in simply as element attribute assignments.

Property binding

You can use property bindings to bind template elements' properties to component's data. A property binding can be applied using the syntax: `property="expression"`, as shown in the following example:

```
<template>
  <div>
    <Child :greet="'John Doe'" />
  </div>
</template>

<script>
import Child from './Child.vue';

export default {
  name: 'Parent',
  components: {
    Child,
  },
}
</script>
```

In the preceding code, the parent component binds the `Child` component's `greet` prop to an expression of a constant value. This is just to illustrate how you can use property binding syntax via a simple attribute assignment.

Property bindings are useful when you bind to the actual data that resides in your component. For this purpose, you will learn about data next.

Data

Often, components need to manage data. In addition to props, which are passed-in immutable input, you can specify mutable component data similar to React's concept of state, as well as props.

Data can be specified as a plain object or a factory function that creates that object. Let's use the latter to rewrite the parent component to bind to mutable data, as shown in the following example:

```
<template>
  <div>
    <Child :greet="name" />
  </div>
</template>
```

```
<script>
import Child from './Child.vue';

export default {
  name: 'Parent',
  components: {
    Child,
  },
  data: () => ({
    name: 'John Doe',
  }),
}
</script>
```

Now the parent component binds the `greet` property to a data entry that can now be mutated as part of this component logic. Next, you will complete the pipeline and update the data as you learn about events and methods.

Methods

Methods allow you to implement functions associated with the component instance which can then be used as event callbacks, data manipulation, and more.

Let's define a method in the `Parent` component that mutates the data in the following way:

```
<script>
import Child from './Child.vue';

export default {
  name: 'Parent',
  components: {
    Child,
  },
  data: () => ({
    name: 'John Doe',
  }),
  methods: {
    changeName: function(newName) {
      this.name = newName;
    }
  },
}
</script>
```

In the preceding code, the `changeName` method is implemented as part of the component's methods. Currently, this method isn't really executed yet, but this changes next.

Like Vue template's expression context explained before, Vue takes care of setting `this` to the component instance; that is, the viewmodel. This means, you should have access to all relevant entries, such as data and props, in your methods; just make sure you're not using arrow functions.

Events

Events are used in two ways — the recipient that subscribes to an event and the emitter that fires it, very much like Angular's concept of output and `EventEmitter`.

To subscribe to an event, you use the at sign (@) — `@event="expr"`. On the left side of the equation, the event corresponds to the event name, while the expression on the right specifies what to execute, usually a certain method.

On the other end, when a child component needs to trigger an event, you use a function provided to you by Vue called `$emit`, passing it the event name and relevant payload if needed, as shown in the following example:

```
this.$emit('click', 'some payload');
```

To demonstrate events, let's change the `Parent` component to subscribe to an `update` event fired by the child component, as shown in the following example:

```
<template>
  <div>
    <Child @update="changeName" :greet="name" />
  </div>
</template>

<script>
import Child from './Child.vue';

export default {
  name: 'Parent',
  components: {
    Child,
  },
  data: () => ({
    name: 'John Doe',
  }),
  methods: {
```

```
      changeName: function(newName) {
        this.name = newName;
      }
    },
  }
</script>
```

Then, let's change the `Child` component to fire an `update` event when a button is pressed, as shown in the following example:

```
<template>
  <div>
    <span>Hello {{ greet }}</span>
    <button @click="changeNameClicked">Change Name</button>
  </div>
</template>

<script>
export default {
  name: 'Child',
  props: {
    greet: String,
  },
  methods: {
    changeNameClicked: function() {
      this.$emit('update', 'Jane');
    }
  },
}
</script>
```

What happens here?

When the button is clicked, the child component fires an event named `update` with a string payload of `Jane`. Having the parent subscribed to this event triggers the parent component's `changeName` method.

Then the method changes the data called `name`, which eventually triggers the Vue rendering process, resulting in passing down the new value to the child component and, finally, in the rendering of `Hello Jane`.

Computed

The fact that Vue brings a reactive system provides you with another useful tool — computed properties.

There are cases in which components have some minor data projections, usually implemented as simple properties that depend on underlying data.

To demonstrate computed properties, let's change the `Parent` component to separate the data called `name` to both `firstName` and `lastName`. The template still binds to `name`, though. Given that it should be a simple concatenation, it is a good candidate for use with computed properties, as shown in the following example:

```
<template>
  <div>
    <Child @update="changeName" :greet="name" />
  </div>
</template>

<script>
import Child from './Child.vue';

export default {
  name: 'Parent',
  components: {
    Child,
  },
  computed: {
    name: function() {
      return this.firstName + ' ' + this.lastName;
    }
  },
  data: () => ({
    firstName: 'John',
    lastName: 'Doe',
  }),
  methods: {
    changeName: function(newName) {
      this.firstName = newName;
    }
  },
}
</script>
```

The preceding code showed us that the component now has `firstName` and `lastName` as the mutable data, and `name` is implemented as a computed property.

This allows the template to remain intact, meaning that it can still bind to name as it did before. Additionally, Vue is really smart about it. Along with its reactive system, Vue knows when relevant data is changed, and eventually renders the update to the DOM as expected.

> Computed properties support defining both getters and setters for mutable computed properties.
> You can read more about computed properties and watchers (uncovered in this chapter) here:
> https://vuejs.org/v2/guide/computed.html

Armed with all this information, you can proceed to implement the category menu using these exact features.

The category menu

You can begin to build the product listing page and implement the categories menu as depicted in this diagram by following these next steps:

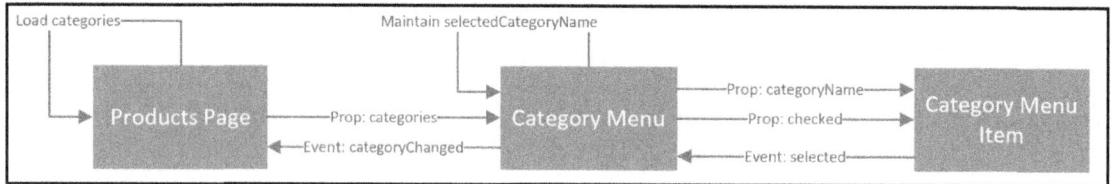

1. Create the folder /src/components/market.
2. Implement the CategoryMenyItem component:
   1. Create the file /src/components/market/CategoryMenuItem.vue
   2. Write the following code:

```
<template>
  <div class="container" @click="onSelected"
:class="{selected: checked}">
    <span>{{ categoryName }}</span>
  </div>
</template>

<script>
export default {
  name: 'CategoryMenuItem',
  props: {
```

```
      categoryName: String,
      checked: Boolean,
    },
  methods: {
    onSelected: function() {
      this.$emit('selected', this.categoryName);
    },
  },
}
</script>

<style scoped>
.container {
  display: inline;
  padding: 5px 3px 5px 3px;
  border: 1px solid black;
  padding: 2px 5px 2px 5px;
  cursor: pointer;
}

.container:hover {
  background-color: lightgray;
}

.selected {
  background-color: bisque;
}
</style>
```

This code is an example of a specialized binding in Vue, the class binding
`:class="{...}"`.
This is a useful feature because toggling elements' class names according to state
is often needed. In this case, the `div` element is set with a `selected` class name
when the component's prop `checked` is true; otherwise, `selected` is removed.

> Vue supports another specialized binding for styles, and you can read
> more about it here: `https://vuejs.org/v2/guide/class-and-style.html`.

3. Implement the `CategoryMenu` component:
     1. Create the file `/src/components/market/CategoryMenu.vue`
     2. Write the following code:

```
<template>
  <ul>
    <li v-for="c in categories" :key="c.name">
      <CategoryMenuItem
        :categoryName="c.name"
        :checked="c.name === selectedCategoryName"
        @selected="onCategorySelected"
      >
      </CategoryMenuItem >
    </li>
  </ul>
</template>

<script>
import CategoryMenuItem from './CategoryMenuItem.vue';

export default {
  name: 'CategoryMenu',
  components: {
    CategoryMenuItem,
  },
  props: {
    categories: Array,
  },
  data: () => ({
    selectedCategoryName: String,
  }),
  methods: {
    onCategorySelected: function(categoryName) {
      const cat = this.categories.find(c => c.name ===
categoryName);
      this.selectedCategoryName = cat.name;
      this.$emit('category-changed', cat);
    },
  },
}
</script>

<style scoped>
ul, li {
  list-style: none;
  padding: 0;
  margin: 0;
```

```
        display: inline;
    }
    </style>
```

Here, the component renders the child menu items using the `v-for` directive. This is related to list rendering and is described later, after the category menu feature implementation steps.

4. Implement a service for retrieving categories and products:
   1. Create file `/src/services/marketService.js`
   2. Write the following code:

```
const baseUrl = 'http://localhost:55564/api/';

function loadCategories() {
    return fetch(`${baseUrl}products/categories`)
        .then(r => r.json());
}

function loadProducts(categoryName) {
    return
fetch(`${baseUrl}products/searchcategory/${categoryNam
e}`)
        .then(r => r.json());
}

export default {
    loadCategories,
    loadProducts,
};
```

Vue provides features one can leverage to set up shared context, or a simple dependency resolution.
You can read more about plugins and provide/inject here:
`https://vuejs.org/v2/guide/plugins.html`
`https://vuejs.org/v2/api/#provide-inject`

Additionally, there's a popular library that serves as an http client in Vue-based apps that you can consider using as well: `https://github.com/pagekit/vue-resource`.

5. Implement the `ProductsPage` component:
    1. Create the file `/src/components/market/ProductsPage.vue`
    2. Write the following code:

```
<template>
  <div>
    <CategoryMenu
      :categories="categories"
      @category-changed="onCategoryChanged"
    />
  </div>
</template>

<script>
import MarketService from
'../../services/marketService';
import CategoryMenu from './CategoryMenu.vue';

export default {
  name: 'ProductsPage',
  components: {
    CategoryMenu,
  },
  data: () => ({
    categories: [],
  }),
  async created() {
    this.categories = await
MarketService.loadCategories();
  },
  methods: {
    onCategoryChanged: async function(category) {
      console.log(category); //eslint-disable-line
    },
  },
}
</script>
```

Here, the use of the service is made in a function called `created`. Vue components have a certain lifecycle, which you can hook into. One of these hooks is `created`, which is executed after a component is initialized, making it a useful place to load related data asynchronously. You can read more about lifecycle hooks here: `https://vuejs.org/v2/guide/instance.html#Instance-Lifecycle-Hooks`.

6. Modify the `App` component:
   1. Import and render the `ProductsPage` component
   2. Add the relevant CSS, as shown in the following example:

```
<template>
  <div>
    <Header />
    <div class="main-area">
 <ProductsPage />
    </div>
  </div>
</template>

<script>
import Header from './components/common/Header.vue';
import ProductsPage from
'./components/market/ProductsPage.vue';

export default {
  name: 'app',
  components: {
    Header,
    ProductsPage,
  }
}
</script>

<style>
.main-area {
 margin: 10px;
}
</style>
```

Great! You can now the run the app and see the category menu in place. It should look similar to this:

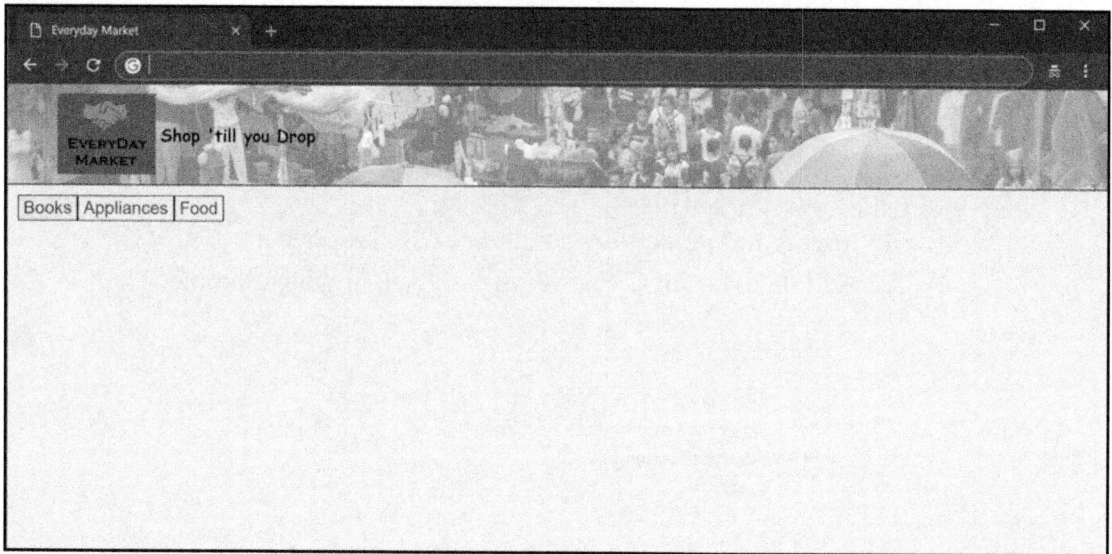

List rendering

Pay attention to the CategoryMenu component and the way it renders the child menu items off the categories array prop, as shown in the following example:

```
<li v-for="c in categories" :key="c.name">
  <CategoryMenuItem
    :categoryName="c.name"
    :checked="c.name === selectedCategoryName"
    @selected="onCategorySelected"
  >
  </CategoryMenuItem >
</li>
```

In Vue, you can use the v-for directive to generate templates off lists. Essentially, v-for repeats the element the template is applied to, and its sub-tree, for every item in the bound list.

The basic usage is <variableName> in <arrayIdentifier>.
This makes variableName available to the context of the template associated with the v-for directive. This is the reason you can use c.name inside.

Another thing to notice is the use of the `key` attribute. This is a specialized prop that should represent the identity, which means that elements with the same key are considered interchangeable, which can better optimize performance when the collection changes.

> You can read more about list rendering in Vue here:
> `https://vuejs.org/v2/guide/list.html`.

Product listing

Now that the category menu is completed, continue by implementing the product listing using the same tools as depicted in this diagram by completing the following steps:

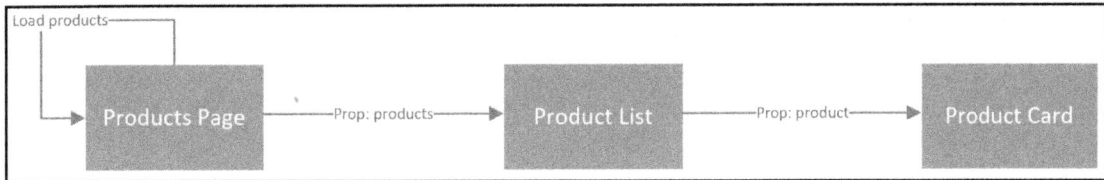

1. Implement the `ProductCard` component:
    1. Create the file `/src/components/market/ProductCard.vue`
    2. Write the following code:

```
<template>
  <div class="item-card">
    <div class="item-card-content-container">
        <img class="item-card-content-container-img"
:src="primaryImageSrc" />
        <span class="item-card-content-container-
title">{{product.title}}</span>
        <span class="item-card-content-container-
text">
          {{product.description}}
        </span>
    </div>
  </div>
</template>

<script>
export default {
  name: 'ProductCard',
```

```
      props: {
        product: Object,
      },
      computed: {
        primaryImageSrc: function() {
          return this.product && this.product.media &&
this.product.media.length > 0
            ? this.product.media[0].url
            : null;
        }
      },
    }
</script>

<style scoped>
.item-card {
  box-shadow: 0 4px 8px 0 rgba(0,0,0,0.2);
  transition: 0.3s;
  background-color: white;
  width: 280px;
  height: 200px;
  float: left;
  margin: 10;
}

.item-card:hover {
  box-shadow: 0 8px 16px 0 rgba(0,0,0,0.2);
}

.item-card-content-container {
  padding: 2px 16px;
  display: flex;
  height: 100%;
  flex-direction: column;
  align-items: center;
  justify-content: center;
  cursor: pointer;
}

.item-card-content-container-img {
  display: block;
  max-width: 80px;
  max-height: 80px;
  width: auto;
  height: auto;
  text-align: center;
}
```

```
.item-card-content-container-title {
  display: block;
  font-size: 1.6rem;
}

.item-card-content-container-text {
  word-wrap: normal;
  font-size: 1.2rem;
  overflow: hidden;
}
</style>
```

2. Implement the `ProductList` component:
    1. Create the file `/src/components/market/ProductList.vue`
    2. Write the following code:

```
<template>
  <div>
    <ul class="products-container">
      <li v-for="p in products" :key="p.productId">
        <ProductCard :product="p" />
      </li>
    </ul>
  </div>
</template>

<script>
import ProductCard from './ProductCard.vue';

export default {
  name: 'ProductList',
  components: {
    ProductCard,
  },
  props: {
    products: Array,
  },
}
</script>

<style scoped>
ul, li {
  list-style: none;
  padding: 0;
  margin: 0;
  display: inline;
}
```

```
.products-container {
  display: flex;
  justify-content: space-around;
  flex-wrap: wrap;
}
</style>
```

3. Modify the `ProductsPage` component:
    1. Add an empty `products` array as the default starting data
    2. Load products when the selected category changes
    3. Import and render the `ProductList` component, as shown in the following example:

```
<template>
  <div>
    <CategoryMenu
      :categories="categories"
      @category-changed="onCategoryChanged"
    />
    <ProductList :products="products" />
  </div>
</template>

<script>
import MarketService from
'../../services/marketService';
import CategoryMenu from './CategoryMenu.vue';
import ProductList from './ProductList.vue';

export default {
  name: 'ProductsPage',
  components: {
    CategoryMenu,
    ProductList,
  },
  data: () => ({
    categories: [],
    products: [],
  }),
  async created() {
    this.categories = await
MarketService.loadCategories();
  },
  methods: {
    onCategoryChanged: async function(category) {
      this.products = await
MarketService.loadProducts(category.name);
```

```
        },
      },
    }
    </script>
```

That's it! You have just completed implementing the product listing, so go ahead and run the app to see it in action. It should look similar to this:

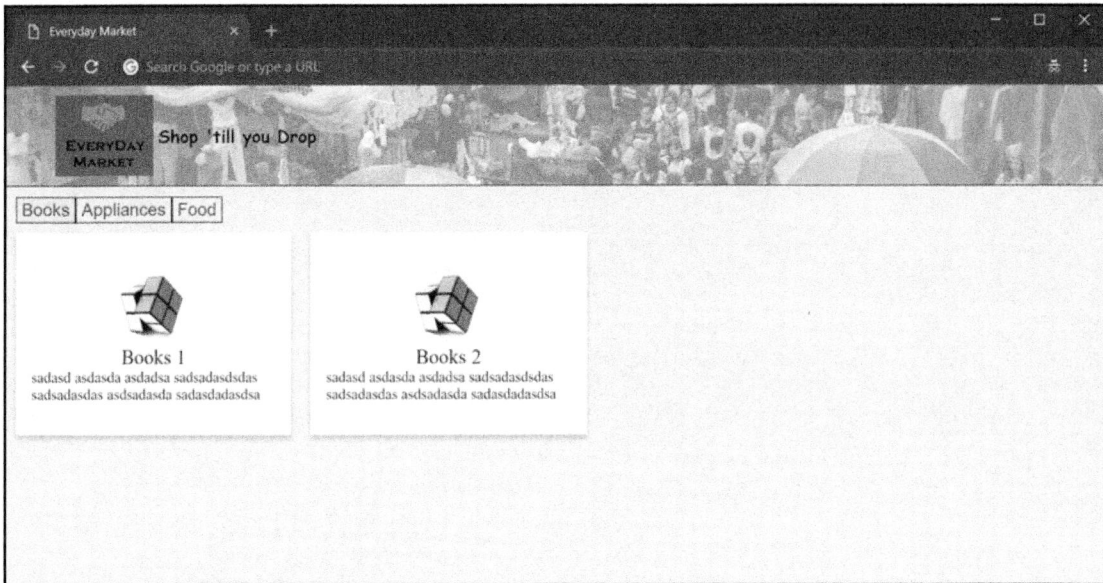

Busy indicator

Finally, implement a Busy indicator in the page by taking the following steps:

1. Implement the Busy component:
    1. Create the file /src/components/common/Busy.vue
    2. Write the following code:

```
<template>
  <div class="loader-container">
    <div class="loader"></div>
  </div>
</template>

<script>
```

```
            export default {
              name: 'Busy',
            }
            </script>

            <style scoped>
            .loader-container {
              position: absolute;
              left: 0; right: 0; top: 0; bottom: 0;
              background-color: azure;
              opacity: 0.5;
              display: flex;
              align-items: center;
              justify-content: center;
            }

            .loader {
              border: 16px solid #f3f3f3;
              border-top: 16px solid #3498db;
              border-radius: 50%;
              width: 80px;
              height: 80px;
              animation: spin 2s linear infinite;
            }

            @keyframes spin {
              0% { transform: rotate(0deg); }
              100% { transform: rotate(360deg); }
            }
            </style>
```

2. Modify the `ProductsPage` component:
    1. Add the `busy` dataset to false as the default starting state
    2. Change the `busy` state when the loading data is initiated and completed
    3. Import and render the `Busy` component when the `busy` data is true, as shown in the following code:

```
            <template>
              <div>
                <CategoryMenu
                  :categories="categories"
                  @category-changed="onCategoryChanged"
                />
                <ProductList :products="products" />
                <Busy v-if="busy" />
```

```
        </div>
      </template>

      <script>
      import MarketService from
      '../../services/marketService';
      import CategoryMenu from './CategoryMenu.vue';
      import ProductList from './ProductList.vue';
      import Busy from '../common/Busy.vue';

      export default {
        name: 'ProductsPage',
        components: {
          CategoryMenu,
          ProductList,
          Busy,
        },
        data: () => ({
          categories: [],
          products: [],
          busy: false,
        }),
        async created() {
          this.busy = true;
          try {
            this.categories = await
      MarketService.loadCategories();
          } finally {
            this.busy = false;
          }
        },
        methods: {
          onCategoryChanged: async function(category) {
            this.busy = true;
            try {
              this.products = await
      MarketService.loadProducts(category.name);
            } finally {
              this.busy = false;
            }
          },
        },
      }
      </script>
```

Congratulations! You have just completed the Busy indicator, and with that, the page functionality in this chapter.

Conditional rendering

Look closely in the `Busy` component's template. It uses another built-in directive you have not used yet in Vue, as shown in the following example:

```
<Busy v-if="busy" />
```

Vue provides a built-in directive that affects the HTML DOM layout: `v-if`.
When applied to an element, the element is rendered to the DOM when the assigned expression evaluates to `true`; otherwise, it is removed from the DOM. Therefore, the `Busy` indicator is displayed only when the `busy` data is true.

Summary

In this chapter, you learned about Vue and many of its core features, including components, component definition objects, data binding, and events.

Vue certainly shows great promise due to it being flexible and more easily adoptable than Angular. It also provides a more feature-complete solution to SPA projects than React does, along with its official complementary libraries for other aspects, such as routing and state management.
Currently, Vue is less popular in comparison to React and Angular, although Vue is gaining popularity at a great pace and many developers find it a middle ground by having strengths of both worlds.

This chapter concludes our journey of Web SPA development. By now, you should have a general understanding of how to implement such apps using the most popular and leading frameworks available today.
Now that you have several tools in your arsenal, hopefully, you already have a favorite one, which you can pick for your next SPA project.

While the recent chapters focused on the development of these projects, this is not where the story ends in software development. Next, you will learn about other aspects of the application life-cycle, specifically distribution and deployment.

14
Moving Your Solution to the Cloud

Up until now, we have only discussed the development side of your application, but have hardly touched anything related to its hosting and deployment. In this chapter, you'll be introduced to the concept of the **cloud** and the value it brings when deploying your application. There are a few known players in the world of cloud computing—Amazon AWS, Microsoft Azure, and Google GCP, to name just a few. For the purposes of this book, we will only concentrate on one of them, and since we are already working with Microsoft technology, we will choose to look at another Microsoft product—Microsoft Azure. At the end of this chapter, you will have a Microsoft Azure account that we will use later to create an environment where we can leverage the different services that the Azure cloud has to offer to make your application production-ready in a short amount of time.

This chapter will cover the following topics:

- What is cloud computing?
- Creating a Microsoft Azure account
- Getting familiar with the portal and with the command line
- Understanding the basic terms: subscription, account, and ARM
- Cost and billing

What is cloud computing?

Eventually, your application needs to run on a machine somewhere in the world and not just on your local development machine. For many years, when someone wanted to run a web application and make it available to the external world, they would buy designated hardware and spent time maintaining it. Over the years, the hosting model has changed and moved to external hosting that, besides running the machine at some data center outside, felt very similar to what you had when you ran it locally—however, the big part was that you didn't have to worry about the machine maintenance, the server room air conditioning, and the procedure that should be performed in case of hardware failure. Then came the cloud.

The **National Institute For Standards and Technology (NIST)** defines the cloud like this:

> *"Cloud computing is a model for enabling ubiquitous, convenient, on-demand network access to a shared pool of configurable computing resources (for example, networks, servers, storage, applications, and services) that can be rapidly provisioned and released with minimal management effort or service provider interaction. This cloud model is composed of five essential characteristics, three service models, and four deployment models."*

> - https://csrc.nist.gov/publications/detail/sp/800-145/final

NIST published this definition in 2011. Since then, there have been some changes, and now the cloud offers more than four service models.

NIST defines the following five characteristics as essential for making the cloud what it is:

- **On-demand self-service**: The ability to provision and remove resources with minimal effort
- **Broad network access**: The ability to manage your resources from any location and the ability to work with resources in a global scale
- **Resource pooling**: Virtualization of resources that allow you to consider the available capacity as infinite
- **Rapid elasticity**: The ability to add or remove resources based on the real usage without prior investments
- **Measured service**: Being able to retrieve metrics on the resources you use to make decisions based on real data

One of the things that hides in these characteristics is that the cloud allows you to automate many (if not all) the operations needed to run your application, and this is made possible above all because of the virtualization that the cloud hypervisor uses.

In the rest of this book, I will delve deeper into how those characteristics come in to play, and in this chapter, I will explain the service models and the connection between the cloud, virtualization, and automation.

Virtualization and automation

Running on bare metal has its benefits: you can get the maximum out of your hardware, latency of operations is minimal, and you can argue that it takes away some complexity from your system design. But managing physical machines is a challenge that requires ongoing administrative operations. In addition, in many cases, buying expensive hardware is not cost-effective because systems tend to use the hardware for a fraction of the total time the machines are running and utilize the full hardware power even less than that. For example, consider an application that provides vacation planning services: it makes sense that this application will be very busy when a holiday is approaching, but for the rest of the time, it will be pretty much idle. Still, you'll have to pay for hardware that is capable of running the maximum load of the system.

Virtualization, on the other hand, abstracts the host you're running on from the actual hardware and allows you to share the infrastructure between multiple applications and workloads. With virtualization, you can start by providing an application with a certain amount of resources and giving the rest to another application, and later on, when needed, reduce the resources from one and give it to the other. All this happens without making any changes to the running application or restarting it.

Virtualization existed many years before the term *cloud* was even coined, but what makes the cloud different from classic virtualization is the ability to automate the procedures that are needed to provision servers, network, and storage, and make the system self-adjusted based on the real usage that takes place in production. You see, until the cloud, when a development team needed a resource of some kind in their environment, there was a lot a bureaucracy that was needed until the resource was provisioned. With the cloud, which embraces virtualization and automation capabilities, development teams can now self-serve themselves and be more agile. These are the main strengths of running in the cloud:

- Access to virtually infinite resources
- Being elastic and changing resource capacity on demand
- Adjustable pricing model—pay for what you use

The cloud gives you the freedom to choose what's best for your application, and there are a few models you can choose from.

Cloud service models

There are four main models for running an application in the cloud:

- **Infrastructure as a Service (IaaS)**: The cloud provider is in charge of the infrastructure, but you are responsible for configuring it and the application that runs on it.
- **Platform as a Service (PaaS)**: The cloud provider fully manages the infrastructure, and you are responsible for the application and the configuration of running it on the infrastructure.
- **Function as a Service (FaaS)**: The cloud provider manages the infrastructure and platform, and based on some trigger (HTTP call, message in a queue, a scheduled time, and so on), activates your application; you are only responsible for writing the single function code that will be run when triggered.
- **Software as a Service (SaaS)**: The infrastructure, platform, and the application itself is managed for you; you only configure and adjust it to your needs. Users use the application without installing anything on their machines.

Another way to look at the different models is to compare them to eating a pizza:

- When you host your application on premises, it's the same as making your own pizza at home: you control the ingredients, the making process, and the eating itself
- IaaS is similar to buying a half-baked pizza base: you still need to put the toppings and bake it, but a lot of the infrastructure has already been supplied to you
- PaaS is like ordering pizza: the entire pizza making process was done for you, but you still need to take care of setting the table and cleaning the dishes
- FaaS is like buying pizza at a counter: you can buy as many slices as you like and pay accordingly
- SaaS is like eating pizza in a restaurant where you get the full service: you can select the style of pizza and special additions, you sit at a nice table, and you don't need to worry about the mess—you just pay for it

The following diagram summarizes the differences between the cloud service models:

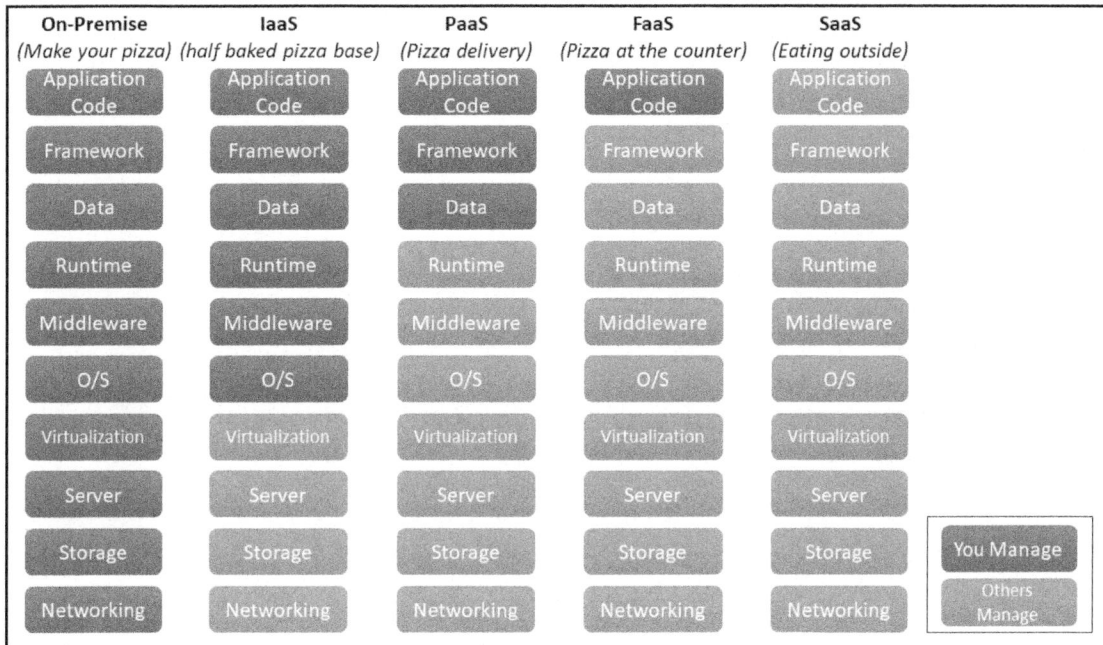

On-Premise *(Make your pizza)*	IaaS *(half baked pizza base)*	PaaS *(Pizza delivery)*	FaaS *(Pizza at the counter)*	SaaS *(Eating outside)*	
Application Code	Application Code	Application Code	Application Code	Application Code	
Framework	Framework	Framework	Framework	Framework	
Data	Data	Data	Data	Data	
Runtime	Runtime	Runtime	Runtime	Runtime	
Middleware	Middleware	Middleware	Middleware	Middleware	
O/S	O/S	O/S	O/S	O/S	
Virtualization	Virtualization	Virtualization	Virtualization	Virtualization	
Server	Server	Server	Server	Server	
Storage	Storage	Storage	Storage	Storage	You Manage
Networking	Networking	Networking	Networking	Networking	Others Manage

Working with Microsoft Azure

Microsoft Azure is a set of services that run in a cloud that's owned and operated by Microsoft. Microsoft Azure data centers are located in more than 50 global regions that run thousands of machines.

Microsoft Azure includes many services as part of its cloud computing platform:

- **Compute services**: Services for hosting and running applications, such as virtual machines, app services, container orchestration clusters, and high-performance batch-processing services.
- **Data services**: Services for persisting data, manipulating it, and retrieving it. This includes storage services for files and **Binary Large OBjects** (**BLOBs**), and databases of different kinds and for different purposes.

- **Cognitive, ML, and AI**: Services that enable you to add intelligence to your applications, such as computer vision, language understanding, text analysis, statistical inference and prediction, and many others.
- **Networking**: Enables connectivity of different machines, applications, and services with full control of security.

The list goes on and on, and it's growing every day. The main point is that for almost every requirement of your system, there's a service that can give the solution with little effort and with great power.

Creating a Microsoft Azure account

To work with Microsoft Azure, you need to create an account that is used to handle the billing of the payable services you use. Each account contains one or more subscriptions that allows for the creation and management of the Azure services.

The following steps will guide you in creating a free Azure account (you can read about the free account at `https://azure.microsoft.com/en-us/free`):

1. Log in to your Microsoft account or create a new one (`https://account.microsoft.com/account`).
2. Navigate to `https://signup.azure.com/` and click on the **Sign Up** link.
3. Fill in the requested details and validate your identity with your phone and credit card numbers (a credit card is needed to allow the use of resources that are not free, but will not be charged otherwise):

Microsoft Azure   endtoendweb@outlook.com   Sign out

Azure free account sign up

Start with a $200 credit for 30 days, and keep going for free

1 About you   ∧

Country/Region ❶

[United States   ▾]

First name

[ ]

Last name

[ ]

Email address ❶

[ ]

Phone

[Example: (425) 555-0100]

By proceeding you acknowledge the privacy statement and subscription agreement

---

i   Your card will not be charged in the free account unless you explicitly increase the spending limit:
https://docs.microsoft.com/en-us/azure/billing/billing-spending-limit

4. Once registration is complete, you will be redirected to the Azure portal, where you can start a tour or continue without it:

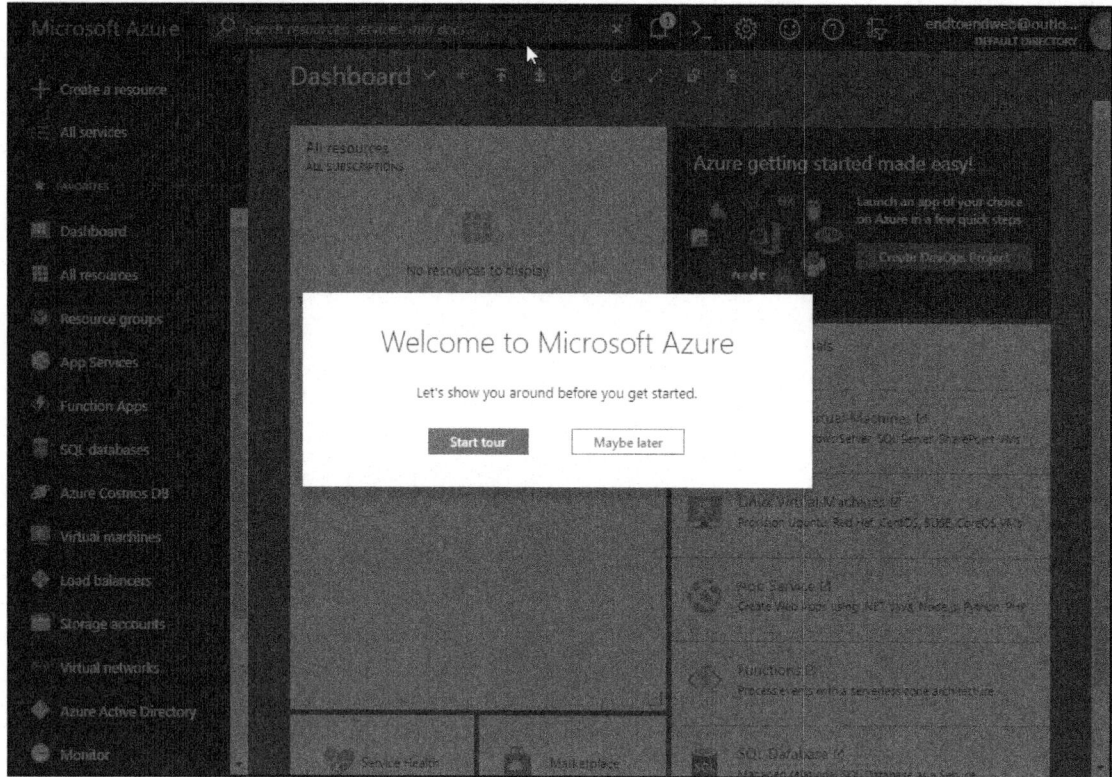

Getting familiar with the portal and with the command line

There are a few ways you can create and manage Azure services:

- **Azure portal**: A graphical interface that's accessible through `https://portal.azure.com`
- **Command-line (CLI) tools**: Cross-platform CLI tools or Azure PowerShell extensions that make it easy to automate and script your tasks
- **Azure SDK**: Templates, tools, and programmable libraries for accessing, creating, and managing your Azure resources from the IDE and code

The Azure portal

The Azure portal is feature-rich and the easiest way to manage the resources in your subscriptions. The main view of the portal is called the **Dashboard** and it contains customizable widgets that allow you to get a fast glimpse of the status of your environment.

The Azure portal is structured from three main areas: the navigation menu (left-hand side), the upper bar (top), and the main content area. The following screenshot explains some of the components that you'll be using throughout the rest of this book:

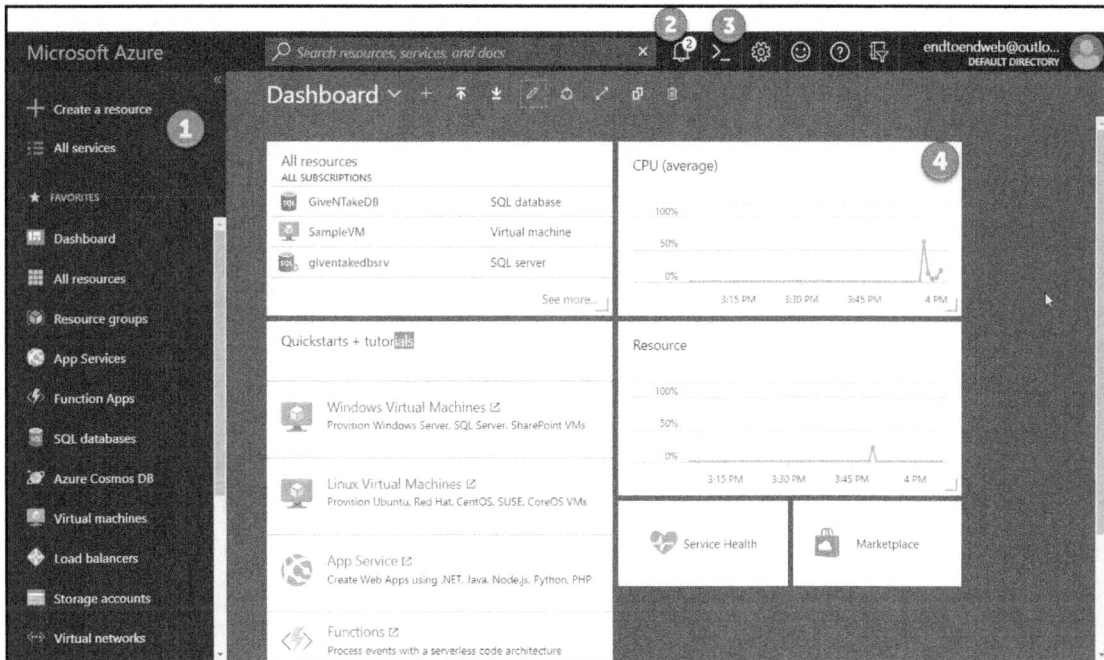

The following is an explanation the various of menus:

- **Navigation menu**: Contains entries for different resource types that allow you to quickly explore the resources and create new instance of the resources in your account.
- **Notifications**: The bell-shaped icon will show an indicator if there's a notification you should be aware of. Clicking on it will show a pop-up screen with further details, for example, when a resource's creation has been completed.
- **Azure Shell**: Clicking on the button will show a shell window in the bottom of the screen. In the shell window, you can write commands or scripts in PowerShell or Bash.
- **Dashboard**: You can pin widgets and customize their look. Widgets can display resource status, graphs of metrics, links for fast access, and so on.

Azure portal blades

The navigation model in the Azure portal is built around the concept of **blades**. Blades are the visualization elements used to describe a resource or to display a form as part of a workflow. Blades open from left to right in a continuous manner, so you always know what your position in a flow is and can always go back. We will now look an example of what I just described in the process of creating a new resource.

To create a new resource, perform the following steps:

1. You usually start by clicking the **Create a resource** button in the navigation menu:

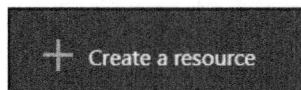

2. This will open the new resource blade:

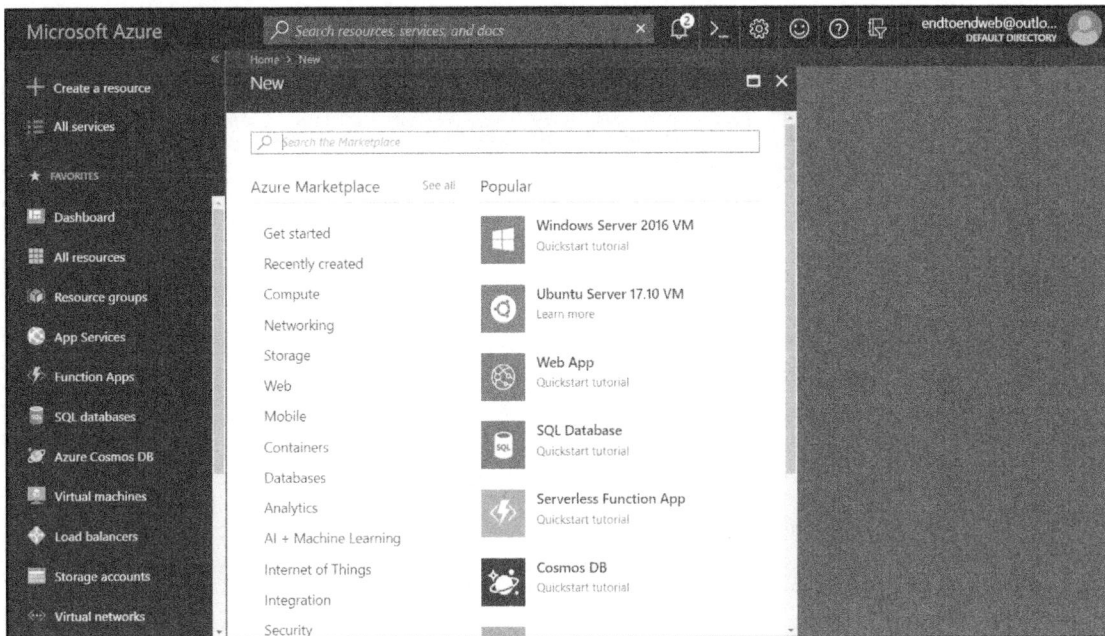

3. Select a resource type, for example, **Windows Server 2016 VM**, to create a new **virtual machine** (**VM**). This will open the VM creation blade to the right of the previous blade:

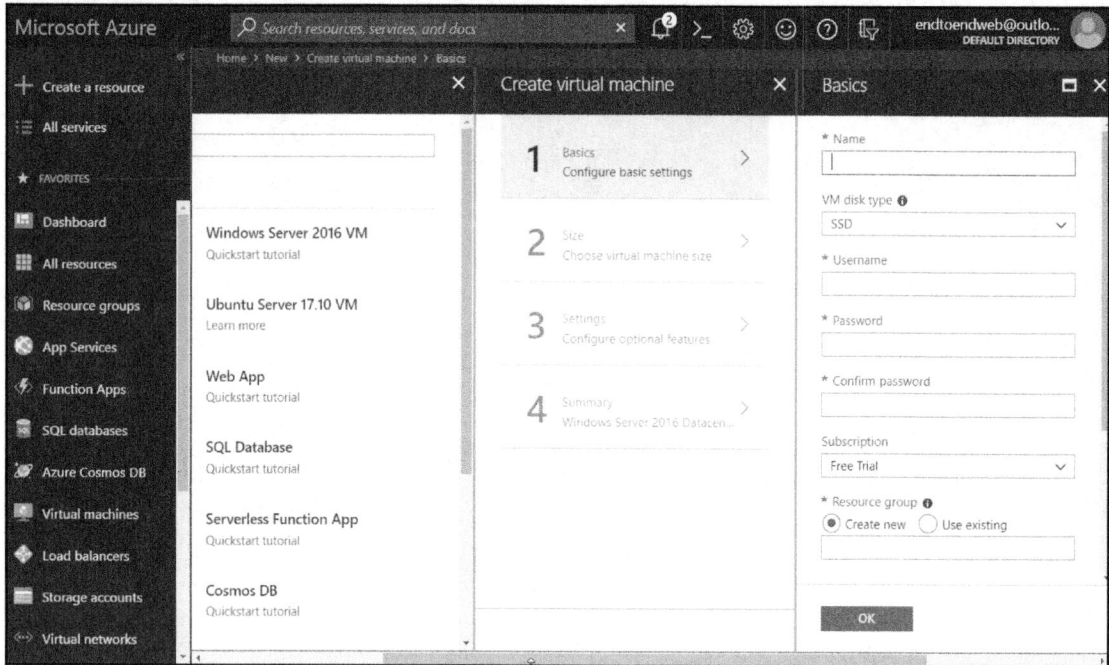

4. The blade infrastructure always shows you your current position in the flow in the breadcrumb control in the top-left corner and allows you to go back:

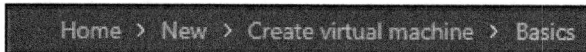

Using the Azure CLI

The Azure portal gives an easy and quick way to experiment with the Azure services that are available, but requires you to perform operations in a manual way. As your application reaches maturity and as your environment becomes large, you should prefer to work in an automated and repeatable way that will reduce the risk of human error and will increase the speed at which you can make changes and provision resources.

The Azure CLI is a cross-platform, command-line utility that allows you to manage your Azure resources in an automated and scriptable way. To use the Azure CLI, download and install the latest bits from https://docs.microsoft.com/en-us/cli/azure/install-azure-cli.

You can work with the Azure CLI from any shell, such as PowerShell, the Windows command line, Base, and so on. Alternatively, you can work with the Azure Cloud Shell inside the portal.

To start working with the Azure CLI, you first need to log in. Type az login into your shell window. This will redirect your browser to a login page, where you'll need to enter your credentials.

If the login is successful, you should see the selected account and subscription details in the shell, for example:

```
PS C:\Users\tamir.dresher> az login
Note, we have launched a browser for you to login. For old experience with
device code, use "az login --use-device-code"
You have logged in. Now let us find all subscriptions you have access to...
[
  {
    "cloudName": "AzureCloud",
    "id": "bd51f004-5a88-4282-bc5c-ec1518068dfb",
    "isDefault": true,
    "name": "Free Trial",
    "state": "Enabled",
    "tenantId": "0d1731c3-13a6-470a-9906-fab677548576",
    "user": {
      "name": "endtoendweb@outlook.com",
      "type": "user"
    }
  }
]
```

The basic command-line structure of the Azure CLI looks like this:

```
az [group] [sub group] [command- create/delete/list] paramteres
```

For example, to display all the web applications (webapp) in your subscription, type the following command:

```
az webapp list
```

In this case, webapp is the group and the requested command was list.

> To see all the available groups, type `az --help`.
> To see the subgroups of a certain group, type `az group --help`.

The Azure account and resources model

The Azure cloud gives services to thousands of organizations worldwide. Each organization has an isolated environment where it can create resources and configure them to the organization's needs. Inside each of these isolated environments, there can be more levels of separation that make it easier for the organization to manage the resources and their billing. From an Azure standpoint, it doesn't matter whether you represent a large enterprise or whether you are a single developer; the configuration model and billing work the same way, so it's best to understand the concepts that comprise your Azure environment, as shown in the following diagram:

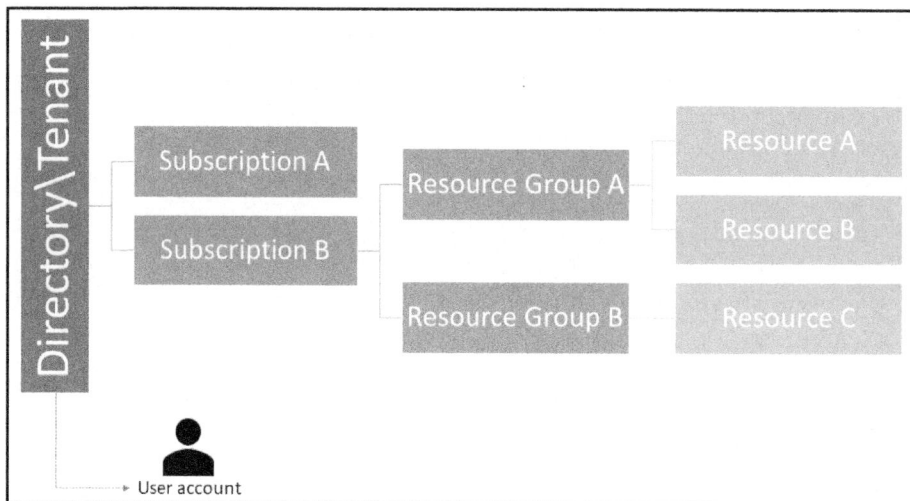

Let's explain the different levels of the Azure environment:

- The root of the Azure environment is the **directory** (or **tenant**). This represents the organization that the Azure environment belongs to. Technically, the directory is an Active Directory tenant that holds the user account, roles, and permissions of the given organization.

- Each directory can hold one or more Azure **subscriptions**. The subscription is the billing container that allows the grouping of expenses that are related to all the resources inside the subscription. For example, an organization might decide that each product will run in a different subscription so that it will be easier to see the expenses related to each product. Alternatively, an organization might decide to give each team a different subscription to run resources related to development activities, and control the budget of each team separately.
- Resources inside a subscription reside inside a **resource group.** The resource group is a logical container of resources that makes it easier to manage their life cycle together. For example, a product that has a global distribution might be implemented so that all the resources that are deployed to different regions will be grouped together as a resource group. This way, adding or removing a region is easier.

Now that we have covered the basic terms related to accounts and subscriptions, let's delve into the real meat in our environment—resources.

Azure Resource Manager

In the past, every resource you created in your Azure environment was a standalone entity without any relation to other resources. To create an operable environment for your system, you had to create each resource separately and configure the links by yourself. It was hard to see the full picture and it was hard to host different systems inside the same account as well as manage them and their billing. Microsoft solved those problems with a way to manage resources—**Azure Resource Manager** (**ARM**).

Azure Resource Manager is the engine that allows you to group resources together and create them (as a resource group) in a declarative way via **ARM templates**.

Resource groups

A resource group is a logical container that functions as a unit of management. With resource groups, you can do the following:

- Manage security policies with access control
- See and manage the costs of the resources in the group
- Export and import resource groups
- Delete a resource group and all the resources it holds atomically

Whenever you create a resource in Azure, you need to create or select a resource group that the resource will be created in:

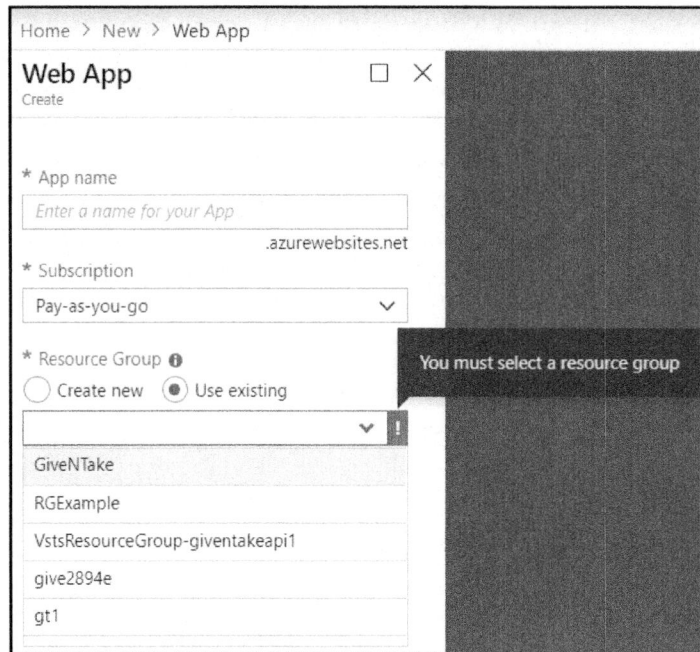

You can later inspect the resource groups you have and their content through the button in the left-hand side menu, and is shown in the following screenshot:

Alternatively, you can use the `az group` CLI commands to list, create, delete, and configure the resource groups in your account.

ARM templates

ARM templates are JSON format documents that declaratively describe the structure of a resource group and provide an infrastructure-as-code solution to your Azure environment. With ARM templates, you can deploy a full environment into your Azure account in a repeatable way that is source-control friendly.

You have a few options for creating an ARM template:

1. Write it from scratch. The syntax and schema definition for ARM templates can be found at `https://docs.microsoft.com/en-us/azure/azure-resource-manager/resource-group-authoring-templates`.

2. Create it with Visual Studio by using the **Azure Resource Group** project:

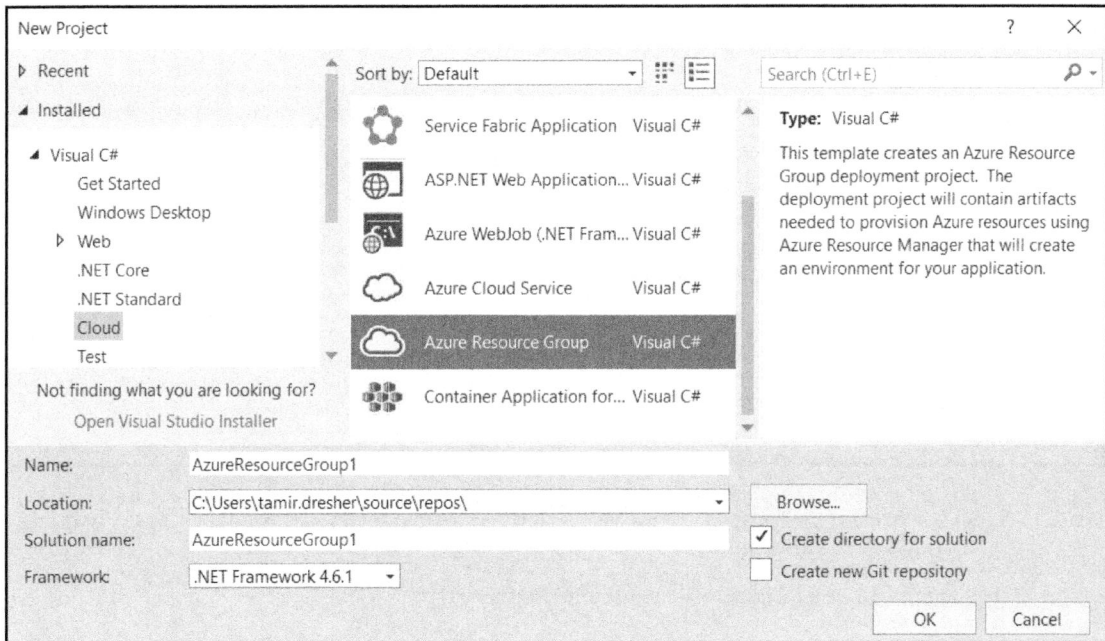

3. Add resources to the ARM template using the **JSON Outline** tool:

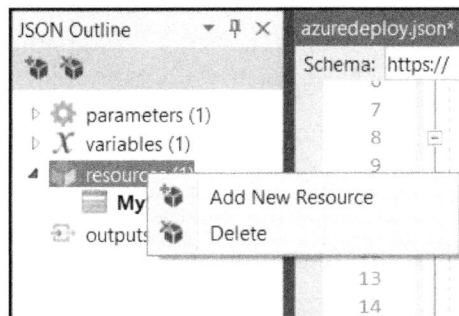

4. Export a resource group from the Azure portal:

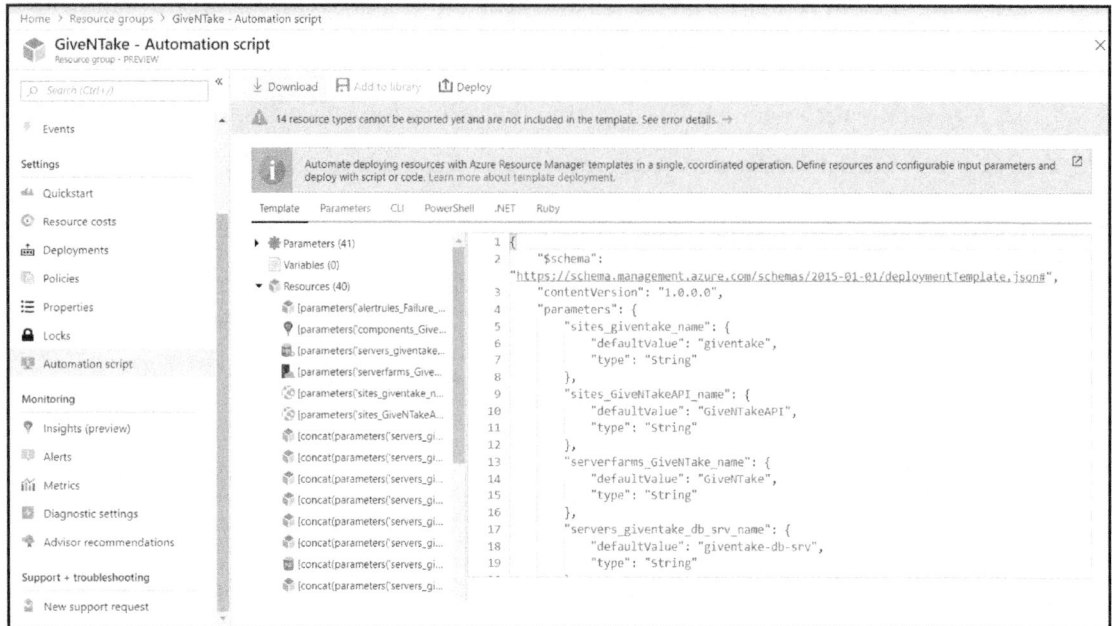

5. Use a pre-made template and modify it to your needs. Microsoft offers a catalog with many templates that you can use: `https://azure.microsoft.com/en-us/resources/templates/`.

Pricing and billing

Each resource you deploy in Azure has a different price that depends on many factors (location, size, support, time, and so on). If that's not enough, the prices in Azure are hardly constant, and you can expect changes in the pricing of different resources as time goes by.

To get a better understanding of what you're going to pay, it's a good practice to use the Azure calculator: `https://azure.microsoft.com/en-us/pricing/calculator`.

The Azure calculator allows you to select the resources you want to provision and their performance, and as you change your selection, the pricing tag is updated to reflect your estimated monthly bill.

For example, here are the steps to build the pricing for the GiveNTake environment:

1. Click **Compute** | **App Service**. Scroll down and change the location to **East-US** and the **Tier** to **Free**.
2. Click **Storage** | **Storage**. Scroll down and change the location to **East-US**.
3. Click **Databases** | **Azure SQL Database**. Scroll down and change the location to **East-US**, the **Type** to **Single Database**, and the pricing model to **DTU**.
4. Click **DevOps** | **Application Insights**, as demonstrated in the following screenshot:

Microsoft Azure		Contact Sales: 1-909-349-115 📞 Search 🔍 My account Portal endtoendweb@outlook.com 👤	
Why Azure ⌄ Solutions Products ⌄ Documentation **Pricing** Training Marketplace ⌄ Partners ⌄ Support ⌄ Blog More ⌄			Free account ⟩

Your Estimate

App Service	🗐 🗑	Free Tier; 1 F1 (0 Core(s), 1 GB RAM, 1 GB Storage) x 73...	$0.00
Storage	🗐 🗑	Block Blob Storage, General Purpose V2, LRS Redundan...	$21.84
Azure SQL Database	🗐 🗑	Single Database, DTU Purchase Model, Basic Tier, B: 5 D...	$4.90
Application Insights	🗐 🗑	5 GB Logs collected, 0 Multi-step Web Tests	$0.00

Support

SUPPORT:

Included ▾ ❶	$0.00

Programs and Offers

LICENSING PROGRAM:

Microsoft Online Services Program (MOSP)   ▾ ❶

• ⊘ SHOW DEV/TEST PRICING ❶

Estimated monthly cost	$26.74
🗐 Export 💾 Save 💾 Save as 📤 Share	US Dollar ($) ▾

5. To see the cost of your resources, click on the **Cost Management + Billing** button in the left-hand side menu:

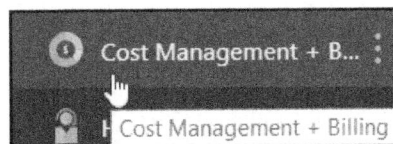

6. Then, you can select your subscription and see a drilldown of the costs and tools for deeper analysis:

Summary

In this chapter, you learned the basic concepts that are needed to move your application into the Azure cloud. First, I covered what exactly the cloud is and the benefits you get when using it. Then, I listed the hosting models that exist in the cloud world and when you should consider each of them for your system. In this book, we are using the Microsoft Azure cloud, and so I showed you how to open your account and explained how the subscription and account model works and the fundamentals you need to work efficiently with resources using ARM templates and resource groups.

Deploying to Microsoft Azure

15

In this chapter, we will take our application to the next step and start its productization by deploying it to a production environment that is running in Azure. There is more than one option for hosting your backend services and application frontends in Azure, but I'll focus on only one of them, *Azure App Service*, as it is both powerful and easy to use. To make it simpler to teach the concepts, I'll first show you how to deploy it manually from Visual Studio, but by the end of this chapter, you will have learned how to create an automated build server in **Visual Studio Team Services** (**VSTS**) to make repeatable tasks easy and with a lower risk of mistakes.

These are the topics covered in this chapter:

- Creating a production environment with Azure App Service and Azure SQL
- Deploying the GiveNTake backend service from Visual Studio
- Creating an automated build and release pipeline in Azure DevOps (formerly VSTS)
- Deploying the GiveNTake frontend to Azure App Service

Creating a production environment with Azure App Service

Azure App Service is a family of services that are provided as PaaS in Azure and help you to build apps that can be used by web and mobile clients. You can use Azure App Service with a wide range of programming languages and technologies—Node.js, Java, PHP, and, of course, .NET—and can create Web Apps, API Apps, Mobile Apps, and Logic Apps without worrying about the underlying infrastructure.

There are many features that Azure App Service provides to assist with application lifecycle development, such as automatic deployment options, the management of application settings that can be modified based on the environment (deployment slots), easy manual and automatic scaling options, security control, monitoring, and troubleshooting utilities, to name just a few.

App Service plan

Azure App Service separates the hosted application and the resources it uses by using a concept called *App Service Plan*. The App Service plan defines the computing resources (virtual machines) that host your applications, and multiple applications can be hosted on an App Service plan.

These are the things that an App Service plan defines:

- Region: the location of the computing resources; for example, West US, East Europe, and so on
- The amount of VM instances
- The size of VM instances (small, medium, large)
- Pricing tier: determines the features you can use and how much you pay (Free, Shared, Basic, and so on)

Creating your App Service

In the Azure portal:

1. Click on the **Create a resource** button in the left-hand navigation menu.
2. In the marketplace window that opens, search for App Service:

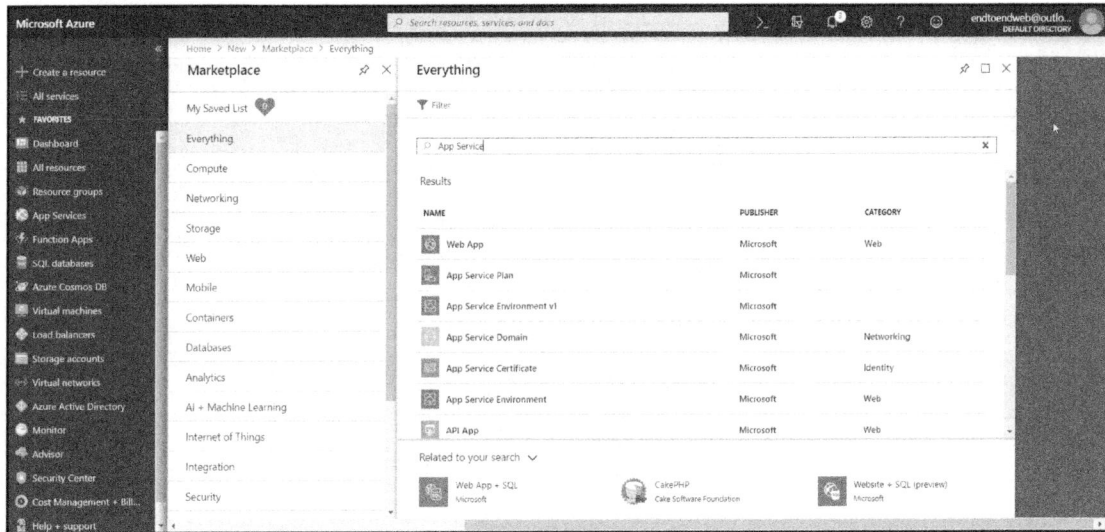

The text in this screenshot is not important. The purpose of this image is to show you what the Azure portal looks like.

3. Click on the **Web App** option, and then click on the **Create** button.
4. In the **Web App** creation blade, enter the name of your application and create or choose a resource group that the application will be created in, as shown in the screenshot below.

In the past, Azure offered a set of services that were called API App, Mobile App, and Web App. Each of them offered specific features for their target application type. At some point, Microsoft merged all these application types into a single one under the name App Service, but the old services are still available. The only difference between them now is the icon.

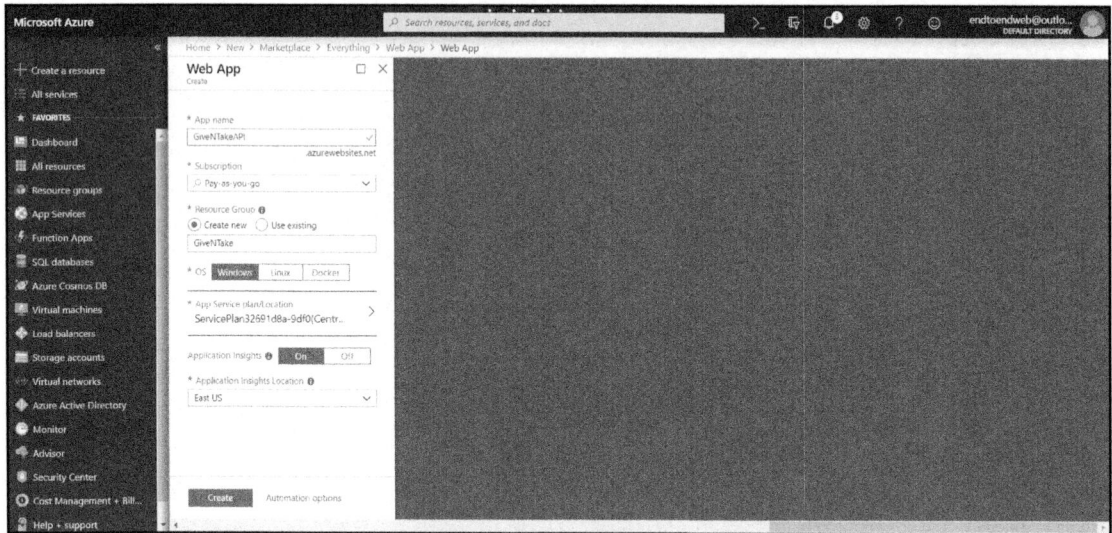

5. Turn on **Application Insights** support, then choose your preferred operating system and the **Application Insights** hosting location.

6. Click on the **App Service plan/Location** area to open the **App Service Plan** configuration blade and select an existing plan or create a new one:

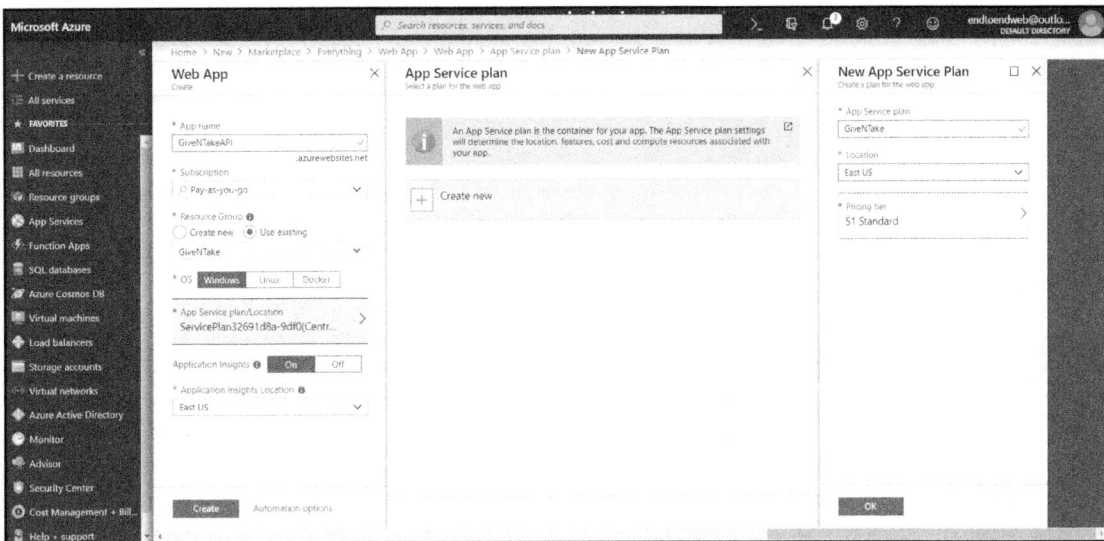

7. Click on the **Pricing tier** button to select the plan you wish to create. You can filter the pricing tiers shown by selecting the appropriate workload you wish to create the App Service plan for in the toolbar:

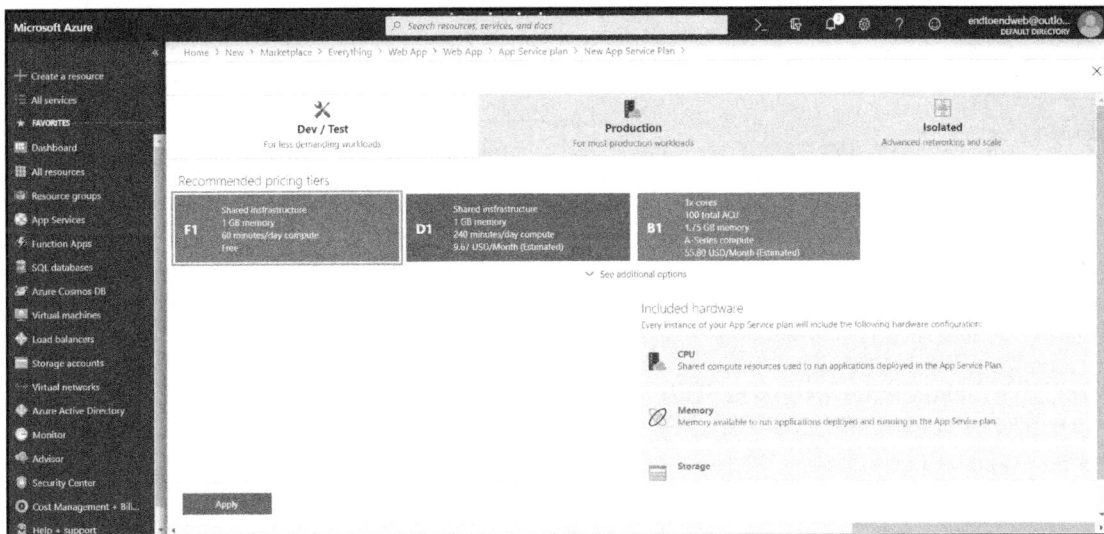

> **TIP**
> You can always change the pricing tier later, increasing or decreasing the feature levels and computing power that your application uses.

8. After filling in and choosing all the required settings, click on the **Create** button and create your Azure App service web app.
9. Once the resource deployment is complete, a notification popup will appear. Click on the **Go to resource** button to open your web app blade:

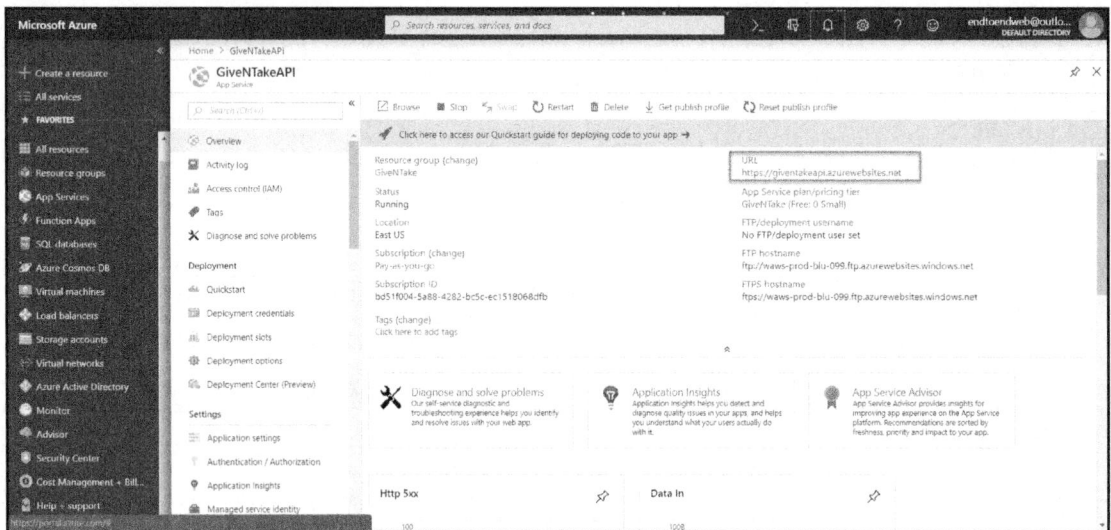

The text in this screenshot is not important. The purpose of this screenshot is to show you what the App Service looks like.

10. In the main view, you can find details of your application and its status, and buttons for quick operations you can perform on it, such as stopping it or deleting it.

The URL that appears is the base URL of your application and is formatted with the name you chose when creating your App Service (GivenNTakeAPI in this example), followed by azurewebsites.net

Linking a SQL server database to the application

The GiveNTake application uses SQL Server as its data store and will not be able to work without it, so we will spend the next section explaining how to create a new SQL Server and database and link it to an application.

1. Scroll through the left-hand menu of your web app, click on the **Data connections** menu item, and then click on the **Add** button:

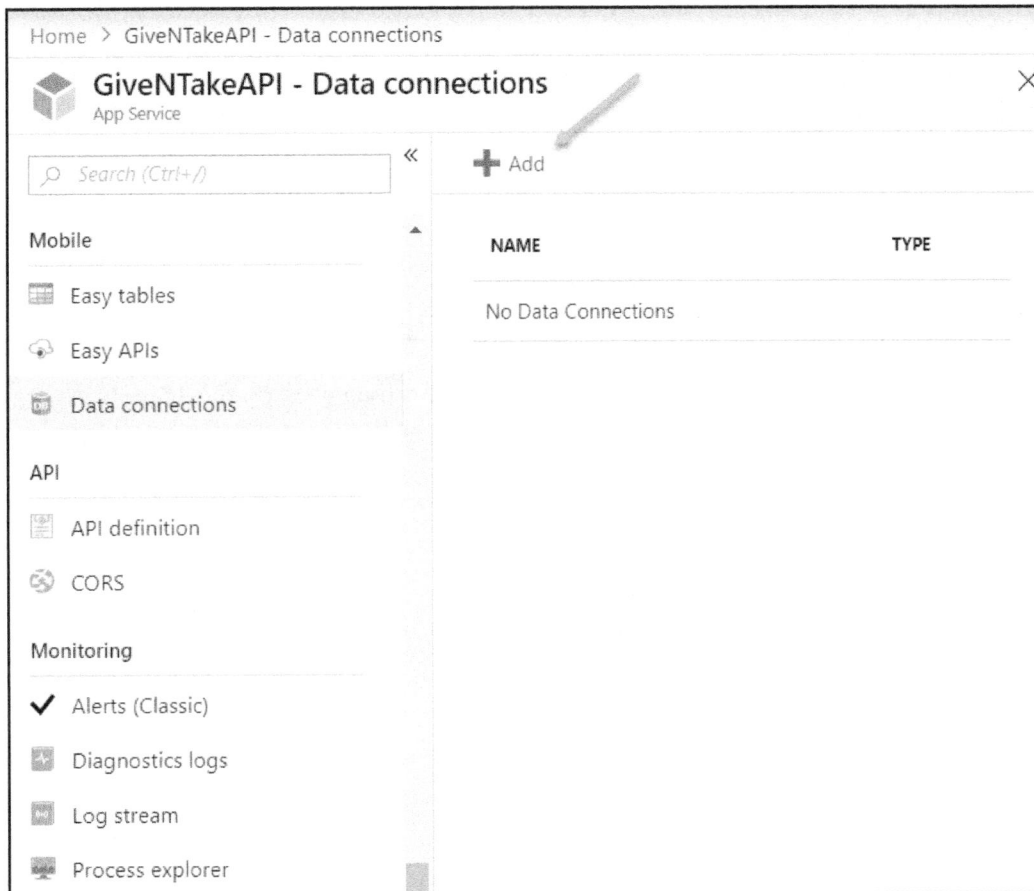

2. Select a **SQL Database** in the **Type** drop-down control and click on the **SQL Database** configuration area:

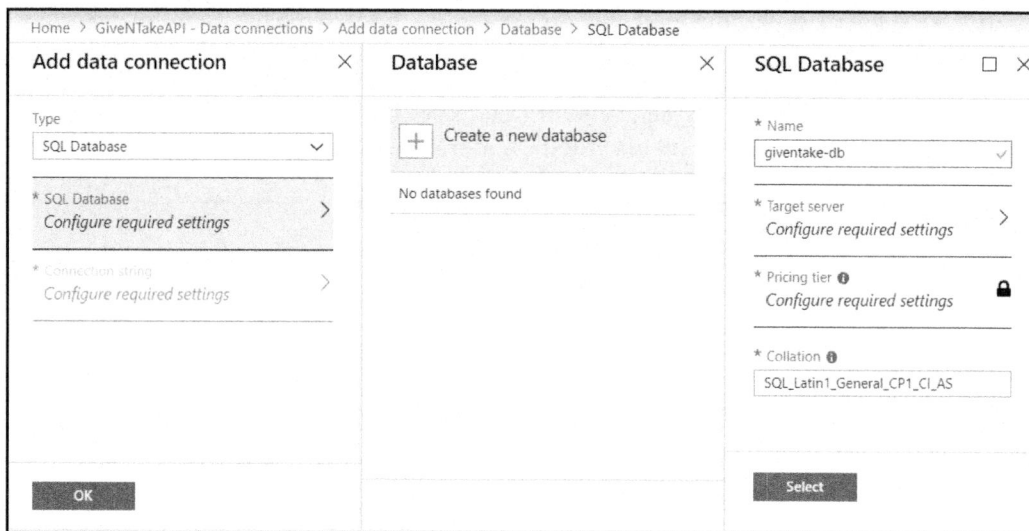

3. Fill in the desired name of your database, and then click on the **Target server** configuration area to create a new server on which your database will run:

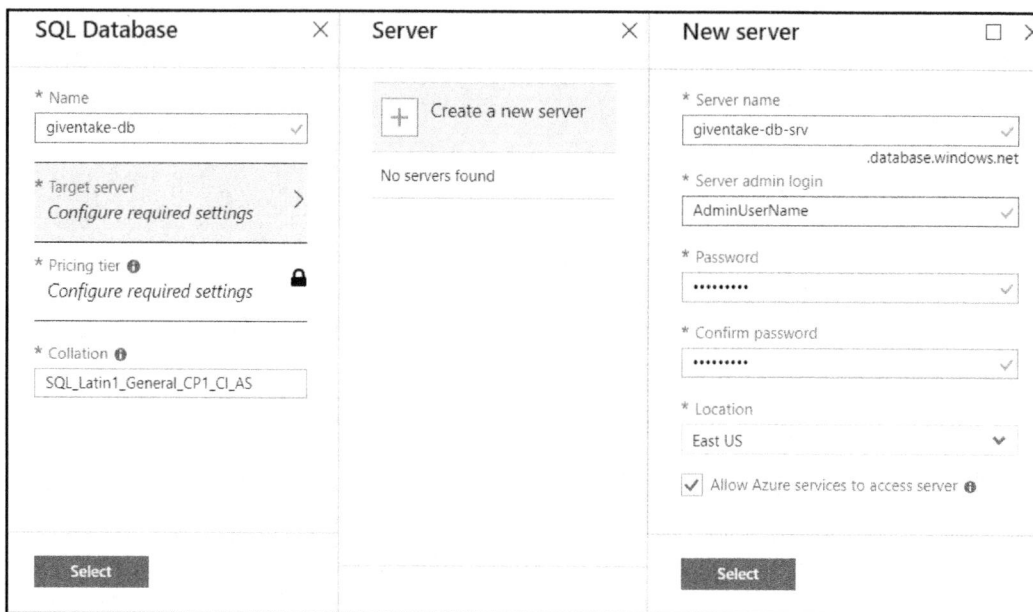

By default, network access to Azure SQL Database is blocked from any IP and can later be opened in the server firewall settings.
When creating a new server, you can check **Allow Azure services to access server** to allow App Service to connect to your database without manual configuration.

Once you complete the server creation, you need to select the pricing tier for your database.

Choosing an Azure SQL pricing tier

Azure SQL is a PaaS offering that allows you to concentrate on application needs rather than the infrastructure and resources that the database server consumes. There are two pricing models you can choose from when working with Azure SQL: DTU-based and vCore-based.

Database Throughput Unit (DTU) is a metric that defines a relative combination of compute, storage, and IO resources. When you purchase an amount of DTUs, you set the limit of the performance your database is able to reach in relation to the service tier you choose (Basic, Standard, Premium). The limits and ratios per tier can be found at: `https://docs.microsoft.com/en-us/azure/sql-database/sql-database-service-tiers-dtu`.

Virtual Core (vCore) represents a logical CPU from a predefined set of physical hardware that you can choose from (memory, number of cores, and storage size). The cost of the vCore model is based on the service tier (General purpose or Critical), the hardware you choose, the amount of storage, and other configurations such as backup retention. You can read more about the vCore model at: `https://docs.microsoft.com/en-us/azure/sql-database/sql-database-service-tiers-vcore`.

To select the pricing tier for your database, click on the **Pricing tier** configuration area in the **SQL Database** blade. Choose the service tier that fits your workload and the DTU level you need. The Free tier provides a fixed amount of five DTUs and 32 MB of shared storage:

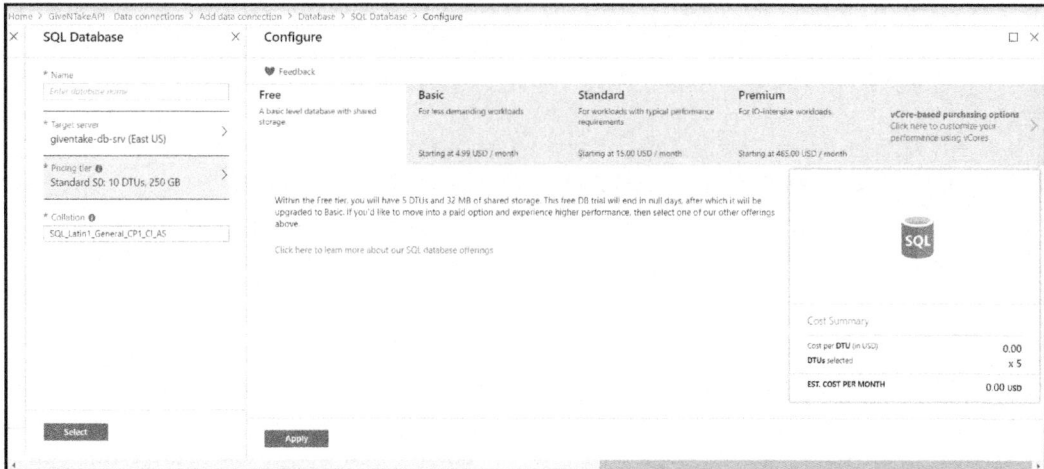

The text in this screenshot is not important. The purpose of this screenshot is to show you what the Pricing tier selection looks like.

After you complete all the necessary steps to create your SQL Database, a data connection will be added to your Web App by adding a connection string to the application settings. You need to provide a name for the connection string, and Azure will then fill it with a value. Since the GiveNTake API uses a connection string with the name GiveNTakeDB, I gave the same name to the connection string that was just created:

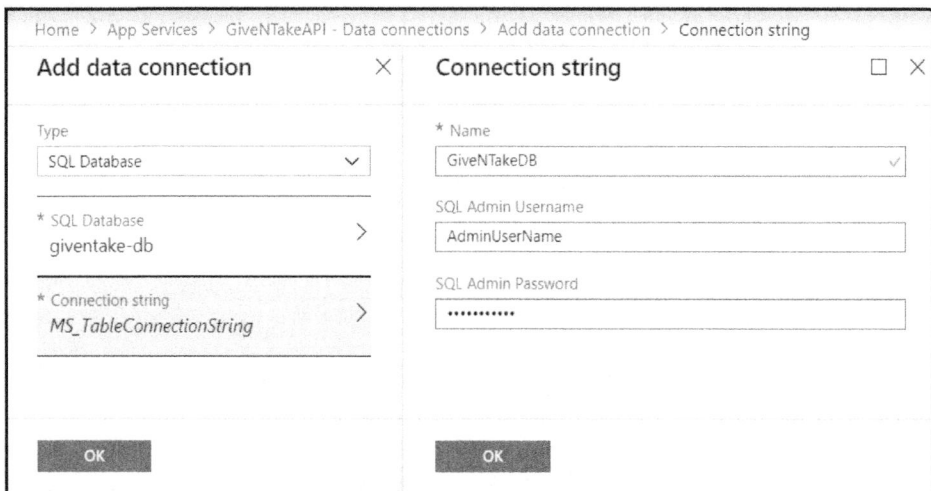

You now have a configured App Service that you can start to work with. The next step is to deploy your application to it.

Deploying the GiveNTake backend service from Visual Studio

Visual Studio provides an awesome environment to manage and control your Azure App Service. It's very easy to see what's going on inside your App Service and to deploy your application from Visual Studio, but you must remember that it is not advisable to do so because it requires manual steps that are error-prone. However, for teaching purposes, it's very useful in terms of understanding, and therefore, I decided to start with it:

1. First, make sure you have opened the Solution Explorer in Visual Studio, and then right-click on the project and select **Publish...**:

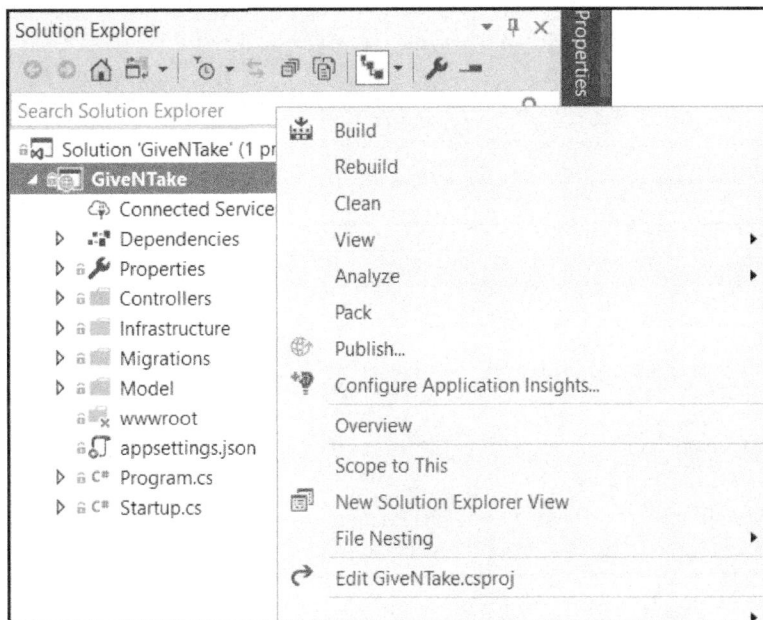

2. In the **Publish...** dialog, you can create a new **App Service** or choose an existing one:

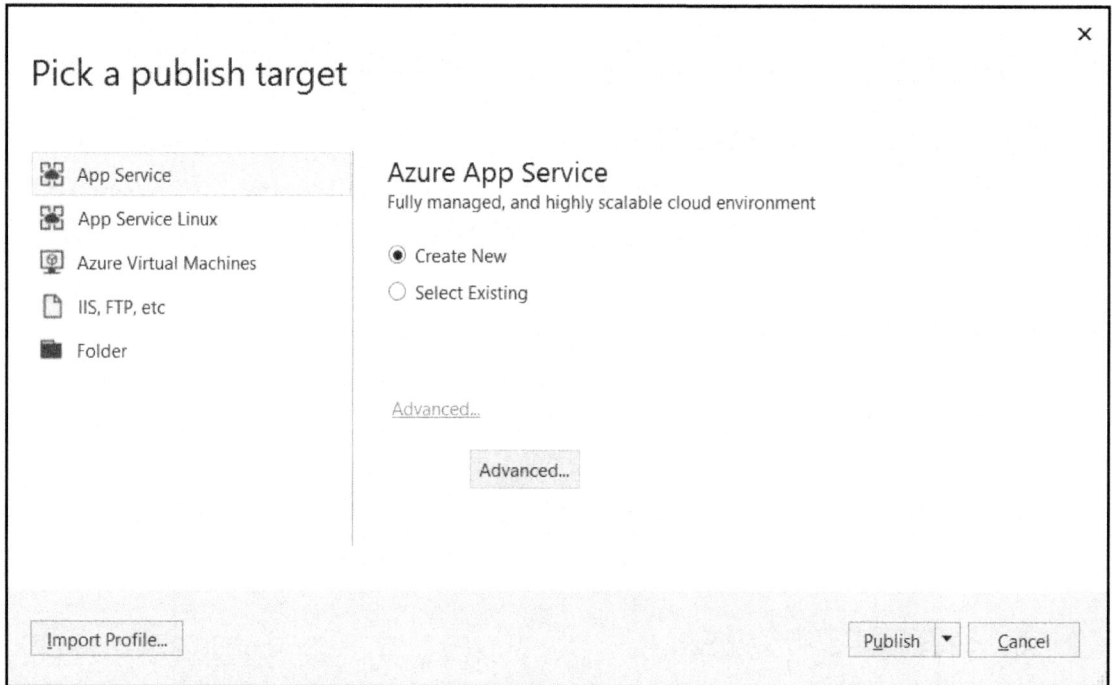

Pick a publish target

App Service

App Service Linux

Azure Virtual Machines

IIS, FTP, etc

Folder

Azure App Service
Fully managed, and highly scalable cloud environment

○ Create New
○ Select Existing

Advanced...

Advanced...

Import Profile...   Publish ▾   Cancel

3. Since I had already created an App Service, I selected the **Select Existing** option and clicked the **Publish** button. You should now see the **App Service** selection dialog. Choose the details of your subscription and the Web App you wish to deploy your application to and then click **OK**:

4. You have now completed configuring the publish profile, and all there's left to do is to click on the **Publish** button. The next time you publish your application, Visual Studio will use the settings you already configured in the profile:

5. The publish operation may take a few minutes, and you can monitor its progress in the **Web Publish Activity** window that will appear at the bottom of the Visual Studio window:

6. After the publish completes, your application is up and running and you can navigate to it:

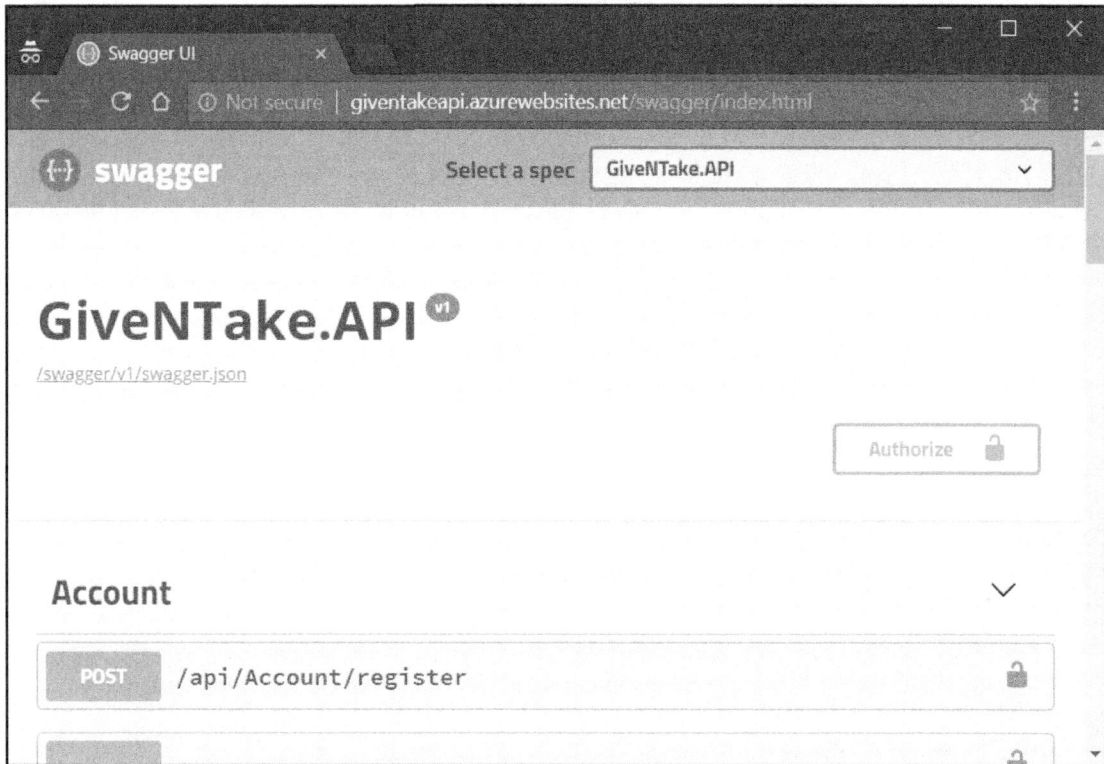

Next up, you'll learn how to create an automated process for building and deploying your project.

Creating an automated build and release pipeline in Azure DevOps

Doing things manually can be useful for getting things done, but in the software industry we call this style of working *quick-and-dirty*, and in many cases, once you remove the *quick*, all you get is the *dirty*.

Deploying your application without an automatic build and release pipeline in the production environment is something you could pay for in the future. These are some of the common issues you might encounter:

- Issues in production can't be easily traced to the code version
- Debugging in production and debugging dump files is hard or impossible
- Human errors in repeatable tasks are hard to overcome
- When working in a team, knowledge transfer becomes hard

This list is not exhaustive, but I'm sure you get the picture. The solution to the aforementioned problems is quite easy — you need to create an automated environment for building and deploying your code. There are a few products that allow you to create a build and release pipeline that you can choose from—Jenkins (`https://jenkins.io/`), Bitbucket pipelines (`https://bitbucket.org/product/features/pipelines`), AppVeyor (`https://www.appveyor.com/`), Azure DevOps (`https://azure.microsoft.com/en-us/services/devops/`), and others. For this book, I chose to use Azure DevOps (formerly known as VSTS) because it provides a free plan, is easy to use, and has a lot of powerful features.

To get started, you need to create an account:

1. Go to `https://azure.microsoft.com/services/devops/` and sign up for a free account.

2. After you have logged in to your account, you'll be asked to create an organization and select the location in which your DevOps projects will be hosted:

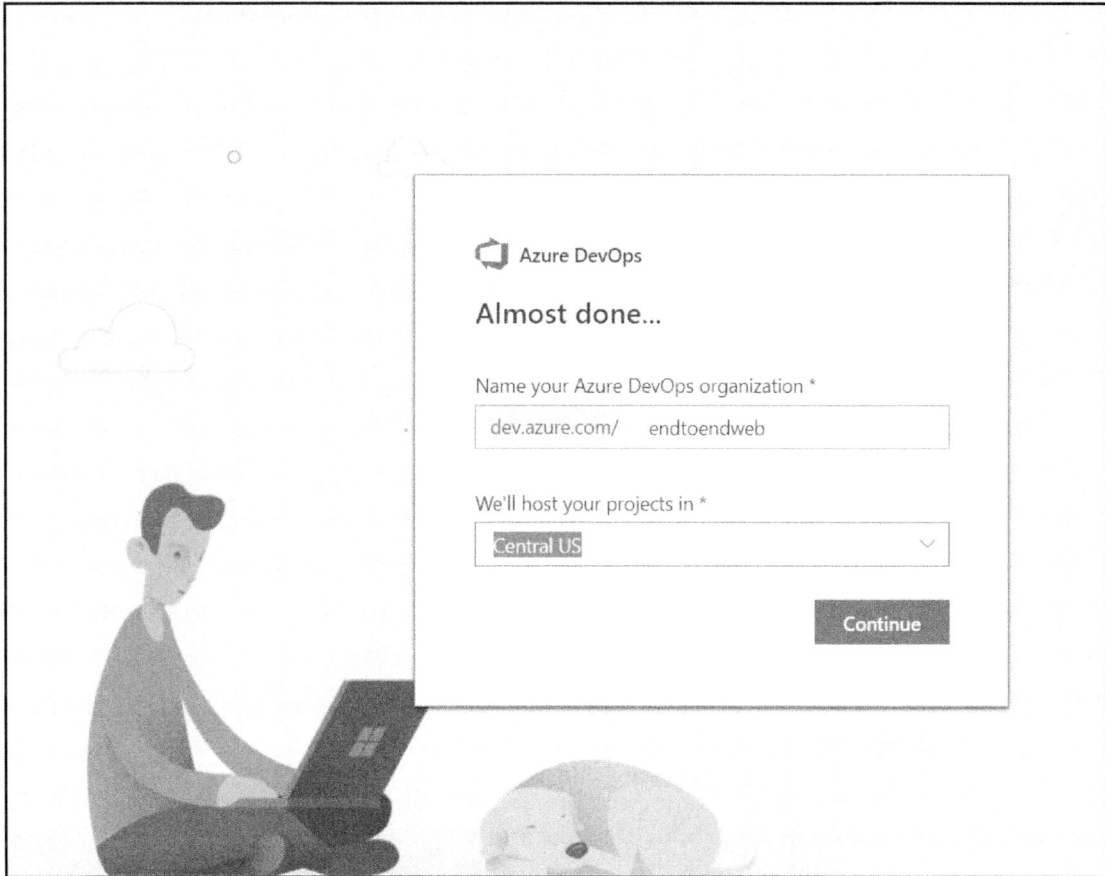

3. Inside your organization, you can work on multiple projects. Azure DevOps provides a source control for each project you create, but you don't have to use it. You can define your project as **Public** and allow anonymous access to your source code, or **Private**, to allow only authorized users you define to access the code, the build and release pipeline, and other areas of your project.

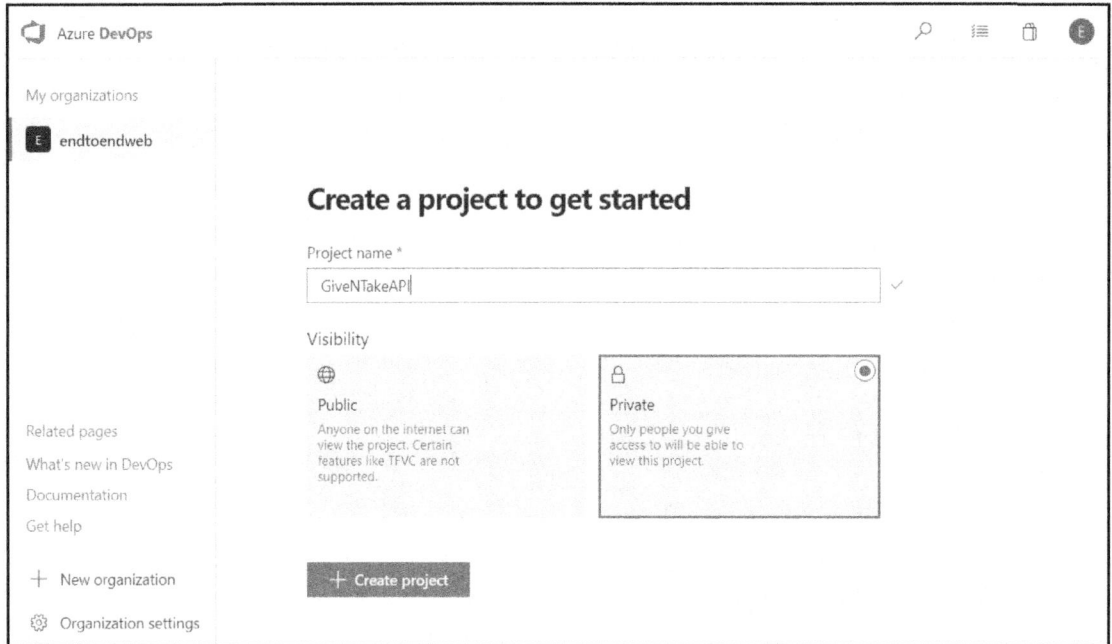

The project you create is currently empty, but not for long. In the next section, you will create the build pipeline that will automate the way you build your application and create artifacts that can be used in the production environment.

Creating a build pipeline

The build pipeline is responsible for running the steps needed to create the artifacts of your application. The artifacts that are produced by the build pipeline will then proceed to another pipeline–the release pipeline–to be deployed to your cloud environment.

Perform the following steps in your Azure DevOps project portal:

1. Click on the **Pipelines | Build** menu item to access the build pipelines of your project:

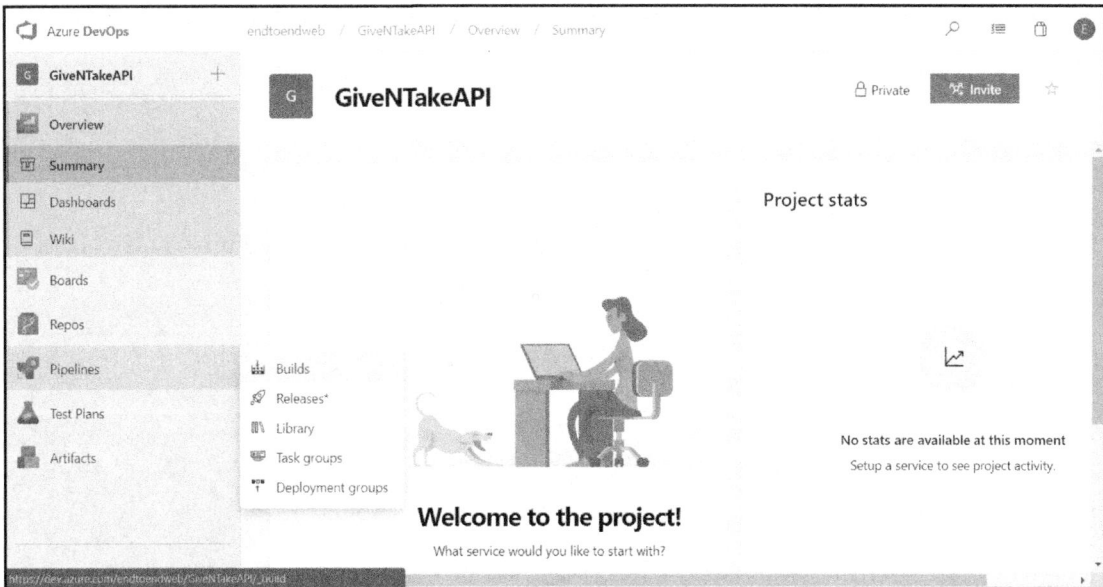

2. Click on the **New pipeline** button. In the **New pipeline** wizard, select the **use the visual designer** option:

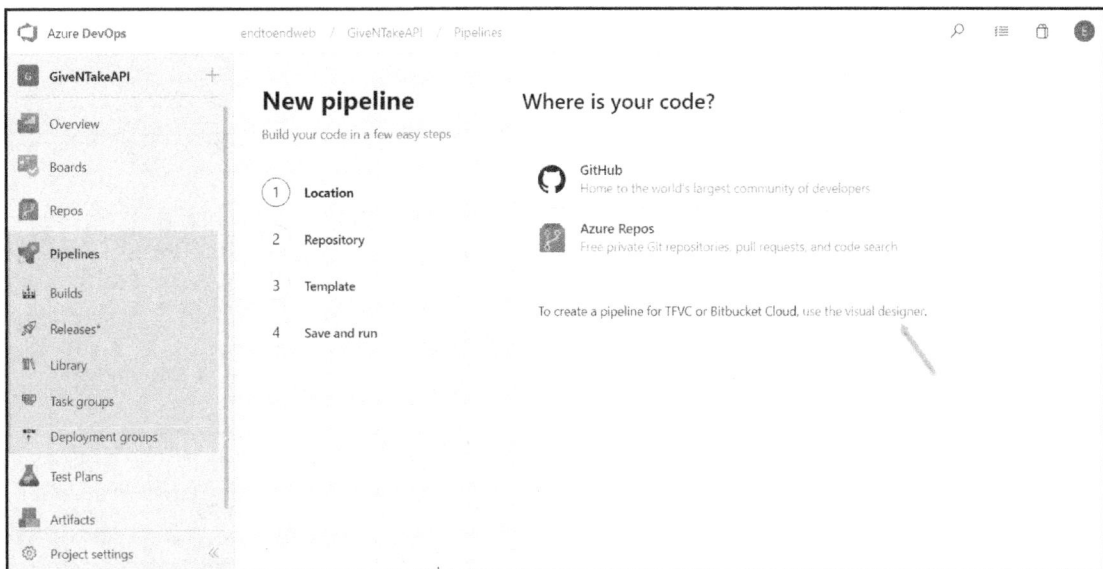

3. Select the source control that your project source code resides in.

The code of the `GiveNTake` API is stored on GitHub at: `https://github.com/tamirdresher/GiveNTake`.

4. I've granted permissions to Azure **Pipelines** to access my GitHub as instructed and have chosen the repository and branch:

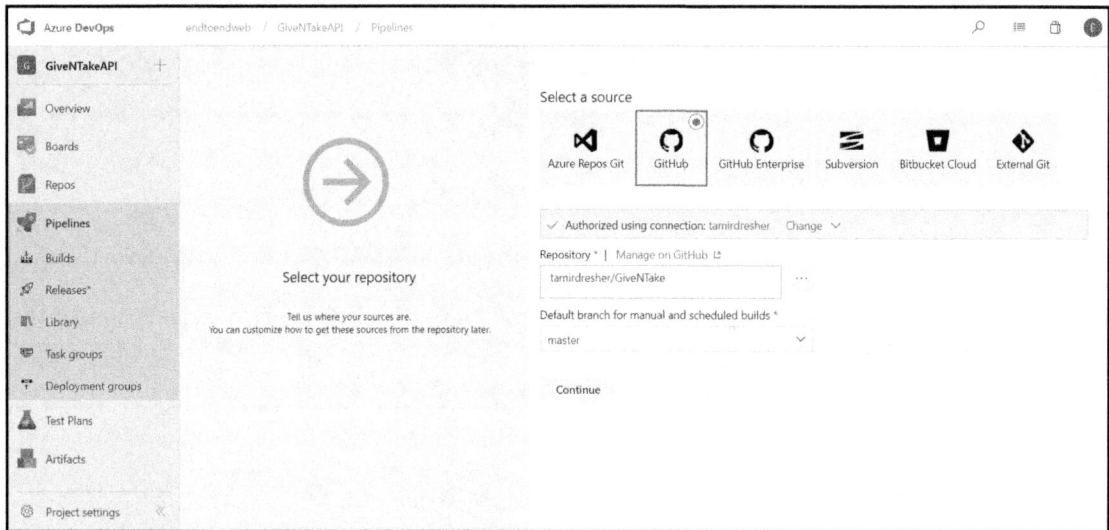

5. Now it's time to select a template for the way the pipeline should work—in our case, **ASP.NET Core**:

This will generate a pipeline with the necessary tasks for:

- Restoring NuGet packages
- Building the code
- Running unit tests (if they exist)
- Publishing artifacts as a ZIP file
- Storing artifacts

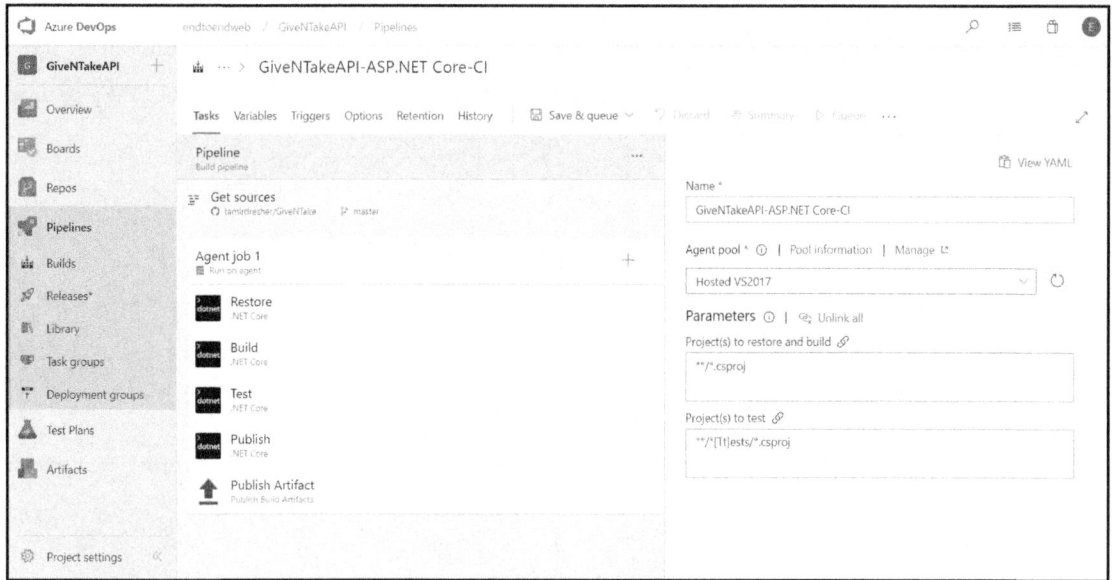

The text in this screenshot is not important. The purpose of this screenshot is to show you what the Build Pipeline looks like.

After creating the pipeline, you need to choose the Agent pool that will be used to run your pipeline.
Make sure you select the **Hosted VS2017** option.

6. By default, the **Publish** task will try to find web projects by looking for a `web.config` file or a `wwwroot` folder in the repository. If your code doesn't include those, you will get an error during the build process. To fix that, click on the publish task and uncheck the Publish Web Projects option:

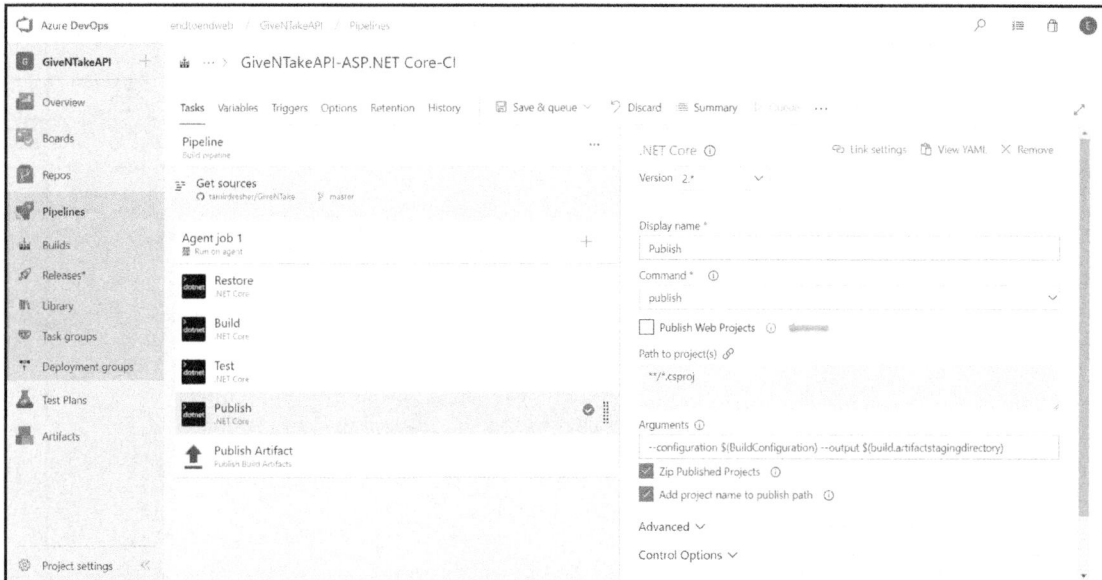

The text in this screenshot is not important. The purpose of this screenshot is to show you what the **Publish** task looks like.

7. Click on the **Save & Queue** button to save your build pipeline and to add a request to run it in the Build Agent queue. This will open the **Queue** build window, where you can set build variables, such as the build configuration and platform, and custom variables that you can add in the build definition:

Queue build for GiveNTakeAPI-ASP.NET Core-CI   ×

Agent pool

Hosted VS2017   ∨

Branch

master

Commit

Variables   Demands

BuildConfiguration   Release

BuildPlatform   any cpu

system.debug   false

+ Add

Queue   Cancel

8. Click on the **Queue** button. You should see a title with the queued build identifier appear on the screen. Click on the ID of the queued build, which will appear at the top of the screen, to see the build progress. Note that the build process could take several minutes to complete:

Creating a release pipeline that will deploy to Azure

To get the artifacts of your build process deployed to the Azure environment, you need to create a release pipeline, as follows:

1. Click on the **Pipelines** | **Release** menu item to enter the release pipelines page, and then click on the **New pipeline** button:

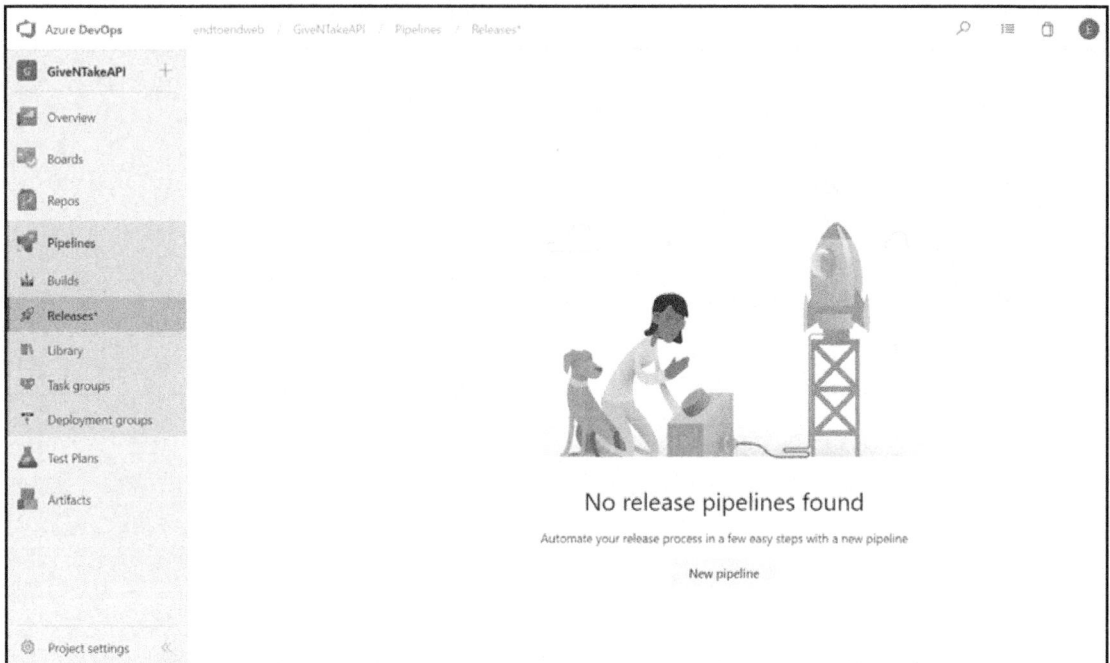

2. Select the **Azure App Service deployment** template:

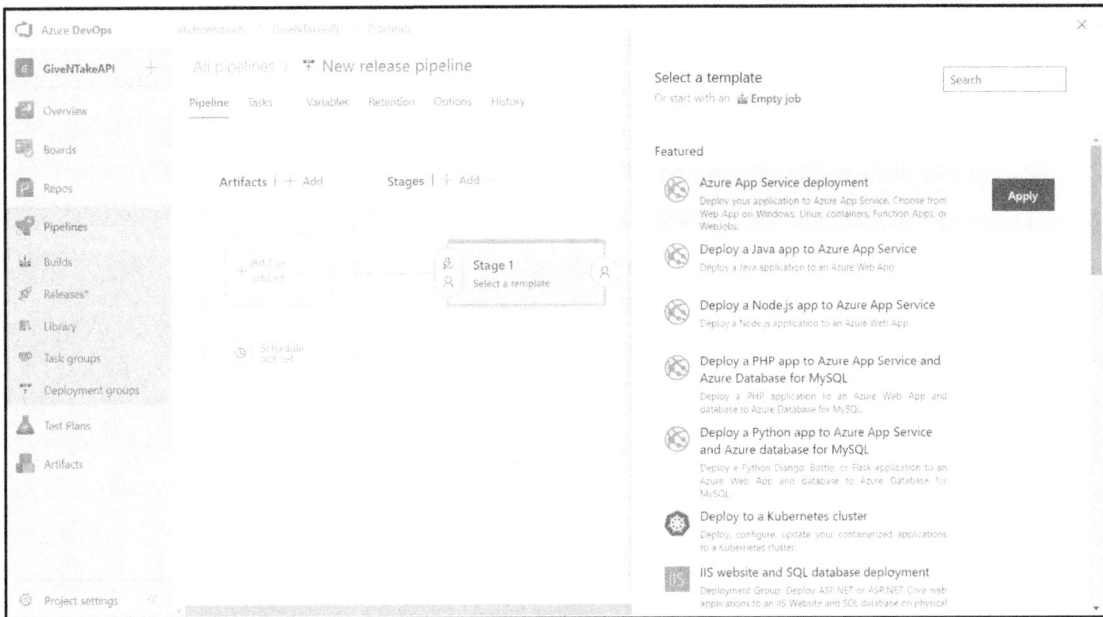

The text in this screenshot is not important. The purpose of this screenshot is to show you what the Deployment template looks like.

The release pipeline has two sections—**Artifacts** and **Stages**.

Configure the release pipeline artifact

An artifact is the deployable unit of your application. Inside the **Artifacts** section, you add the sources from which you want the release pipeline to deploy. There are many sources you can choose from—Azure pipelines, Jenkins, or a source control, among others:

1. Click on the **Add an artifact** button to create the connection between the build pipeline you created earlier and the release pipeline:

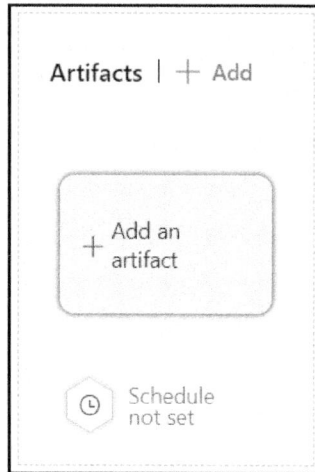

2. Select the details of the build pipeline and click **Add**:

Add an artifact   ✕

Source type

✓ Build	Azure Repos ...	GitHub	Team Found...

4 more artifact types ∨

Project *   ⓘ

| GiveNTakeAPI | ∨ |

Source (build pipeline) *   ⓘ

| GiveNTakeAPI-ASP.NET Core-CI | ∨ |

Default version *   ⓘ

| Latest | ∨ |

Source alias ⓘ

| _GiveNTakeAPI-ASP.NET Core-CI |

ⓘ The artifacts published by each version will be available for deployment in release pipelines. The latest successful build of **GiveNTakeAPI-ASP.NET Core-CI** published the following artifacts: **drop**.

Add

Now that you've set the artifacts to be deployed, you can proceed to configure how those artifacts should be handled by the release pipeline.

Configure the release pipeline stage

The **Stages** area is where you define the logical destinations of your artifacts. The deployment destination can be a physical server, a cloud application, or a container orchestrator cluster, to mention just a few. You can create as many stages as you wish, based on the representation of your environment; for example, a stage for the **Production** environment, another stage for the **Staging** environment, and another for a **Test** environment. You can create a stage as independent, or create it as being dependent on another stage. You can also specify restrictions on stage deployment so that it will only execute if it receives approval from a list of users, and if a collection of conditions called gates are satisfied. For example:

1. You can add a REST API call that makes sure that your service deployment on the staging succeeded and that the service is operational before it is deployed to the production environment:

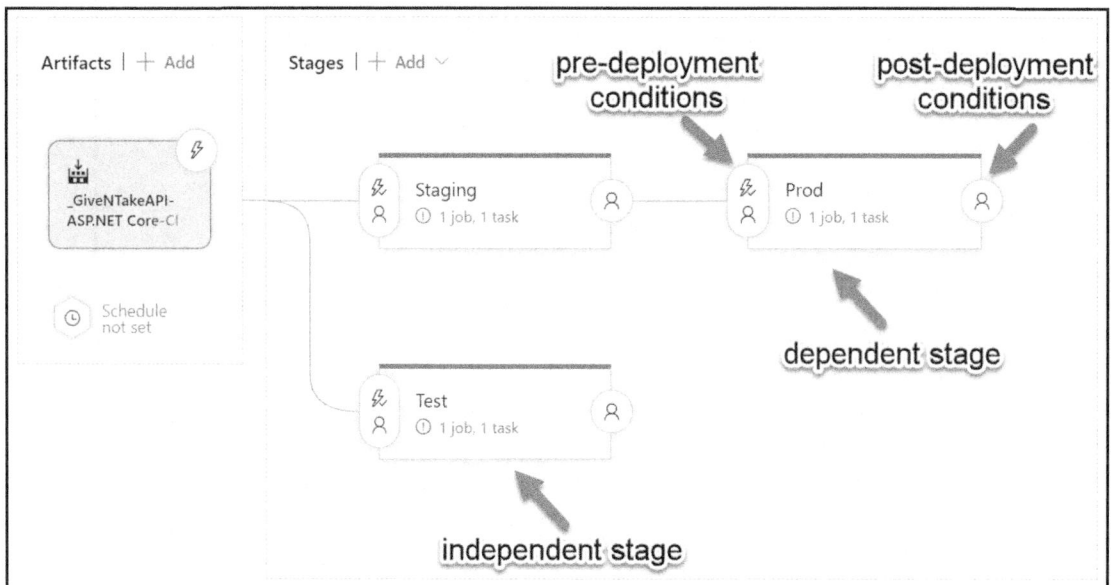

2. When you selected the release pipeline **Azure App Service deployment** template, a default stage was created for you that contains a single task which executes the deployment to Azure App Service.
3. Click on the stage tasks link to navigate to the stage tasks and configure the Azure account information:

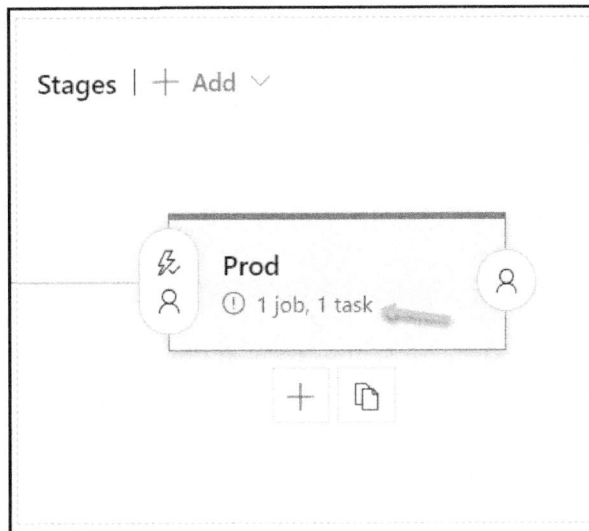

4. On the tasks definition screen, you can add the tasks that will be executed as part of your pipeline. Select the **Deploy Azure App Service** task to enter the information needed to connect to your App Service:

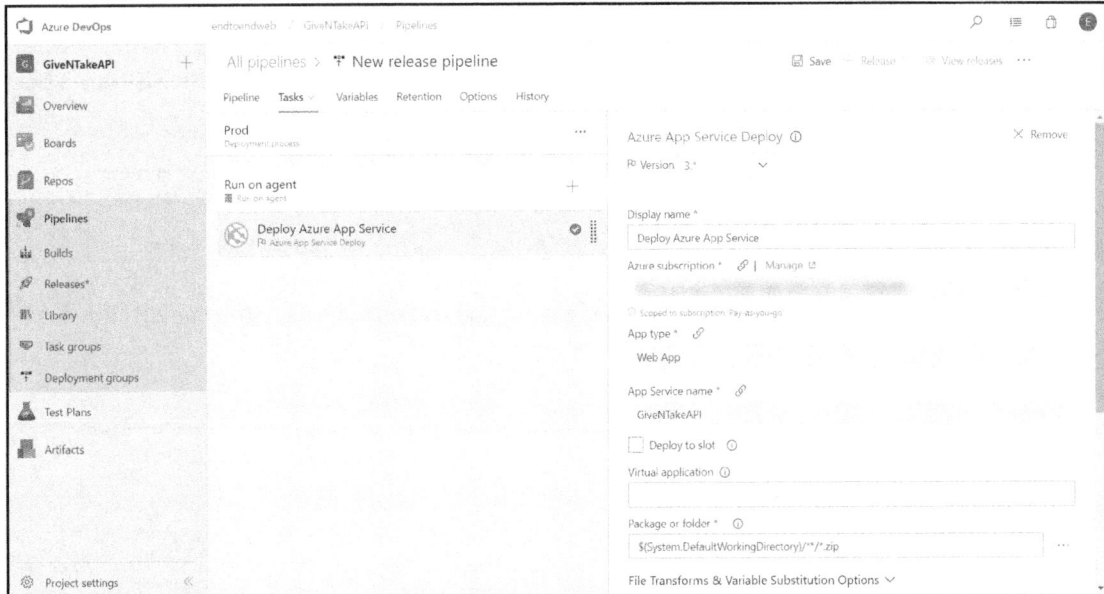

The text in this screenshot is not important. The purpose of this screenshot is to show you what the App Service Deploy task looks like.

5. Click the **Save** button to save the release pipeline.

6. Your release pipeline is currently configured to manual mode, and will only run on demand. Go back to the **Releases** page, select the release pipeline, and then click on the **Create a release** button to trigger a new release:

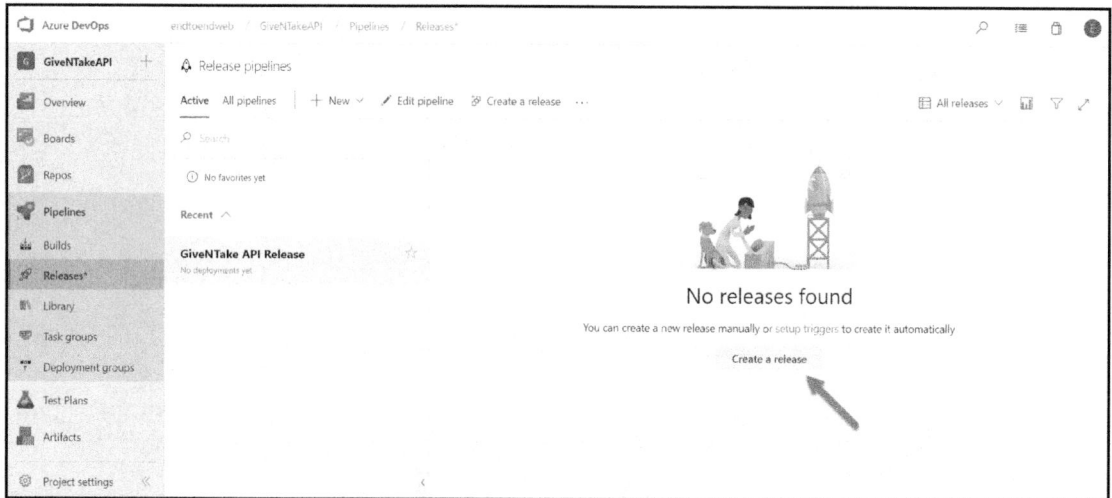

The text in this screenshot is not important. The purpose of this screenshot is to show you what the Release creation screen looks like.

7. After you approve the release configuration and click on the **Create** button, a bar with the release information will appear:

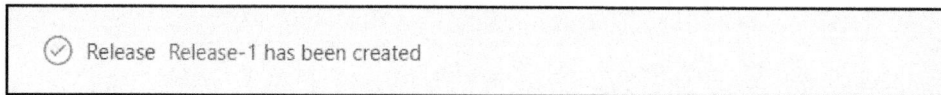

> ✓ Release Release-1 has been created

8. Click on the release identifier (**Release-1**, for example) to see the executed release pipeline:

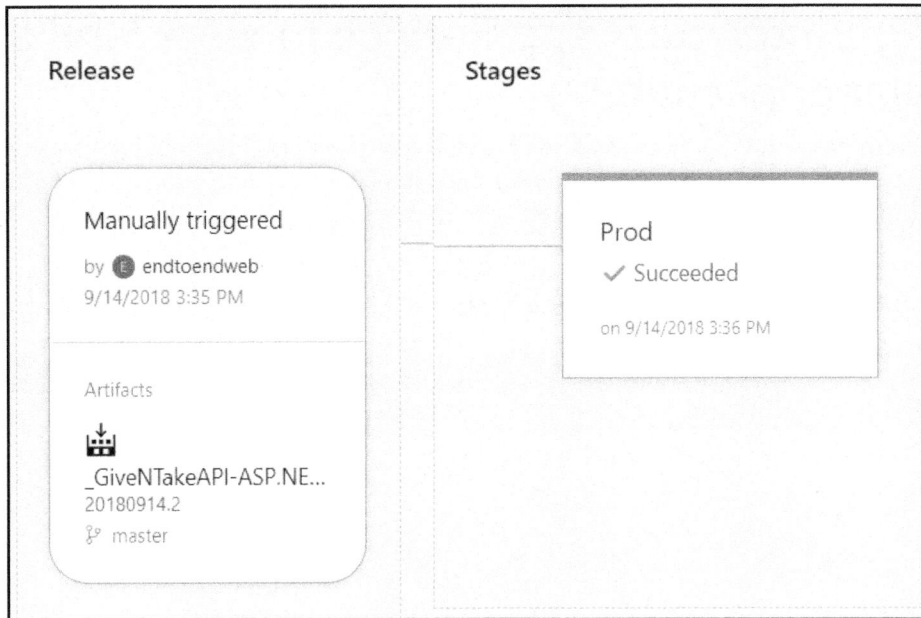

Congratulations, you now have an automated build and release pipelines!

Deploying the GiveNTake frontend to Azure App Service

In this section, you'll learn how to deploy your frontend application to Azure App Service using an Azure DevOps project. I will demonstrate the necessary steps for deploying an Angular application, but you can use the same approach for other SPA frameworks.

As a prerequisite, create a new App Service and a new Azure DevOps project in the way I demonstrated earlier in this chapter.

Configuring Azure App Service to work with an Angular application

By default, the App Service you create will take the request URL and match it to a file. Since Angular (and other SPA frameworks) use an internal router to match the URL to a page, you need to make Azure App Service aware of that.

1. Create a new file with the name `web.config` in the `src` folder of your Angular project and write the following XML in it:

```xml
<configuration>
    <system.webServer>
      <rewrite>
        <rules>
          <rule name="redirect to Angular"
              stopProcessing="true">
            <match url=".*" />
            <conditions logicalGrouping="MatchAll">
              <add input="{REQUEST_FILENAME}"
                  matchType="IsFile"negate="true" />
              <add input="{REQUEST_FILENAME}"
                matchType="IsDirectory" negate="true" />
            </conditions>
            <action type="Rewrite" url="/"
            appendQueryString="true"/>
          </rule>
        </rules>
      </rewrite>
    </system.webServer>
</configuration>
```

2. This file will create a rule inside the IIS web server that Azure App Service provides. The rule defines that any requested URL should be rewritten to the root of the Angular app.

3. In the `angular.json` file, add the `web.config` as an asset. This will make sure that when you build your Angular app, the `web.config` will be included in the artifacts folder:

```json
"assets": [
  "src/favicon.ico",
  "src/assets",
  "src/web.config"
],
```

Now we will move on to create an automated build and release pipeline to deploy the Angular app.

Creating a build pipeline for the Angular app

Angular applications are a bit different than ASP.NET Core applications in whatever needed to create a release and deploy it. Here are the steps you need to take to build the Everyday Market frontend so that we can later deploy it to Azure:

1. Create a new build pipeline in your Azure DevOps project and click on the **use the visual designer** option.
2. Select the source for your project files. The Everyday Market files can be found in `https://github.com/azuker/frontend-web-dev`.
3. Add a new `npm` task to the agent tasks list:

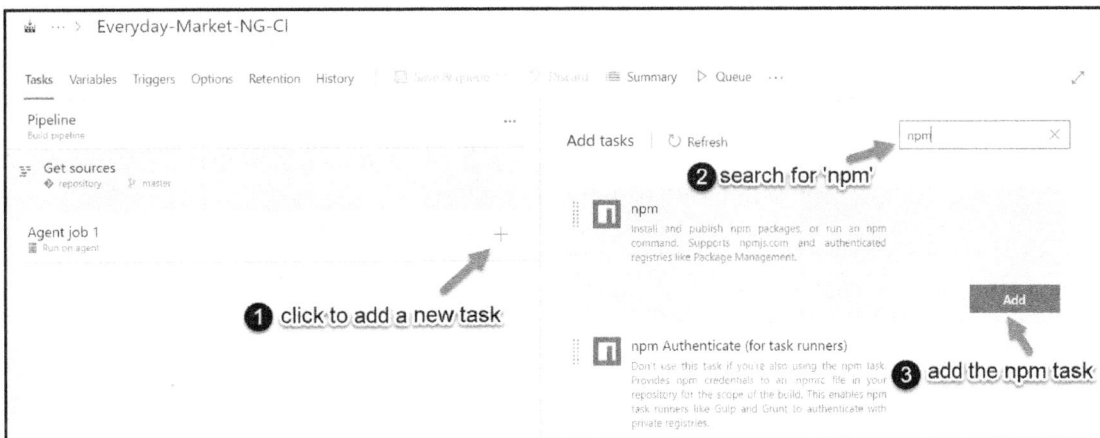

The text in this screenshot is not important. The steps indicated in the screenshot will guide you on how to go about it.

4. Select the `npm` task and change **Command** to **install**. Set the `package.json` path to the correct location:

5. Add another `npm` task to install the Angular CLI. Change **Command** to **custom** and set the **Command and arguments** field to `install -g @angular/cli`:

7. Add a **Command Line Script** task and write the script that will build the Angular, app `ng build --prod --output-path="$(Build.ArtifactStagingDirectory)\dist"`:

8. Finally, add a **Publish Artifact** task. Set the **Path to publish** field to `$(Build.ArtifactStagingDirectory)\dist` and the **Artifact name** to `dist`:

The text in this screenshot is not important. The purpose of this screenshot is to show you how to configure the Publish Artifact task.

9. To enable **Continuous Integration** (**CI**) so that the build pipeline will run every time there's a change, go to the **Triggers** tab and check **Enable continuous integration**:

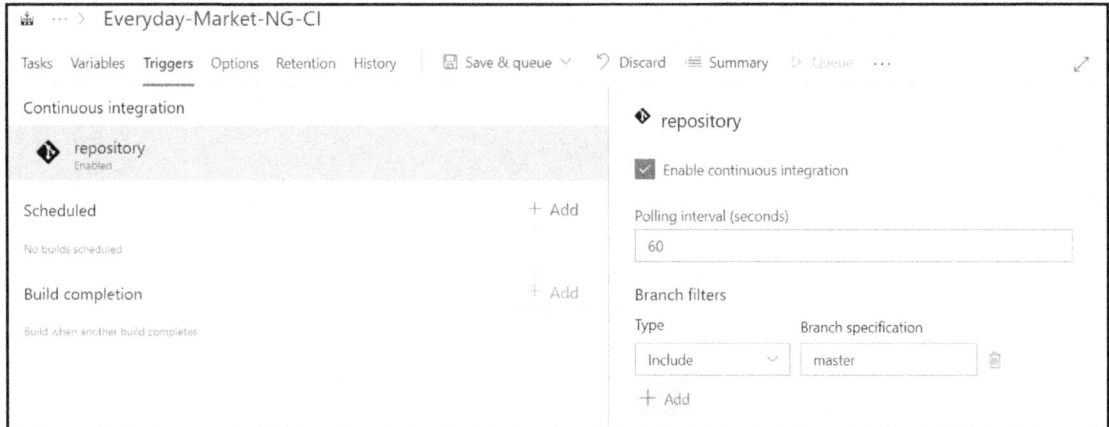

10. Save the build pipeline.

Next, you will create a release pipeline to deploy to the Azure App Service you created.

Creating a release pipeline for the Angular app

Once the Angular application is built, we want to run a release pipeline that will deploy it to Azure. These are the steps needed to deploy the Everyday Marker fronted to Azure App Service:

1. Create a new release pipeline in your Azure DevOps project. Select the **Azure App Service deployment** template, and then set the stage name to `Prod`.
2. Add an artifact and set the source to the build pipeline you created earlier. Change the **Source alias** field to something meaningful to represent that this the `dist` folder:

Add an artifact

Source type

4 more artifact types ∨

Project * ⓘ

| Everyday-Market-NG | ∨ |

Source (build pipeline) * ⓘ

| Everyday-Market-NG-CI | ∨ |

Default version * ⓘ

| Latest | ∨ |

Source alias ⓘ

| Everyday-Market-NG-CI-dist |

> ⓘ The artifacts published by each version will be available for deployment in release pipelines. The latest successful build of **Everyday-Market-NG-CI** published the following artifacts: ***dist***.

Add

3. Go to the **Tasks** tab and set the details of your Azure App Service.

4. Click on the **Deploy Azure App Service** task and set the `Package` or folder field to `$(System.DefaultWorkingDirectory)/[Source Alias]/dist`. Replace the `[Source Alias]` with the value you configured in the previous step:

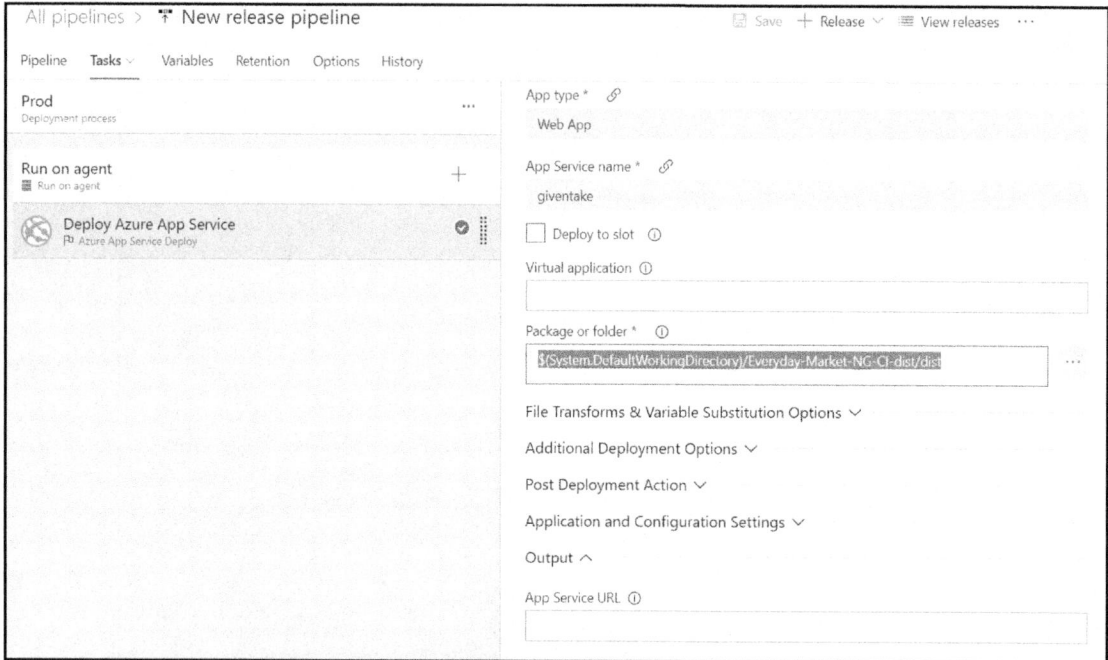

5. Go back to the pipeline and click on the Artifact trigger icon :

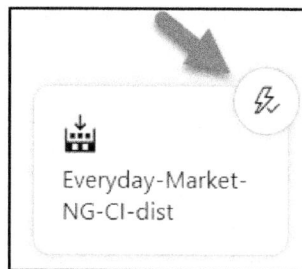

6. Enable the **Continuous deployment** trigger. This will make sure that for every new build, a deployment will be executed automatically:

Continuous deployment trigger

Build: Everyday-Market-NG-CI-dist

Enabled

Creates a release every time a new build is available.

Build branch filters ⓘ

Type	Build branch	Build tags	
Include ∨	master		🗑

+ Add | ∨

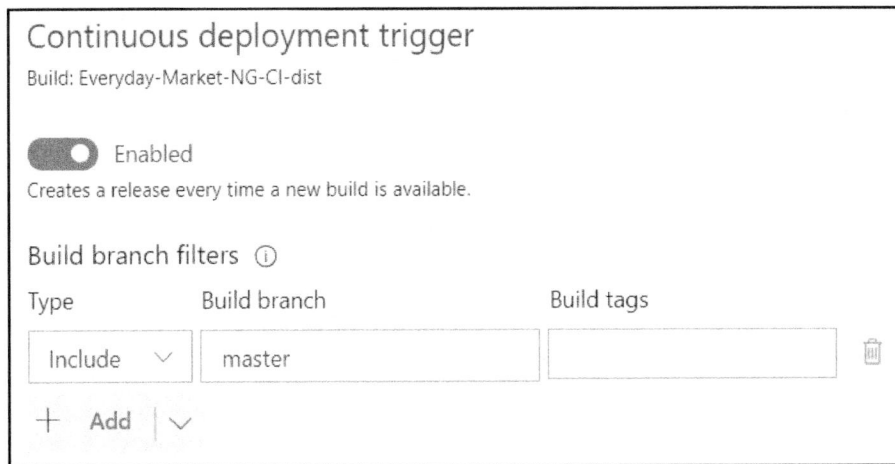

You now have an automated process for building and deploying your frontend application to Azure.

Summary

In this chapter, you've created your production environment on the Azure cloud. You have learned how to deploy your backend services and frontend application to Azure App Service. Azure App Service is a feature-rich solution for hosting and managing your cloud applications, and, in this chapter, you learned how to create it and how charges are made via an App Service plan. You also created an Azure SQL database and connected it to your application. Since performing manual deployment is error-prone, you learned how to create an automatic build and release process using an Azure DevOps project and pipelines, and you also used this technique to automatically deploy your frontend application to the production environment using a CI/CD pipeline that will build and then deploy automatically when there are changes in the source files that are stored in your source control repository.

In the next chapter, you'll learn how to add elasticity and scalability to your cloud application, and will also learn about some services that will allow you to better manage and control your production environment.

16
Taking Advantage of Cloud Services

Running in the cloud opens up a world of capabilities for your application. Things that once took a lot of effort to achieve are now a mouse click away. In this chapter, I want to highlight a few of the services you can use to make your application better–better for your users, who want the best performance they can get, and better for you as a developer, who needs to develop the application, deploy it, and monitor its behavior.

To enhance your application, you will now learn how to enable elasticity to scale based on demand or on prior knowledge of events. You will also connect your application to Application Insights, which runs in the cloud and collects metrics that you can later use to diagnose problems and analyze your application's behavior. Finally, you'll learn how to test your application like the cloud giants, and how to run multiple versions of your app side by side in production using Azure Deployment slots.

Here are the topics you'll learn about in this chapter:

- Scaling your service
- Cloud diagnostics with Application Insights
- Testing in production with Deployment slots

Scaling your service

An application that is running on a web server can only process requests that can fit the computing resources that the server contains. As more requests are sent to the application, resources begin to decrease, and at some point, new requests will start to fail and our customer will start experiencing a degradation of service and performance.

The ability of your service to handle increasing amounts of requests is called **Scalability**, and there are two ways in which your service can scale: *Scale Up* and *Scale Out*.

Scaling up your App Service

To scale up a service means that you add more resources to the infrastructure it is running on: CPU, memory, disk, network bandwidth, and so on. This is also known as *vertical scaling*. The resources that your App Service is running on are represented by the App Service plan that you created in `Chapter 15`, *Deploying to Microsoft Azure*. At any point, you can change your App Service plan and increase or decrease the resources that your service runs on.

In the App Service menu on the left, click on the **Scale up (App Service plan)** menu item to select the service plan that best suits your needs:

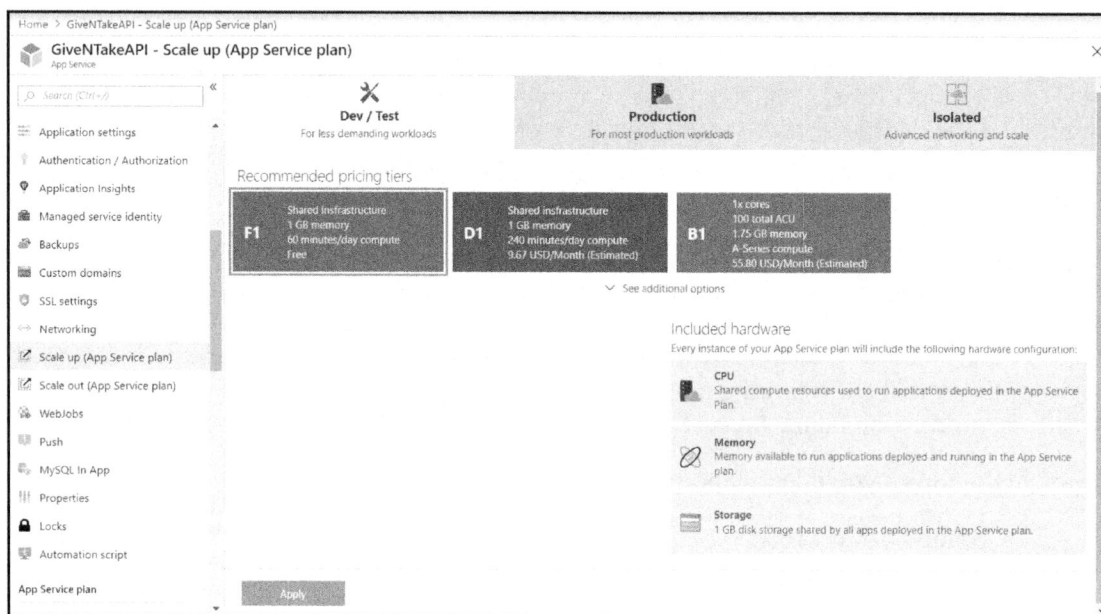

Scaling up is not a silver bullet, and it can't solve every performance issue that your application might encounter. A more scalable approach is to scale your service horizontally with **Scale out**.

Scaling out your App Service

With **Scale up**, the resources you run on can only be increased up to the limit of the existing hardware, and the cost for those resources doesn't increase in a non-linear way.

Scale out means that, instead of increasing a machine's capabilities, you add more machines. With **Scale out** (also known as Horizontal Scaling), you can scale your application indefinably, and then pay in a linearly–multipling the number of machines by the price per machine.

Scaling out allows you to distribute the processing of requests between several machines dynamically. When there is a high load, you can add machines, and when the load decreases, you can decrease the amount of machines you use. This way, you pay for your actual usage instead of paying for under-utilized hardware.

Azure App Service allows you to set the amount of instances your service runs on manually (Manual scale) or automatically (Auto scale).

> To enable Manual scale or Autoscale, you need to configure your App Service plan with a pricing tier that allows their use; for example, the F1 pricing tier doesn't allow any scale options; the B1 pricing tier allows only Manual scale; and S1 allows both Manual and Autoscale. If your pricing tier doesn't allow scaling, you will see this message:

Errors

- Autoscale is currently not available for this resource: The resource pricing tier might have been changed, and autoscale is not supported in the new pricing tier.

In the left-hand App Service menu, click on the **Scale out (App Service plan)** menu item. In the open blade, you can select the amount of instances you wish your service to run on, or click on the **Enable autoscale** button to configure automatic scaling:

Autoscaling

After you enable the autoscaling of your service, you can add a scaling condition to define how and when your service will be scaled out or in, as shown here:

The scale condition can scale out or in based on a metric, or you can specify a specific amount of instances. For a metric-based scale condition, you define rules that will determine how to scale by clicking on the **Add a rule** link. This will open the **Scale rule** blade, in which you need to set the following:

- **Criteria**: The metric (**CPU Percentage**, **Memory Percentage**, and so on) and the aggregation method that will apply to the metric (**Total**, **Average**, **Minimum**, and so forth), together with the condition that will determine whether the **Action** will be applied.
- **Action**: The **Operation** (increase or decrease) and by which amount of instances. Also, you can define how long the system should wait before applying the **Scale rule** again (how long the cooling down takes):

Scale rule ✕

Criteria

* Time aggregation ⓘ

Average ⌄

* Metric name

CPU Percentage ⌄

1 minute time grain

* Time grain statistic ⓘ

Average ⌄

* Operator

Greater than ⌄

* Threshold

70

* Duration (in minutes) ⓘ

10

Action

* Operation

Increase count by ⌄

* Instance count

1

* Cool down (minutes) ⓘ

5

You can add more than one rule and make sure your service will stay balanced based on its usage. For example if the average CPU usage is above 70% then an instance will be added, and when the average CPU usage is below 20% an instance will be removed:

Default Auto created scale condition 🖉   🗑

| Scale mode | ● Scale based on a metric   ○ Scale to a specific instance count |

Scale out

| | When | ServicePlan1753cb... (Average) CpuPercentage > 70 | Increase instance count by 1 |

Rules

Scale in

| | When | ServicePlan1753cb... (Average) CpuPercentage < 20 | Decrease instance count by 1 |

＋ Add a rule

| Instance limits | Minimum ❶
 2 | Maximum ❶
 5 | Default ❶
 2 |

| Schedule | **This scale condition is executed when none of the other scale condition(s) match** |

The first scale condition you create is the default one, and will be executed when no other scale conditions match. When you create scale conditions other than the default, you can also set a schedule for them to be applied. For example, if you know that your service will have a higher load on a specific day, such as Black Friday, you can prepare for that load beforehand:

Black Friday ✏   🗑

Scale mode   ◯ Scale based on a metric   ⦿ Scale to a specific instance count

Instance count | 5   ✓ |

Schedule   ⦿ Specify start/end dates   ◯ Repeat specific days

Timezone | (UTC-10:00) Hawaii   ⌄ |

Start date | 2018-11-23   🗓 | | 12:00:00 AM |

End date | 2018-11-24   🗓 | | 12:00:00 PM |

Cloud Diagnostics with Application Insights

In `Chapter 7`, *Troubleshooting and Debugging*, you learned how to add logging to your application and then query it with Application Insights on your local development machine. When moving to the cloud and dealing with multiple services and instances of them, you need a central location in which you can query all log messages, monitor the behavior of your entire system, and define alerts for anomalies in system components. This is where Azure Application Insights shines.

Application Insights can monitor any type of application–backend services or frontend applications. Once you configure it to your App Service, it collects telemetry on requests and failure rates, usage statistics, exceptions, and different flavors of availability and performance.

Connecting Azure Application Insights to your App Service

When you created your App Service, you were asked if you wanted to enable Application Insights.

1. If you switched it on, then you can proceed to the next section:

2. If you chose to keep it switched off, or can't remember, continue reading.
3. In the left-hand App Service menu, click on the **Application Insights** menu item:

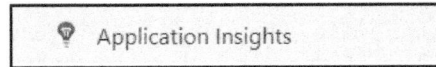

4. Then click on the **Setup Application Insights** link to open the creation blade:

> If you already connected **Application Insights** to your App service, you will see a link to navigate to the **Application Insights** dashboard instead.

5. Select an existing Application Insights resource or create a new one.

Connecting the ASP.NET Core logger to Azure Application Insights

In `Chapter 7`, *Troubleshooting and Debugging*, you added the Application Insights provider to ASP.NET Logger Factory. The Application Insights provider searches for an instrumentation key in your application's configuration, and if it finds it, it uses it to send log messages (called Trace messages in Application Insights) to your cloud resource.

You can find the instrumentation key of your Application Insights when you navigate to the **Application Instance** resource in the Azure portal and click on the **Properties** menu item:

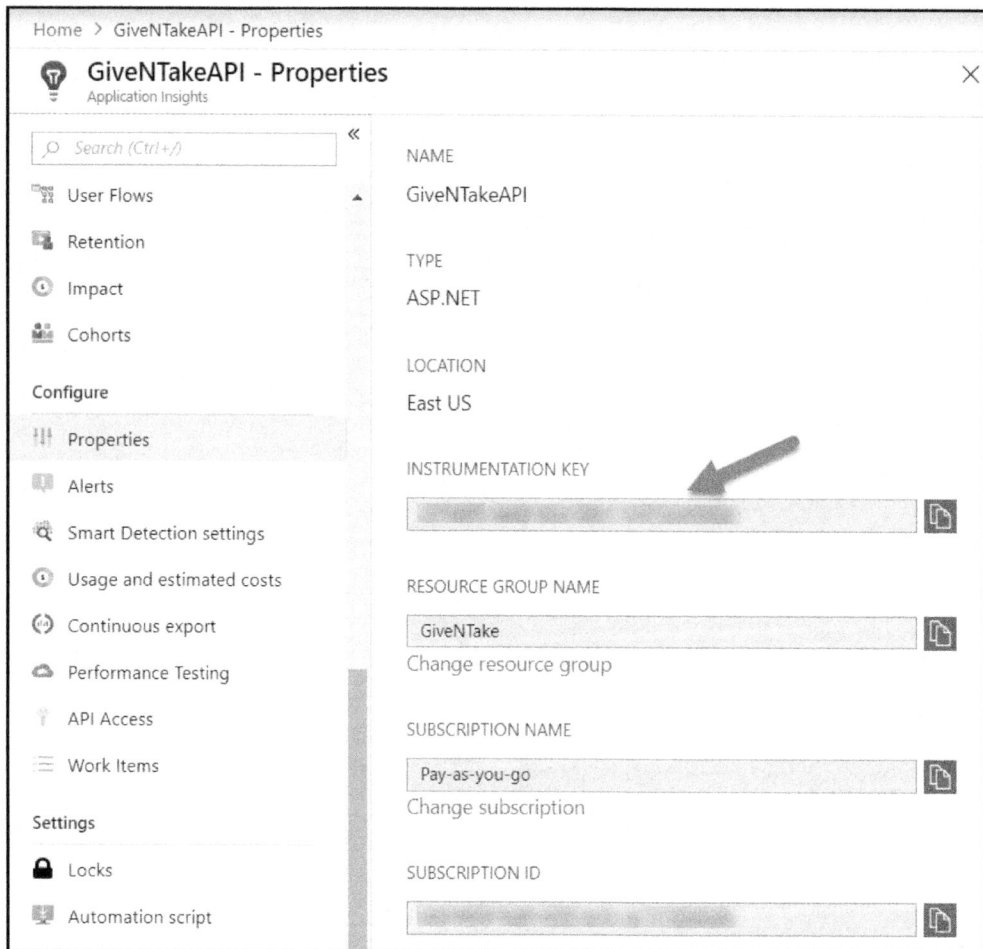

You can add the instrumentation key directly to your `appsettings.json` file, which is useful for writing logs to Azure even from the local machine, but it's advisable not to store the instrumentation key in your source control, so be careful.

```
{
    ...
    "ApplicationInsights": {
      "InstrumentationKey": "XX7b8ff5-YY88-ZZaf-XXb1-YY47d2d958bb"
    }
    ...
}
```

Another option is to take advantage of the way Azure App Service manages Application settings and how ASP.NET Core configuration works.

Setting the Instrumentation Key in Application settings

In ASP.NET Core, the configuration system is built in a hierarchy in a way that a higher-level provider can override the configuration values that were set by a lower-level provider. By default, environment variables are highest in the hierarchy and will override other values for the same key.

To set environment variables inside your App Service environment, click on the **Application settings** menu item in the left-hand menu:

The `APPINSIGHTS_INSTRUMENTATIONKEY` setting was added automatically when you connected your App Service to Application Insights.

When the Application Insights logger is created in your ASP.NET Core application, it will look for this key and load the instrumentation key from it.

This way, you can set the instrumentation key in your cloud environment without risking it by storing it in the source control.

Analyzing Application Insights telemetry

Application Insights collects data about requests that are processed by your application, together with traces that you send from your code. With all this information, Application Insights can be used to search for patterns by querying events, and Application Insights adds some machine learning algorithms to find anomalies automatically.

1. In the **App Service** menu on the left, click on the **Application Insights** menu item:

   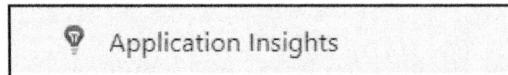

2. Then click on the **View more in Application Insights** link, which will open the Application Insights dashboard:

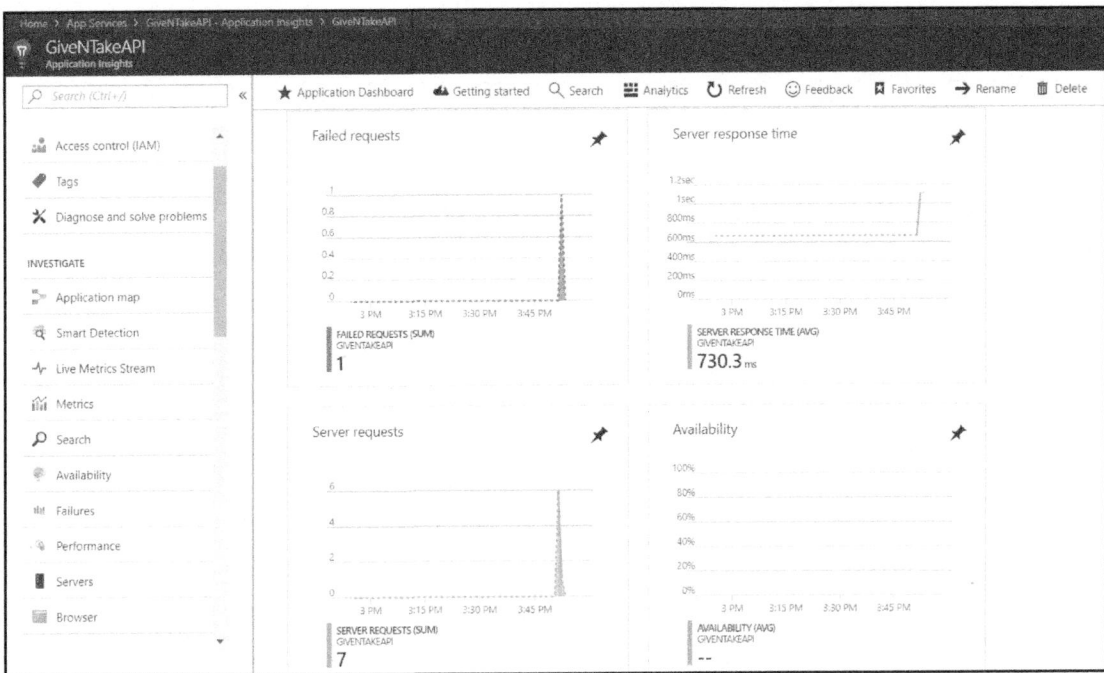

The dashboard contains a few widgets that allow you to quickly see what the status of your application is

3. Click on the **Search** menu item to see the list of events and query them:

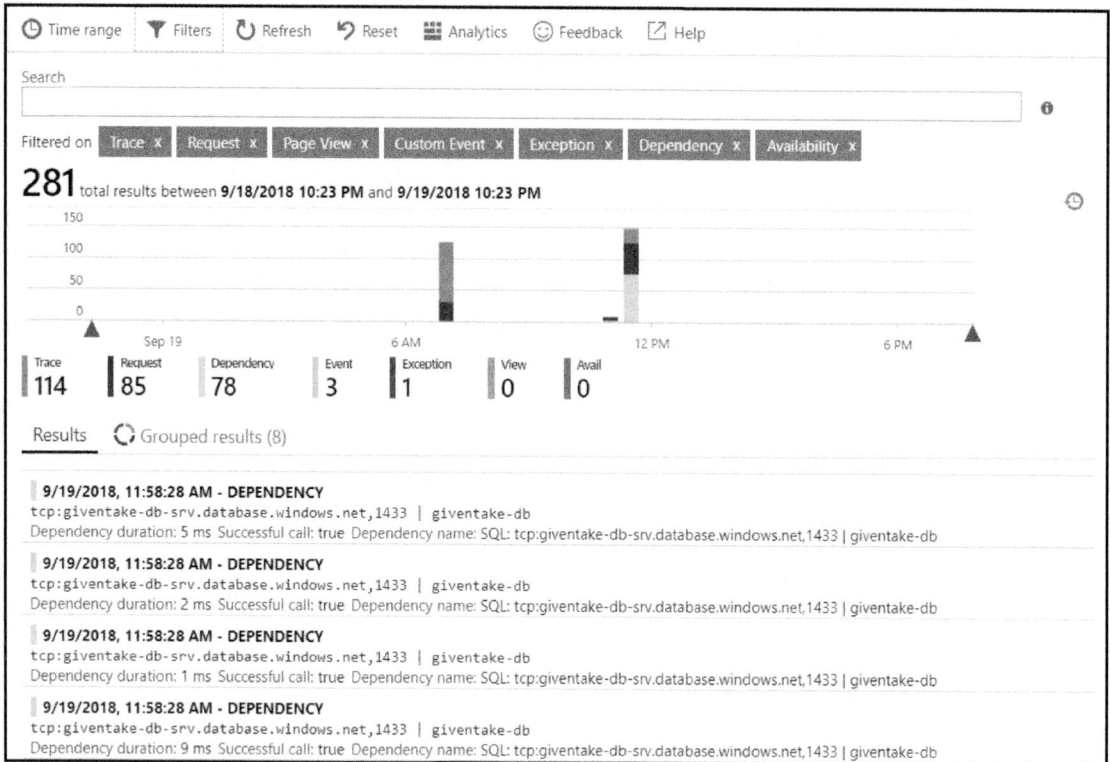

4. You can click on the **Filters** button to see a list of the properties and the set of values that exists in the events, and also select the filters you want to narrow your searches:

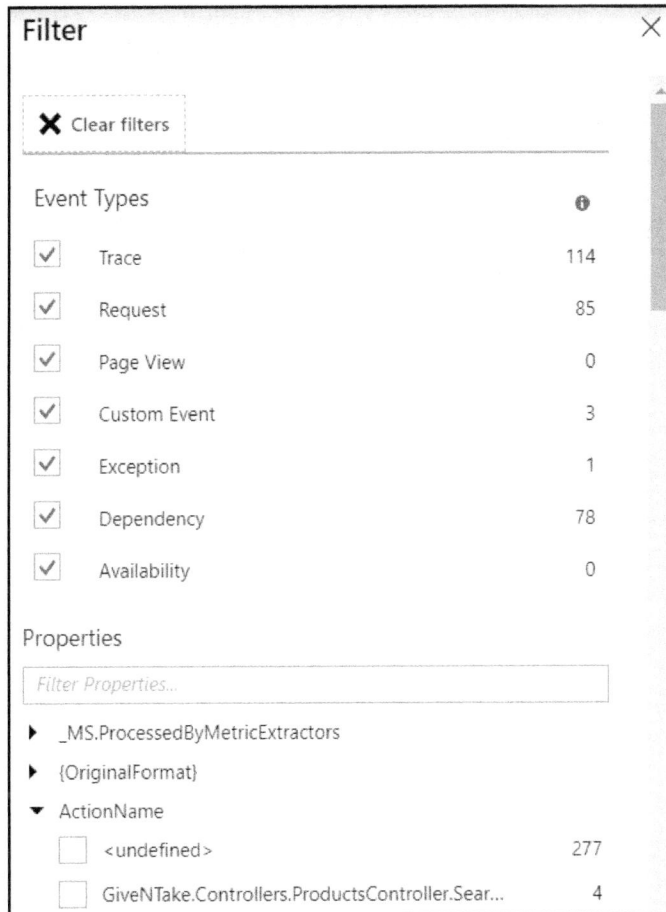

End-to-end transaction analysis

One of the benefits of putting all your services and resources in Azure is that Application Insights can track a logical transaction from end to end and display all the related telemetry of that transaction. For example, the `GiveNTake` application uses SQL Server as a database, and therefore, when clicking on one of the log events that belong to a request that used the database, you can see all the SQL queries that were sent as part of it, as well as the timeline of when each sub-event was made and how long it took:

Advanced querying and visualizing with Analytics

The **Search** tool in Application Insights is useful for quickly querying data, but it's not suitable for complex searches where you try to find correlations between different events, nor for visualizing your data.

The Analytics web tool is a more advanced query and visualization system, through which you can inspect the data that Application Insights collects. Click on the **Analytics** button in the **Application Insights** search blade:

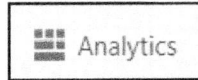

The Analytics web tool will open with a default query to search all the events that happened in the last 24 hours:

The query language that is used in Azure Log Analytics is very rich and can only be used to control the rendering of results. For example, this query will show a time chart with the `requests` duration percentiles for the last 12 hours:

```
requests
    | where timestamp > ago(12h)
    | summarize percentiles(duration, 50, 90, 95) by bin(timestamp, 1m)
    | render timechart
```

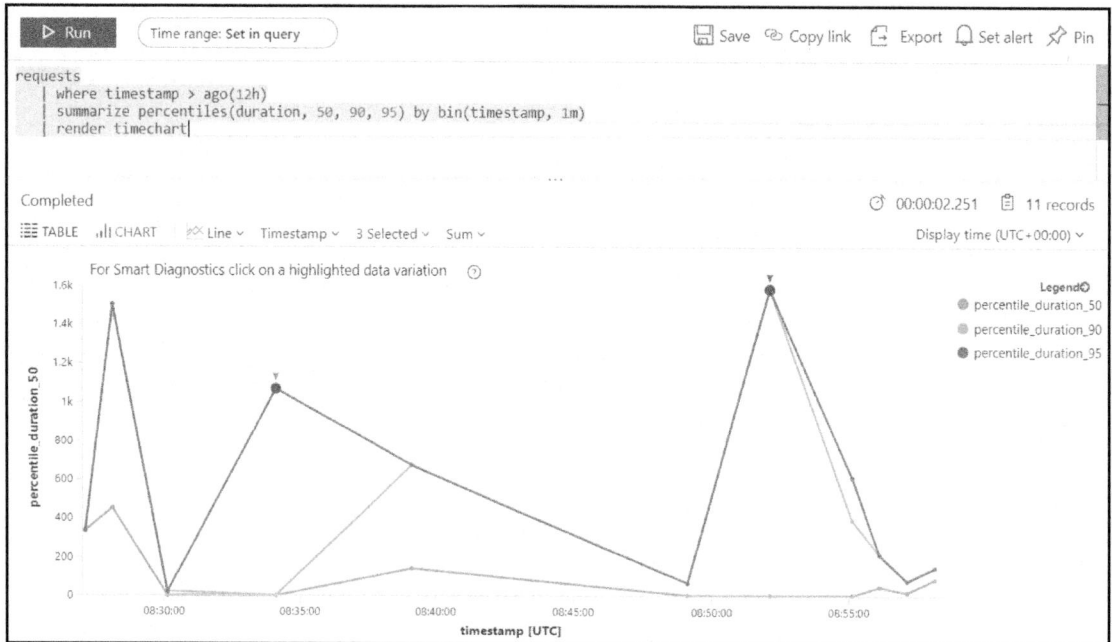

Azure Log Analytics is a complex system with many features. To read more about it and learn how to use it, check out the *Getting started* guide
at: `https://docs.loganalytics.io/docs/Learn/Getting-Started`.

Application map

Application Insights uses the information it collects to understand the structure of your system–which resources exist and how they interact.

Click on the **Application map** menu item to open the application map that Application Insights created based on the events it collected:

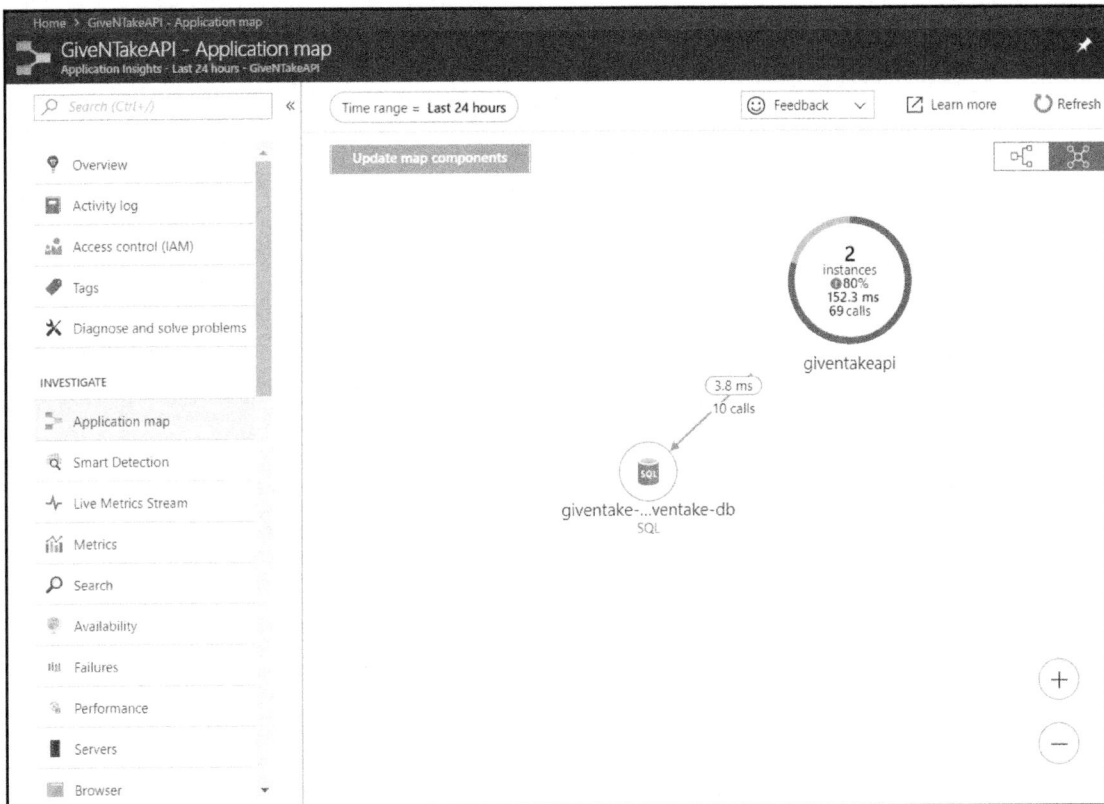

The application map can be very useful for explaining the structure of your application and finding bottlenecks.

Testing in production with Deployment slots

Deployment slots in Azure App Service is a capability that allows you to run multiple versions of your application side-by-side on an App Service plan and control its settings in a central place.

There are two main reasons for running multiple versions of your application:

- **Testing in production**: As your application evolves, you'll add features and make changes that you want to see the effects of in the wild in a real production environment. You will only want to expose changes to some users, or to a specific testing group.
- **Blue-green deployment**: A technique to reduce downtime, in which you deploy the new version of the application, validate that it's operable, and switch to it at once. This is as opposed to the rolling-upgrade technique, where in some instances run the old version and some run the new version, but requests arrive at any one instance.

To add a deployment stage, click on the **Deployment slots** menu item in the **App Service** menu on the left, and then click the **Add Slot** button:

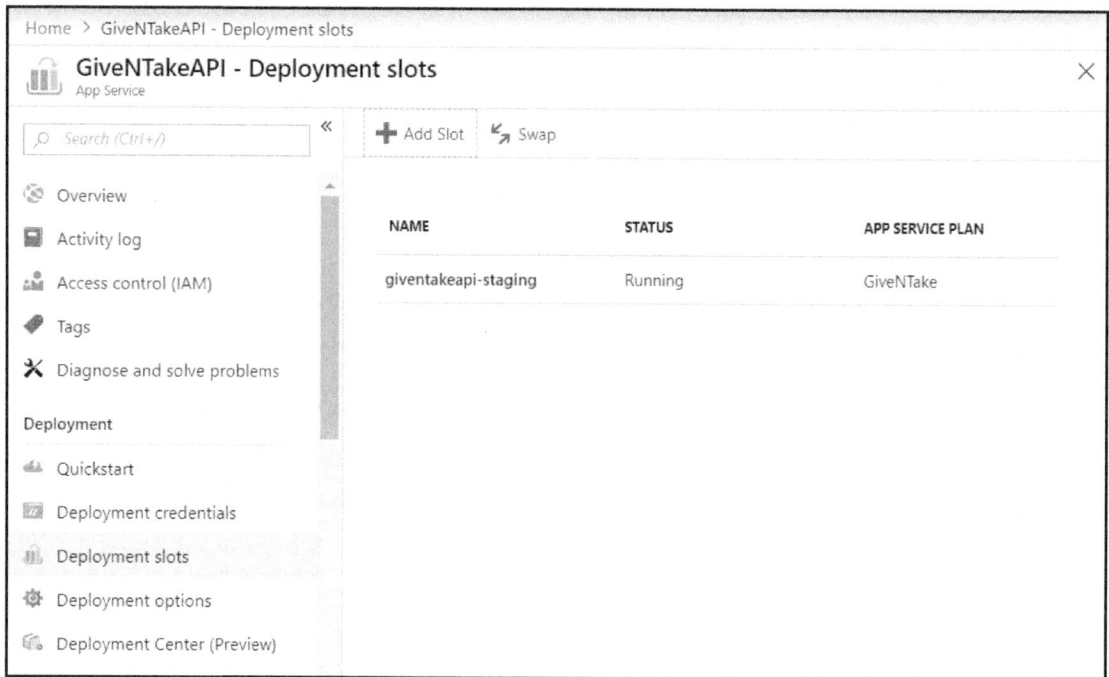

Clicking on one of your Deployment slots will transfer you to slot configuration, and you can see that the URL has now changed and includes the Deployment slot name:

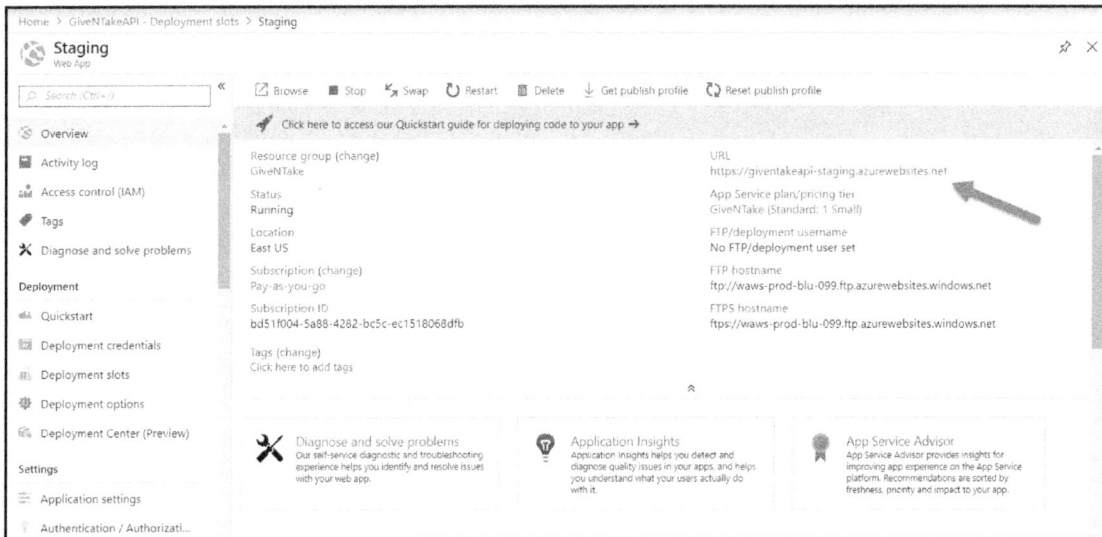

Deploying to a Deployment slot

In a way, the Deployment slot is just like having another App Service, but the tools that you use for deployment are aware of the Deployment slot, making it easier to select where you want to deploy to.

In Visual Studio, when you create your publish profile, you can select the **App Service** slot:

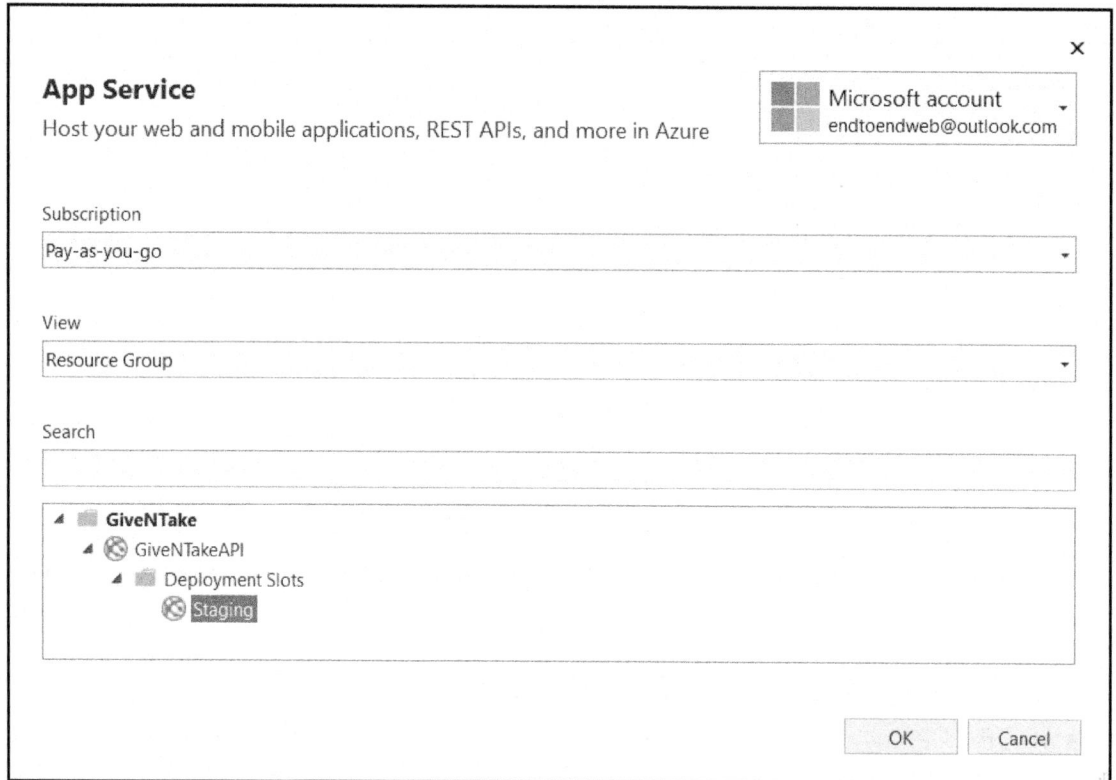

With an Azure DevOps project, you can configure your release pipeline to deploy to a Deployment slot:

Swapping between Deployment slots

Each Deployment slot has a URL that you can use to send the request to the application that is deployed in it. In some cases, you may want to replace the application that is deployed in the production Deployment slot (the one that poses the URL of your App Service) with one that is deployed in one of the Deployment slots. Instead of redeploying the application to the production Deployment slot, you can use the `Swap` operation, which switches between the two Deployment slots, such that the swapped Deployment slot becomes the production one.

1. Click on the **Swap** button:

2. In the App Service overview blade, or from the Deployment slots blade, select the source and destination slots:

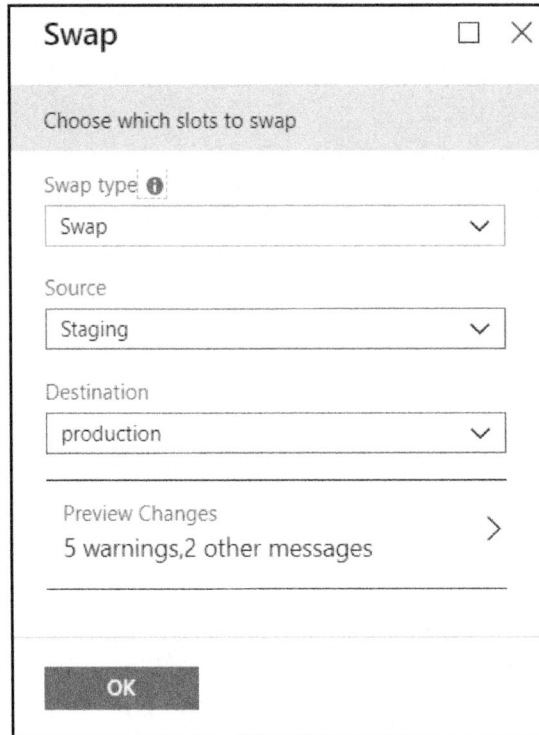

3. In the **Application settings** blade, you can configure a specific setting to retain its value even after a swap:

APP SETTING NAME	VALUE	SLOT SETTING	DELETE
APPINSIGHTS_INSTRUMENTATIONKEY	237b8ff5-eb88-42af-85b1-3347d2d958bb	☑	✖
MSDEPLOY_RENAME_LOCKED_FILES	1	☐	✖
WEBSITE_HTTPLOGGING_RETENTION_DAYS	5	☐	✖

Deployment slots are not only useful for isolating application changes when you have a new version to deploy, they also allow you to test different configurations and features in a controlled way, with what is usually referred to as **Testing in production**.

Testing in production

Testing in production allows you to distribute requests that are sent to your App Service between different Deployment slots. This way, you can check new functionality that you add without affecting the entire user base, or only a small percentage of it.

1. Click on the following menu item in the left-hand **App Service** menu:

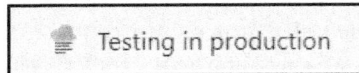

2. Select the Deployment slot you want to distribute traffic to and set the traffic percentage:

Summary

Running your application in the cloud gives you the flexibility to reach millions of users from all regions of the globe. When dealing with such scale, you need to know that your application can handle it, and if something goes wrong, then you want to know about it as soon as possible. In this chapter, you learned about some of the tools that will help you control the state of your deployed application. Azure App Service's Scale up and Scale out are two options you can use to make sure your application can reach higher and higher scales and can handle an increase in the number of requests received. You can set your App Service to autoscale out or in based on metrics or other rules that you define. With Azure Application Insights, you can see events happening in your application, query them, and let Application Insights monitor them and alert you to anomalies. Finally, when you make changes and want to make sure they work as expected in the production environment, you can use Deployment slots and swap when you are ready, or you can use the test in production capability and distribute traffic to different slots at the same time so that you can monitor the effects without affecting your entire user base.

Finally, we are here–the last words of the chapter. You've come a long way and have learned many new concepts. Well done!

While reading this book, you have developed a full and complete application that is production-ready. You have worked on both the frontend and backend, have created a domain model and stored it in a database, and have created a cloud environment and configured it to scale. You've also created a fully automated process to deploy your application into production. You are now a real full-stack developer, and we want to take this moment to say thank you and congratulate you on your success. We are sure you will use the techniques you learned in this book to create wonderful applications, and we wish you good luck in the rest of your full-stack career.

Other Books You May Enjoy

If you enjoyed this book, you may be interested in these other books by Packt:

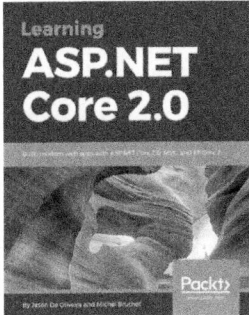

Learning ASP.NET Core 2.0

Jason De Oliveira

ISBN: 9781788476638

- Set up your development environment using Visual Studio 2017 and Visual Studio Code
- Create a fully automated continuous delivery pipeline using Visual Studio Team Services
- Get to know the basic and advanced concepts of ASP.NET Core 2.0 with detailed examples
- Build an MVC web application and use Entity Framework Core 2 to access data
- Add Web APIs to your web applications using RPC, REST, and HATEOAS
- Authenticate and authorize users with built-in ASP.NET Core 2.0 features
- Use Azure, Amazon Web Services, and Docker to deploy and monitor your applications

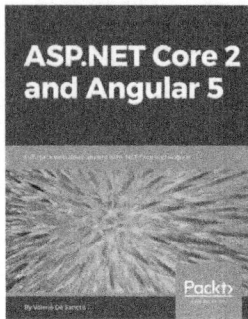

ASP.NET Core 2 and Angular 5
Valerio De Sanctis

ISBN: 9781788293600

- Use ASP.NET Core to its full extent to create a versatile backend layer based on RESTful APIs
- Consume backend APIs with the brand new Angular 5 HttpClient and use RxJS Observers to feed the frontend UI asynchronously
- Implement an authentication and authorization layer using ASP.NET Identity to support user login with integrated and third-party OAuth 2 providers
- Configure a web application in order to accept user-defined data and persist it into the database using server-side APIs
- Secure your application against threats and vulnerabilities in a time efficient way
- Connect different aspects of the ASP. NET Core framework ecosystem and make them interact with each other for a Full-Stack web development experience

Leave a review - let other readers know what you think

Please share your thoughts on this book with others by leaving a review on the site that you bought it from. If you purchased the book from Amazon, please leave us an honest review on this book's Amazon page. This is vital so that other potential readers can see and use your unbiased opinion to make purchasing decisions, we can understand what our customers think about our products, and our authors can see your feedback on the title that they have worked with Packt to create. It will only take a few minutes of your time, but is valuable to other potential customers, our authors, and Packt. Thank you!

Index